THE PARTITION OF AFRICA:
ILLUSION OR NECESSITY

MAJOR ISSUES IN HISTORY

Editor
C. WARREN HOLLISTER,
University of California, Santa Barbara

THE PARTITION
OF AFRICA:

Illusion or Necessity

EDITED BY

Robert O. Collins

Department of History
University of California
Santa Barbara, California

John Wiley & Sons, Inc.
New York   London   Sydney   Toronto

Library of Congress Catalog Card Number: 75-81334
SBN 471 16579 4 (cloth)
SBN 471 16580 8 (paper)

10 9 8 7 6 5 4 3 2 1

Printed in the United States of America

SERIES PREFACE

The reading program in a history survey course traditionally has consisted of a large two-volume textbook and, perhaps, a book of readings. This simple reading program requires few decisions and little imagination on the instructor's part, and tends to encourage in the student the virtue of careful memorization. Such programs are by no means things of the past, but they certainly do not represent the wave of the future.

The reading program in survey courses at many colleges and universities today is far more complex. At the risk of over-simplification, and allowing for many exceptions and overlaps, it can be divided into four categories: (1) textbook, (2) original source readings, (3) specialized historical essays and interpretive studies, and (4) historical problems.

After obtaining an overview of the course subject matter (textbook), sampling the original sources, and being exposed to selective examples of excellent modern historical writing (historical essays), the student can turn to the crucial task of weighing various possible interpretations of major historical issues. It is at this point that memory gives way to creative critical thought. The "problems approach," in other words, is the intellectual climax of a thoughtfully conceived reading program and is, indeed, the most characteristic of all approaches to historical pedagogy among the newer generation of college and university teachers.

The historical problems books currently available are many and varied. Why add to this information explosion? Because the Wiley Major Issues Series constitutes an endeavor to produce something new that will respond to pedagogical needs thus far unmet. First, it is a series of individual volumes—one per problem. Many good teachers would much prefer to select their own historical issues rather than be tied to an inflexible sequence of issues imposed by a publisher and bound together between two covers. Second, the Wiley Major Issues Series is based on the idea of approaching the significant problems of history through a deft interweaving of primary sources and secondary analysis, fused together by the skill of a scholar-editor. It is felt that the essence of a historical issue cannot be satisfactorily probed either by placing a body of undigested source materials into the hands of inexperienced students or by limiting these students to the controversial literature of modern scholars who debate the meaning of sources the student never sees. This series approaches historical problems by exposing students to both the finest historical thinking on the issue and some of the evidence on which this thinking is based. This synthetic approach should prove far more fruitful than either the raw-source approach or the exclusively second-hand approach, for it combines the advantages—and avoids the serious disadvantages—of both.

Finally, the editors of the individual volumes in the Major Issues Series have been chosen from among the ablest scholars in their fields. Rather than faceless referees, they are historians who know their issues from the inside and, in most instances, have themselves contributed significantly to the relevant scholarly literature. It has been the editorial policy of this series to permit the editor-scholars of the individual volumes the widest possible latitude both in formulating their topics and in organizing their materials. Their scholarly competence has been unquestioningly respected; they have been encouraged to approach the problems as they see fit. The titles and themes of the series volumes have been suggested in nearly every case by the scholar-editors themselves. The criteria have been (1) that the issue be of relevance to undergraduate lecture courses in history, and (2) that it be an issue which the scholar-editor knows thoroughly and in which he has done creative work. And, in general, the second criterion has been given precedence over the first. In short, the question "What are the significant historical issues today?" has been answered not by general editors or sales departments but by the scholar-teachers who are responsible for these volumes.

University of California,   *C. Warren Hollister*
Santa Barbara

CONTENTS

vii

PART THREE: Italy: The Imperialism of Personalities

PART FOUR: Britain's Nilotic Imperative

PART FIVE: French Conflict of Interests

Africa on the Eve of the Partition

Africa after the Partition: 1914

INTRODUCTION

During their four centuries of contact with Africa, the European powers had been content to restrict their holdings to a handful of scattered trading stations along the coast, the control of which passed from one state to another as its strength in Europe waxed or waned. Finally, in the nineteenth century European explorers penetrated into the interior and opened the enormous hinterland of Africa; yet no European government rushed to follow in their footsteps. Stimulated by the fires of evangelism and the humanitarianism produced by the crusade against the slave trade, missionaries began to work out from the coastal enclaves, but they never regarded themselves as agents of the home governments. In fact, until the European acquisition of Africa the missionaries argued that, with proper training, the Africans themselves were the best equipped to carry Christianity among the peoples of the continent. Even the commercial interests were reluctant to see the extension of European control. All along the coast, but particularly in West Africa, an equilibrium existed between European traders and African middlemen. The more astute merchants on both sides realized that they would not necessarily gain by the intervention, occupation, and rule by any single European power. The others traded freely in practice, as well as spirit, satisfied to derive reasonable gain for the many rather than monopolistic profits for the few. Thus, on the threshold of the partition of Africa a balance of influence existed among the Europeans themselves, on the one hand, just as an equilibrium was maintained, except in South Africa, between the European and African societies on the other. To be sure, the presence of missionaries, merchants, explorers, and soldiers had cleared the way for the expansion of Europe in Africa, but nothing in history is inevitable until it occurs. Yet within less than twenty years, the continent was conquered and divided amidst rising national feeling at home and increasing belligerency abroad. Why? The explanations are nearly as unsatisfactory as they are numerous. The interpretations are as controversial as they are doctrinaire. The misconceptions are as enduring as they are erroneous. To scholar and student alike, the search for understanding this dynamic period which dramatically altered the future of a vast continent, if not the non-Western world, holds out an intellectual challenge more than equal to the intellectual rewards.

The nineteenth century was an age of European expansion not only in territory but also in knowledge. The foundations of science laid down in the seventeenth and eighteenth centuries permitted the construction of an ever-enlarging structure of scientific learning, the practical application of which produced a new technology to meet the insatiable demands of an expanding industry whose products provided Europeans with undreamed of power and more time for more people to undertake intellectual inquiry and political participation. On the one hand, the technological advances of the industrial revolution upset the balance of power between Europe and Africa. On the other, machines began to release men from time-consuming drudgery, providing the means and the leisure for Europeans to satisfy their newly aroused curiosity about far-off lands. Even Christianity expanded. Under assault by secular and scientific thinkers, the Church lost its former hold on men's minds at home and sought to make good its losses by seeking new recruits overseas. Stimulated by an outburst of evangelism, Christian missionaries set out not only to convert the heathen but also to accomplish social and scientific objectives. Thus, David Livingstone was more interested in exploration than conversion, in abolition of the slave trade than evangelism, yet his writings focused British attention on Africa and his personal experiences inspired many to leave Europe to spread the word of Christ in Africa.

The expansion of knowledge, the triumphs of science and technology, and the improvement in the standard of living of the many produced a cultural self-confidence in Europe that found popular and political expression in nationalism. Technological superiority was often confused with national superiority, and it certainly helped to create a rationale for conquering technologically primitive peoples and an Olympian confidence in the superiority of European rule over them. National self-confidence was characteristic of all the European powers but particularly Germany, which, after the victories of the Franco-Prussian War of 1870, became the greatest continental power. Unified by blood and iron, the military monarchy ruled uncontested in a Germany where the threat of a radical uprising rapidly receded before the vision of an unlimited but ill-defined future in which colonialism seemed, for the first time, a viable solution to the problems resurgent Germany would face in the future. Like the great nations of Europe, Germans argued that they, too, must acquire colonies overseas in order to establish protected markets for German industry, while not ignoring her responsibilities to provide enlightened administration and economic progress for backward peoples. By the last quarter of the nineteenth century, German enthusiasm for overseas expansion was irrepressible and sponsored by a network of organizations such as the German Colonial League, (Gesellschaft für Deutsche Kolonisation) characterized by a romantic chauvinism and consisting of a vociferous mixture of economic, geographical, and naval interests.

Germany was not alone in looking beyond Europe after 1870. In 1871, the preeminent position of France on the continent came to an end. Many Frenchmen began to seek overseas for the greatness that had vanished in Europe. The loss of Alsace-Lorraine could be regained in Africa and Asia where vigorous colonial enterprise would regenerate France. The French were not without examples of prosperous colonization. By 1876, over 300,000 Europeans, mostly French, had emigrated to Algeria where French farmers had acquired new vinelands to replace losses sustained on the continent. An outpouring of colonial literature also appeared in these years as French intellectuals—journalists, scholars, civil servants, army officers—began to write on colonial questions. Most argued that colonies were proof of national vitality and would result in economic gain. Not only would the acquisition of new territories broaden man's intellectual horizons but they would also provide raw materials for French factories, markets for French manufactured products, and investment for French capital. What Frenchman could resist the combination of scientific inquiry, intellectual enterprise, and profits. The colonial challenge was for the brave and the bold, the men of the future who were not content to remain in their appointed stations in a Europe characterized by international peace and internal quiescence.

Much the same attitude prevailed among colonial enthusiasts in England, marked, however, by a growing apprehension as the Olympian confidence of the men of midcentury Britain gave way to the hesitancies of the late Victorians. Throughout the first three quarters of the nineteenth century, Great Britain's worldwide naval and commercial supremacy had remained unquestioned. Thereafter, the British had to face, for the first time, very real competition from America and continental Europe, particularly the newly unified nation-states. Perhaps, after all, colonies might not be an unwanted financial burden for the mother country, but rather economic and human assets with which to meet the challenge from land-based powers like Germany, Russia, and the United States. Like the advocates of colonialism in France, British imperialists argued that colonies were an economic benefit but for opposite reasons than their continental counterparts. Instead of regarding the colonies as protected markets, assured sources of raw materials, and isolated opportunities for investment, some viewed the empire as representing a powerful free trade union that would act as a counterweight to the protectionism of the continental powers. Others still retained the old idea of colonies as an outlet for overpopulation and, consequently, a remedy for poverty at home. More pervasive was a new mood that captured the minds and imagination of many Englishmen. The growing emphasis on bigness in industry and society carried over into empire—expansion not so much for the acquisition of new markets as for prestige. To many, particularly the British working class, this sentiment was expressed in the jingoist, flagwaving assertion of British power. To others, it was the duty of an advanced civilization, like Britain, to guide backward peoples out of darkness. Trusteeship was the price of power and prestige was the reward for carrying the torch of civilization into the unknown. Together these ideas created persuasive new arguments in favor of imperialism and a popular enthusiasm for empire in striking contrast to the parsimony of the little Englanders and the pacificism of the Liberals. Disraeli sensed the changing mood in his famous speech at the Crystal Palace in 1872 when he linked Tory conservatism to expanding empire. Imperialism had become not only popular but also good politics.

The assumption and growing acceptance of the idea that overseas expansion was characteristic of national greatness did not cause the partition of Africa; the changing climate of opinion only made the scramble possible. So, too, did the technological gap between Europe and Africa. By the last quarter of the nineteenth century, scientific and technological advances not only made partition possible but also proved decisive in the subsequent conquest and occupation of the African continent. The use of quinine no longer made the malarial areas of tropical Africa a white man's grave. The steamship revolutionized maritime trade and naval strategy, obliterating hitherto formidable distances, opening precarious ports of call, and carrying enormous cargoes both human and material. The locomotive accomplished on land what the steamship achieved on the high seas, and formerly remote hinterlands could now be exposed to large numbers of intruders whether they be soldiers, settlers, or traders. The disparity between African and European technology was even greater in the development of weapons. The invention of repeating rifles and automatic weapons, like the Maxim gun, invested the Europeans with an enormous military superiority. True, Africans obtained considerable numbers of modern rifles, but they never acquired quick firing guns, against which their massed armies were of little avail.

If European imperialism in Africa had become acceptable in the closing decades of the nineteenth century and European technological superiority could make that imperialism possible, the political weakness of the traditional African states vis-à-vis the European nation-state made the European conquest a reality. Many African states fought a valiant if futile struggle against European invasion, and in many parts of Africa a long period of pacification, in fact, followed the initial European conquest. Nevertheless, traditional political institutions generally failed to meet the European challenge. The inequality between the administrative, bureaucratic, and diplomatic resources of the greatest African states and even the weakest European colonial power was too great for African authorities to maintain their independence without the aid of a rival European nation, and almost without exception whatever the political and economic conflicts in Europe, the European powers consistently supported one another when faced by a strong state in Africa. Everywhere thrown on the defensive, African polities certainly influenced and conditioned the scramble, but the European powers determined the partition, occupation, and pacification of Africa.

There were hesitant beginnings to the partition of Africa in the 1870's. The discovery of diamonds in South Africa in 1869 provided the incentive and capital for a large influx of Europeans that ultimately spilled across the Limpopo into Central Africa. The opening of the Suez Canal in the same year, made possible by the steamship, not only made the East African coast more accessible but also soon became the great pivot in British imperial strategy, shifting British interest from Constantinople to Cairo with re-percussions as far south as the great lakes of equatorial Africa and as far west as Wadai and Lake Chad. In 1881, the French reluctantly extended their control over Tunis. Like the British in Egypt, Zanzibar, and Turkey, the French had hoped to main-tain their influence by supporting the government of the Bey and avoiding annexation. Like the British, the French discovered to their dismay that financial and diplomatic manipulation was insufficient to maintain French influence against indigenous re-vulsion to their interference. They had to control Tunis or leave it to the Italians. The French chose to control it. The Italians had hoped to acquire Tunis, but their reaction to the French seizure was to turn against the monarchy rather than to clamor for al-ternative territory in Africa. The occupation of Tunis did not precipitate or signal the beginning of the scramble for Africa. In Tunis, the French were reluctant empire builders, and the reper-cussions might reverberate in North Africa and Europe, but not south of the Sahara. The partition of Africa required greater stimuli than the discovery of diamonds in South Africa or polit-ical intrigue on the Mediterranean littoral. The partitioners did not have long to wait.

On the morning of September 13, 1882, the British Army under the command of General Sir Garnet Wolseley assaulted the en-trenchments of the Egyptian forces at at-Tall al-Kabir. Spear-headed by the Scots of the Highland Brigade, the British troops carried the Egyptian fortifications in twenty minutes and within the hour had routed the Egyptian forces. At-Tall al-Kabir was a complete and decisive British victory. The Egyptian Army had been destroyed and a somewhat muddled British government found itself absentmindedly in sole control at Cairo. Like the French in Tunis, the British occupied Egypt with the greatest reluctance. Like the French, the British had sought to maintain their influence at Cairo by supporting the Khedivial government, not by doing away with it. Like the French, the British had failed. The profligate spending of the Khedive Ismail, in his valiant attempts to simultaneously modernize and expand his empire, had driven Egypt into bankruptcy in 1876. Britain and France intervened and assumed control of Egyptian finances. Intervention, however, produced a strong reaction. Led by Colonel Ahmad Urabi Pasha, a nationalist uprising swept through Egypt destroying European property and lives and disrupting European control until the British Army crushed the nationalists and occupied the country.

British statesmen intended the occupation to be temporary, at best a few short months, at worst a few short years. They had invaded Egypt to protect European financial interests. They had invaded Egypt to restore European political influence. They had invaded Egypt to secure the Suez Canal, lifeline to Britain's Oriental empire. When these objectives were achieved, the British were prepared to depart. No one envisaged a long occupation, and no one ever imagined that the British presence on the shores of the Mediterranean Sea would result in British commitments in tropical Africa. To contemporaries, the British occupation of Egypt appeared to have no relation to Africa south of the Sahara. British officials refused to support the Egyptians in the Sudan and, comforted by the thought that they would soon be leaving, assured the European powers that they had no territorial ambitions elsewhere on the continent. The partition of Africa seemed the least likely outcome of the occupation. Yet even before Britain imposed its rule on Egypt, Henry Morton Stanley, the famous explorer and journalist, was laying claims to the south bank of the Congo on behalf of his employer, King Leopold II of Belgium, while Savorgnan de Brazza had already concluded treaties on the north bank for France. If Egypt were not the beginning of the partition, then what of the activities of Stanley and Brazza in the Congo?

Leopold II had always wanted a colony. In 1876 he founded the International African Association and between 1878 and 1879 dabbled in East African schemes. After Stanley had descended the Congo River in 1877, thereby opening the great basin of that river, the King's interests turned increasingly to the Congo. In 1879, Stanley returned to the Congo as the representative of King Leopold to establish on the river stations of the *Comité d'Etudes du Haut-Congo* (Committee for the Study of the Upper Congo), which Leopold had created to further his growing interest in the region. Leopold had virtually no support in Belgium for colonization, and the penny-pinching burghers of Brussels were not about to embark on expensive schemes of colonization with little prospect of profit or prestige. Nevertheless, Leopold engendered sympathy by appealing to European sentiment against the slave trade, geographical curiosity, and the economic potential of tropical products. By skillful diplomacy, intrigue, and the judicious use of his own wealth, he was determined to establish himself in Africa. During the next five years, Stanley worked assiduously for the King to negotiate treaties with the Africans, to build stations, and to construct lines of communication a thousand miles up the river to Stanley Falls. He was not alone.

In 1880, Savorgnan de Brazza arrived on his second expedition to Gabon. He traveled up the Ogue River, passed over the height of land, and marched down to the Congo River where he signed a treaty in September 1880 with Makoko, Chief of the Bateke, by which Makoko ceded his territory to France. Brazza established a small post under a Senegalese sergeant on the site of the future city of Brazzaville and raised the French flag. In July 1881, nearly a year later, Stanley arrived to find himself forestalled. Making the best of a bad job, he claimed the south bank for Leopold and his *Assocation Internationale du Congo* (International Association of the Congo), which had replaced the *Comité d'Etudes du Haut-Congo* and which was neither international nor an association but an instrument and screen for the king's activities. Brazza returned to France as a hero in June 1882, just two months before at-Tall al-Kabir. In November, 1882, two months after the British occupation of Egypt, the French Chamber ratified Brazza's treaty with Makoko and appropriated 3.5 million francs to organize the new territory. In April 1883, French protectorates were declared over Contonou and Porto Novo on the coast of West Africa. With a surge of patriotic fervor, the French press and Brazza himself overcame past reluctance for empire by French legislators, local economic groups, and statesmen and almost overnight captivated the imagination and interests of the French public with the promise of prestige and riches where before imperial adventures had brought only humiliation and expense. Having failed to act on the Nile, France could not ignore the Congo. True, Brazzaville could not compensate for Cairo nor could Contonou overcome the disgrace of indecision in Egypt. Nevertheless, the Makoko Treaty put France squarely on the map of interior equatorial Africa, and Egypt had been a decisive factor in that decision. The partition of Africa was beginning. Had King Leopold been left behind?

Leopold had not been idle. Brazza's intervention had dramatically demonstrated that Leopold could not maintain his trading stations in the Congo against foreign competition without the protective mantle of sovereignty. Without sovereign rights, Leopold's International Association could hardly hope to continue its commercial activities when faced by the power of those European nation-states, France and Portugal, with claims in the Congo, and the King was now forced to seek more actively sovereign rights for what had been ostensibly a scientific and commercial association. To be sure, Stanley had momentarily countered the French threat north of the Congo by laying claim to the south bank, but Portuguese rights to the mouth of the river presented a more immediate danger to Leopold's presence in the Congo basin. The Portuguese claims were ancient, going back to the first contacts between Portugal and the Kingdom of the Kongo in the fifteenth century. Thereafter, they languished— paper rights of past greatness. No empire, however, no matter how feeble or inefficient, could permit its claims to vanish by default. In fact, the very antiquity of Portuguese rights seemed to demand their vigorous defense. Portugal did not have to act alone. Alarmed by the aggressive activities of Leopold and Brazza, Great Britain sought to close the mouth of the Congo and thereby neutralize the interior. In 1884, Britain recognized Portuguese claims in the Congo by the Anglo-Portuguese Agreement concluded in February.

The Anglo-Portuguese Treaty was in trouble from the start. Portugal was Catholic and long the purveyor of slaves. British Protestant missionary and humanitarian interests were shocked by the association of liberal Britain with the corrupt and decaying Portuguese empire. Moreover, British commercial interests were equally furious that the England of free trade should support the narrow protectionism of Portugal. And, of course, cajoling, intriguing, and supporting the opposition to the treaty was King Leopold who worked frantically to save his claims upriver by insuring the vital access to the sea. By skillful diplomacy and clever propaganda, he created the myth that only his *Association Internationale du Congo* could keep the protectionist powers, France and Portugal, out of the Congo while bringing civilization to darkest Africa. His propaganda did indeed rally support for Leopold both in Britain and elsewhere, but it also exacerbated old rivalries, stimulated national fears, and stirred up suspicion in the chancellories of Europe. Only in an atmosphere of tension, jealousy, and chauvinism could Leopold offer himself as the least threat to the contending interests in the Congo of the other powers.

Suddenly, in the midst of this diplomacy of apprehension, a new and awesome competitor appeared—Imperial Germany. In 1883-1884, Bismarck decided that Germany needed colonies. His motives still remain unclear, and historians today are divided between those who argue that Bismarck's colonial policy was an instrument for resolving domestic or foreign problems while others believe that it was designed, in fact, solely for the sake of having colonies. In Africa, Bismarck could utilize German diplomacy to support French dreams against British pretensions and thereby hopefully take the first step toward the Franco-German reconciliation that the occupation of Alsace-Lorraine had hitherto made impossible. In Africa, Bismarck could acquire colonies to stimulate patriotic feeling within Germany and, consequently, gain support for the empire and himself. Clearly, Bismarck's control of the German government was much too authoritarian to permit a handful of German merchants trading in Africa or even the more powerful German Colonial League to dictate policy, but if they profited from colonies abroad they would surely support the Chancellor at home.

Once determined to seize colonies, Bismarck set out to collect them swiftly and ruthlessly. In a year and a half between 1884 and 1885 Germany acquired extensive regions in South-West Africa, Togoland, the Cameroons, and East Africa. Before the German annexations, the European powers had yet to overcome their hesitancy to precipitate a land rush in tropical Africa. The British were particularly reluctant to take on new commitments in Africa, and their diplomacy was aimed more at preventing the partition of Africa than encouraging it. The French had been aggressive, but the first flush of empire soon wore off to be followed by a hangover of hesitancy. By this time, Leopold could hardly contain his desire for the Congo, but his weak position in Europe and his limited resources in Africa forced him to remain in the shadows until his diplomacy and luck illuminated the way to sovereignty in equatorial Africa. As for Portugal, she did not count.

German intervention resolved all these doubts. Not only did Bismarck seize territory on both sides of the continent, but he joined with France in October, 1884 to invite twelve other states to a conference in Berlin to discuss free trade in the Congo basin, freedom of navigation on the Niger and the Congo rivers, and the requirements for international recognition of European occupation in Africa. The conference opened in November 1884. It passed an act incorporating vague and pious pronouncements regarding the slave trade, free trade, and the ground rules for occupation. In practice, they were to prove largely ineffectual. Of greater consequence was the recognition by the powers of King Leopold's claims to the Congo, but even this international investiture was a foregone conclusion after France, Germany, and the United States had individually recognized the sovereignty of Leopold's International Association in the Congo before the opening of the conference. The real importance of the Berlin Conference in the partition of Africa, however, was neither the Berlin Act, which it produced, nor Leopold's rule in the Congo, which it sanctioned, but the realization that partition was now practicable. When the Berlin Conference ended in February 1885, the scramble for Africa should have been in full swing. Paradoxically, it was not.

Once having agreed on the rules for the partition, each of the contestants seemed reluctant to scramble for African territory. Bismarck had taken much in a short time. Perhaps he was satiated; certainly he had lost interest. In addition, Bismarck required British support for Austria in the Balkans more than British animosity in Africa. Germany made no additional acquisitions in Africa, confining herself in later years to extending the colonies acquired in 1884-1885. Leopold, of course, had the Congo; he could hardly claim more, at least for the moment. France had been the most energetic, but in March 1885 the leading architect of French colonialism, Jules Ferry, fell from power, and it was another five years before the French colonial movement succeeded in overcoming the obstinate and vocal opposition to French overseas expansion that had been momentarily stilled during the heady days of the Makoko Treaty. In the meantime, the French officers who sought the military glory in Africa that they could not win in Europe were checked, if not defeated, by the heroic defense of the Africans—Ahmadu and Samori in the Sudan, King Gele and Behanzin in Dahomey, and later, Rabih Zubayr in the Chad. If none of their rivals seemed imminently aggressive, neither did the British. Bechuanaland in southern Africa had been annexed in 1885 to counter the Germans in South-West Africa and the Boers in the Transvaal, but thereafter in southern Africa the initiative was in the hands of individuals from the Cape Colony whose avaricious and patriotic motives did not immediately commit the imperial government south of the Zambezi. But here the British had no serious European rivals. True, the Portuguese after 1886 had sought to revive their claims to the interior of Central Africa linking Angola and Mozambique, but neither Lusitanian pride nor manipulation could overcome British power, represented not so much by the imperial government but by a private individual—Cecil John Rhodes.

Cecil Rhodes had gone to Africa for his health and drifted to the diamond fields where, by buying up small bankrupt claims, he formed the DeBeers Consolidated Mining Company and became a very wealthy man. He regarded money not as an end in itself, but rather as a means to extend British control into Central Africa. Rhodes' interest in Central Africa was stimulated by the discovery of gold in the Transvaal, and he predicted that additional gold reserves would be disclosed north of the Limpopo. Founding the British South Africa Company to spearhead the drive to the northern interior, Rhodes utilized his great wealth and political position as Prime Minister of the Cape Colony to secure Rhodesia and frustrate Portugal's claims to the interior. Only when a Portuguese expedition was sent into the Shire Highlands in 1889 did the British government, with strong support from Rhodes, directly intervene to prevent Portuguese acquisition of Malawi and clear the way for the formulation of British claims north of the Zambezi River. Having brushed aside their only European rival in southern Africa, the British had even less to fear from the indigenous people. The Bantu groups had, by the 1880's, been subdued. The conflict with the Boers, who counted for little in international relations, was a decade away. Thus, immediately after 1885 the scramble for Africa appeared in slow motion. It could not last. Once again the decisive factor was Egypt.

In the autumn of 1888 (some think in the spring of 1889), the Prime Minister of Great Britain, Lord Salisbury, decided that the occupation of Egypt would have to become more permanent. The implications of this decision were far-reaching. It precipitated the second round in the scramble for Africa. Once the British determined to remain in Egypt, they were committed to its defense. Egypt is a desert that is made to bloom only by the waters that pour out of equatorial Africa and from the highlands of Ethiopia. No African people possessed the technological skills to interfere with the northward flow of the Nile waters. The European powers did. Thus, to protect Suez, that lifeline of empire, the British had to remain at Cairo. When they decided to take up permanent residence in Egypt, they had to defend the Nile waters, wherever they might be—Khartoum, Lake Tana, Fashoda, Uganda. The Berlin Conference may have presaged the partition of eastern Africa; Egypt made it inevitable.

The first threat to the Nile Valley came from Italy. In the great battle of Al-Gallabat between the Mahdists of the Sudan and the forces of King John of Ethiopia, the King was killed by a chance bullet and the Ethiopians routed. The Mahdists marched all the way to Gondar before retiring from the cold and consumption of the hill country. As for Ethiopia, the country was thrown into chaos by the rival factions competing for succession to the Crown of the Lion of Judah, King of Kings, and Emperor of all the Ethiopians—well nearly all. In this fluid situation Menelik, the King of Shoa, sought Italian support to consolidate his position as the emperor. In May 1889, he signed the Treaty of Uccialli. To the Italians, Ethiopia had become a protectorate. To Menelik, he had merely found an ally. The Premier of Italy, Francesco Crispi, was an avowed imperialist, prepared to recreate in Africa the grandeur of Imperial Rome. The Treaty of Uccialli was followed by the big battalions. As long as the Italians remained in the highlands, the British were happy to have someone keep Menelik busy and out of the Nile Valley. When the Italians proved more aggressive, however, and occupied Kassala below the Ethiopian escarpment, Lord Salisbury wasted no time in warning them to keep out of the Nile Valley. Deeply embroiled with Menelik, they agreed.

Having gotten rid of the Italians, Salisbury next had to face the more powerful Germans. Although Bismarck had disclaimed any designs on the Central Africa lakes, his successors did not. The Kaiser was particularly smitten with "equatorial madness" and Carl Peters, one of the most sinister of German imperialists, had eluded naval patrols, reached the German enclave of Witu, and raced inland to sign a treaty in 1890 with Mwanga, Kabaka of Buganda, situated on the shores of Lake Victoria, the enormous reservoir of the White Nile. Peters' movements had not gone unnoticed. With the support of Sir William Mackinnon, a leading British advocate of imperialism and founder of the Imperial British East Africa Company, Salisbury struck a bargain with the Germans, the Anglo-German Agreement of 1890, restricting them to the southern shore of Lake Victoria in return for the island of Heligoland off the coast of Germany. The vital region north of the lake in Uganda had been preserved for Britain. By 1890, the Nile sources seemed secure—but from whom?

During the negotiations with the Germans in 1890, Salisbury had been faced with a dilemma. He wanted to save Uganda and the Upper Nile for Britain. To do so, however, meant abandoning to the Germans the territory south and east of Lake Victoria between Lake Albert Edward and Lake Tanganyika. Unfortunately, this triangular region formed a strategic link in the Cape-to-Cairo Railway, a scheme that had captured the imaginations of Britain's leading and most powerful imperialists—Mackinnon,

Rhodes, and their supporters. Salisbury could not have cared less for an All-Red Route from Capetown to Cairo, but he cared a great deal for the political support of those who did. Thus, how could he defend the Nile without losing the Cape-to-Cairo Railway and its proponents? King Leopold supplied the answer. In a treaty with Sir William Mackinnon's Imperial British East Africa Company, which at that time was carrying British interests into the interior of East Africa, Leopold leased to the company a corridor behind German East Africa, thereby providing the all-important link between Lake Tanganyika, which touched on the British sphere in the south, and Lake Albert Edward whose shores met the British sphere in the north. The price of Leopold's cooperation, for that astute monarch never did anything for nothing, was to extend the sphere of influence of his Congo Free State to the Nile. Salisbury had kept out the Germans but had let in King Leopold.

In 1890, Salisbury did not regard King Leopold as a Nilotic rival. Like many other European statesmen, he seriously underestimated Leopold, for no sooner was the ink dry on the Mackinnon Treaty than the King began to make plans to march to the Nile. His forces reached the Upper Nile in 1892 and at Wadelai raised the blue banner with the golden star of the Congo Free State. The British were stunned. The Mackinnon Treaty was immediately repudiated, and Leopold told in blunt terms to stay out of the Nile Basin. He might have resisted, but his forces had to retire before the Mahdists and with them went King Leopold's principal weapon for negotiation.

While Leopold's forces withdrew from the Nile, the French were on the move. Under the direction of Eugène Etienne, the Under-Secretary for the Colonies in 1887 and 1889–1892, the French colonial movement had revived. Employing the economic arguments of Jules Ferry, Etienne fashioned an aggressive and coordinated program for French imperialism in Africa. The colonial enthusiasm that he generated in France was reciprocated by the bronzed and spurred young officers in Africa. Virtually unchecked by Paris, they frequently committed France to policies which the statesmen privately disapproved but which they publicly could not disavow. If heroism and glory had been sufficient, the French would have occupied the interior of West Africa in a few months. In fact, African resistance was determined enough to prolong the conquest for several years. But then, as long as the French won, a hard-fought campaign was invariably more glorious than a peaceful promenade. In this pursuit of prestige, the French drive for the Nile was launched.

On January 20, 1893, the French hydrologist, Victor Prompt, delivered a paper entitled "Soudan Nilotique" before the Egyptian Institute in Paris. Prompt did not confine his remarks, however, simply to Nile hydrology. He suggested that a dam constructed on the Upper Nile could destroy Egypt. He who controlled Fashoda controlled Cairo. Prompt's lecture had a profound impact on the new Under-Secretary for Colonies, Théophile Delcassé. It was circulated among the French ministries at precisely the time when the British Foreign Secretary had peremptorily re-buffed a French offer to negotiate an agreement to withdraw the British from Egypt. If the British refused to discuss the Egyptian question upon invitation, they must then be intimidated by a threat of interference with the Nile waters. In May 1893, Prompt was summoned to the Elysée Palace where, in private discussions with Sadi Carnot, President of the Republic, Commandant P.L. Monteil, the well-known French explorer, and Delcassé, the great French Fashoda expedition was born. Founded on the superficial speculations of Prompt, the intrigue of Delcassé, who after all was only a very junior minister, and the enthusiasm of President Carnot, the march to Fashoda began. The only one who appeared reluctant was Commandant Monteil. He insisted on obtaining the support of the Congo Free State, but King Leopold was in no hurry to help the French get to the Upper Nile before him. His obstruction not only delayed the Monteil Mission but also provided the opportunity for the new Premier of France, Casimir-Périer, to terminate the mission of which he strongly disapproved.

Although frustrated in France, the Monteil Mission was not forgotten either by the men of the Pavillon de Flore, the French Colonial Ministry, or by officials in Whitehall, the British Foreign Office. British intelligence knew of the Monteil expedition; it required little imagination to guess its destination. Thus, the Liberal's Foreign Secretary, Lord Rosebery, was faced with the same problem as his Conservative predecessor, Lord Salisbury—

how to keep European rivals out of the Nile Valley without actually occupying it? Salisbury had frightened off the Italians by threats and, with an assist from King Leopold, had bought off the Germans with Heligoland. Rosebery obviously could not bully France, and he certainly was not going to withdraw from Egypt. In desperation he turned to King Leopold. On May 12, 1894, the Anglo-Congolese Agreement was signed. It was, in essence, a revised version of the Mackinnon Treaty and leased to King Leopold, on various terms, the whole of the Upper Nile basin west of the river and south of Fashoda. The French were blocked but not, however, for long.

The French were indignant when they learned of the treaty, but that was to be expected. What was not foreseen was the violent reaction in Germany. In return for the loss of the Upper Nile, the British had received a corridor in Congolese territory behind German East Africa. The Tanganyika strip had been more an afterthought than a condition, a sop to the Cape-to-Cairo crowd who still clamored for a passage to link British territories north and south of German East Africa. Unwilling to anger the Germans, Britain did nothing to support King Leopold. Deserted and thoroughly frightened by the veiled threats from Berlin, Leopold gave way and abrogated the article ceding the Tanganyika corridor. Having given way to the Germans, the King could not refuse the French. On August 14, 1894, he signed an agreement with France, limiting his once vast lease to an insignificant enclave at Lado on the Nile. The way to Fashoda was free and clear.

The failure of the Anglo-Congolese Agreement marks the beginning of the last great act of partition in tropical Africa. Not only in the Nile Valley but in West Africa as well the pace of partition quickened. As in East and Central Africa the British advance into Nigeria was led by a commercial concern—the National African Company. Throughout the 1870's, the European coastal traders began to penetrate up the Niger River to the markets of the interior. This was an expensive and fiercely competitive operation, particularly when dealing with the powerful Fulani emirates of northern Nigeria, and resulted in the amalgamation of rival British firms under the brilliant direction of George Goldie to undercut the French and German concerns and establish

a virtual monopoly on the river. In 1886, Goldie's African National Company became the Royal Niger Company under a
royal charter permitting the company to administer justice and
maintain order as well as trade in the Niger interior. The French
responded with political support for their faltering commercial
concerns, and although the struggle for control never reached
the intensity of the Nile quest, the race for Borgu between the
French Captain Decoeur and C ptain Lugard of the Royal Niger
Company signaled another and more militant round in the contest for control of the lower Niger. Joseph Chamberlain, the new
and energetic British Colonial Secretary, was not about to bargain
away deserts in West Africa for interests in eastern and southern
Africa as Salisbury had done in 1890. Vigorously supporting
British men of action in West Africa and stubbornly rejecting
Salisbury's concessions in London, Chamberlain sanctioned an
expedition to occupy Ashanti in 1896, consolidate British control
in the hinterland of Sierra Leone, and, by 1897, was determined
to resist, with imperial forces if necessary, French encroachment
into the lower Niger.

In 1898, the charter of the Royal Niger Company was ter-
minated and the British Government accepted the direct responsibility for defending the British sphere in northern Nigeria,
which had proved too expensive for a private company. Convinced by Chamberlain's firm stand, the French compromised
and signed the Niger Convention in June 1898. The agreement
virtually ended the scramble for West Africa. Now all that the
imperialists had to accomplish was the conquest and occupation
of the spheres drawn on the maps in London and Paris. Within
less than a decade and a half that vast land had been partitioned.
It came none too soon. Three months later the struggle to control the Nile came to a climax. The French had reached Fashoda.

In September 1895, Captain J.P. Marchand, with the support of
the permanent officials of the Colonial Ministry, revived the
Monteil Mission and proposed to lead a French expedition to the
Upper Nile. The project met with a cool reception at first, but
was finally approved in the spring of 1896 following a change of
government in France. Marchand left for Africa in June. The
march to Fashoda had begun, but Marchand was not alone. King
Leopold had never abandoned his Nile quest, and although his

forces had retired from Wadelai in 1892, he laid plans in the summer of 1895 for a new assault. Led by Baron Dhanis, the Congolese
Nile expedition was to march from Stanleyville to the Nile
and then down the river to Fashoda. Unhappily, Dhanis attempted to pass through the terrifying rainforest of the
Aruwimi valley. Here his troops mutinied, and although a second
column under Captain Louis Chaltin did eventually reach the
Nile at Rajjaf and drive off the Mahdist defenders, Chaltin had
neither the men nor the supplies to push northward to Fashoda.

While the French and the Belgians made their way laboriously
toward the Upper Nile, the British became increasingly alarmed.
The disastrous defeat of the Italian Army at the Battle of Adua in
March 1896 ended for a generation Italian attempts to find greatness by conquering Ethiopia. But if Adua kept the Italians out
of Ethiopia, it seemed to let in the French. With Marchand
pressing up the Ubangi and Nile tributaries from the west and
several French expeditions preparing to march from Ethiopia in
the east, British concern turned to outright alarm. Lord Salisbury,
who had returned to power in 1895, began to apply all of his
diplomatic skill and political acumen to defend the Nile. He had
two options: to conquer the Mahdists in the Sudan at great expense and bloodshed or to send a flying column from East
Africa down the Nile to Fashoda. Salisbury had always preferred
to defend the Nile from East Africa rather than Egypt, but
when the construction of the Uganda Railway from Mombasa
to Lake Victoria was delayed and Captain Macdonald's expedition
from East Africa to the Nile was diverted in Uganda, the Prime
Minister ordered General Horatio Herbert Kitchener and his
Anglo-Egyptian army into the Sudan.

In 1896, Kitchener had conducted a limited but successful
campaign along the Dunqula Reach in the northern Sudan. Here
he paused to consolidate his base, construct the all-important
railway across the Nubian Desert, and strengthen his army with
British battalions. By 1898 Kitchener was ready, and in February
he received orders to advance. In April, the Anglo-Egyptian
forces defeated the Mahdists at the Atbara River and, after waiting through the heat of summer in the Sudan, pressed on to the
Mahdist capital of Omdurman. Here on the plains of Karari
outside the city machine guns of Kitchener's army destroyed

the massed host of the Khalifa Abd Allahi. With imperturbable courage, the Mahdists charged the lines of Anglo-Egyptian troops and with matchless bravery they died. By noon on September 2, 1898, the Mahdist State was no more. Kitchener had come none too soon. Marchand had reached Fashoda.

Accompanied by a flotilla of gunboats and troop-laden steamers, Kitchener hurried up the Nile to confront Marchand. Their meeting was cordial. The results were not. Fashoda was the greatest Anglo-French confrontation in nearly a century, and the most serious crisis in Africa between European rivals. Britain was determined and united to secure the Nile. France was divided and hesitant to percipitate a European war over a mud hut village on the edge of a swamp hundreds of miles from the nearest French possession. The French gave way, and after drawn out negotiations with King Leopold, which lasted until 1906, the Nile became safely British. The partition of Africa was virtually complete. Only a handful of states on the periphery of the continent remained free of European control and by the outbreak of the First World War only two countries, Liberia and Ethiopia, maintained their independence. Liberia was not only one of the least attractive regions of the continent but its leaders successfully played off the European powers and the United States against one another to maintain a remarkable degree of independence. Ethiopian integrity was preserved more gloriously by the impressive victory at Adua, checking European imperialism in the Ethiopian Plateau and permitting Menelik to consolidate his rule and extend his control to the south and west. The others, Morocco and Libya, had slipped under French and Italian administration, respectively. France acquired Morocco in 1912 only after facing two crises precipitated by German designs to assert imperial power for the sake of prestige and the ultimate loss of large portions of the French Congo to the German Cameroons. Italy found compensation but not greatness in a desultory war with Turkey that resulted in the annexation of Tripoli and Benghazi. Neither the Franco-German dispute over Morocco nor the Italian-Turkish struggle for Libya possessed the drama or the danger of the Fashoda crisis and were, in fact, the peripheral and rather sandy remains of the scramble for the more tropical regions further south.

PART ONE

Leopold II Takes the Initiative?

MOTIVES

1 P. A. Roeykens: Leopold—Patriot and Philanthropist

A Capucin monk and former missionary in the Ubangi region of the Congo, Father Roeykens has been one of the most prolific historians and staunchest defenders of King Leopold II and his African enterprise. He regards Leopold not only as an unselfish patriot work-ing for the welfare of Belgium but also as a great humanitarian who regarded his intervention in the Congo as the beginnings of civiliza-tion in Africa.

At this point it is impossible to isolate two essential conclusions from the study of the incessant efforts employed by Leopold II with rare energy from 1855 to assure "the external development of Belgium." At the same time they constitute the two funda-mental theses of the history of the origins of the Belgian Congo.

From 1875 the King had no other objective in Africa than that which had inspired all his previous expansionist attempts: the ex-tension of the homeland by the complete delegation of the public power in an overseas domain.

From 1865–1866 the King was convinced that he could only realize that objective by giving the political creation he desired a personal character: it was only indirectly that he could assure

SOURCE. P. A. Roeykens, *Leopold II et L'Afrique, 1855–1880*, Brussels: Académie Royale des Sciences D'Outre-Mer, 1958, pp. 312–317. Translated for this book by Nell Elizabeth Painter and Robert O. Collins. Reprinted by permission of the Académie Royale des Sciences D'Outre-Mer and the author.

for Belgium the external development of which he dreamed. By acquiring for himself the possession and sovereignty of an independent state and by tying the destiny of that overseas empire indissolubly to that of Belgium in the person of their common sovereign, could he expand the structure of the Congress of 1830![1]

Thus it was for the foundation of an Independent State that Leopold II searched in Africa from 1875! Yet we still lack a decisive document to prove definitively this theory. Let us hope that our work will stimulate not only the wisdom of historical critics, but above all, the passion of researchers to complete our documentation.

* * *

The King acted in Africa for Belgium!

All personal considerations on the subject were superfluous for him. Let the King himself tell us in his proud language, which vibrates with all the ardent soul of the great Belgian, of the sentiments which guided him throughout his whole life:

"It is by serving the cause of humanity and progress that the peoples of second class [powers] appear as the useful members of the great family of nations. More than any other, a manufacturing and commercial nation like ours must force itself to assure markets for all its workers, for those of intellect, capital, and labor."

"These patriotic preoccupations have dominated my whole life. They determined the creation of the African accomplishment."

* * *

The King acted for Africa!

What was the center of Africa before 1876? A vast region, mysterious, inaccessible, backward; the fertile terrain of customs which were still barbarous and abominable; the reign of ignorance and poverty; a land of all sorts of horrors; the hunting ground of the slaving hordes.

---

[1] After the revolution in the summer and declaration of Belgian independence in October 1830, an international congress met in London, recognized the independence of Belgium, and in the Protocol of January 21, 1831, guaranteed the perpetual neutrality of Belgium. *Ed.*

It is true that Leopold II tried to open markets for Belgian industry and commerce there, but it is no less true that he wanted to open to Belgium a vast territory awaiting a noble mission of civilization. He wanted to bring to Africa the liberation from the horrors of the slave trade, the blessings of Christian civilization, progress in all areas, work and prosperity, order and peace, capital and energy which would make this land one of the richest and happiest parts of the world.

* * *

The King acted in Africa for the entire world!

Sovereign of a small neutral country, he protected the center of Africa from the egoistic cupidity of those more powerful than himself; in Africa he made himself the arbiter of everyone's interests. He understood that the interests of Belgium and of his Congolese state were identical with those of all other nations. He opened wide his empire to the most enterprising. His initiative, his energy, and his genius preserved the center of Africa from a cruel war among nations preoccupied above all with maintaining their power and wealth at the expense of others. Leopold II realized in Africa a work of international equilibrium. In working for Belgium and the Congo, he was working for all nations! Leopold II created in Africa an international balance of power. In working for Belgium and the Congo, he worked for all nations.

* * *

Leopold II attempted to realize a personal work in Africa!

The attitude of his fellow citizens forced him to do this. He explains it himself:

"The beginning of enterprises, like those which have preoccupied me so much, is onerous and difficult. I have insisted on sustaining their burdens. To serve his country a king must not be afraid to conceive and carry out the development of a work, even if it appears foolhardy."

He appropriated absolute powers for himself in Africa!

This was not because his goal was a conceited satisfaction of his own omnipotence, but because for him these powers were the indispensable leverage to attain the results he envisaged and to complete his projects for the advantage of Belgium. Such was always the dominant thought of the King-Sovereign.

* * *

A great lesson emerges from the history of the beginnings of the African accomplishment of Leopold II. Beernaert expressed it to the Belgium Chamber on April 23, 1889:

"It is for Belgium that the King has worked. It is for this country that he has surmounted ever recurring difficulties that would have tried even the most indefatigable. It is for this country that he has spent so much money . . .

"In our hands the enterprise would have been less successful and certainly would have cost more. The partisan spirit, which spoils all it touches, would have taken it over. We would have discussed when we should have acted."

"Thus the King has alone supported the weight of this enterprise, so vast that it almost seemed foolhardy and above the strength of one man. He wanted to carry out alone what he considered the great idea of his reign."

* * *

In 1880 the *Congo* affair was definitively launched. The King had only to bring it to a successful conclusion. It needed the master's touch.

Since 1861 Lambermont had been his confidant and wise counselor, and he continued to be during the Congolese enterprise. The Duke of Brabant had found and the King continued to meet in the Belgian diplomatic corps eminent men who shared his patriotic passion and his ardent desire to assure the future of Belgium and to open wide the horizons of expansion. Among them were Blondeel van Cuelenbroeck, Du Jardin, Greindl, Solvyns, Banning, and many others who are less well known. Among businessmen he found people full of energy and the spirit of initiative who were able to appreciate the views of the prince and King, and who did their best to second him—among them Sadoine, Verheyden, and Lambert occupy a place of honor. In the officer corps of the army the King found select men whose aspirations were noble and entirely oriented towards the greatest interests of the country. The greatest among them were Thys, Brialmont, and Strauch. And when from 1877 it was a question of going into the heart of Africa to carry out the royal projects, officers of the Belgian army presented themselves for this pioneering task. Let us give them the honor they merit. Their efforts were not always crowned with success. Many sacrificed their lives to the cause of Belgian expansion and African civilization. We would like to [be able to] cite Belgian politicians of the period 1875-1878 as well who espoused the African cause, but they alone missed the call. The reason: the incorrigible, small-minded partisan spirit which rendered them incapable of rising to the superior level where great ideas are born and which makes great nations. Only several years later would the King meet a Belgian statesman of sufficient stature to appreciate the situation and who would completely espouse the Congolese cause: Auguste Beernaert.

Finally, Leopold II was able to ally himself with precious friends outside the country, particularly De Lesseps, Sanford, MacKinnon, Hutton, Rabaud, and many others less well known.

Belgian journalists? Taken together their contribution was hardly positive or favorable during the first three years of the African enterprise. In addition, when the King began the grand affair in Africa itself, from the time of the sad experience at the death of the leader of the first expedition, he asked silence and discretion of them as the greatest service they could render to a good cause.

The Belgian people? In the beginning they answered with enthusiasm and generosity worthy of the great cause in question: the liberation of African peoples, and the introduction of civilization in the center of the dark continent. The movement did not continue because it was not supported by those who should have provided the leadership for the masses and because the press, with its harmful ideological quarrels, falsely interpreted public opinion.

Finally, the King found in Stanley the energetic man who would lay down the material base for his African empire.

2   *Jean Stengers: The Place of Leopold II in the History of Colonization*

Jean Stengers is Professor of History at the Free University of Brussels and one of Belgium's leading historians of imperialism in the reign of King Leopold II. Neither an apologist for the iniquities of the King, on the one hand, nor convinced that Leopold's quest for a colony sprang from base and avaricious motives on the other, Professor Stengers argues that Leopold was unique, not only because his imperialism was guided by economic theory, but also because he pursued his objective as a Belgian patriot without regard for personal profit.

The originality of Leopold II's imperialism was, first of all, his point of departure.

His imperialism, which was the triumph of action, was the product of theory. With Leopold II the politics of colonialism can only be understood as a function of [economic] doctrine.

What is this doctrine? It is one of extreme simplicity. Leopold II, considering the industrial character of Belgium, professed that the principal effort of the country should tend towards the conquest of markets. Now of all markets, the most sure and the most stable, for products as well as for capital, is obviously that of a colony. Belgium's interest therefore commanded him to create a colonial domain.

Such is the thinking, very much simplified but not at all distorted, which the young Duke of Brabant expressed with force after 1860. He expressed it in his speeches in the Senate, he expressed it in his letters to Brialmont and others; he also expressed

SOURCE. Jean Stengers, "La place de Léopold II dans l'histoire de la colonisation," *La Nouvelle Clio*, No. 9, October 1950, pp. 517–536. Translated for this book by Nell Elizabeth Painter and Robert O. Collins. Reprinted by permission of the author.

it when, returning from a trip to Greece, he gave the Prime Minister Frère-Orban a "souvenir of Athens"—in deplorable taste by the way—on which he had had engraved the inscription: *Belgium must have a colony.*

This colonial doctrine, which Leopold II possessed from the age of 25, would remain his own during the whole of his life. It would inspire the whole of his politics. And because of it, I think, Leopold II is original.

In fact when one reviews at a glance the whole of the history of European colonization during the nineteenth century —at least up to the years 1880–1885—one cannot but remark that the part played by doctrine in this history was very weak beside that played by events. The colonial policies of Europe, from 1880–1885, were almost never guided by theoretical considerations. The English and French statesmen who conquered colonies had, most certainly, more or less firm ideas on the subject of the utility of a colonial domain, but it was not these ideas which guided them: events, contingencies, played in almost every case the decisive role.

What determined colonial conquest was nearly always practical considerations or necessities: the government decided on conquest because it wanted to assure the security of neighboring colonies, because it wanted to defend its citizens against the vexations of a native prince, because it wanted to prevent the installation of a foreign power in the country, or yet again, simply because it was casting about for an easy and brilliant victory which would augment its popularity. . . .

And so the colonial policies of the nineteenth century appear to us, in their totality, dictated infinitely more by facts than by theories. Leopold II was himself an exception to the rule. All his policies were modeled on his doctrine. Nothing, in the facts, urged him on to colonial enterprises. He pushed himself into it because such was his program. This is, and I repeat it, what confers a completely unusual character to his work.

If the motives for action were carefully weighed and thought out by Leopold II, the action itself was for an impetuosity which left only a subsidiary place to reason. General Strauch, who was one of the first and one of the most active collaborators of Leopold II, observed in the twilight of his life that the King began his

Congo adventure with "no previous study." Following Leopold II in his first colonial attempts—watching him successively try to colonize the Pacific Islands, try to establish himself in northern Borneo, attempt to buy the Philippines, put proposals of purchase before both Holland and Portugal—the words of Strauch come invincibly to mind. It is clear that the King, in these attempts, was not guided by a reasoned knowledge of the resources of the countries which he sought to acquire. He wanted a colony, he sought one everywhere, he was ready to seize the first offered. And at the end of this obstinate quest, he threw himself on the Congo.

This is the decisive moment, and we must pause here for a moment.

Stanley's departure for the Congo, at the head of an expedition sent by Leopold II, was at the beginning of 1879. Now, at least four years earlier, the region where the King of the Belgians began his conquest had been officially offered to England. In fact, in 1874–1875 the English explorer Cameron, crossing the upper Congo Basin, concluded treaties with the local chiefs which accorded a protectorate of the country to England. Before leaving Africa, Cameron had even issued a proclamation by which he took possession of the Congo Basin in the name of his sovereign. On his return to London in 1875 Cameron eagerly submitted his treaties and his proclamation to the English government. The Foreign Office scornfully put them aside. It was the same indifferent welcome which English opinion would make to Stanley when he, as the good Englishman that he remained, tried to interest England in the immense countries that he had just discovered. England was not interested in Central Africa.

Who, in truth, was interested? It would have been very difficult to say. The general opinion was that these were countries whose economic value was too slight to permit a rational exploitation. In 1884 still, the Portuguese Minister of Foreign Affairs, talking with our [Belgian] envoy in Lisbon, explained his conviction—sincere from all indications—that an enterprise such as that of Leopold II in Central Africa would never be lucrative—or at least, that it would only be after a long passage of time. This was certainly the general sentiment within European political circles.

How then can we explain the initiative of Leopold II? Had the

King assembled data on the subject of the Congo Basin which convinced him of an error in this opinion? Nothing permits this belief. In actual fact his information was no more than that of his contemporaries. Like that of his contemporaries, it was taken almost exclusively from the works of Stanley. Now Stanley had brought back only very vague accounts of his grand expedition. He was, we must not forget, an explorer of extraordinary energy, but of rather limited education; during the course of his descent of the river Congo he was unable to analyze in a scientific manner the wealth of the country which he had traversed.

Leopold II had, therefore, no valid reason to believe in the wealth of the Congo. If he set off into a practically unknown region, it was simply because he was animated by faith in the colonial idea: he wanted a colony, he set off into that one offered to him. The rest was a question of luck. It was luck alone that the regions he took contained wealth of the first order.

But when one evokes the good fortune which favored Leopold II, it is not only of the prodigious resources of our present Congo that we must think—in Kasai, Katanga, or in Kilo-Moto. We must also—and above all—think of the immediately exploitable resources which the Congo offered its sovereign. In order to realize the importance of this factor it suffices to compare the economic evolution of the Congo with German East Africa. In 1907, when the Congo had already yielded considerable profit for more than ten years, East Africa still had to call on the metropole for nearly 60 percent of its expenditure. The Congo had what East Africa did not: it had rubber. There is no doubt that without rubber, which the creepers of the equatorial forest furnished immediately and in abundance, Leopold II would have met catastrophe. With his limited resources he would have been unable to support the State during the period of its development; and could he, before a permanent and hopeless deficit, count upon aid from Belgium?

And so we see that the god of chance doubly blessed Leopold II. The mineral resources of the Congo—which the King could not suspect—its wealth in rubber—which was not fully realized until rather late, in 1893–1894—appear to us as the double triumph of a lucky gambler.

For there was something of the gambler in Leopold II. There was something of the gambler in the man who, in 1897 upon giving his forces the order to march on Khartoum, confided to his general secretary that he "did not believe in success, but that the risk was necessary because the ends might be very favorable."

There was something of the gambler in the sovereign who, twice during the Berlin Conference and to the great stupefaction of his collaborators, threatened to abandon everything in the Congo. It was not a question there, as has been thought, of a simple diplomatic maneuver; the intention was very serious: his attempt to secure the Congo seeming to have failed, the King preferred to pass.

In the Sudan, where he spent a disproportionate effort, Leopold II gambled and lost. In the Congo, he gambled and won.

Let us understand each other well however: the real throw of the dice, in the case of the Congo, was the decision of principle, the decision to rush into the conquest of a vast region which was still mysterious. But in the execution of this design it is far more than the countenance of a gambler. It is that of a vigilant chief, tenacious and obstinate, which reappears incessantly. Leopold II controlled, in the full sense of the word, an enterprise which joined the difficulties of a political creation with all those of a commercial organization. He held all its strings in his hands, and in all domains he gave the full measure of that creative perseverance which left him only during his final moments.

In the firm and vigilant manner in which the chief directed the whole of his work, one can recognize another of the originalities of Leopold II. In colonial history, indeed, great results are nearly always explained by the conjuncture of two factors: the action of the metropolitan authorities and the action of the colonizers themselves. Beside the initiatives of the metropole there have nearly always been those—often much more daring—of the men in the colony. In the history of the Congo there was not this conjunction of two initiatives. Everything came from Leopold II. The King's agents in Africa, tightly held in hand by their master, never did anything other than conform to instructions.

The thousands of square kilometers of the French colonial empire—to begin with, as E. F. Gautier has effectively shown, the immensity of the Sahara—are due to the initiative of the colonizers. In the Congo, there is not one square kilometer of territory that can be attributed to them. The entire Congo was forged in the offices of the Palace in Brussels.

Is this to say that all that happened in the Congo during the reign of Leopold II was desired and decided by the King? It would be a great exaggeration to pretend so. One could say without paradox that what escaped the will of the King is that which, in history, carries his name: I mean to speak of the Leopoldian regime. The King was never able to fully control the regime of the Congo. He made the rules of this regime; he was never master of their application. On this point, the last word reverted to the agents in Africa, to men who grappled with the concrete realities of colonial life—and this we know was often brutal and without mercy.

I do not want to discuss here the question of the abuses of the Leopoldian regime. It is not that I am afraid of the subject—a historian must know how to face it squarely—but I vow that, at present I have not been able to clearly define the attitude of Leopold II on this question. There is here, from the point of view of the psychology of the King as well as from the point of view of his policies, a problem which the lack of documents does not yet permit resolving. But at least one thing seems certain: that is that the King did not anticipate the abuses which took place. When he knew that they had taken place—it was in 1899—he was profoundly upset. "I am tired" he wrote at the time, "I am tired of being soiled with blood and filth." This angry utterance was that of a man who sensed that, on one point, the control of the mechanism which he had shaped had escaped him.

* * *

In the study of the power of Leopold II there is another aspect which ought to occupy our attention here; it is his own anachronism.

In his African reign Leopold II was a profoundly anachronistic sovereign. He was such both by the nature of his power and his concept of it.

"The sovereignty of the Congo," wrote Félicien Cattier in 1898, "is invested in the person of the Sovereign. Leopold II is not the depository, but the titulary of sovereignty. All governmental rights and duties are summed up and incorporated in his person. . . . He is the direct source of legislative power, of executive power, of judicial power. . . . His will can encounter no judicial obstacle." These sober words of a jurist sufficiently describe the anachronism of this fact. In a universe where absolutism was everywhere vehemently attacked, Leopold II represented pure absolutism. There is no more striking proof than the testament by which the sovereign in 1889 bequeathed the Congo to Belgium: "We declare by those present to bequeath and transmit to Belgium, after Our death, Our sovereign rights in the Independent State of the Congo." Count de Lichtervelde wrote very justly, "this transmission of sovereignty by testimony—as though sovereignty were part of the patrimony—recalls the High Middle Ages and rests without precedent in the modern world."

But as striking as it might seem to us, the absolute power which the King disposed of in the Congo posed no problem: it is a question here of a state of affairs which the history of the Congo's foundation explains perfectly.

The difficulty is greater when one understands the concept which Leopold II had of his power. The King considered himself not only as the sovereign of the Congo, but also as the proprietor, in the strict sense of the word, of the State and its territory. In this regard the texts are precise. In a note of 1901 the King defined himself as the "absolute incontestable proprietor of the Congo and its wealth." Again elsewhere when establishing a balance-sheet of the past, he wrote: "The King was the founder of the State, He was its organizer, *its proprietor*, the undivided Sovereign. . . ."

Assertions of this kind, one could guess, have provoked expressions of horror from the jurists. It was a question there, wrote one of our most eminent specialists of public law, "of a concept which is no longer used in absolute monarchies. Under the last Merovingians it was already crumbling."

But we should not occupy ourselves here with the judicial heresy which such a concept represented. What interests us is the problem posed by the psychological attitude of the King on this point.

For there is a problem here. Let us not forget that in Belgium Leopold II was a perfect constitutional sovereign. Just after his death Jules van den Heuvel, who had been one of his ministers but not one of his courtiers, recalled the words of homage which Gladstone had addressed to him. "King Leopold," Gladstone declared in 1873, "is one of those sovereigns from whom we would not be ashamed, if there were need, to receive those lessons of constitutional government which we sometimes have the pretension to teach." And van den Heuvel added: "The Belgian King, Leopold II, has never ceased to merit this eulogy."

Leopold II not only respected the Belgian constitution; more than that, he seemed to accept it. Leopold I did not hide the fact that he considered perfectly absurd the pact to which he was held to conform. In the correspondence and conversations of Leopold II one would seek in vain for a judgment of this kind. Leopold II certainly desired a reinforcement of royal power—and he did attempt to obtain it at the time of the constitutional revision of 1893—but he nevertheless recognized the legitimacy and the advantages of an essentially liberal constitution such as that which the Belgians of 1830 had given their country.

In this regard, the second king of the Belgians appears to us as a modern sovereign. To cite only one example, it was a modern sovereign who appeared, opposed by one of the *Ancien Regime*, in the extraordinary scene at the Palace of Potsdam in 1904. William II, receiving the King of the Belgians, spread out his extravagant projects. He "spoke of his proud predecessors, the Dukes of Burgundy, adding that if the King wished it, he could reconstitute their state and spread his scepter over French Flanders, Artois, and the Ardennes." Leopold II, opening his eyes wide, answered that neither his ministers nor the Belgian Chambers wanted to hear anything of such projects: "Well then," relates the emperor himself, "I lost patience and I told him I could not respect a monarch who judged himself responsible before deputies and ministers, and not before the Lord who reigns in heaven."

This scene is significant. It shows us that in the circle of European monarchs, Leopold II was an advanced liberal. How can it be explained that as sovereign of the Congo, this modern king would nurse such profoundly backward concepts?

I think the explanation is twofold. It is necessary first to search in the circumstances surrounding the foundation of the Congo. Leopold II had done everything in the Congo—in the beginning at least—with his own resources. It was with his personal fortune that he had built and supported his work. The financial effort

which he had to furnish was very exhausting; more than one
time, it is certain, the King skirted ruin. For that reason would
he not have been tempted to consider this acquisition, which had
cost him such great sacrifices, as his property? The Congo was
his thing, his creation, the work which he had fed with his own
money and his own labor: could he not say that he possessed it?

He had even fewer scruples in saying it because his conception
of colonies perfectly accommodated such an assumption. We know
that his doctrine of expansion was essentially an economic
one. A colony, in his eyes, was valuable essentially for the material advantages which it offered the metropole: it should be
above all, in his concept, a great and profitable commercial enterprise. Now does not the idea of commercial enterprise precisely
recall the idea of property?

And so, when the jurists speak, and when we, following them,
speak of this retrograde concept, we fail to understand, for we
place the problem on a level—the political level—which was not
that on which the thinking of Leopold II moved. It was in reality
the great capitalist, the contemporary of the Rockefellers and
the Carnegies, who declared that he possessed the Congo as
Rockefeller possessed *Standard Oil* and Carnegie his steel mills.

*   *   *

If he was "the absolute and incontestable proprietor of the
Congo and its wealth," the King did not, however, exploit his
estate for personal profit. He was a king of business, as Paul
Hymans has said very correctly, but he made his business for the
country.

The country, the metropole, occupied the principal place in
his system.

Here again, in fact, we must speak of a system. The King, in
his concept of the relationship between the colonies and the
metropole, was profoundly imbued with the theories of the
Ancien Regime: a colony, to his mind, was made for the metropole, it must serve the interests of the metropole. One day, speaking of the Congo he let the word "milk-cow" escape. The
expression was perhaps exaggerated, but it certainly did not
distort his conception of the Congo.

Would we still say in this regard that Leopold II was anachronistic? Quite to the contrary, he was profoundly within his time: a time which, although it did not dare employ the formulas of the *Ancien Regime*, continued, consciously or unconsciously, to think according to its formulas.

There is nothing more characteritsic in this dichotomy—in that concerning Leopold II himself and in that concerning his contemporaries—than the propaganda which the future Sovereign of the Congo put out towards the years 1883–1885, on the eve of his creation of the Independent State.

Leopold II, at that time, presented himself as a philanthropist, as a man totally disinterested, seeking to found what one would call an "ideal colony." The language which he spoke aimed, in a systematic manner, to attract the sympathy of the civilized world to the future state.

Now what was this language by which Leopold II sought to gather the admiration of his contemporaries? In what did the philanthropy of which the King boasted consist? It consisted, of course, in the suppression of the slave trade and of cannibalism. But above all it consisted in opening the Congo, according to the formula which the King affectionately termed, to the "commerce of all nations." It consisted above all in serving the interests of the white nations.

Of the primacy of native interests, which is today the proclaimed principle of colonization, Leopold II, completely occupied as he was in presenting himself as the ideal colonizer, had not even a second thought. In this, at the same time that he characterized himself, one might say he characterized an era.

But here we must immediately introduce a reservation. In regard to the very principle of colonial exploitation, Leopold II thought in keeping with his times. In the application of this principle however, he separated from his contemporaries.

The nineteenth century reserved the profits of colonial exploitation for private enterprise. Its ideas on the advantages of colonies, in other words, were essentially placed on the level of individual interests—and in public interest inasmuch as it was the sum of individual interests. In contrast it was inconceivable that the metropolitan state might itself profit from the resources of its colonies. It was a well-established principle of colonial science that the public finances of a colony should be administered exclusively in the interest of the colony and never in that of the metropole.

Now Leopold II precisely rejected this distinction. He wanted the Congo not only to profit some Belgians, but Belgium herself. From the time that the colony's budget received a surplus he set aside, in a systematic manner, a portion—and a considerable portion—for the metropole. This way of acting seemed absolutely legitimate to him. Belgium, represented by her Sovereign, had opened the Congo to commerce and civilization. She had the right to receive some benefit from it. It is necessary, wrote the King in 1896, that the Congo contribute its "just participation to the embellishment of our territory, in the support of old workers who found themselves in need" and to the creation of a national marine. The first point of this program, we know, was immediately put into effect. It was made concrete in the lavish policy of public and urban works which characterized the last ten years of his reign.

But Leopold II transgressed against the principles. He alone, or nearly so, spoke of "just participation." When he wanted to continue, after the recovery of the Congo by Belgium, the policies which he had practiced during the time of the Independent State, he was abandoned. Even his own government would no longer follow him.

I cannot stop myself from citing here a text which seems to me particularly revealing concerning the opposition which showed itself at that time between the Sovereign and his ministers, or in other words, the opposition between orthodoxy and heterodoxy.

In order to perpetuate the Congo's contribution to Belgium, Leopold II, we know, had created an immense foundation called the *Foundation of the Crown*. When the nature of this institution became known, it precipitated violent criticism. At the parliamentary commission charged with the examination of the treaty [to cede the Congo to Belgium], numerous questions were asked concerning the extent of the Foundation, its statutes, its objectives, etc.

The Independent State—that is to say in the person of Leopold II—answered them point by point. But the royal replies were not directly transmitted to the Commission; they first passed through the hands of the government, where they were carefully dressed up. We have had the good luck to possess both texts: the original text of the King and the revised text of his ministers. The comparison is instructive.

Here is Leopold II.

"What is the Foundation?" asked the King. "It is the approximation of the revenue of certain holdings which the Sovereign has designated for patriotic ends. It has no personal advantage for the Founder; on the contrary, the property of the Foundation is used entirely for the embellishment of the Homeland, the creation of a marine, the development of world instruction, and in Africa, for hospitals and education."

And the King made this more precise:

"The Foundation of the Crown makes possible, without contribution from Belgians, great things of a useful nature which they themselves would have had to finance in the end. . . . The Sovereign Founder does not aim at the construction of a new palace. He aims at the completion of what was begun at Laeken, at the Hôtel de Belle-Vue at Ostend. He forsees the creation of a museum at Ostend, promised to the city, the establishment of a vast covered Hall for exhibitions . . . , and the joining of the street Royale to the area of the Galleries and the Race Track by an architectural ensemble, so as to make Ostend, only a few hours from London, a unique sea-side resort.

"The Foundation should facilitate, in many of the country's congested areas, the progressive enlargement of roads bordering beautiful gardens in the cities, and in Belgian cities everywhere, the establishment of squares and public promenades."

"In Africa," the King adds, "the program of the Foundation will be to establish hospitals, churches, and schools."

But after this short parenthesis, he quickly comes back to public works. "The goal of the Foundation, from the point of view of public works, is thus, in time, and without demanding a centime from the taxpayers, to serve in the beautifying of the country and enjoyment of the public, etc., etc."

The essential point, the capital point, of the program, that is to say, the realization of grand public works, was therefore stressed unequivocally.

But the Belgian government was vigilant. Before the short sentence of two lines relative to works in Africa, a ministerial hand inscribed: "To be developed at length."

And here is the government text. Public works in Belgium? A few lines. It was limited to stiffening the democratic spirit of the program a little by adding, "the creation of certain sensible and reasonably priced model residential areas." But as soon as one comes to Africa, what poetic enthusiasm!

"The philanthropic and social works which the Foundation of the Crown must help to realize are multiple. The instruction and education of the Negroes will be one of its preoccupations. . . . Its role will be to aid the multiplication of the number of schools, erection of buildings, the granting of scholarships to young Negroes during their schooling. . . . The Foundation is equally reserved for the aid of Catholic missionaries in their educational mission, by means of subsidies or otherwise, in the creation, development, and amelioration of their establishments, by aiding, according to its resources, the supply of furnishings and scholastic materials, by favoring the addition of workshops or model farms."

"The needs of the population are even more pressing from the standpoint of their sanitary condition. The establishment of a number of hospitals is urgent. . . . The present hospitals for blacks are insufficient; it is necessary that they be multiplied and equipped. . . . The ravages caused by sleeping sickness require the installation, without delay, of research laboratories, . . . the creation of medical observation posts, the foundation of quarantine-stations. . . . The Crown Foundation considers that one of the best reasons for its existence is its being given the opportunity of contribution . . . to the fight against this frightening disease. . . ."

"The Foundation may also participate, in as much as its resources permit, in the work of evangelizing the black race. The missions, etc."

And it goes on—for here I am only citing extracts—for two whole pages.

One can therefore see the effort made by the government to bring back to colonial orthodoxy—that is to say to the principle of the utilization of colonial resources to the profit of the colony itself an essentially heterodox institution. Even so, this effort was still in vain. Under pressure from parliamentary opinion the Foundation of the Crown had to be abandoned. The endowment voted to Leopold II in exchange for its abandonment was added to the metropolitan budget. It was the return—the definitive return—to principles so long misconstrued.

*   *   *

In these few considerations of the colonial policy of Leopold II, I have brought out in more than one instance the preponderant importance which the King attributed to material interests. The fact is incontestable that Leopold II envisioned all colonization in this light. "The duty of a Sovereign," he declared near his death, "the duty of a Sovereign is to enrich the nation." Such was the meaning which he attributed to his life's work. In giving the Congo to Belgium he had fulfilled his duty, he had enriched his country.

But should all these material formulas lead us to believe that the King's policies were inspired exclusively by considerations of interest? Can we consider Leopold II as one of those powerful businessmen who accord no place to feelings?

That would be both to know him imperfectly and misunderstand him. On the contrary in the policies of the King, feelings played a vital role.

Two great feelings, two great passions, it appears to me, lived in the spirit and the heart of the Sovereign.

And first of all, was his passion for grandeur.

This passion for grandeur in Leopold II was by no means a passion for glory. Glory, just as popularity, hardly counted in the eyes of the King. His pride, which was immense, had taken the form of a haughty distrust of public opinion. He deigned neither to seek the applause of his contemporaries nor the admiration of posterity. One could find no better proof in this regard than in the manner in which he disposed of his enormous profits from the Congo during the last ten years of his reign. Louis XIV constructed royal buildings and had the *Histoire metallique* coined. Now the King-Sovereign never for a moment dreamed of an *Histoire metallique*. He consecrated his millions to the embellishment of Brussels, of Tervueren, of Ostend, but in his enterprises, in which he was everything, he often remained nearly anonymous. The King hid himself behind the Crown or behind men of straw. The fifteenth Anniversary Arcade cost him several millions (more than a hundred million francs today), but in inaugurating it he thanked, without a smile, the "generous donors." He wanted to be a Builder-King, but he cared little about reaping the glory. The administration of the Independent State, which bought so many writers and journalists, used them only to defend the Congo. Be himself celebrated? Leopold II never spent a centime on it. In 1896 he asked Paul Hymans, who submitted to him an article dedicated to his reign, to take out "quite a few passages, all that eulogized him," for, he added with disillusioned realism, "eulogy always begins reaction."

But the King who scorned glory aspired to grandeur. He dreamed of great things, and in the ardor with which he realized them, one senses the satisfying of a passion.

It was truly a passion which made of him the prodigious Builder-King which he was in his last years. It was passion as well which flashed across his whole Nile policy. What satisfied that obstinate will to establish himself on the Nile, that will which cost him super-human efforts, which, at certain moments, made him sacrifice all the other interests of the State? The answer was, in a few words which the King hurled one day at the Secretary of State: "These are my colors," he said, "and I refuse to give them up!"

But beside this aspiration to grandeur, there was another passion which animated the King, and which, far more than the first, was his great source of inspiration: it was patriotism. His contemporaries, both adversaries and admirers, sensed the depth of this patriotism, this ardent love of his country. When, in 1902, the King answered a delegation of the Chamber come to greet him: "I am in my life's decline. I do not know when my hour will sound, but as long as I live, all that I possess of devotion and activity will belong to the nation."—there was no one, even among his worst enemies, who dared scoff. For those words, as each one knew, were true.

His patriotic ideal does not only serve to explain the King, it also explains the exceptional devotion of which Leopold II, during the whole of his reign, was successfully assured. One day a high ranking Congo functionary was asked about the manner in which he took service with Leopold II. "Sir, he answered, "the first time that I saw the King, he spoke to me of patriotism with such passion, that I was profoundly moved; from that moment, I was entirely devoted to him."

And so, even when one speaks only of the colonizer, it is to the man and to the patriot that one is irresistibly drawn. And at the foot of the portrait of this great creator of empire there is no better inscription than that of Leopold II who has bequeathed us the text: "Belgium, our passionately loved homeland. . . ."

3   Neal Ascherson: From The King Incorporated

Although acknowledging the patriotism of King Leopold II, Neal Ascherson, American biographer and writer, does not accept royal altruism as the sole motive for Leopold's African adventure. The King may very well have wanted to beautify Belgium with Congo profits, but he also sought to endow the monarchy with a great private fortune from the wealth of Africa which would make him and his successors independent of the penny-pinching burghers of Belgium, Parliament, and ultimately the Constitution.

THE CAPITALIST KING

In the evolution of monarchy, Leopold II of the Belgians occupies a special position. Like one of those last dinosaurs at the end of the saurian age whose very size or length of fang or desperate elaboration of armour sought to postpone the general decline of their race, Leopold developed in his own person a

SOURCE. Neal Ascherson, *The King Incorporated*, New York: Doubleday & Co., 1964, pp. 11–13, 238–240, 272–280. Copyright © 1963 by George Allen & Unwin Ltd. Reprinted by permission of Doubleday & Company, Inc.

most formidable type of King, designed for the environment of the late nineteenth century, which used the new forms of economic growth to strengthen and extend royal authority. Other monarchs watched the birth of modern trust capitalism with mixed feelings of suspicion, incomprehension and contempt. Leopold understood that the private fortunes of a King remained as much a measure of his power to act freely as they had been in the Middle Ages.

New sources of money provided a new way of escape from the control of Cabinets, now firmly in charge of the King's official allowance through Civil Lists. The Belgian Constitution gave the Kings considerable powers, but little freedom of action beyond those specified duties; Leopold wanted to endow the Belgian Coburgs with a great private fortune to be used for the nation's good as they would see fit, and to liberate them from the control of penny-conscious politicians. To achieve this, he proposed that the King should himself become a grand financier, a tycoon who could offer his creditors the incomparable security of a Crown. Leopold had discovered a way to reverse the historical victory of the middle classes over their kings: a new path to absolutism.

The attempt failed. Leopold made himself one of the richest men in Europe, but he failed either to transmit the body of his wealth to his descendants or to exercise freely the power it gave him. With the rise of international trust capitalism came the parallel growth of Socialism, and by the end of his reign the Belgian Left, inside and outside Parliament, was strong enough to block his way and even to strip him of his greatest private acquisition—the Congo. After his death, the nation and his disinherited daughters tore down the fabric of trusts and endowments which he had created to last for centuries, and fought over the fragments.

⁎ Leopold II is best known as the founder and owner of the ill-famed Congo Free State. To most English-speaking readers, his name evokes the phrase "Red Rubber," and a world of plunder and atrocity: the Congo Reform Association in Britain and America which campaigned against his ruthless exploitation of the Free State has left behind it the notion of an aged, snow-bearded Satan who used black slavery to get money, and money to buy the favours of young girls. To many Belgian historians, on the other hand, Leopold II is still a Crusader, the carrier of Christianity and Belgian civilization into a dark land. The equestrian statue of him in the Place du Trône in Brussels makes an obvious reference to the statue of the Crusader Godfrey of Bouillon which stands on the other side of the Royal Palace. Godfrey's motives also have been somewhat unhorsed by research, but to the average Belgian Royalist, Leopold's critics remain mere jealous merchants or the hacks of greedy foreign Powers.

Belgian apologists for the old King are sometimes so truculent that they throw further discredit on the figure they profess to defend. As recently as 1950, a courtier could write of Leopold II: "How tiny, how minute are those shadowy slanderers, carried away to eternal oblivion by the wind of destiny! They are crushed beneath the massive stone pedestal which bears the bronze image of our splendid sovereign." But with all his impatience at constitutional restriction, Leopold never sought the primitive flatteries suitable for a twentieth-century dictator.

Nor can the "slanderers" be easily dismissed as "shadowy." In the King's lifetime, they came to include King Edward VII, President Theodore Roosevelt, Sir Roger Casement, Lord Cromer, Emile Vandervelde, Mark Twain, Joseph Conrad and many others. So prolonged, in fact, was the outcry against the labour and trading conditions in the Congo Free State, and so notorious the scandal of the King's private life, that when he died the topic of his crimes was dropped by the British and American Press as if from sheer exhaustion. . . .

It is now possible to escape from the "saint or Satan" controversy, and to see Leopold as a statesman of exceptional skill and vision. Few men of his period could assess its possibilities with the logic that Leopold displayed, or emulate the brutal, subtle politics of deceit by which he herded parliaments and Powers down the lanes of his own purpose. Yet the very intensity with which Leopold could see the opportunities of the present seemed to blind him to the general movement of history towards the future. Everywhere, Leopold built fortifications against change which were beginning to crumble at their foundations by the time they were completed. Looking at people and at his times, the King saw only their weaknesses. He had no imagination, and could not feel the movement of change which is the strength of all confused things. . . .

THE KING'S PERSONAL POSSESSION

Even if he had planned to do so, it was now quite impossible for Leopold to work on the assumption that an African dominion, once carved out, could then be handed over to the Belgian government. Belgium was not only unwilling but in his view unfit to receive it. There remained the alternative of somehow placing this unborn dominion under his own personal trusteeship until the day when Belgium and its colony were ready for each other. Two years later, Greindl was to write to Leopold: ". . . with time, the enterprise will become, by the force of circumstances, as Belgian in name as in fact. It is advisable, especially at the outset, that the business should shelter under the international flag. The colonial concept still rouses sharp antipathy in Belgium, where the memory of our unfortunate attempts is not yet obliterated. In the preliminary conferences of 1876, strong opposition broke out against anything that might lead to isolated action. A project advanced in too exclusively Belgian a light would rouse almost certain resistance, whereas it would have a much better chance of being well received by public opinion if it presented itself under an international flag."

This much was now clear: that Leopold had founded the Association Internationale Africaine with the ostensible purposes of furthering exploration and repressing the slave trade, but with the real purpose of using it as a smokescreen to confuse stronger nations while he laid the foundations of a colony in Central Africa. He had further decided that this colony would have to be his personal possession, until Belgium was ready to accept it. It would be located in the Congo basin, and if a "tramway" really could be built, it would open on to the Atlantic with an ocean port at the river mouth. It remained for Leopold

to set his men to work on the chosen ground, and to find a man
to lead them. . . .

PROFITS FROM THE CONGO

All over the world, Leopold's little team of financiers was at
work, responding to the innumerable minutes which suggested
to them some new point of opportunity by injecting doses of
Congolese money into railways, fisheries, mining concerns and
timber trusts. Shadowy "Sociétés" rose and fell, and secret emissaries hustled about the world, bribing newspapers, buying
lunches for politicians, and filling notebooks with trading figures.
Morocco again became a target of Leopold's intelligence services,
and Empain prepared an abortive expedition to lay hold of
Agadir for a Belgian fishery station. The Congo State, in its
official capacity, made Spain an offer for the Canaries. In
Mongolia and Manchuria and on the Yenisei in Siberia, the
King's agents sought openings for Belgian syndicates in collaboration with Russian capitalists; in Korea, he and Wiener
worked with the Americans. Belgian interests were helped forward by Leopold in Persia, where Belgians organized the postal
and customs staff, and in Siam, where they worked as lawyers.
At different times, Leopold formed ambitions towards Albania;
the Baghdad Railway; mining concessions in Greece; Fiji; the
New Hebrides; rubber in Bolivia; the Solomon Islands; Meso-
potamia; the West Indies.

A part of Leopold's design for monarchy now stood completed. The huge financial resources and the liberty of action
which he possessed as soverign of the Congo State were already
altering his position as King of Belgium. In a very real sense, he
was the leader of the nation's industrial expansion. He did not
merely open industrial fairs and award medals to inventors, he
formed the very lance-head of Belgian penetration into remote
and well-defended markets. First came the Congolese emissaries,
with their portfolios of attractive propositions; then came the
Royal investor himself, using to the full his prestige as a reigning
monarch to secure the entry of his bewildering menagerie
of study-companies and holding-groups; lastly, when the con-

cession was signed and sealed, came the Belgian industrialists to build and carry and sink shafts and sell their tramcars. All this, and a considerable income of such deals, was made possible by the revenues of the Congo. But this was not appreciated by the majority of the Belgians. They tended to see the Congo only the means for the King's increasing absolutism, and intelligent Belgians feared that the Congo would eventually become the object of an international brawl which would involve the safety and the reputation of Belgium herself. As the rumors about Leopold's methods in the exploitation of the Congo grew and united into a running scandal in the Anglo-American Press, this fear seemed to have been fully justified, even though few Belgians, as yet, believed that such reports were true. . . .

THE SCRAMBLE

4 *Roland Oliver and J. D. Fage: Leopold and the
Scramble for Africa*

*Who started the scramble for Africa? The question has tantalized
historians of Africa as well as scholars of imperialism. Two of the
foremost historians of Africa, Roland Oliver, Professor of African
History in the University of London, and Professor J. D. Fage, Professor of African History in the University of Birmingham, believe
that Leopold, if not actually precipitating the scramble, created the
atmosphere in which the partition took place.*

Two decades later, however, at the beginning of the twentieth
century, European governments were claiming sovereignty over
all but six of some forty political units into which they had by
then divided the continent—and of these six exceptions, four
were more technical than real. This partition of Africa at the end
of the nineteenth century was by no means a necessary consequence of the opening up of Africa by Europeans during the
first three-quarters of the century. Very few indeed of the explorers of Africa had been sent by their governments to spy out
the land for later conquest. It is probably safe to say that not a
single missionary had ever imagined himself as serving in the
vanguard of colonialism. In so far as there was an economic

SOURCE. Roland Oliver and J. D. Fage, *A Short History of Africa*, Baltimore: Penguin Books, 1965, pp. 182–184. Reprinted by permission of Penguin Books Ltd. and the authors. Copyright Roland Oliver and J. D. Fage,
1962.

motive for partition of the kind suggested by Marxist writers, it
was a motive which appealed to those European powers which
had no colonies and little commercial influence in Africa, rather
than to those whose influence was already established there. The
partition of Africa was indeed essentially the result of the appearance on the African scene of one or two powers which had
not previously shown any interest in the continent. It was this
that upset the pre-existing balance of power and influence and
precipitated a state of international hysteria in which all the
powers rushed in to stake claims to political sovereignty and to
bargain furiously with each other for recognition in this or that
region.

The first of these new factors to enter the African scene was
not strictly speaking a power. It was a European sovereign acting
in his personal capacity, though using his status as a sovereign to
manipulate the threads of international diplomacy in pursuit of
his private objective. King Leopold II of the Belgians was a man
whose ambitions and capacities far outran the introverted preoccupations of the country he had been born to rule. His
interest in founding an overseas empire had started in the
1850's and 1860's when as Duke of Brabant he had travelled
in Egypt and had also scanned possible openings in places as
remote as Formosa, Sarawak, Fiji, and the New Hebrides. Suc-
ceeding to the throne in 1865, he bent most of his great energies
to the study of African exploration. Ten years later he was
ready to act. His cover was the African International Association,
created in 1876 to found a chain of commercial and scientific
stations running across central Africa from Zanzibar to the
Atlantic. The stations were to be garrisoned, and they were to
serve as bases from which to attack the slave trade and to
protect Christian missions. The first two expeditions of the
Association entered East Africa from Zanzibar in 1878 and 1879,
and attached themselves to mission stations of the White Fathers
at Tabora and on Lake Tanganyika. From this moment, however,
Leopold's interests switched increasingly to the west coast of
Bantu Africa. Stanley, who in 1877 had completed his coast-to-
coast journey by descending the Congo River, took service under
King Leopold in 1879, and during the next five years established
a practicable land and water transport system from the head of

the Congo estuary to Stanley Falls, more than a thousand miles upstream, at the modern Stanleyville.

Leopold, meanwhile, was deftly preparing the way for international recognition of his rule over the whole area of the Congo basin. Although his real intention was to develop his colony on the basis of a close-fisted commercial monopoly, he was successful in persuading a majority of the European powers that it would be preferable to have the Congo basin as a free-trade area under his "international" régime than to let it fall to any of their national rivals. The skill of King Leopold's diplomacy has been widely recognized. What has received less notice is the extent to which it sharpened the mutual suspicions of the European powers about their activities in Africa as a whole. Probably it was Leopold, more than any other single statesman, who created the "atmosphere" of scramble.

5 Henri Brunschwig: Leopold II's Intervention in Central Africa

Henri Brunschwig, Professor of African History at the Institut des hautes études d'outre-mer and a leading scholar of French colonialism, argues that the French and, consequently, the other powers, would not have scrambled for Africa if not provoked by King Leopold's designs on the basin of the Congo.

Perhaps the French would have taken a long time to put their theories into practice if a foreigner had not provoked them into doing so. Since his youth, Leopold II, the king of the Belgians, had kept abreast of geographical developments. During the

SOURCE. Henri Brunschwig, *French Colonialism, 1871–1914,* William Glanville Brown, tr., New York: Frederick A. Praeger, 1966, pp. 31–34. Reprinted by permission of Frederick A. Praeger, Inc. and the author. Copyright 1960 Max Leclerc et Cie. English translation by William Glanville Brown, Copyright 1964 Pall Mall Press Ltd.

liberal epoch, he alone of the men exercising political authority had questioned the economic views then generally accepted. As early as 1863, two years before he came to the throne, he had written and was planning publication of a book, *Les Belges à l'Etranger,* with a view to influencing public opinion away from its devotion to free trade. (In the event, the book was not published.) It criticised the Manchester school and expressed the view that "the fact that we have free trade and that this includes the colonies of all peoples, does not prevent its being more advantageous to possess one's own territories overseas." Leopold concluded with these words:

"I should be happy to see Belgians trading with and in colonies in general, but I think the country must also, in its own interests, possess territories overseas. I see in this a means of giving us a more important place in the world, of opening up fresh careers for our fellow citizens, of supplying ourselves with a new financial structure which might, as in Java, yield a surplus and give an opportunity for investing capital in places where our own laws hold sway, and much more advantageously than in the metal industry or even in railways, which yield between 3 and 3½ per cent. Belgians are not profitably utilising the world's resources. A desire to do so needs to be awakened in them; since this idea requires fostering, let me say that I would rather see my fellow countrymen working for the nation's benefit and remaining its citizens, with property in parts of the world over which our flag flies, than see them dispersed to the United States and elsewhere where they will be absorbed without benefit to Belgian society."

The king was actuated both by trading and by political motives. He had independently come to hold the views which were subsequently held by the "geographic" school in France. In temperament an absolute ruler, he was also in investor of capital. All voyages of discovery fascinated him and all great public works. He had thought of China, of Egypt and of Borneo; between 1873 and 1875 he had planned a settlement in the Philippines, while between 1875 and 1878 he actively sought to penetrate the Transvaal. A treaty of friendship, settlement and trade between Belgium and the Transvaal Republic was signed on September 3,

1876 during the visit of President Burgers to Brussels, and a Belgian consul was appointed in Pretoria. Leopold supported the Cockerill company which was negotiating a mining and railway concession, and went on with his Transvaal scheme until 1878, despite British opposition—perhaps seeking thereby to distract the attention of the European powers from the course he was by then pursuing in Central Africa.

Until then, African exploration had been carried out mainly by persons of British nationality. The Royal Geographical Society of London, the protestant missions and the trading companies had made a considerable contribution to mapping the interior of the "dark continent." Livingstone had just discovered the great lakes of East Africa, when on November 10, 1871 H.M. Stanley found him at Ujiji on the Tanganyika. In 1875, at the International Congress of Paris, there was much talk about Lovett Cameron, a naval officer to whom the Royal Geographical Society had given the task of finding Livingstone. He left Zanzibar in 1873 and learnt at Tabora of the death of Livingstone, who had been seeking to establish that the Lualaba river was a tributary of the Nile. Cameron decided to explore further to the west and Leopold made an offer to the Royal Geographical Society to subsidise him. Cameron crossed the continent and reached Loanda in November 1875. Leopold was also on the look-out for news of the expedition which Stanley led in 1874–1875 (sponsored by the *Daily Telegraph* and the *New York Herald*), and of the French journeys of discovery by the Marquis de Compiègne, by Marche, the naturalist and by Brazza, along the Ogwai river.

The Congress of Paris caused Leopold to cast his eyes definitely on Central Africa. He could not let it be seen that he had plans for conquest and, indeed, perhaps he had none, for there has been much dispute as to the motives which caused him to call an international geographical conference in Brussels. But it need not necessarily be assumed that the king knew precisely what he planned to do. What is clearly shown, by the steps he took before the 1876 conference met, is that he did not wish to be left out of future developments, and Central Africa was very much in people's minds. Brazza was seeking to reach it along the Ogwai river, British missionaries were extremely active in the area of the great lakes, and Stanley was following the course of the Lualaba river, with a view to determining to which drainage basin it belonged. There was no question of sending out Belgian missionaries and explorers as well, for there were none ready to undertake the task and the necessary finances for it did not exist.

Moreover, large geographical congresses were international gatherings and missionary societies were usually international in their scope and influence. The struggle against the slave trade and against slavery had been put on an international basis as early as the treaties of Vienna of 1815. Although some countries had been markedly less enthusiastic than others in this field, suppressing the slave trade had certainly led to international co-operation in naval "slave-patrols" and in mixed courts. Since no one envisaged the possibility of Leopold's suddenly laying claim to any part of Africa, it seemed perfectly natural, in view of his well-known deep interest in geography, that he should become patron of a movement concerned with scientific exploration or action of a humanitarian nature. His interest in geography and international humanitarianism enabled Leopold II to take his place amongst those concerned with Central Africa. He may at this time have had not other aims, but he had emerged from the wings onto the African stage. He was now ready to play a major role.

6 Ronald Robinson and John Gallagher: Egypt and the Partition of Africa

Ronald Robinson, Fellow of St. Johns College, Cambridge, and John Gallagher, Beit Professor of History, Oxford University, are among the foremost scholars of British imperialism in Africa. Their

SOURCE. Ronald Robinson and John Gallagher, with Alice Denny, *Africa and the Victorians: The Official Mind of Imperialism*, London: Macmillan & Co., 1961, pp. 163–166, 168–175, and 177–180. Reprinted by permission of St. Martin's Press, Inc. and The Macmillan Co. of Canada, Ltd. Copyright Ronald Robinson, John Gallagher, and Alice Denny, 1961.

study, Africa and the Victorians, *occupies a central place in the parti-tion and occupation of Africa by the European powers and has be-come one of the most influential works in modern imperialism. The scramble for Africa was begun, not by the intrigues of King Leopold or the heroics of Brazza, but rather by the British occupation of Egypt in 1882. From that decisive event the powers maneuvered them-selves into partitioning the African continent.*

Without the occupation of Egypt, there is no reason to suppose that any international scrambles for Africa, either west or east, would have begun when they did. There seem to have been no fresh social or economic impulses for imperial expansion which would explain why the partition of tropical Africa should have begun in the early 1880's. Gladstone's second administration was totally devoid of imperial ambitions in west Africa. Granville was unimpressed by the dingy annals of the west coast. Kim-berley, at the Colonial Office, was eager to give sleeping dogs every chance of lying. The pessimistic Derby, who succeeded him in 1882, was temperamentally opposed to any suggestion, however modest, for expansion on the west coast. Finally there was Gladstone, himself, who knew little and cared little about the problem. In so far as these men possessed any coherent view of the situation in tropical Africa, it was the view sometimes of Cobden, sometimes of Palmerston and the mid-Victorian im-perialism of free trade. As in Gladstone's first ministry, they still concurred in looking on tropical Africa as a third-rate adjunct of the British economy, which might be worth the exertion of coastal influence, but did not justify the effort of administration inland. There were none of them likely to plant the flag in the middle of the African bush in a fit of absence of mind.

For decades all the European governments concerned with the coast of Africa both east and west had tacitly agreed not to allow the petty quarrels of their traders and officials to become oc-casions for empire. The ministries in London and Paris wanted nothing more than to continue their gentleman's agreement, al-though each faintly suspected the other of wanting to break it.

There was little reason for this. Napoleon III had nourished a few sporadic projects for African expansion, but the catastrophe of 1870 had halted them. The Third Republic had pulled out of the Ivory Coast, contemplated renouncing its options in Dahomey, and had hoped to get rid of Gabon and the unpromising claims in the Congo. In Senegal, however, there was a stronger interest. The colonial government there had gradually developed a local expansive power of its own, which derived not so much from its economic potential as from the French army's proprietary feeling and its influence in Paris. In 1879 Brière de l'Isle began the portentous advance from the old colony towards the Upper Niger; two years later the Chambers voted credits for a railway which should link the Senegal to the Niger. Analysis of this line of policy does not concern us here, but it had implications for Gladstone's Cabinet. The rulers of Senegal were extending not only eastwards but southwards. In 1877 they took a further step towards the encirclement of the Gambia; in 1881 Brière de l'Isle made a treaty with Fouta-Djalon which threatened to cut off the hinterland of Sierra Leone; at the same time private French firms had started to compete for the trade of the Niger Delta.

To Granville and Kimberley in London, these moves were faintly disturbing. Poverty-stricken though they were, it would have been feckless to stand idle while Sierra Leone and the Gambia lost their hinterlands, and with them, all chance of ever becoming solvent. Hence the British Cabinet tried to amplify the traditonal understanding by a formal agreement. In 1880 they made two separate suggestions to Paris. They proposed that the frontier between the Gold Coast and the French settlement at Assinie should be delimited; and secondly that there should be a standstill arrangement between the two Powers to the north of Sierra Leone, to be followed by a commission of demarcation. The French government accepted both these suggestions. They had to do with regions which in themselves meant little to the diplomats of the Quai d'Orsay. To their minds it was much more important to keep in alignment with Great Britain because of "the interests of our policy in general." The French government wanted to go into Tunisia and keep in line with London over Egyptian policy. Obviously, it would go more than half way to meet the wishes of the Gladstone government in west Africa. The

British wishes, for their part, were plain enough. Best of all, they would have liked to continue the standstill arrangement along the whole line of coast, so as to save the hinterlands of Sierra Leone and the Gold Coast for any future development, and to keep the Deltas of the Congo and the Niger free from French interference. Unwilling to advance their own formal authority, their simple ambition was to ward off French tariffs. All the political problems of the west coast would go on being shelved; there would be no bidders for its territory; there would simply be a partition of informal influence. Britain and France could still both consent to a policy of self-denial. Nobody would annex anything, and furthermore France would promise not to raise any discriminatory tariffs against British trade. Such were the maximum demands of the British. In practice they had to settle for less. A commission of demarcation in 1881 agreed that Britain should not interfere on the coast between the northern frontier of Sierra Leone and the Gambia; while France bound herself to non-intervention between the southern frontier of Sierra Leone and Liberia. The expansion of Senegal had been checked. The Quai d'Orsay could console themselves by recalling that ". . . the British Government promised us more co-operation in our other affairs if we regulated the west African question to their satisfaction."

Granville and Kimberley were able to stick to the old ruts of west African policy. The delimitation talks with France in 1881 were based on the assumption that the north-eastern hinterland of Sierra Leone was expendable. In the same year Kimberley refused to sanction any step intended to pacify the warring tribes behind Lagos. The following January, the Cabinet had to consider a new offer fudged up by the traders of the Cameroons, and he told Gladstone firmly that "we have already quite enough territory on the West Coast." The Colonial Secretary took an equally strong line about the Niger Delta. When Consul Hewett urged that a loose protectorate should be formed between Benin and the Cameroons, Kimberley would not hear of it:

"Such an extensive protectorate as Mr. Hewett recommends would be a most serious addition to our burdens and responsibilities. The coast is pestilential; the natives numerous and unmanageable. The result of a British occupation would be almost certainly wars with the natives, heavy demands upon the British taxpayer. . . ."

Looked at commercially, the Niger was the best of a poor lot of trading prospects, and it was worth keeping open to British merchants. But it was not worth the expense of administration. If a protectorate were set up, it would certainly not pay for itself. Moreover, there seemed to be no immediate danger that any other Power would rush in where Kimberley feared to enter on tip-toe. True, Galliéni had made a treaty with Segou, and Borgnis-Desbordes was moving on Bamako; but there are more than three thousand kilometres of Niger between Bamako and the Delta. Since 1880 a French firm had been established in the Oil Rivers, but there were plenty of British firms as well. As late as 1882 the British and French governments saw no reason to upset the old coast arrangements for territorial self-denial.

It was the British invasion of Egypt which shattered this system, because it shattered the general Anglo-French collaboration. When France came out in open opposition to the new *régime* in Egypt toward the end of 1882, she began to cast around for ways of putting pressure on London. There was plenty of scope for a policy of pin-pricks in west Africa, and these now began in earnest. Two French firms were on the lower Niger, trading not only at the coast, but pushing into the interior. The alarming feature of this activity was that the French consular agent in the river was now hard at work making treaties as far upstream as the kingdom of Nupe and along the Benue. In Paris they had no illusions about their chances on the lower Niger, for the British position seemed too strong. But the Minister of Marine and Colonies had high hopes of the Benue. . . .

At the same time, another British sphere looked like slipping away. Trade in the Delta of the Congo was dominated by British firms; in the interior Lieutenant Cameron had made a set of treaties in the Seventies which gave the United Kingdom an option on the inner basin of the river. Then Her Majesty's Government had rejected it. Now French and Belgian private enterprises were ready to take the Congo seriously. There was a vast river behind the mouths of the Congo, as Stanley had shown; and it had become possible to break into the hinterland, as Brazza had found. King Leopold II of the Belgians, who had floated an International Association to explore central Africa at the end of the Seventies, launched Stanley on another mission to open communications between the navigable Congo and Stanley Pool in the interior. At the same time Brazza too went back, acting in the name of the French section of the International Association. Here was a scramble, but only at the personal level of two explorers racing each other to the interior, each with the skimpiest of credentials. Stanley was little more than the personal agent of a petty monarch, for the International Association was a piece of mummery, and the Belgian Parliament would have nothing to do with its King's speculations. The status of Brazza was no less peculiar. He too was nominally the agent of the International Association. Although his expedition was given a tiny grant by the French government, the chief inspiration of his mission came from his own pleadings. Paris had little desire to be involved in his adventures. Brazza however had heard that Leopold intended to seize all the interior basin of the Congo, and this would cut off the French colony of Gabon from its hinter-land and cast it into bankruptcy. To avoid the ruin of their colony, the French government in 1879 authorised Brazza to make a treaty at Stanley Pool. Just as the Foreign Office in the Eighteen-fifties had worked to open the Niger hinterland, so the French government in the Eighteen-seventies worked to open the Congo basin. They were far from wanting to extend their political control into the interior; their aim was simply to block the political extensions of others. Brazza's treaty was meant to "reserve our rights, without engaging the future."

Between 1880 and 1883 Stanley and Brazza played out their game in the Congo. This raised awkward questions for the British government. Leopold was a puny rival, and his Association could be pushed into the wings if the need arose. But after Brazza had made his treaty at Stanley Pool, the Foreign Office had to rely on the French disinclination to move in central Africa. In April 1882 the British ambassador in Paris asked the Quai d'Orsay whether the Congo mission had an official character. The discussion that followed showed that in the opinion of the Ministry of Marine and Colonies Brazza had no right to have made a treaty at all. But on the Congo, as on the Niger, all this was to change. After the Egyptian affair had reached its climax, Paris did not feel the old need to pay deference to British susceptibilities; on 10 October the Foreign Minister over-rode the protests of the Marine, and announced that he intended to ask the Chamber to approve the treaty. Ratification followed on 30 November. On 15 December the Foreign Office countered by recognising Portugal's claims to the Congo and its hinterlands—claims which Britain had steadily rejected for the past forty years. In return Britain was to enjoy most favoured nation treatment in the trade of the Congo, a maximum tariff rate, and the setting up of an Anglo-Portuguese commission to supervise the traffic on the river. The treaty took fifteen months to complete, because the Portuguese went on hoping to get better terms from France than from the United Kingdom; but its purpose was always painfully clear. When it had at last been signed, the French ambassador in London caustically defined it as:

". . . A security taken by Britain to prevent either France or an international syndicate directed by France from setting foot in the Congo Delta. . . . The British Government . . . would rather parcel it out with Portugal, whom it can' influence at will, than leave France with an open door."

That was true enough. During 1883 and 1884 the Gladstone Cabinet hoped to use the Portuguese as a sort of holding company which would decently veil the pre-eminence of British interests. Lisbon would do the governing, London would do the trade. In fact, British optimism went further than that. It was rumoured in the Foreign Office that King Leopold's own organisation might become ". . . as I hear is not unlikely, an English company." Both these sanguine hopes are very revealing. As a direct result of the Egyptian occupation, British interests in the Congo were now threatened by Leopold and the French. If their sphere were to be saved, then ministers could no longer rely on the old gentleman's agreement; from now on, official acts of policy would be needed. This they understood. Yet they refused to meet the new situation by any territorial extension of their own. Instead, they fell back on a variant of their technique of informal empire. Others could administer on paper, while they enjoyed the trade.

With the King of Portugal as their caretaker on the coast and the King of the Belgians as their manager in the hinterland, all might still be saved, thanks to these regal subordinates.

For all the apparent dexterity of this solution, it was full of difficulties. As negotiations for the treaty with Portugal dragged on in 1883, the French hostility to the project became plainer. In London they badly wanted Egyptian concessions from Paris. Was the Congo worth the cost of rendering those concessions harder to get? Already in May the First Lord of the Admiralty was expressing his doubts to Granville: "I presume we don't want to get into a quarrel with anyone in order to carry out a measure of which the advantage is so doubtful." The Congo was not much of a prize, that was common ground; and from there it was a short step to draw a new conclusion. Since the British position on the west coast was under pressure, ministers would have to resign themselves to the loss of some sphere or other. If the Congo was expendable, then what could be bought with it? Kimberley by June was arguing that the treaty should be scrapped and moreover that the Gambia should be sacrificed, if in return the government could ". . . above all get control of the Niger so as to prevent the possibility of our trade there being interfered with." Now at last ministers were compelled to work out their priorities for the west coast.

But precisely how was the Niger Delta to be kept? In November, a Cabinet committee decided "to establish an efficient Consular Staff in the Niger and Oil Rivers District," which should make treaties with the chiefs and induce them to accept British protection. Action to forestall official French encroachment had become urgent. This was the largest possible measure of agreement that could be found in that distracted Cabinet, but it represented the smallest possible measure of official commitment in the threatened region. At most, it meant a wider and a more intensive system of consular rule; but even this was to be whittled down by the caution of ministers. More consuls would mean more salaries; who ought to meet the bill? The traditionally-minded group in the Cabinet were clear that government should not find the money, and the Treasury took the same view. The whole plan was delayed, while efforts were being made to cajole the British firms in the Niger trade to help with the costs. None of them, except Goldie's National African Company, would do so. The outcome of all this shilly-shallying was that not for another six months did the government nerve itself to pay, and Consul Hewett did not sail on his treaty-making mission until 28 May, 1884. He was to go down in the folk-lore of the west coast as "Too-late Hewett"; but the real procrastination was that of his masters.

In fact, British plans went astray both in the Niger and in the Congo. Ministers had had their doubts already over the Anglo-Portuguese Treaty. They were to end by thoroughly repenting of it. Although the treaty had been designed to guarantee the interests of British traders, they were loud in opposition to it, because of the nominal Portuguese control and the actual Portuguese tariff. Their protests were joined by the ancestral voices of the Anti-Slavery Society and the Baptist Union. Behind all this agitation there may have lain, as Granville suspected, the fine hand of King Leopold. The complaints of these pressure groups however were not enough to stop the treaty. That it failed was another of the consequences of the Egyptian crisis. After the occupation of Cairo, it seemed to French observers that Britain was driving for African empire. French diplomacy attacked the Anglo-Portuguese arrangement, both as a way of keeping the Congo open, and of putting pressure on the British in Egypt. The treaty was signed on 26 February, 1884, and during March the Quai d'Orsay was actively inciting opposition in Belgium, Holland and the United States, the Powers with trading interests in the Congo. But in his search for supporters Ferry hooked a bigger fish than these. On 31 March he tried to get the Germans to join the resistance. This overture was to begin the partition of west Africa.

Bismarck too had his grievances against British policy. To his rooted dislike of Gladstone as a man fit only to chop down trees and make up speeches, he could now add a splenetic indignation at Granville's dawdling. In February 1883 he had enquired whether Britain would be ready to protect the German settlement at Angra Pequena; in December he repeated the enquiry. But for a further six and a half months the only reply he could get from London was a series of vague observations about British claims in that region. In part the muddle was caused by the objections of the Cape, in part by the British feeling that the colonial politicians had to be listened to, if south Africa was one day to be united around that province. But it was an important muddle. The occupation of Egypt gave Bismarck the chance to deepen the rift between Britain and France and to enter the African game. In March and April of 1884 the Germans took steps to assert their own protectorate over Angra Pequena, but the ambiguity of their statements and the imperceptiveness of Gladstone's ministers (one of whom as late as June did not know where Angra Pequena was) left the British as naively ignorant as ever about where their attitude was taking them. It was beginning to take them a long way. On 5 May Bismarck hinted at this in two messages to London, in which German colonial claims and the question of the Congo were ominously linked. By another in this chain of muddles the messages were not delivered. Thereafter Bismarck swung the weight of Germany behind the Congo revisionists and then against the whole British position in west Africa. On 7 June he let the Foreign Office know that Germany refused to recognise the Anglo-Portuguese Treaty and wanted a conference to settle the Congo question. Granville was too discouraged to press on with ratification, and that was the the end of the Treaty. But the retreat did not stop there. On 4 August the Germans suggested to the French that they should co-operate over west African questions generally at the impending conference, and at the end of the month the French persuaded their new collaborators to join in an onslaught against the least expendable of the British spheres—the Niger.

By now the whole of the British position along the coast seemed to be in danger. The Germans were established at Angra Pequena; on 5 July they had proclaimed a protectorate over Togoland, and on 14 July another over the Cameroons, where Hewett had indeed been too late. In addition, British designs in the Congo had been blocked, and now, as a final twist of the knife, their control of the Lower Niger was being challenged.

What had brought about this rout? Fundamentally, the cause was the British intervention in Egypt and its effects on the European balance. In the aftermath a resentful France had been driven into repudiating the former standstill arrangement throughout west Africa; and now Germany was enabled to press heavily upon the British government. One of the worst penalties of the Egyptian occupation, so ministers found, was the torment of the Egyptian budgets. By 1884 it looked as though they might have to ask the British taxpayer to meet the deficits. Rather than run this political risk, they summoned a conference of the Powers to modify the law of liquidation. This was the moment Bismarck chose to withdraw his grace and favour. The desire to discipline Gladstone, the chance of having a colonial flutter in Africa, the decision to edge closer to France, all these worked to change Bismarck's approach to the Egyptian question. When the Egyptian conference opened on 28 June, the French stated their opposition to the British request. That was predictable; but Lord Granville suddenly woke up to the fact that the Germans were opposing it too and he hurriedly dissolved the conference on 2 August.

This fiasco made a number of points clear. The Foreign Office had long been uneasily aware of how much they depended on Bismarck to underpin their position in Egypt. Rather than risk a drubbing from his *bâton égyptien*, they had gone into retreat in west Africa. They had abandoned Angra Pequena, they had given up the Portuguese treaty, yet Berlin was still not satisfied. Soon it was to be the turn of the Niger.

By the end of September 1884, Bismarck and Ferry had reached agreement over the official bases of the west African conference. It was to regulate the division of Africa by defining the concept of effective occupation, and to discuss the measures needed to assure free trade in the Congo and liberty of navigation on that river and on the Niger—issues which brought up the whole question of jurisdiction in those regions. In October, Granville accepted an invitation to the conference, but in doing so he specifically objected to any form of international control over the Lower Niger. Routed elsewhere along the coast, he was at last beginning to defend the British sphere in the Delta. . . .

Why, amid their general retreat along the west coast, had ministers decided to hold the Lower Niger? Here was the region with the best trade. Here was the best waterway into the interior. Here lay the best opportunity for breaking the power of the African middlemen. In so far as British policy during the west African "scramble" was governed by any clear motive, it was to protect trade.

Yet the motives were very different from those postulated in the theory of economic imperialism. It was not the case that the merchants pressed the Crown to pacify and develop the Lower Niger for them. Most of the traders still wanted to operate in a *res nullius*, where there would be a fair field and no tariffs, without an imperial authority to tax them and get in their way. All they asked for was protection against the interference of foreign governments and help in breaking the power of the middlemen. Neither was it the case that industrialists and investors at Home looked on west Africa as the remedy for their difficulties during the Great Depression. Nor had government when it claimed the Niger the slightest intention of employing the power of the state to administer and exploit it. Indeed, the traditionalists of the Cabinet acquiesced in the sphere on the Niger because they thought it the one region where merchants could be made to pay the bill. The official programme fell a long way short of administering the region or turning it into a colonial estate. There is no sign that British public opinion was hungry for west African territory. In 1884 and 1885 opinion was agitated about the Franchise Bill, anxious about the crisis in Ireland and in Afghanistan, agonised about the fate of Gordon. The scramble for the west coast aroused very little interest. At no time before, during or after the Berlin Conference was there a parliamentary debate about its aims or its results.

It seems then that any attempt to analyse British policy in terms of some one decisive factor breaks down before the facts. There is nothing for it but to approach the problem from another direction. Instead of postulating a single, necessary and sufficient cause of these events, it is well to be less pretentious and to define them as the result of an interplay between non-recurrent factors in the early Eighteen-eighties. Government policy in west Africa seems to have evolved as a by-product of three major crises, one in Egypt, another in Europe, a third in the domestic politics of Great Britain, and a minor crisis on the west coast itself.

The Egyptian affair had started off the "scramble." It had ended the standstill arrangement in Africa. It had run British policy into a noose held by Bismarck. When Germany's policy swung towards France, the two of them squeezed hard on the British position in west Africa. That postion was already susceptible to change, as the bases of tribal societies and economies were eroded by the gradual commercial penetration of the interior. So long as other things stayed equal, Gladstone's Cabinet thought it could cope with the results of this erosion by making only small adjustments in its traditional policy. But things did not stay equal, and the Egyptian aftermath shifted the European balance, blowing these calculations sky-high.

This left the Cabinet in a dilemma. On a rational view of priorities, it was sensible to give ground in such places as Angra Pequena, Togoland, New Guinea, Samoa, the Congo and the Cameroons, so as to hold ground in Egypt. But this involved some political fiction at Home. During the nineteenth century the political nation was seldom interested in the expansion of British frontiers, but opinion in general, and vested interests in particular, were usually averse to the contraction of their trading empire.

The Liberal administration had come a long way since the glad, confident morning of 1880. By now the Whigs and the Radicals were at each others' throats, and their quarrels had riven the Cabinet apart. The Egyptian misfortunes and Parnellite manoeuvres had brought its prestige so low that in March the government was beaten by seventeen votes. From February until December 1884 the government was pushing its Franchise Bill through the Commons and then wrestling over its consequences with the Lords. Whig ministers were alarmed at the prospect of Irish peasants with votes, their Radical colleagues were alarmed lest there should not be enough of them. On top of all this friction and intrigue were superimposed the Franco-German *entente* and Bismarck's bid for colonies. On this issue the forward party in the Cabinet was able to exploit the Cabinet splits to press their policy on the traditionalists who kept their rooted dislike of African adventures. The Radicals, Chamberlain and Dilke, wanted action. For tactical reasons they were both willing to stomach the German irruption into the Cameroons, but they were determined to make a spirited stand somewhere. They could see the political risks of passivity, and anyhow it did not agree with their temperaments. This was the spirit of Chamberlain when he wrote, "I don't give a damn about New Guinea and I am not afraid

of German colonisation, but I don't like being checked by Bismarck or anyone else;" and by Dilke when he blamed ministerial
dawdling for letting the Germans into the Cameroons. But it was
not only the Radicals who wanted to do something in west
Africa. Granville himself came to think that the Lower Niger
must be safeguarded, if need be by the extension of official control. Even so orthodox a Whig as the Lord Chancellor, Selborne,
wrote:

"I must confess to a feeling of humiliation at the passive part
which we have played, and are still playing, under the idea that
a breach with Germany, at this juncture, would make our chances
of honourable extrication from the Egyptian difficulty even less
than they are."

The restiveness in the Cabinet finally overbore the moderates.
It was common knowledge that the right-wing ministers, Hart-
ington, Northbrook and Selbourne might split off, and that Chamberlain and Dilke might do the same on the left. Gladstone in the
middle might dislike the whole quarrel over these west African
affairs, but under pressure from both the dissident groups in his
government he had no alternative but to let the spirit blow where
it listed. The future of the Delta cut only a small figure amid
the many racking dissensions of that government; but the dangers
contained in those other dissensions helped to decide the fate of
the Lower Niger.

It would seem that the claiming of the Niger in 1884 was
motivated neither by increased enthusiasm for enlarging the empire nor by more pressing economic need to exploit the region.
The incentive to advance here was no stronger than of old. It
sprang from a passing concatenation of minor trade rivalries in
west Africa with major changes of front by the Powers in
Europe and the Mediterranean, mainly provoked by British
blunders and difficulties in Egypt. The Liberals claimed the Lower
Niger merely to prevent an existing field of British trade from dis-
appearing behind French tariff walls; and they limited their new
commitment to this negative purpose. They had not decided to
found an ambitious west African empire. All they had done in
the face of French hostility was to make a technical change in

the international status of the Lower Niger. Henceforward the
Powers recognised this country as a British sphere, but government still had no serious intention of administering, developing
or extending it.

7   Jean Stengers: The Beginning of the Scramble for Africa

*Professor Stengers argues that it was not Leopold but the French
that precipitated the scramble for Africa by ratifying Brazza's treaty
with Makoko followed by the declaration of protectorates in West
Africa. Chauvinism made possible the acceptance of the Makoko
Treaty, economic motives resulted in the West Africa protectorates.
Thus, at the beginning of the scramble new forces emerged, nationalism and prestige, to exacerbate old economic rivalries that would have
then led to the partition of Africa even if Egypt had never existed.*

Was it Leopold II who began [the scramble for Africa]? One
could so imagine when reading the first treaty signed by the
agents of the expedition which he sent into Africa. In this treaty—
which was published in 1884 by the American Senate to whom
the King had sent it—the political idea was apparently the most
important: the Vivi chiefs of the lower Congo ceded their rights of
sovereignty over a part of their territory to the *Comité d'Etudes*
[du Haut Congo], the organ which served as a screen for
the King. This was June 13, 1880. If the text was authentic, the
political initiative would be striking. Unfortunately, it is not.
Leopold II had sent the American Senate a falsified version. The

SOURCE. Jean Stengers, "L'Impérialisme Colonial de la fin du XIXᵉ Siècle;
Mythe ou Réalité," *Journal of African History*, Vol. III, No. 3 (1962), pp.
471–491. Translated for this book by Nell Elizabeth Painter and Robert O.
Collins. Reprinted by permission of Cambridge University Press and the
author.

real Vivi treaty of June 12, 1880, has been found, and it does not provide for any abandonment of sovereignty.

At its beginnings, Leopold II's enterprise in Africa had no political nature. This does not mean that the King, from time to time, did not envision or contemplate political projects, but they never progressed beyond the stage of ephemeral plans. The central idea, the program, in every sense of the word, of Leopold II was elsewhere. It consisted in the organization of the commercial exploitation of Central Africa. To establish trading stations, to get started a big commercial enterprise, this was Leopold's first objective.

It was not until 1882 that he was forced to change direction, to impress a new orientation upon his enterprise. It was necessary to face a danger, that is, Brazza. Was he not going to plant the French flag in the regions of the Congo where Leopold II wanted to penetrate, even as far as the stations where the *Comité d'Etudes* [du Haut Congo] was already established? In order to stop Brazza, to prevent his annexations, the only method was to plant another flag before his and one which would also be the emblem of a political power. Henceforth, Leopold II sought for a way to acquire sovereignty: now began the march toward the formation of the Congo State.

But all this, which began in 1882, was only a counterweight to Brazza's policies, to the intentions reputed to be Brazza's. In our search for first initiatives, should we not turn directly towards France?

It is in France, in fact, that we think the two real initiatives of the "scramble" began. The first was the conclusion of the Brazza-Makoko treaty and, even more, its ratification in 1882. The second was the protectorate policy inaugurated in West Africa in January 1883. The first episode is well known, although France's reasons for installing herself in the Congo have never been sufficiently analyzed. The second, we believe, has never been brought into focus.

In 1882 Brazza returned to France. He brought what he himself called, and what everybody would soon be calling, his "treaty" with Makoko. It was, in fact, two documents in bizarre legal form—and which were certainly not the work of a specialist in international law—dated September-October 1880. The explorer declared in the first that he had obtained from King Makoko, reigning sovereign north of Stanley Pool, the "cession of his territory to France." Makoko had put his "mark" on this declaration. In the second, he declared that he had occupied, in the name of France, part of this territory situated on the edge of Stanley Pool itself (that is to say, what became Brazzaville). This "treaty," to use Brazza's expression, installed France in a small territory whose strategic and commercial importance was great, being situated on the doorstep of the navigable Congo, but which was isolated by hundreds of kilometers from both the coast and the existing French possessions.

Treaties of this type—a little bizarre and very adventuresome were signed by countless French and British officers and proudly brought back to Europe, only to be left without further issue by smiling authorities in the metropole. Cameron, to cite only one example, drew up, in December 1874, a solemn treaty in the midst of Central Africa by which he took possession of the Congo basin in the name of the Queen of England. The views of Lieutenant Cameron are interesting, but "are not designed to be carried out in our generation" observed a civil servant at the Foreign Office, after which the solemn treaty was added to others in the file without further ceremony.

Did not Brazza risk the same fate of so many officers judged too bold by the metropole? He thought so himself and feared that this "treaty" would not be ratified. Visiting Brussels in September 1882, he confided his pessimism to Lambermont, Secretary-General of the Ministry of Foreign Affairs. He told him that he was "convinced that neither the government nor the Chambers would do anything in Paris." Considering Brazza the most dangerous of his rivals, Leopold II, on his part, used his influence to dissuade France from ratifying the famous treaty. "If Brazza's ideas triumph," he wrote to Ferdinand de Lesseps, "I'm very afraid that he will put his country on the road towards annexations and conquests which will invariably lead other nations to take over other parts of the Congo, and also to try and monopolize a traffic which is now open to all. This would be the end of all our efforts, the installation of politics in Africa: the field that we would like to open would be suddenly closed. Instead of having attained a great goal of civilization and humanity the goal at which Leopold II declared himself to be aiming and to have opened all the barriers of Africa, we would see all the rivalries of the rest of the world transplanted there."

In actual fact, in Paris the Minister concerned, that is to say, the Minister of the Marine, was completely ready to bury the Brazza affair. After having declared in July 1882 that he held himself "aloof" from the arrangements concluded by Brazza, he adopted the most efficient administrative attitude so that nothing would come of it: he remained completely silent.

However, on October 12, Lesseps replied to Leopold II. He had seen Duclerc, President of the Cabinet, and Minister of Foreign Affairs, who had told him of his intention to bring up the Brazza-Makoko treaty for approval by Parliament.

What happened? The government had decided to act, for the French press was stirred up. With the help of a few friends, Brazza had established remarkable public relations with the newspapers and organs of public opinion. He had zealously communicated to the press, not only a record of his explorations, but also arguments for the advantages that his treaty would procure for France and of the immense economic prospects which would open in the new colony: the French Congo. From the second half of September, the newspapers reacted one after another to his eloquent appeals. One after another they came out with enthusiasm for Brazza's exploits, his treaty with Makoko, the French Congo. On September 30 the *Temps* reported that "the press is unanimous in this Congo affair . . . for once, all the shades of opinion are in accord." It was a sort of national plebiscite: "the whole French press, with an enthusiasm that has never been seen towards colonial questions, invites the government to ratify the treaty made by Mr. de Brazza with the riverine people of the Congo." When expressing its wishes on October 3 in favor of ratification, the Society of Colonial and Maritime Studies could write that it associated itself with the "national movement."

Woe betide the government if it did not give way to this outcry of opinion! "Are we going to refuse a colony so rich and desired by others? It would be a mistake, . . . for which we cannot possibly find an excuse." "Public attention has been so sharply solicited, national susceptibilities have been so carefully awakened, that a Minister who let an exceptionally favorable chance to extend our colonial power by clumsiness or negligence would be at pains to exonerate himself before the Chambers and before public opinion."

The government, as we have seen, would propose approval of the Brazza-Makoko treaty to Parliament. This would be accepted unanimously in November 1882, by the Chamber. "The Chamber," commented the *Temps*, "high spirited and warm hearted, has put aside all dissension: it was truly French. . . ."

In this enthusiasm, it is easy to distinguish the dominant major part played by national pride. It could be felt alive everywhere. A competition was opened in Africa between two rivals: Brazza and Stanley. France supported her champion and wanted his triumph. Stanley, who had returned to Europe in 1882, attacked Brazza and declared that the treaty with Makoko was worthless. One more reason for French public opinion to form a solid block around the man who wore its colors.

While making the cause of Brazza in the Congo triumphant and achieving this victory for France, it was possible to get even with England. It is here that we rediscover the question of Egypt—but from a point of view, it must be emphasized, that Robinson and Gallagher [*Africa and the Victorians*, London, 1961] have not noticed. After the hurt, the humiliation that the occupation of Egypt caused it, French public opinion instinctively looked for a way to compensate for the British success. It needed a French success. The Congo offered itself at this point. For us it is, wrote a Parisian newspaper, "the best and the surest revenge" to the "frustrations" that we have just suffered. Brazza, of course, did not fail to play on these sentiments. "A speaker who preceded me," he declared during a ceremony at the Sorbonne, "said that the English have left us behind everywhere. There is, however, one place where we have put our mark before them; that is the Congo [prolonged applause, notes the report]. The French flag flies over this land and the Parliament has only to say the word for it to be ours forever."

The psychological relation between the Congo and Egypt, noted by diverse observers, prompted the very intelligent correspondent of the *Kölnische Zeitung* at the moment of the voting of the Brazza treaty by the Chamber to write: "The matter was considered as a work of pure patriotism. Having been supplanted by the English on the Nile, France wants to make it up by supplanting in turn the Belgians and Portuguese north of the Congo."

The Egyptian question, therefore, contributed in a decisive manner, and in a manner without a doubt important, to the installation of France in the Congo.

With the approval of the Brazza-Makoko treaty in the autumn of 1882, the political appropriation of Central Africa began. It was the decision taken by France which would, in reality, set off the process of appropriation. . . .

Leopold II . . . would embark upon a course towards sovereign acquisitions more and more wide spread. The "scramble" in this region of Africa was launched.

In the Congo the French policy had been more chauvinistic than calculating, dictated far more by patriotic exaltation than by considerations of economic matters. In West Africa—where the second French initiative took place in January 1883—the game was completely different. It was, without interference by public opinion and without public outcry, a game calculated to promote the interests of national commerce.

Commercial interests and territorial occupation had been linked on the West Coast more than once during the nineteenth century. These were always limited occupations, responding above all to local or regional preoccupations. The last of these local maneuvers carried out "to support national commerce" had been the reestablishment in 1882 of the French protectorate over Porto-Novo.[1]

In January 1883 the designs apparently were enlarged. Texts came from the Ministry of the Marine and Colonies in Paris which, when brought together, defined a new policy, and which one would be tempted this time to call grand policy. . . .

A protectorate on the coast from the Gold Coast to Dahomey, political treaties on the Benue, agreements with the chiefs in the eastern delta of the Niger, eventual protectorates at Bonny, Old

---

[1] The declaration reestablishing a French protectorate at Porto Novo was signed in Paris in 1882, but not carried out in Africa until April 1883. *Ed.*

Calabar, or in that region, treaties to the south of the Cameroon estuary: one recognizes that there is here, in the treaties of January 1883, a far-reaching political program.

By whom had it been elaborated? Under what influences? What had been the personal role of Jauréguiberry?[2] Had the commercial establishments whose interests were at question—and notably the huge commercial enterprises of Marseilles—taken a direct part in the elaboration of these plans? Here are many questions to which the documents, at least up to the present, do not give an answer: this is the secret, still to be solved, of the Ministry of the Marine in 1882-1883.

What is clear is that the Marine had obtained, apparently without difficulty, the adherence of the Quai d'Orsay [French Foreign Ministry] for at least part of its plans. The annotation: "Write to Mr. Mattei on this matter" (Mattei being the French consular agent at Brass River) is found on a letter of January 25, 1883, relative to the Niger and the Benue in the hand of a civil servant responsible to the Quai d'Orsay. On March 6, 1883, instructions were telegraphed to Mattei.

The plans were grand, but the means actually employed were mediocre, and all in all, the policy defined in January 1883 produced only very minor results.

To the west of Dahomey action was reduced to really very little. It was put off essentially for fear of diplomatic complications. Farther to the east, in the Niger and the Cameroons, those who tried to execute the new policy with slender means hardly succeeded at all.

The first to appear in these areas was an officer of the Marine, Godin, commanding the gunboat the *Voltigeur*, who was charged with executing the instructions of January 3rd. In March 1883 Godin went first to Bonny, whose chiefs had concluded a treaty of commerce and friendship with France some time before. Could one transform that accord into a protectorate treaty? Godin found out immediately that "it was not even thinkable."

"How and by what right to demand a protectorate from a

---

[2] Jean Bernard Jauréguiberry was Governor of Senegal, 1861–1863, and Minister of Marine (which handled colonial affairs) 1879–1880 and 1882–1883. *Ed.*

country where there are eight English commerical houses, of which two are big companies with steamboats, and where commercial movement is such that in 11 days I counted 10 steamships entering and 9 leaving, all under the English flag, when since forty-two years ago, the age of our treaty, not a single French house of commerce bothered to establish itself?"

The commander of the *Voltigeur* limited his ambitions thus to obtaining the renewal of the old commercial treaty. He could not even do that because, from all the evidence, the chiefs were so afraid of displeasing the British consul.

After this failure, Godin went to the "country of Cameroon" in April. There also, he found the English influence preponderant (to the point, he notes, that "my pilot was worried about what the English consul would say when he learned that he was in my service"), but on the banks of the river Quaqua, which his instructions had specifically designated, he found a "king" very well disposed towards him, the King Malimba Passall, who signed, with no difficulty whatsoever, a treaty ceding half his territory to France. Such ascquiescence appeared strange even to Godin:

"Since I was surprised by the facility with which he alienated his independence, Passall said to me: governing pains me; when you are here, I won't mix in anything and I will sleep all day."

Passall, whose English name meant that his power surpassed that of all his neighbors, evidentally hardly merited his glorious appellation.

If one adds to this treaty with Passall the renewal of the old treaties with the chiefs of Banoko, it is there that the success of the passage of the *Voltigeur* ends.

Mattei, a little later in the year 1883, had even less success. At Brass River, where he had his consular post, he gathered all the local chiefs together in August and submitted a treaty to them placing "their country and its dependencies as well as all their subjects under the protection and suzerainty of France." After a momentarily favorable welcome (for the chiefs wondered, without a doubt, if it would not be possible to play France off against Goldie's English company, whose competition had become detrimental), the refusal was clear; England was too powerful. Mattei then went to the middle Niger and the Benue, where he was a little more lucky, but from a commercial (he was at the same time the general agent of the French Equatorial Africa Trading Company) not from a political point of view. It was the same thing at Ibi, rather far up the Benue, where he succeeded in obtaining from the Emir of Djebon, before English commercial agents, a "space to use as market," but this was not a political agreement.

Thus, between the program conceived on paper in January 1883 and its realization in West Africa, there was a world of difference. The little that the French did was sufficient however—just as the approval of the Brazza-Makoko treaty had been sufficient in Central Africa—to set off the "scramble." In fact, there is no doubt, once the English documents are taken in hand, that it was the French initiatives which, taken together and, in a way, regarded as one by the Foreign Office and the Colonial Office, were at the origin of the decision taken by the British government to act.

Already the Brazza-Makoko treaty had begun to cause worries for West Africa, as well as for the Congo, for a "coup" like that which Brazza had succeeded in pulling off might well be repeated elsewhere, and, for example, on the Niger. "The tactics of M. de Brazza may be imitated on the Niger, and that great highway into the interior of Africa be converted into a French river," wrote a British trader to the Foreign Office, where his words were listened to. Then came the news of the reestablishment of the French protectorate at Porto Novo, which reinforced the alarm. Then came the announcement that a French warship was at Bonny and that the officers of the ship were trying to obtain a treaty from the native chiefs. Under these conditions, it became "a question of the first importance to consider . . . how British interests are to be protected." From June 1883, Percy Anderson, in the Foreign Office, makes the point. He brought together the different elements of the French activity and particularly emphasized the last.

"The Captain of the *Voltigeur* is trying to induce the natives of the mouths of the Niger to accept his treaties. If he succeeds in this, the final step will have been taken, and British trade will have no chance of existence except at the mercy of French officials."

The conclusion, from that point onwards:

"Action seems to be forced on us. . . . Only one course seems possible; that is, to take on ourselves the protectorate of the native states at the mouth of the Oil Rivers, and on the adjoining coast. . . . Protectorates are unwelcome burdens, but in this case it is . . . a question between British protectorates, which would be unwelcome, and French protectorates, which would be fatal."

Later news from the west coast—the treaty concluded with Passall, the activities of Mattei—did nothing but further reinforce the reasoning so well defined by Percy Anderson. This reasoning resolved the British government to act. In a second region of Africa, the "scramble" began. . . .

In analyzing the events of 1882-1883, we see the new face of imperialism emerge, which it acquired from that moment and which it kept to the end of the parcelling of the lands that were still free in the world. Three characteristics particularly emerge: the development of colonial chauvinism; the new type of occupations designed to safeguard economic interests as their end; finally, the role of public opinion. National pride, national *amour-propre*, and chauvinism entered into colonial affairs with a force which they had never before had. In this case, Brazza appeared as a great instigator. His propaganda in 1882 used, without a doubt, numerous economic arguments; it indicated to France the direction of rich and fertile lands. But Brazza would never have been acclaimed if, in a moral sense, he had not waved the national flag. It was when he invoked the tricolor which he had planted in the heart of Africa that he had his audience in his hand, that he carried off the country. Even the economists who agreed with his views did so more as patriots than as economists. Leopold II, a great admirer of Paul Leroy-Beaulieu, sadly reported that "chauvinism seemed to have possessed" the eminent author of *Colonisation chez les peuples modernes* [The Colonialism of Modern Peoples].[3]

In the settling of African questions, the prestige of each coun-

---

[3] Pierre Paul Leroy-Beaulieu, French economist and writer. *Ed.*

try—and no longer just its interests—henceforth entered into the discussion. At the end of 1884 negotiations began in Berlin between the French ambassador and the representatives of the International Congo Association, alias Leopold II. There were territorial disagreements to be settled. A question of frontiers? Also a question of prestige, explained Jules Ferry to the French ambassador.

"Even the most suspicious opinion will approve the Berlin arrangements on one condition: that they do not result in an indirect victory for the Association over Mr. de Brazza. Mr. de Brazza is popular, he has a large following, national honor has been conferred upon him. We must have an arrangement that will flatter the national pride of the French public."

Here we see the new aspect of colonial policy; it satisfied a need for grandeur which, in more than one case, passed well above considerations of material interest. Yves Guyet in 1885, shocked by the mental habits of the traditional economist used to serene calculations in all matters, wrote of the psychological evolution of his colleagues, and particularly of their attitude vis-à-vis the British colonial empire:

"We are jealous of that vast domain, and we want to have one like it to oppose theirs at any price. We no longer count, we listen only to passion. We want annexations, of which we see only their size, without worrying about their quality."

In virtue of the opinion it has of itself a great country must spread overseas. And thus it proves to itself and shows to others its national vigor. "One believes," said the German chancellor in 1890, "that if we only had colonies, and bought an atlas and colored Africa blue, we would then be a great people." Not to act, not to expand, is to give to oneself the label of incapacity, the prelude of political decadence. Jules Ferry proclaimed in 1885:

"It is necessary that our country put itself in a position to do what the others are doing, and because colonial expansion is the most important means at this time used by all the European powers, it is necessary that we play our part. Otherwise what hap-

pened to other nations which played a great role three centuries
ago and which now find themselves, no matter how great they
once were, fallen to the level of third or fourth class powers,
will happen to us."

The rank: it was their rank in the world—an absolutely new
phenomenon whose appearance is vainly sought before this time—
which the European countries would defend by means of overseas partitions.

This was especially so in the partitioning of Africa. There,
more than in Asia or Oceania, the process is definite and well
defined: it was a continent that could be taken apart piece by
piece. The success of each one was visibly measured on the map.
"In this partitioning," declared the *Comité de l'Afrique française*
[Committee on French Africa], "France has the right to the
largest part." And in trying to realize this program, the majority
of those who supported the work of the *Comité*—secondary school
students, for example, or officers, which were found in such
great numbers among the subscribers—evidentally thought above
all of the grandeur of their homeland.

On the race which was begun, economic preoccupations of
course were present, but they very often changed their character
in comparison with those of the past. During the period which
Jules Ferry very correctly called that of "modest annexations
and of little actions, of bourgeois and parsimonious conquests," a
well-planned annexation was sought more than once, in order
to gain economic advantages or to improve the condition of
national commerce. Those were the classic and traditional objectives. French commercial houses on the west coast pushed
for annexations; they wanted to procure a privileged position
there. The British consul in the Gulf of Benin, Hewett, recom-
mended the protectorate policy. In his eyes the best way to
stimulate national commerce would be to establish direct commercial relations with the hinterland. Calculations of this kind
had a positive character. But after 1882-1883 the fear of annexations
by others would be substituted for positive calculations. Conquest would be made in the name of protection to defend an
area considered endangered by the interventions of another power
because it was necessary to make good one's own commercial

interests there. The "tariffs" of others: that was what became, on the economic plane, the major obsession which seized all minds.

In the program of the French Ministry of Marine in January 1883, the English tariffs were evoked as the possible peril against which measures should be taken. But in this aggressive program, both political and economic, the positive aspect was still dominant. The English reply was itself essentially defensive; annexations were made without enthusiasm because it was indispensable to forestall the French. By pushing the Portuguese forward at the mouth of the Congo, England was only defending herself against the French menace: French traiffs would mean the death of British imports in this region.

Was a policy of this type really new? It is obvious that nothing is completely new and one finds precedents for everything. But listen to Gladstone speaking in 1885 of "the demands now ripe . . . for a system of annexations intended to forestall the colonising efforts of other countries." He explained to Queen Victoria:

"Mr. Gladstone could not honourably suppress the fact that he himself, for one, is firmly opposed on principle to such a system, and he believes that herein he is only a humble representative of convictions, which were not general only but universal among the Statesmen of the first thirty years of his political life."

When one sees to what degree, even in the eyes of Gladstone, the policy that he considered contradictory to traditions would be practiced, it is clear that an innovation had indeed taken place.

Finally the third new element: the role of public opinion. In the autumn of 1882, in the affair of Brazza and the Congo, observers were unanimous in agreeing that such an unleashing of the press and public opinion had never before been touched off by a colonial question. Thus began in colonial matters a series of movements of public opinion at the end of the nineteenth and the beginning of the twentieth century. It is necessary to speak in the plural of movements and not of a movement, for it was never a question of one emotion, such as we know in politics, that literally take over and dominate imaginations in a lasting manner. It was by sporadic spurts that colonial enthusiasm would flare up in one country after another separated by periods of indifference which so upset the champions of the colonial cause.

These flare-ups, however, spread over a period of nearly thirty years—for the last one was in Italy just before the war of 1914—and would more than once have a real importance in the development of history. The example of 1882, which opened the series, is one of the most characteristic. Carried away by a nationalist ardor which went far beyond economic considerations, French opinion in 1882 practically dictated the policies to follow. The government and the Chambers could not, according to the expression of the historian Henri Martin, "fail in the task imposed upon them by the unanimous desires of the country." Let us mark this fact and this date. For the first time in the partition of Africa, imperialist agitation by the public opinion of the metropolitan country played a decisive role.

Two years later Germany in turn was seized by colonial fever. It was in quasi-clinical terms that witnesses in 1884 described the phenomenon: "national craving," "colonial mania," "colonial fever," "honest to God fever," "mania for colonial adventure." The excitement reached such a degree that the president of the *Kolonialverein* [Colonial Union] felt in October 1884 that he should warn his compatriots against the illusions born of excessive enthusiasm. Bismarck was a man, however, whose temper differed from that of Duclerc, President of the French Cabinet in 1882. It is hardly believable that—as the ambassador of Great Britain in Berlin thought at the time—he would let himself be led by public opinion. His taking of a colonial position must have been deliberate, wise, and analyzed in terms of major political strategy. But there was, nevertheless, a direct relation between the policy decided upon by the chancellor and German public opinion. One of Bismarck's objectives in entering the domain was, without doubt, to find a theme which would help him win the 1884 elections. Once again, by this detour, metropolitan public opinion played a major role. . . .

In 1883–1884, when the British began to act in order to stay ahead of France, British leaders did so with deep reluctance, if not sometimes in anger, because of the terrible French protectionism which would not allow commercial expansion. In 1897, Salisbury said to the French ambassador, "If you were not such hard line protectionists, you would not be so greedy about territories."

One finds a permanent way of thinking here which was always in action. In a speech of 1898, Sir Edward Grey described English expansion [as reported by *The Times*] as having been a means, above all, to escape exclusion:

"We had got on the Continent the undeserved reputation of being a jealous, grasping and greedy nation, but the truth was we had been forced into the policy of expansion, because if we had not expanded we should have been excluded. He did not entirely accept the doctrine that trade followed the flag, but it had been unfortunately true that where the foreign flag went British trade was certain to be excluded."

Grey perhaps exaggerated, but he diagnosed one of the evidently major characteristics of a policy which he knew well.

"Greediness." Was it from that time outside of British policy? Did England, in its approach to African problems, escape the psychosis of national grandeur, of one's place in the sun? There is sufficient evidence to show that from a certain moment—incontestably later than in France or Germany—this psychosis played a powerful role in public opinion and among the men who made the partition. . . .

To conclude, let us come back again to Egypt. Without the occupation of Egypt, would things have happened as they did in Africa south of the Sahara? If the Egyptian question had not inspired a desire and a need for revenge, would French opinion have embraced Brazza's cause as it did? When it is a question of movements of collective emotion, the "what would have happened if," we must recognize, is nearly always a futile question. There are always too many imponderables in emotions which escape analysis.

But the "scramble" also had a basis in economic reasons. And here there is no doubt possible: Egypt or no Egypt, economic factors would have in any case begun the movement sooner or later.

The fundamental element that must be kept in mind is the following: from the moment when the economic penetration of the dark continent was begun, the temptation to reserve certain advantages for oneself in the regions penetrated was strong, even irresistible. The march towards the interior became almost of necessity synonomous, in many cases, with the acquisition of economic privileges.

The great incontestable precurser in this regard was Leopold II. Confiding to a Belgian diplomat in 1877 he wrote:

"We must be prudent, clever, and prompt to act . . . so as to procure for ourselves a piece of this magnificent African cake."

"A piece of the cake": unless there is an error, the first use of this expression by a political leader is found in this letter of 1877. We must nevertheless be careful. What the King envisioned, in his first rather vague projects, was not the conquest of a part of Africa; he wanted above all to take his place, his "party," in the economic exploitation of new lands. When he sent Stanley into the interior of the continent in order to execute his plans, he charged him to take over from the very first, not political power, but economic advantages, and these exclusively. The treaties signed by Stanley during the course of the first phase of his expedition—and for example the authentic treaty of Vivi in 1880—were agreements which strictly reserved all economic privileges to only the agents of the *Comité d'Etudes*. "The sole and exclusive right of all foreigners and strangers to cultivate any portion of Vivee district. . . . The sole and exclusive right of all foreigners and strangers to trade in any part of Vivee district. . . . The sole and exclusive right, etc. (the expression is repeated like a litany)."

A "privileged position": we have seen that that was also what the French wanted to acquire on the Benue; that was what Goldie succeeded in obtaining in fact on the Niger.

Attempts to acquire privileges in the new markets of Central Africa, reactions of the opposing currents of these attempts: the "scramble" would have been the inevitable outcome of any such process.

Remarkably, despite his forward entrance on the scene, Leopold II did not set off the process. From 1882, in fact, by a political about face whose genius must be acknowledged, he abandoned his designs on a privileged exploitation to make himself, to the contrary, the champion of free trade in Central Africa. In this way he played the card which would lead to triumph. When some of the exclusive treaties that Stanley and his collaborators had signed at the beginning were brought to light, they evidently made the King uncomfortable, but he was able to overcome the bad effect they produced by burying them under torrents of solemn promises to respect free trade. And so the bomb was dismantled.

Whether by Leopold II in the first phase, whether by Goldie, whether by the French eyeing the Benue, Africa in the 1880's, or rather, the interior market of Africa, was opened for commercial competition, which would have engendered the "scramble" in any case. And this would have been so had Egypt never existed.

PART TWO

Germany's Place in the African Sun

MOTIVES

1 Erich Eyck: Bismarck's Colonial Policy

Erich Eyck, German lawyer and historian, regards Bismarck's interest in German overseas expansion as the product of the Chancellor's domestic difficulties. With no genuine interest in colonies and little prospect of any permanent reconciliation with France, Bismarck was more concerned with acquiring the support of the German colonial movement at the polls and in the Reichstag. The price he had to pay was to participate in the partition of Africa.

The colonial policy of Bismarck which came into the political foreground in the years 1884 and 1885 is of particular biographical interest, because he had in former years peremptorily rejected any colonial policy for Germany, and during his final years of power he returned to this mood of aversion. In one of his last speeches to the Reichstag he cried: "I am not a colonial man" *(Kolonialmensch)*, and we now know from the diary of a member of the Prussian cabinet that at a meeting of the Staatsministerium in August 1889 Bismarck thundered against the "German colonial humbug" which was clumsily upsetting his arrangements. We can therefore say that his short period of colonial enthusiasm is only an episode in his life. But it was an episode of momentous consequences, both for Germany's relations with other countries,

SOURCE. Erich Eyck, *Bismarck and the German Empire*, New York: W. W. Norton, 1964, pp. 272–277 and 279–280. Reprinted by permission of George Allen & Unwin Ltd. Copyright 1958 by George Allen & Unwin Ltd. First published in 1950: Copyright under the Berne Convention.

especially with Britain, and for the whole outlook of the German people. Hence it is all the more interesting to solve the riddle of Bismarck's reasons for embarking on this policy. Many historians have tried to unravel it.

When Bismarck began to be interested in colonial problems, only two areas of the world were open to German colonization: the southern part of Africa and the South Sea Islands. In both these regions British colonies occupied the paramount position: the Cape Colony in South Africa, and Australia in the South Seas. The success of German colonial policy would therefore in a certain degree depend on the attitude of Britain and her colonies. Britain was by far the greatest sea-power and did indeed "rule the waves." But her international position had undergone a very important change by her occupation of Egypt in 1882. This occupation brought her into sharp political conflict with France, which for generations had considered Egypt as falling within her sphere of interest. We cannot doubt that Bismarck had foreseen this consequence, and that he had included it in his calculations when he repeatedly advised the British government "to take Egypt." Britain was all the more vulnerable by reason of her presence in Egypt, as many of the problems of Egyptian administration and finance were of an international character, so that to maintain their foothold the British were dependent on the goodwill and approval of other Powers, especially France. . . .

Shortly after his policy of conciliation towards France had ended, Bismarck's colonial interest had evaporated. He was now much more interested in fostering relations with Britain.

We can therefore say that this particular alignment of circumstances—Britain's embarrassments with Egypt and the improved relations between Germany and France—gave Bismarck the opportunity for his experiment in colonial policy. But I do not believe that we have here found his motive. A much more likely motive was, in my opinion, the state of domestic politics in Germany itself.

We have seen how the election of 1881 had produced a Reichstag in which the Conservative Parties combined with the remains of the National Liberty Party were in a minority. Whenever the Centre Party joined the Secessionists and the Progressive Party, Bismarck had to face an Opposition which wielded a majority. Although the Centre voted for the government in tariff questions, there remained many political issues over which it joined the Opposition. In the summer of 1884, six months before the elections to the next Reichstag, the Secessionists and the Progressive Party amalgamated and formed a united radical Liberal Party which took the name *Deutschfreisinnige Partei*. It began with more than a hundred deputies, among whom were some of the most prominent parliamentarians—Eugen Richter and Haenel from the Progressives, and Bamberger, Forckenbeck, and Stauffenberg from the Secessionists.

Lasker died just at this time in New York, where he had gone to see something of the New World. His death gave Bismarck an opportunity to show that he never forgave or forgot, and that not even death could assuage a personal hatred. The American House of Representatives had passed a resolution expressing its sympathy with the German Reichstag for the loss of an excellent and patriotic member. Bismarck declined to pass on this resolution to the Reichstag and sent it back to the U.S.A. When the matter was brought before the Reichstag by a friend of Lasker, Bismarck made a speech in which he condemned the political activities of the dead man, root and branch. When we compare this speech with those in which in the British parliament the leaders of all parties are accustomed to bid farewell to an opponent who has died (the speech of Lord Salisbury in which he praised his lifelong antagonist Gladstone as a "great Christian statesman" is but one example), we can see the striking difference in the political culture of the two countries.

But there was one thing about the new party which irritated Bismarck more than anything else. It was supposed to be the Crown Prince's party, *die Kronprinzenpartei*. There was a rumour that the Crown Prince had welcomed the unification of the radical Liberals in a telegram to Forckenbeck in which he expressed his congratulations on the founding of the new party. Bismarck was afraid that the Prince, when he succeeded his father, would choose the members of his cabinet from among the leaders of this party who would then supplant him. For this imaginary cabinet Bismarck coined the phrase "a German Gladstone Ministry," a name which expressed his detestation and derision. The moment when the Crown Prince would succeed to the throne could not be far off, for old William was now eighty-seven years of age. To destroy the *Deutsch-freisinnige Partei* and to kill the "Gladstone Ministry" before it was born were now the principal aims of the Chancellor. He looked for a political project likely to strengthen his own popularity and opposition to which would make his adversaries unpopular. In 1881 Bismarck had outlined a programme of social reforms, providing for social insurance covering sickness, accidents, and later, old age and infirmity. A part of this programme was realized by the law for the insurance of working men against sickness. But the programme had not been as popular as Bismarck had expected, and his hopes of tempting voters away from the Social Democrats by this means had not been fulfilled.

⅄ Now a colonial policy had a good deal of attraction for a section of the upper middle classes, particularly in certain maritime towns like Hamburg and Bremen, and it was considered by many an eminently national policy. On the other hand, Bismarck knew it would meet with vigorous opposition from the *Freisinnigen*. One of their leaders, Ludwig Bamberger, distinguished himself as an energetic opponent of a colonial policy. It would bring, he said, no practical benefit to the Reich, as all the territories worth having were already in the possession of other nations. On the other hand, it might easily bring Germany into collision with other states. Bismarck could therefore foresee that it would be possible to utilize the colonial movement at the coming election to the detriment of the *Freisinnigen*, who could be accused of lack of national feeling. Besides, he might also entertain the hope of bringing this party into conflict with the Crown Prince, who was supposed to favour the idea of German colonization. ✝

But Bismarck seems to have had yet another motive, which is hinted at in a very curious utterance on the part of his eldest son Herbert, who at this time was his intimate collaborator. In March 1890 General von Schweinitz had a conversation with Herbert Bismarck, and asked him how Bismarck's enthusiasm for a colonial policy could be explained, as it was in striking contrast to everything the Chancellor had previously said or done. Herbert answered: "When we entered upon a colonial policy, we had to reckon with a long reign of the Crown Prince. During this reign

English influence would have been dominant. To prevent this, we had to embark on a colonial policy, because it was popular and conveniently adapted to *bring us into conflict with England at any given moment.*" While it is hard to credit a great statesmen with such a motive, we cannot doubt that Herbert had heard an argument in this vein from his father's lips.

At this time of Bismarck's colonial policy Gladstone was in power in Britain. In view of his personal hostility towards Gladstone, we may suppose that it was a particular joy to Bismarck when he succeeded in defeating the man whom German Liberals considered the foremost Liberal statesman of the age. But it was not so easy to fall out with Gladstone over colonial questions, because he was quite ready to acquiesce in German colonial expansion, and he was far from claiming that England enjoyed a privileged position in these matters or had a real interest in excluding Germany from other continents. But it was only in the later stages that Gladstone took personal cognizance of Bismarck's demands and protests; as a rule, they were dealt with by the departmental Ministers. The German notes were, of course, addressed to the Foreign Office, at the head of which was Lord Granville, the Foreign Secretary. But Granville, in making a decision, had to consult the Colonial Secretary, Lord Derby, and the Colonial Secretary had, in his turn, to consult the cabinet of the colony concerned—that of the Cape Colonies, for instance, if a demand of Bismarck's touched on an African matter. Such a complicated organization is likely to lead to procrastination if the Ministers in question do not put forth their best efforts to quicken the tempo. But that was neither Granville's nor Derby's way, and so it came about that an important question submitted by Bismarck was left unanswered for six months.

That such a delay made him furious we can well understand, and we shall not be surprised to find that he was quick to turn any mistakes made by the British government to good account. But he was certainly wrong when he put the blame on a hostile disposition on the part of Granville. Granville was far from being anti-German; Bismarck himself knew his friendly feelings, for Granville had received Herbert Bismarck, who was for some time Secretary to the German Embassy in London, with the greatest kindness.

The chief reason for the misunderstandings between Bismarck and the British government was that the British learned only too late that Bismarck was bent on a colonial policy at all. All that they knew was that Bismarck opposed German colonial expansion, and the British Ambassador Odo Russell, now Lord Ampthill, continued to report in this sense from Berlin. This was not only due to his failing health—he died in August 1884—but still more to the fact that *Bismarck purposely concealed from him his change of policy*. In all the months that Granville could have adapted his attitude to Bismarck's wishes, not a word reached him from either the British Ambassador in Berlin or the German Ambassador in London, Count Münster, which would have enlightened him about these aspirations. Bismarck kept his intentions secret from Münster as well. When Hatzfeld, the Secretary of the German Foreign Office, suggested to Bismarck that he should inform Münster quite confidentially of his plans, he expressly forbade this in his order of 21st May 1884. . . .

The climax of this controversy came when Bismarck, simultaneously with the publication of these polemical articles, openly attacked Granville in the Reichstag. His speech is perhaps the most vehement attack made by the Minister of one state on the Foreign Minister of another in time of peace. True, Granville had given him an opening for this attack by an indiscreet remark in the House of Lords, where he mentioned Bismarck's advice to the British government "to take Egypt." When Bismarck asserted that he had never given this advice, he was certainly not telling the truth. But even so, Granville was in the wrong in making this suggestion public without first seeking Bismarck's permission.

Bismarck's speech caused an enormous sensation. Many people thought it the prelude to a rupture with Britain. But what did Bismarck really do? The next day he sent his son Herbert to London to bring about a settlement with the British Ministers. This settlement was, indeed, very soon reached, not because Herbert was such a skilful negotiator, but because Gladstone was resolved to come to an understanding in any case. He himself talked things over with Herbert and made it quite clear that he was willing to go to any lengths to meet Germany's just claims, but that Britain would find it more difficult to entertain them if they were presented in the form of blackmail. This word "blackmail" was without doubt plainly heard by Herbert, but he did not mention it in his very arrogant report on his negotiations. Instead, he had the impudence to write in this report to his father: "To discuss with Mr. Gladstone the essence of the foreign policy of a great state is useless, because he is quite unable to understand it." This was the tone in which the Chancellor liked to hear of a man whom his fellow-countrymen called the "Grand old Man" and whom Bismarck himself used to call "Professor Gladstone," "Professor" being an expression of his most utter contempt. Bismarck handled his controversy with Granville so cleverly as to leave the impression ultimately that the British Minister had been worsted. This had much to do with his being transferred to the Colonial Office when Gladstone formed his third cabinet in 1886.

2 A. J. P. Taylor: FROM Germany's First Bid for Colonies

Alan John Percival Taylor, Fellow of Magdalen College, is one of Britain's most controversial and influential historians. In an early work, he argued that Bismarck had no real interest in German overseas expansion and was motivated to embark upon colonial adventures in order to draw France and Germany together over imperial quarrels with Great Britain.

Thirty years of European concussions came to an end at the Congress of Berlin. In the ensuing period the European powers shrank from European conflicts, and the problems which continued to divide them were, as the French said of Alsace-Lorraine, *"reserved for the future."* European rivalries were temporarily diverted to the less dangerous field of *extra-European expan-*

SOURCE. A. J. P. Taylor, *Germany's First Bid for Colonies*, London: Macmillan & Co., 1938, pp. 1–7. Reprinted by permission of Macmillan & Co. Ltd.

sion, and in the years between 1881 and 1912 the European powers extended their influence or their empires over Africa and large parts of Asia.

This imperialist expansion was of two kinds. The more important was the struggle for the heritage of decaying states, themselves very often the relics of earlier epochs of imperialism. The struggle over the succession to the Turkish Empire had gone on since the end of the seventeenth century; but what distinguished the "Age of Imperialism" was that more of these decadent states came into the market and that the process of absorption was rendered more and more difficult by the interference of some other European (and in one case of an Asiatic) power. Thus France was able to establish her control over Tunis, Annam, and Madagascar without serious difficulty; but she extended her influence over Morocco only after coming twice to the brink of war with Germany. Great Britain annexed the Boer republics (relic of an earlier Dutch empire) after a period of conflict with Germany; and she asserted her predominance in Egypt after a period of conflict with France. It was owing to the rivalry of England and Russia that Persia and Afghanistan preserved their independence—though Persia nearly lost it to Russia in the last years before 1914; and, thanks to the jealousy of all the powers, China preserved her independence, except for the loss of a few ports in what proved to be an abortive partition in 1898. It is not necessary to speculate at length on the reasons for these imperialist activities: the objects of conflict were going concerns; their economic and political importance was known; and in many cases they adjoined possessions or strategic routes of European powers (Morocco on the frontier of Algiers, Egypt and Persia on the route to India, the Boer republics on the frontier of Cape Colony, and so on). The rival powers were still primarily influenced by European considerations; and though the extra-European questions provoked crises, it was the old problem of the Balkans which produced the War of 1914, with the even older problem of the Franco-German frontier as a contributory cause.

The predominance of European considerations is even greater in relation to the second form of European expansion in these thirty years—the occupation of hitherto ownerless territories, or rather of territories with no ruler substantial enough to be treated as an independent power. Under this head come most of Africa and the islands of the Pacific. The enormous areas of tropical Africa appear impressive on the map; but of most of them the plain truth is that they had remained so long ownerless because they were not worth owning. The principal exception was the basin of the Congo, which, curiously enough, slipped through the hands of the two traditional colonial powers, England and France, and was secured by a royal speculator, Leopold II, of Belgium, masquerading as a philanthropic society. Portugal, with a shadowy traditional claim to all Africa, managed to retain one colony on the west coast, and one on the east. France, who created a great North African empire within a few years, had intelligible political reasons for doing so: the republican government wished to demonstrate by colonial expansion that France was still a great power despite the humiliations of 1870; part of the expansion was undertaken to protect the frontiers of the existing colony of Algiers; and much of the rest aimed at opening for France an overland route to the Sudan, where—it was commonly believed—it would be possible to divert the upper Nile and so make the English position in Egypt untenable. France regarded Egypt as part of the heritage of Napoleon, and, in endeavouring to oust the English, was seeking to recover what had once been hers.

England had two interests in Africa, which she meant to preserve—a settlement of British colonists in South Africa, and a predominant influence in Egypt, which was both valuable in itself and a vital point on the route to India. The new English acquisitions were made in order to protect what England already possessed by cutting off the Nile from foreign interference, and the Boer republics, the neighbours of Cape Colony, from foreign help. It is true that these new possessions sometimes proved to have a value of their own, such as the diamond mines of Kimberley and the cotton plantations of the Sudan; but it was not for this that they had been undertaken.

In these years of "the scramble for Africa" there was suddenly added to the old colonial rivals, France and England, a power which had hitherto confined itself strictly to the European continent. The German colonial empire, or rather the formulation of

its theoretical claims, was virtually the work of a single year: the
Cameroons were established in July 1884, German South-West
Africa in August, New Guinea in December 1884, and German
East Africa was begun in May 1885 (though its frontiers were
not settled until 1890); Samoa was added in 1899; otherwise—
apart from some minor adjustments of the Cameroons frontier
at the expense of France after the second Moroccan crisis
(1911)—the German colonial empire was complete. The success
of Germany, as previously of Prussia, had been due to freedom
from all concern in non-German questions: Prussia had been
able to secure the support of Russia because of her indifference
to the Near East, and of Italy, because of her indifference to the
maintenance of the treaty settlement of Europe. It is therefore
surprising that Germany should have deliberately pushed her
way into the hornets' nest of colonial conflicts. The explanation
of this German outburst of colonial activity has usually been
found in the rising enthusiasm for colonies, and it is true that
there was in Germany a certain amount of colonial agitation.
Imperial Germany was a "made" state, an artificial reproduction
of French nationalism tinged with echoes from the Holy Roman
Empire; the new Germany had no political tradition, and had
therefore to ape the political traditions of others. Many Germans
demanded a colonial empire simply because other great powers
had colonial empires, and their demand was reinforced by the
current belief that the possession of colonies was in itself a profitable thing. Many writers, not only German, at this time failed
to grasp the truth about the British empire—that it had come into
being as the result of British commercial enterprise and industrial
success; and they asserted the reverse, that the prosperity and
wealth of Great Britain were due to the existence of her empire.
The German campaign for colonies rested on the simple dogma—
give Germany colonies and the Germans will then be as prosperous as the English.

It is difficult to believe that this primitive outlook was shared
by the German government, particularly in the days of Bismarck.
It has often been suggested that Bismarck was driven into a policy
of colonial expansion against his will. Lord Sanderson, who was
a member of the British Foreign Office in 1884, put forward this

explanation in a defence of Bismarck written some twenty years later: "Prince Bismarck was personally opposed to German colonisation. . . . He therefore encouraged us to make fresh annexations on the West Coast of Africa, to which we had been previously indisposed: hoping that the clamour for such annexations by Germany would subside. Suddenly he found that the movement was too strong for him, and that his only expedient, in order to avoid a crushing Parliamentary defeat, was to make friends with the party which urged the acquisition of Colonies. He went to Lord Ampthill [the British Ambassador], explained his dilemma, said he should have to take up the Colonial policy vigorously, and begged that we should give him our support."

To imagine that Bismarck was influenced by public opinion, or that he was swayed by fear of "a crushing parliamentary defeat" is to transfer to Germany the conceptions of constitutional government as practised in England or France. The Imperial German government did not depend upon a parliamentary majority, and the German press was only slightly freer than the press in Russia. There are, of course, plenty of instances—the history of the Schleswig-Holstein affair is full of them—when Bismarck gave the signal for a popular campaign to compel him to do what he wanted to do, but there seems to be no other case in which Bismarck is supposed to have bowed to the force of public opinion. Nor is it conceivable that Bismarck was suddenly converted, after years of scepticism, to a belief in the value of colonies. He was contemptuous enough of those who were ready to disturb the quiet of Europe for the sake of the "sheep-stealers" of the Balkans. But even Bismarck could not have found words of condemnation strong enough for a policy which provoked a quarrel with Great Britain for the sake of the "light soil" of South-West Africa or of the head-hunters of New Guinea.

It is the purpose of the following chapters to discover an explanation of Bismarck's colonial policy by fitting it into the structure of contemporary European politics. His colonial policy alone seems meaningless and irrational; but when to the relations of England and Germany are added those of Germany and France, and those of France and England, Bismarck's policy in 1884 and 1885 becomes as purposeful as at any other time in his career. Such an examination shows that Bismarck quarrelled with England in order to draw closer to France; and that the method of quarrel was the deliberately provocative claim to owner-less lands, in which the German government had hitherto shown no interest. These lands had a certain negative value to Great Britain, in that they adjoined existing British colonies or lay near British strategic routes; but their value was not such as to provoke the English government into a war. Moreover, they were of no concern to any other power, and claims to them would not cause any international complications, such as would have been occasioned by German demands in China or Persia. The German colonies were the accidental by-product of an abortive Franco-German entente.

It may be asked whether the later colonial disputes and discussions between England and Germany were similarly related to the European situation. It would be rash to attempt to discover in German policy after 1890 any such persistent and successful planning as in the days of Bismarck, particularly when to the gross incompetence of his successors were added the planless impulses of William II. Moreover, with the passing of time the German colonies did acquire a spurious ideological value; they became a white elephant, a sacred relic of Bismarck's era. He could contemplate passing on their useless burden to England, and even in 1890 the German government could surrender vast theoretical claims in East Africa in exchange for the really valuable island of Heligoland. Ten years later the value of colonies was taken as an axiom by the Germans, and from the failure of their colonial ventures they drew the moral not that colonies were a mistaken luxury, but that they ought to have more, and better, colonies. In the first decade of the twentieth century the Germans demanded "a place in the sun"; by this they meant someone else's place in the sun, their own having proved too hot.

3   Henry A. Turner: Bismarck Changes His Mind

After nearly thirty years, A. J. P. Taylor's hypothesis of Bismarck's colonial initiative has been reexamined by Henry A. Turner, Associate Professor of History at Yale University. Professor Turner remains unconvinced that Bismarck's change of policy can be attributed to ulterior motives. He offers an alternative explanation that, in fact, Bismarck simply changed his mind in 1884 and decided that Germany must expand overseas.

It is not difficult, however, to point out circumstantial evidence that casts considerable doubt on the validity of Taylor's reasoning. For example, just prior to Bismarck's move into the colonial world his utterances to his most trusted confidants contain strong indications that he was very skeptical about the prospects for reconciling France and Germany genuinely and permanently. The attempt to placate the French was, contrary to the impression conveyed by Taylor, nothing new, having been a basic component of Bismarck's policy at least since 1878. But even while pursuing this goal, Bismarck did not cease to doubt the possibility of quickly overcoming French resentment at Germany's possession of Alsace-Lorraine. It therefore seems questionable whether the Chancellor would have been willing to saddle his new German Reich with the sort of uncertain obligations and dangers that overseas possessions entailed, solely in order to pursue a goal he suspected was unattainable in the foreseeable future.

As Taylor himself admits, if Bismarck had really been looking for a quarrel with Britain in order to test the possibility of a Franco-German entente, there was a simpler and less risky alter-

SOURCE. Henry Ashby Turner, Jr., "Bismarck's Imperial Venture: Anti-British in Origin?", in *Britain and Germany in Africa*, Roger Louis, Prosser Gifford, and Alison Smith, eds., New Haven: Yale University Press, 1967, pp. 49–53. Reprinted by permission of Yale University Press. Copyright 1967 by Yale University.

native to the seizure of overseas possessions: he could instead
have sided with France against Britain in the dipute over Egypt.
Taylor dismisses this alternative in characteristically apodictic
fashion. It would not, he states, have served Bismarck's purpose,
"which was to convince the French that he had a grievance of
his own and therefore actually needed French help. A grievance
had to be created, and Bismarck turned to the colonial topics,
which he had hitherto despised." However, if Bismarck had actually been seeking a rapprochement with Paris he would certainly,
as a master diplomat, have sought it initially at the lowest price.
Before resorting to such extravagant means as an imperialist policy he surely would have at least tried playing the Egyptian
card.

More important than these objections to Taylor's theses is the
fact that, like all the other interpretations that attribute Bismarck's
change of policy to ulterior motives, it fails to accord with the
documentary record of the Chancellor's words and actions. Some
of this documentary evidence is new, having come to light only
after Taylor's book was written. But much was available in print
even in 1938, in German monographs and in documents published
by the Reich in the 1880s. As will be shown below, these sources
indicate clearly that Bismarck was not primarily motivated by
any of the ulterior motives imputed to him. They reveal instead
that he simply changed his mind and decided there must be
German overseas possessions. This is not to say that Bismarck
suddenly became an ardent imperialist. From all indications he
was a very reluctant convert and retained a high degree of skepticism even while presiding over the founding of Germany's overseas empire. This was obviously because he was moved to reverse
his policy not by the confident expectation of gaining concrete
advantages but rather by a mounting concern about the possible
adverse consequences of continued abstention. He acted, that is,
only in order to avert what he feared might be the damaging
effects of not doing so.

Bismarck's apprehensions stemmed initially from his growing
concern lest the failure to stake out a German claim in the
colonial world might have grave economic consequences. This
was by no means an immediate possibility. Although Germany's
commerce with Africa and Asia had been increasing rapidly since

the mid-1870s, it remained only a miniscule fraction of the country's total foreign trade. But the non-European world was still the great unknown factor: there was always the chance that the extravagant predictions of the colonial zealots would eventually be borne out. As long as the principle of free trade prevailed in the colonial world, this possibility caused Bismarck no apprehension, for there was no reason to assume that Germany would lack access to Africa and Asia if those continents should prove to be of great economic importance. What brought Bismarck to reconsider his policy were the multiplying signs in the early 1880s that the era of free trade, which he himself had dealt such a heavy blow in Europe by the adoption of the protectionist German tariff of 1879, was also drawing to a close in the colonial world. Quite clearly, his attitude began to change under a barrage of reports to the effect that the colonial powers were beginning to favor their own nationals by means of differential tariffs and other discriminatory policies.

The Chancellor's doubts about the wisdom of continued opposition to German overseas possessions were further heightened by the developments that foreshadowed the partition of Africa, beginning with the well-publicized de Brazza-Stanley race to claim territory along the Congo in the early 1880s. As long as large parts of the non-European world were free of colonial rule, German commerce could get access to the markets and resources of Africa and Asia regardless of the discriminatory policies of the imperialist powers. But if those powers were to carve up all of the non-European world, German overseas merchants would be at their mercy. And without territorial possessions of her own overseas, Germany would be unable to obtain for her subjects the sort of economic privileges the colonial powers could gain for theirs through reciprocity agreements. The indications are that Bismarck had these eventualities in mind and that they contributed to his decision to break with his old policy.

Bismarck was also not immune to the *Torschlusspanik* that was to play such an important role in the partition of the non-European world—the fear that the gate was rapidly closing and that the last chance was at hand. A major factor in his turn to imperialism was the thought that if he failed to authorize the hoisting of the German flag, the flag of another European power would quickly go up. In Germany's case at least, it is impossible to account for the new imperialism of the late nineteenth century without taking into account the dynamics of the highly competitive European state system.

Finally, it should be said that there was undoubtedly a domestic political dimension to Bismarck's reversal of policy. He was, after all, primarily a man of politics who instinctively sought out the political significance of almost everything that came into his purview. Still, it would be a mistake to conclude, as have some, that he limited his assessment of the political ramifications of such a major policy decision to tactical, short-range considerations such as the impact on a single election campaign. He was without question aware in 1884 that the popular colonial issue would be a useful cudgel against the anti-imperialist Radical Party in the campaign for the autumn Reichstag elections. However, the line of argument that would attribute the origins of his imperialist venture to his concern about those elections founders on the fact that he continued to enlarge Germany's overseas commitments even after the Radicals had been dealt a resounding setback at the polls. It is far more likely that long-range considerations played a greater role in Bismarck's assessment of the domestic aspects of overseas questions than did the campaign of 1884. This was, it must be remembered, the mature Bismarck, who was seeking to stabilize the political system he had imposed on the German people and to convince them his government really served their interests. Moreover, the early 1880s was a period when, under the impact of a severe economic depression, Bismarck had committed his government to the task of restoring and furthering the material welfare of Germany. The possible effect that continued abstention from the colonial arena might have on the attitude toward the government of such an important component of society as the business community, particularly if Africa and Asia became as important economically as the imperialists had predicted, must therefore have given the Chancellor pause. There are also indications that he was very much concerned about the effects on his own place in German history. In remarks that have an unguarded, sincere ring, he later explained that in considering whether to take the plunge into colonial affairs he had to ask himself "whether after twenty, after thirty years, people will charge that faint-hearted Chancellor back then with not having the courage to ensure for us a share of what later became such valuable property."

It was this complex of economic and political considerations that brought Bismarck to reconsider his position. Formerly, he had opposed overseas possessions for Germany on the grounds that they would be a two-fold liability, externally because the country lacked a fleet adequate to defend them, and internally because the costs of administering them would "widen the parliamentary parade ground" by increasing the government's financial dependence on the Reichstag. In searching for solutions to the new developments described above, however, he began to relax his rigid attitude, gradually moving away from his old position. When he finally became convinced he had found an administrative formula that circumvented at least his domestic objections, he acted to commit Germany to the imperialist scramble.

THE BERLIN CONFERENCE

4 J. D. Hargreaves: The Work of the Berlin Conference

J. D. Hargreaves, Professor of History in the University of Aberdeen, has long been one of the most perceptive students of the partition of West Africa. His analysis of the Berlin Conference of 1884–1885 has destroyed many of the myths that have emerged concerning the work of the conference. Not only did the conference not partition Africa, but the vague provisions of the Berlin Act had little real effect upon the scramble.

Early in October France and Germany joined in inviting twelve other states to a conference in Berlin to discuss three problems. The first was liberty of commerce in the basin and mouth of the Congo ("liberty of commerce" having been redefined, at French initiative, so as to permit the imposition of duties to cover administrative costs). The second was the application to the Congo and the Niger of the principles adopted by the Congress of Vienna in 1815 to safeguard liberty of navigation in international rivers; the third, definition of formalities to be observed before new occupations of territory on the coasts of Africa should be internationally recognized. The British government at once accepted the invitation in principle, while adding their own glosses to that ambiguous term, "liberty of

SOURCE. J. D. Hargreaves, *Prelude to the Partition of West Africa*, London: Macmillan & Co., 1963, pp. 334–338. Reprinted by permission of St. Martin's Press, Inc., Macmillan & Co., Ltd. Copyright John D. Hargreaves 1963.

commerce." Their main concern was to establish a clear distinction between the position on the Congo, where internationalization would be both justifiable and advantageous, and that on the Niger, where Britain herself, thanks to the efforts of Hewett and Goldie, was now "the Niger power." Until quite recently the government might well have been content with international guarantees for its commercial interests on the Niger; but many Ministers were now determined to stand by the previous year's decision to assert British national claims, partly because of Goldie's insistence, but also in reaction to French and German policy elsewhere. Right-wing Whigs and Radicals had alike been greatly irritated by the set-backs recently suffered by Britain in Africa; Kimberley and Chamberlain, among others, now insisted on excluding both Germany and France from political control in Niger. Gladstone and other pacifically-minded Ministers, already threatened with resignations from both wings of the disunited Cabinet over a wide range of Irish and domestic issues, had to agree to resist any real internationalization of the Niger. Derby, still loyal to his principles, saw no reason why the Niger should not be treated in the same way as the Congo, but his officials too advised against accepting any effective international Commission.

In fact, Britain had little real difficulty in avoiding the internationalization of the Niger. The question of enforcing commercial liberty there, it will have been noted, was not even on the Conference agenda; the French Ministry for Foreign Affairs had not thought it worth making the attempt. (The Ministry of the Marine, however, regretted this, and and even seemed willing to pay the price of including its own sphere of influence on the *upper* Niger within the scope of such an international arrangement.) As for navigation, the British could claim that, since they now held treaty rights and a *de facto* trade monopoly over that whole portion of the river which was navigable from the sea, there was no justification for an International Commission; the Niger, for purposes of navigation, was not an "international river." But Britain was *herself willing* to guarantee free navigation on the same basis as in the Congo. Two days before the Conference opened Bismarck, whose relations with France were passing through a strained period and who may have anticipated

a need for British support over the Congo, agreed to accept this
case; and on 16 November the French delegation too accepted
the distinction between the two rivers. (In making this concession they may have been influenced by fears that, if they
pressed for a Commission on the Niger, Britain might demand
one on other African rivers than those mentioned in the Conference programme, such as the Senegal.) In the final Berlin
Act, therefore, Britain and France simply bound themselves to
apply similar conditions to those imposed on the Congo along
such reaches of the Niger as they respectively controlled, but no
machinery for international supervision was established.

On the Congo question too the upshot of the Conference
proved satisfactory to Great Britain, who gradually realized
that by supporting Leopold she could secure the essential purposes pursued by the abortive treaty with Portugal. During 1884
Leopold showed great diplomatic skill in obtaining recognition
of his International Association as a sovereign power in Africa,
initially from the United States and France. Even the right of
pre-emption, which he openly conceded to France as the price
of her recognition, served the cause of Congolese independence,
for it gave those powers hostile to French expansion the strongest
possible interest in strengthening international guarantees for
the new state. In this task, and in the formulation of safeguards for trade and navigation through the wider area known
as "the conventional basin of the Congo," Germany and Britain
eventually found a high degree of common interest.

The importance of the Berlin Conference has often been mis-
represented and exaggerated. Diplomatically, though it seemed
a significant novelty that France and Germany should jointly
sponsor such a conference, their African interests proved to be
widely divergent, and the idea of a Franco-German entente soon
lapsed. Wilhelm II's belief that the continental powers had
united in an anti-British league was a myth. Nor is it true that
the Conference "partitioned Africa." Territorial questions were
specifically excluded from the agenda, and those requiring
settlement were dealt with in a series of bilateral agreements
extending over many years (though it is true that important
questions affecting boundaries in the Congo basin were discussed
by delegates in Berlin outside the Conference sessions).

One aim of the Conference, as defined in the third 'basis', was to limit the effects of future African disputes upon international relations in Europe by prescribing some new code of conduct. The final Act provided that any power acquiring territory or establishing protectorates on the coasts of Africa should at once notify all other signatory powers; and declared that possession of territory on those coasts implied a responsibility for "the establishment of authority . . . sufficient to protect existing rights, and, as the case may be, freedom of trade and of transit upon the conditions agreed upon." But both these provisions were restricted to the coastal districts, virtually all of which were already appropriated by 1885; and protectorates were not covered by the wording of the second. (This was a victory for the British, who, although they had formerly questioned the French claims to Cotonou and Porto Novo on the grounds that there was no effective occupation, were not ready to assume extensive administrative commitments in their new Niger protectorates.) These provisions of the Berlin Act, like its vague references to the abolition of slave dealing and to the welfare of the peoples of the Congo basin, had little practical effect on the coming partition of Africa.

PART THREE

Italy: The Imperialism of Personalities

MOTIVES

1 Donald A. Limoli: Francesco Crispi's Quest for Empire—and Victories—in Ethiopia

In this original essay, which reflects the themes from his larger, forthcoming work on Italy and the First Ethiopian war, Donald A. Limoli, Assistant Professor of History at the University of California, Santa Barbara, delineates the origins of Italy's Ethiopian adventure,

Italian Imperialism in Ethiopia

its advocates and enemies, its successes and ultimate failure. Through the speeches of the personalities involved, the dreams of empire and the dress of reality vividly emerge.

On February 5, 1885, Italy occupied the port of Massawa on the coast of Ethiopia with, probably not by accident, about 1000 troops—the same number of men that had comprised Garibaldi's famous Expedition of the Thousand to Sicily in 1860. Previously, in 1882, Italy had acquired some territory around Assab, further south on the Ethiopian coast. But no one had paid much attention to this; and, when the occupation of Massawa was announced by the government, there was universal amazement. Most Italians, undoubtedly, remained unaware of the event, for most, particularly the massive Italian peasantry who were illiterate and poverty stricken, were not politically conscious or part of the political life of the Italian state at this time. Those, however, who were politically conscious and who made up the directing class of the Italian state formed in 1860, were almost all in agreement that Italy's vital interests lay in the Mediterranean and North Africa, and could not understand why the government had directed itself to the Red Sea and Ethiopia. Nor could they understand why, of all places, it had chosen to occupy Massawa, a hot, malarial, unhealthy port—indeed, one of the hottest places in the world.

To this day, one may wonder why Italy went to Massawa and Ethiopia. Italian explorers, it is true, were in the vanguard in opening up Ethiopia, and, in their enthusiasm, they brought or sent home tales of a rich trade Italy could develop in Abyssinia. Many, moreover, held that Italy's poor or landless peasants, who were beginning to emigrate in large numbers across the Atlantic, could be settled on the Ethiopian high plain. On the high plain, conditions were more hospitable than along the coast; the climate was more bearable and a long rainy season and prairie soils made the cultivation of crops such as coffee and grain possible. Over 300,000 peasants, one ardent explorer argued, could be settled on the high plain of Ethiopia. But, as Ferdinando Martini devastatingly pointed out in a speech to the Italian

Chamber of Deputies [see pp. ooo-ooo], Abyssinia had no
products or needs that would support any kind of trade, let
alone a rich one; and as Andrea Costa pointed out in a speech of
his to the Chamber [see pp. ooo-ooo], Italy had no surplus
products to send to Abyssinia, for her own industrialization had
just begun. Furthermore, the high plain had to be approached
through wild, precipitous mountains in the Tigrè, where there
were no roads, but only trails and paths, and the cost of transport-
ing and settling Italian peasants in Ethiopia was prohibitive. It
would have been much cheaper to undertake land improvement
and reclamation for them at home.

In addition to all this, the head of the Italian government in
1885, Agostino Depretis, was strongly opposed to foreign or
colonial adventures of any kind. He knew Italy was a weak
power—she was the weakest of the great powers—and believed
that they might lead her to disaster. He was also a masterful
parliamentary manipulator intent on preserving his parliamentary
majority, which he feared dangerous adventures might upset.
Perhaps even more curiously, his foreign minister, Pasquale
Stanislao Mancini, was an eminent professor of international
law, well known as a champion of peace, international arbitration,
and the right of all peoples to be free and independent—that is,
the principle of nationality on which the whole Italian *Risorgimento* had been based.

Why, then, did Italy occupy Massawa? Most important, Italy
had suffered a series of disappointments in international affairs:
in 1878, she got nothing at the Congress of Berlin; in 1881, she
was caught by surprise when France seized Tunis; and in 1882,
she turned down an English invitation to participate in the
pacification of Egypt, whereupon England occupied Egypt by
herself. The French seizure of Tunis particularly hurt Italians,
for Tunis lay just three hours across the Mediterranean from
Sicily, and some 20,000 Italians had settled there. But all these
"reverses," were denounced by Italian nationalists and colonialists,
who, beginning to become vocal around 1881, declaimed that
Italy was being humiliated by the other powers and strangled
in her own sea, the Mediterranean. Thus, Depretis undoubtedly
hoped to quiet these ardent spirits by giving them a little
colonial undertaking. He also probably hoped to divert attention

away from internal problems, such as peasant disorders and the first signs of working class unrest, which were now causing him a good deal of trouble. As for Mancini, he seems to have been overcome by the colonial fever that gripped Europe around 1884–1885, and to have feared that Italy might again be caught by surprise and humiliated by new colonial coups on the part of the other powers—especially France. He was, in fact, ready to send an Italian expedition into Tripoli if France made a move in Morocco. The French, however, did not move there; rather, in the wake of the Mahdist revolt in the Sudan and the collapse of Egyptian control all along the Red Sea in 1884–1885, they seemed ready to occupy various points along the coast of Abyssinia, where they already held the port of Obock. In addition, on October 20, 1884, the British government, even more concerned than the Italian about possible French occupations along the Red Sea coast, asked the Italian government if it would be interested in occupying Massawa. In view of this, it has generally been assumed that, faced with the Mahdist revolt and the necessity to abandon the Sudan, the English enticed the Italians into occupying Massawa in order to keep the French out of it and to prevent a French advance from Massawa to the high Nile in the Sudan. But the English never really wanted any European power at Massawa or the approach to the Sudan from there; from start to finish, it was Mancini and the Italians who were the suppliants and not the English. Intent on action somewhere, Mancini bombarded London with telegrams requesting England's approval for the occupation of Massawa. He even went so far as to offer to send an Italian expedition to help relieve Gordon at Khartoum! Not only was he intent on action, but he also fell under the illusion that if Italy helped England out of her difficulties in the Sudan, she would support Italy in the Mediterranean, where British support was deemed essential by all Italians. This was the meaning of his famous declaration, made to justify the occupation of Massawa, that the keys to the Mediterranean were to be found in the Red Sea. This was an unfortunate illusion that, later shared by Crispi, was to cost Italy dearly. So it was, that instead of going to Tripoli, Italy went to Massawa.

The occupation of Massawa caused an uproar in the Italian press and parliament. The colonialists in Italy were always a small

minority; most Italians believed that Italy had too many problems
at home to be solved to waste her resources in colonial adventures. A common refrain, which was raised by moderates
as well as radicals and socialists, was that she had many Africans
at home to civilize, especially in the Italian South, so much like
North Africa in its arid climate, poor, parched soils, and massive,
hopeless poverty, before she turned to expansion abroad. Moreover, colonialists as well as anticolonialists almost unanimously
held that Ethiopia was worthless, and that if Italy was going to
expand, this had to be in the Mediterranean. Many Italians also
denounced colonialism as immoral and impossible for Italy,
whose whole existence, they at once reminded Mancini and the
government, was based on respect for the principle of nationality.
So, except for a few extreme nationalists, for example, Rocco
De Zerbi, who had for years been saying that Italy needed a
great and successful war to increase her self-confidence and
cohesion and who spoke of the Ethiopian venture as "poetry" that
the nation needed, almost everyone condemned the occupation of
Massawa. And in the parliamentary debate over the occupation,
a voice was heard that for the first time powerfully, eloquently,
and movingly, spoke of the workers' cause and charged the
government with betraying that cause—by wasting in colonial
ventures the resources of the nation needed for social reform
at home. This was the voice of Andrea Costa, the first socialist
ever to be elected a deputy to the Italian parliament, and his
speech, previously mentioned, constitutes an historic moment not
only in the history of Italian colonialism, but in that of Italian
socialism and the Italian workers' movement.

So great was the opposition to the occupation of Massawa
that, not long after, Depretis disembarrassed himself of Mancini.
But Depretis had no intentions of expanding into the interior of
Ethiopia; and after the initial furor died down, most Italians forgot about Massawa and the unfortunate detachments of the Italian
army stationed there. Two years went by in this way.

Then, on January 26, 1887, 500 Italian troops were annihiliated
at Dogali, not far from Massawa, by Ras Alula, one of the
Emperor John's chieftains. The Emperor, or Negus, as he was
called by his Ethiopian title, resented the occupation of Massawa,
which was the natural outlet of his realms in the north. For

defensive reasons, the Italians had moved inward from Massawa a few miles to the positions of Saatio and Ua-a. Beseiged at Saatio by Alula, they sent a column of 500 men to relieve it. This column was caught by 5000 of Alula's soldiers in the open. The Italians fought bravely, choosing to stand and fight rather than to retreat, but the odds aganst them were obviously too great: 413 men and 21 of 22 officers fell at Dogali.

The news of Dogali shocked Italy. It was another military defeat for a nation that had suffered many in the past: at Custozza in 1848, at Novara in 1849, and at Custozza on the land and Lissa on the sea in 1866. A profound reaction set in against Depretis and the immobilism he seemed to represent in both foreign and domestic policy. Dogali, in short, brought the hour of Francesco Crispi, the most ardent nationalist and imperialist among Italy's leaders. As one contemporary put it, Dogali brought Crispi's name to everyone's lips. In April, 1887, Depretis took him into the government. In July Depretis, who was old and ailing, died, and Crispi became the head of the government and master of Italy.

Crispi himself was no youngster; he was 67 years old when he finally achieved power. Power, he had wanted for a long time, but power, sensible Italians had feared to entrust to him. For Crispi seemed—and was—a dangerous, headstrong leader who could—and did—lead Italy to ruin. He believed that Italians were a great people and that Italy must play the part of a great power in Europe and imperial power in the Mediterranean. He had been in his younger years a follower of Mazzini and learned from him to believe in Italian greatness and the idea of an Italian mission in the world. But whereas Mazzini had looked for Italians to carry out a new civilizing mission in the world, Crispi translated this mission into one of asserting Italy's power over other peoples. Crispi had been, too, a member of Garibaldi's Expedition of the Thousand—in fact, the man behind it—and could never forget the remarkable feats the Thousand had performed. United Italy, he believed, had to perform similar feats so that the "age of poetry," as many Italians spoke of the *Risorgimento*, would not end. Crispi fell, finally, under the fatal influence of ancient Rome, the Rome of the Caesars, and believed that as Rome had dominated the Mediterranean, so must Italy. No one more than he denounced the Congress of Berlin, the loss of Tunis, and the decision not to go into Egypt as great national disasters and humiliations. No one more than he, also, did more to swing Italy into the Triple Alliance with Germany and Austria.[1] With all his other ideas and passions, Crispi was bitterly anti-French and strongly pro-German. France he hated for her opposition to Italian unification and seizure of Tunis; Germany he admired for her military power and respect for authority. He himself had an authoritarian temperament. With his assumption of office, he took to exercising authoritarian powers at home. Abroad, he set out in haste to assert Italy's greatness, to expand in the Mediterranean—and to avenge Dogali.

After Dogali, Italy could have withdrawn from Ethiopia and called it an act of wisdom. This is what Ferdinando Martini called on the government and the Chamber of Deputies to do in his speech of June 2, 1885, previously mentioned. Dogali showed that the Ethiopians were capable of mounting strong resistence and that a major military effort would be necessary to subdue them. Such an effort was difficult to make in Ethiopia, for not only did troops have to make their way along precipitous mountain trails, but all their equipment, munitions, and supplies had to be transported by pack animals. In addition, Italy had to defend her possessions not only against the Ethiopians, but also against the Mahdists of the Sudan. Martini was a well-known and respected representative of the moderates, who were men of balance and common sense. Speaking in their behalf, he appealed to the government and the Chamber not to make Dogali a point of national honor, outlined all the perils of military operations in Ethiopia, and argued not only against the folly of trying to conquer Ethiopia, but of trying to avenge Dogali and expand even on a limited scale. His speech is also noteworthy for what he said about the idea of bringing civilization to the Ethiopians and about their aspirations for independence on the basis of the principle of nationality. The majority in the Chamber was opposed to any further expansion. Almost all the deputies felt, however, that Dogali had to be avenged. Laboring under the stigma of her military defeats, Italy could not take Dogali in

---

[1] The Alliance was concluded in 1882. *Ed.*

stride. Even the leader of the radicals or democrats, who were ardently anticolonialist, declared that England could withdraw from the Sudan and call it an act of political wisdom, but that Italy, with her record of defeats, could not effect the pose of England. She had to redeem herself on the field of battle first. Such views opened the door of opportunity to Crispi.

The speech Crispi made on June 3, 1887 (given on pp. 130–32), was a direct reply to Martini's speech of June 2. As can be seen, he assured parliament that the government did not intend to conquer Ethiopia. And at this time, he spoke truthfully. Crispi did not have any systematic plans of expansion in Ethiopia. He was among those, as a matter of fact, who in 1885 called the occupation of Massawa senseless. His main objective was to acquire Tripoli for Italy in the Mediterranean. But, intensely nationalist, he could not conceive of abandoning Massawa; and needless to say, he believed that Dogali had to be avenged, as he made clear in his speech with his words about how the cannons would thunder. He also believed that something had to be made of the Massawa undertaking; and he made this clear too when he said that the government could not renounce taking any action in Ethiopia that circumstances might favor or make possible. What happened was that he failed to get Tripoli and wound up making his big imperialist effort in Ethiopia. His imperialism was politically, not economically, motivated. Through expansion he sought mainly to raise Italy's national prestige, and just as important, to redeem the reputation of the Italian army. In addition, he was always restless and avid for action. The Ethiopian enterprise thus became, above all, his enterprise.

To vindicate the massacre of Dogali, an expedition of about 10,000 men was sent to Ethiopia. Its objective was to inflict a military defeat on Emperor John. Vastly outnumbered by John's hordes, the Italians took up a fortified position at Saatio, hoping that John would attack them and that they could destroy his forces with superior fire power. But the Emperor wisely chose not to assail the Italian position; and the Italians wisely chose not to come out in the open. In the end, John retreated. No military victory, consequently, was achieved, and this left Crispi more dissatisfied and restless for action than ever.

The course of action he took was one laid out for him by one of the most irresponsible of Italy's colonial adventurers, Count Pietro Antonelli. According to one authority, Antonelli wanted to be for united Italy what Cavour had been for the *Risorgimento!* Antonelli believed he had won the absolute confidence of King Menelik of Shoa, a kingdom in southern Ethiopia. The kings of Shoa in the south and of the Tigrè in the north had historically vied for control of all Ethiopia. John was king of the Tigrè, and Menelik hoped to depose him as Emperor and assume the imperial title of Ethiopia himself. Antonelli thus advised Crispi to back Menelik in this conflict and to supply him with the arms he needed to overthrow John. In return, he held, Menelik would concede Italy a protectorate over Ethiopia and a portion of the high plain in the Tigrè. Antonelli's plan looked simple, and Crispi, placing his entire confidence in Antonelli, made it his own.

The opportunity to put it into effect came in 1889. In March of that year, John was killed by the Mahdists fighting at the Battle of Al-Gallabat. Soon after, Menelik, whom Crispi helped arm, took the crown of Ethiopia. On May 2, 1889, he concluded with Antonelli the famous, or infamous, Treaty of Uccialli. Its crucial article was Article XVII, which presumably gave Italy a protectorate over Ethiopia by granting her the right to represent Ethiopia in international affairs. Crispi, on his part, ordered his military commander in Ethiopia, General Antonio Baldissera, to occupy the points of Keren and Asmara on the edge of the high plain in the Tigrè. (The first was about 108 and the second about 86 kilometers from Massawa.) Baldissera actually opposed this move, for he well knew what the difficulties of military operations in Ethiopia were. He argued that he would need at least 20,000 troops, and he did not have anywhere near that number. Crispi never appreciated such arguments. He knew nothing about conditions in Ethiopia; and never able to forget his experience in the Expedition of the Thousand, he could not see why a few European troops, animated by the spirit and fervor of the Thousand, could not prevail over African savages. In the end he had his way. Keren and Asmara were occupied; and on January 1, 1890, he proclaimed into existence the colony of Eritrea. Extending from Massawa to Assab to the south, it extended far beyond Keren and Asmara in the Tigrè—to the Mareb River which he claimed as a strategic frontier for the new colony.

With this, Crispi announced that the objective of his colonial policy would be to settle Italy's landless peasants on the high plain. Plans for this were drawn up, but only fifteen peasant families—a paltry number—were ever sent to Ethiopia. Crispi's objective remained to expand. He now turned his attention to the Sudan, setting his sights on an advance to Kassala, 400 kilometers from Keren! He wanted to undertake joint military operations with the British in the Sudan to share in the martial glory of reconquering the Sudan with the great English nation. England, however, would have none of this.

Moreover, almost as soon as the Treaty of Uccialli was concluded, Menelik objected that he had not, by the treaty, granted Italy a protectorate over Ethiopia. As is well known, there were two versions of the treaty, one in Italian and one in Amharic. By the Amharic, or Ethiopian text, Article XVII stated that Menelik could, *if he wished*, avail himself of Italy's services in international affairs; by the Italian, it stated or implied that *he must*. It can never be known for certain, but it is possible that, desirous of fame and success, Antonelli knew of this difference and never informed Crispi or his superiors in Rome of it. That Menelik would sign away his independence is unlikely, for his objective was to consolidate Ethiopia under his control, and he was the founder of the modern Ethiopian state. In May, 1892, he denounced the Treaty of Uccialli.

This occurred while Crispi was out of power. On January 31, 1891, he lost his office because of a host of serious problems he created. Most important he ruined the Italian budget by making vast expenditures on the Italian army and navy, while, following an anti-French policy, he engaged Italy in a series of diplomatic contests and in a commercial war with France that ruined large sectors of the Italian economy. In Ethiopia, his successors instituted a policy of retrenchment. But they could not solve the many problems he created, and in December 1893, Crispi returned to power.

Reassuming control of the government, Crispi had to pledge himself first and foremost to the solution of the crisis of the Italian budget. To this end, he was obliged to cut expenditures to the bone in Ethiopia and to pledge that he would not try to expand any further. But Crispi was determined to compel Menelik to abide by the Treaty of Uccialli. In addition, he was now faced by vigorous opposition from the Democrats and the Socialists of the Extreme Left. The Socialists, who formed their own party in 1892, were now gaining strength, and both parties, the Socialists and the Democrats, came out in vigorous opposition to his dictatorial, militaristic, and imperialist policies. What he hoped to do was to silence this opposition and to entrench himself in power by achieving a great victory in Ethiopia and founding a great Italian empire in East Africa. He began to move again in 1894.

In July of 1894, General Baratieri, now in command in Ethiopia, marched to Kassala and defeated the Mahdist forces centered in that locality. Enthused by this victory, Crispi ordered him to retain and occupy it. Then in December of 1894 and January of 1895, Baratieri won three victories over the Tigrens, who, under the leadership of Ras Mangasha, had risen in revolt. This seemed to open the way for Italian penetration into the heart of the Tigrè, and Crispi could not restrain himself. He threw Baratieri's victories into the face of the acrid Democratic and Socialist opposition against him, and pressed Baratieri to cross the Mareb River and occupy the Tigrè. This, now, Baratieri opposed unless he was sent major reinforcements. But this Crispi refused to do, for his cabinet would not allow him to imperil the budget by increasing expenditures in Ethiopia. Yet he kept up the pressure on Baratieri, who finally succumbed. On March 25, 1895, he crossed the Mareb River and occupied Adigrat near Aduwa. Subsequently, as Menelik advanced against him, he set up advanced outposts ever further south, the farthest being at Amba Alagi.

In terms that the Italians had used in the *Risorgimento*, Menelik called on his people to expel the foreigner from the soil of Ethiopia. He now had a well equipped army. In retaliation against Crispi's anti-French policy, the French government opposed his policy in Ethiopia and allowed its agents to run guns, cannons, and munitions to Menelik from the French ports of Obock and Djibouti. Crispi protested in Paris time and again against this to no avail. In the fall of 1895, Menelik began his advance north. On December 7, 1895, he annihilated the Italian garrison at Amba Alagi, made up of 1500 troops, who once again fought bravely, but were overwhelmed by superior numbers.

As can be seen from Crispi's speech on Amba Alagi, he tried to disclaim all responsibility for expansion in Ethiopia and to place all the blame for Amba Alagi on General Baratieri—a friend and former comrade of his in the Expedition of the Thousand. This was morally inexcusable. But he called on the nation to persist in Ethiopia and to vindicate Amba Alagi. And now, in fright, he offered and sent Baratieri troops by the thousands.

Baratieri, however, could not get the vast majority of these troops to Adigrat or supply them there. For, as Menelik advanced, revolts occured on the Italian rear lines to Massawa. By February, 1896, when Menelik and Baratieri's forces were finally facing each other, his supplies were cut down to a trickle. In desperation, he proposed that some of these troops be used to launch a diversionary expedition into Ethiopia in the south from the English port of Zeila. Throughout, Crispi had relied on England for support in colonial affairs. Like Mancini earlier, he deluded himself that he could base a Mediterranean entente with England on cooperation in the Sudan and East Africa. But the English regarded his Ethiopian policy as suicidal. Also, England was now being challenged by Germany, and given this, the English were not willing to offend France in Italy's behalf. The French objected to the Zeila operation, and England made their support conditional on French approval, which France refused. Italy's allies, Germany and Austria, also regarded Crispi's policies as foolhardy and refused Italy support. So, on the eve of Aduwa, Italy was isolated in Europe.

To the end, Crispi demanded a victory from General Baratieri. Baratieri's strategy was to entrench himself at Adigrat and hope he could repel the Ethiopians with his fire power. But bombarded by telegrams from Crispi demanding decisive action, and down to a few days' supplies, he decided on the night of February 28 to advance to Aduwa, entrench himself there, and challenge Menelik to battle. The Italians marched to Aduwa on the night of February 29, in three columns. Baratieri had about 23,000 troops, half of which were African soldiers, and 50 mountain guns; Menelik had 80,000 to 100,000 men, armed with rifles, and 42 mountain guns. Baratieri's maps were faulty, and as March 1 dawned and wore on, the three columns became separated from each other in the mountains of Aduwa. The Ethiopians attacked and destroyed each column separately. Bravery, of which there was much, was to no avail. The defeat of the Italians was complete and stunning: 3772 Italian soliders and 262 officers, including two of the generals, were killed; 2000 were taken prisoner. Over 3000 of Baratieri's African troops were also killed. The news of Aduwa caused widespread disorders and near civil war in Italy. Crispi was overthrown, and his successor, the Marquis di Rudini, concluded peace with Ethiopia.

2   *Andrea Costa: The Workers' Opposition to Expansion in Ethiopia, Speech in the Chamber of Deputies, Session of May 7, 1885*

Gentlemen, do not expect a speech on colonial policy from me: after so many that have been made, my speech would be superfluous.

I do not have any other pretension than of being, here, for a single instant (the Chamber may calm itself) the most feeble echo, alas, of thousands of voices that are raising themselves from the factories and the fields, the echo of those classes that do not have the time or the leisure to think of the *costly poetry* of the honorable De Zerbi, but must instead, unfortunately, think of daily bread.

Gentlemen, Italy that works, Italy that produces, working Italy, true Italy I dare to say, does not want colonial policy. It has no need, honorable minister of war, that the insult once hurled against the Italian by General Oudinot, if I am not mistaken, namely that *les italiens ne se battent pas*, be repudiated today. This insult has been efficaciously repudiated by the events

SOURCE. "Discussioni della camera dei Deputati. Tornata del 7 maggio 1885," *Atti Parlamentari* (Sessione 1882–1885), Vol. XIII, pp. 13480–13481. Selected and translated for this book by Donald A. Limoli.

that took place from 1849 to 1870; and when there is need to repudiate it again, I do not think that strong and audacious men would go to look for their field of battle on the sands of Africa, but would look, oppositely, to Tripoli, or would raise their eyes to the Giulian Alps.

Italy that works . . . is thirsty for liberty, thirsty for justice, thirsty for culture; and as the base of its every intellectual, political, and moral improvement, wants the improvement of its economic conditions; for that reason it sees, with horror, the public patrimony squandered in easy conquests of African sands; it sees, with horror, its strongest sons sent there; nor does it think that in the present very wretched conditions of our national production there is any need of seeking outlets for our commerce.

It wants, instead, our production increased; or, rather than to increase production, it . . . [wants] to make the products accessible to the producers.

This Italy that works wants, this the great mass of the Italian people wants. And, instead of squandering the public money in this way, in colonial adventures, . . . it wants that the public patrimony be employed for the relief of the miseries we have in our house, for the relief of the thousands of peasants who (this is not rhetoric) slowly die of hunger and pellagra in Venetia and Mantova and for whom the government has only manacles; it wants that one would think to better the conditions of those human multitudes that in the underworld of all the large cities live a life more of animals than of men; it wants that the conditions of those who every day leave a bit of their living flesh in the mines and in the factories be improved.

This the great mass of the Italian people wants, all those who work and who are the true wealth, the true strength of the nation. . . .

Let us recall, consequently (I say it frankly), our legions from Africa, where we have sent them with so much frivolity; and before thinking of carrying civilization into the house of others, let us, we, disembarrass ourselves of what remains with us from a very sorrowful past; and turn all our strength, all our energy to the solution of that which is the torment and the honor of our century; the social question.

3 *Ferdinando Martini: Dogali and the Necessity to
   Liquidate a Hopeless Venture, Speech in the
   Chamber of Deputies, Session of June 2, 1887*

I have said that it is not possible for us today to seek out the
reasons for the occupation of Massawa; judging from the results,
I have no difficulty in affirming freely that I think this was an
error in which everyone had a share with our acts, and with our
vote [of confidence in the government] . . . we all have a sad
responsibility.

But, if, as I think, it was an error, whoever intends to continue
on there will from now on bear the responsibility himself, which
is separate and distinct from that of us all.

Having said this, I come to the main subject.

The Ministry, presenting itself to the Chamber on April 18,
read its program, in which there were these words: "Italy cannot, without offense to the national dignity, leave the glorious
sacrificial slaughter of Dogali unvindicated," and it continued,
demonstrating the necessity of "reestablishing the prestige of
our arms . . . [with assurances that] it would not let itself be
carried away by sudden impulses, in an undertaking that was not
prepared, thought over, and carried out at the opportune time."

I hope that the Government will not be carried away by impulses in the future; but certainly, it gave in to an impulse the
day on which it said the unmeditated words that I have read.

The national dignity was not compromised in the battle of
Dogali. The honorable Depretis repeated that phrase here, a few
days ago, and interrupted by the outcries of the Chamber, he
changed *national dignity* into *national interest*, a correction, in
many respects, unhappy. But of interests we will talk later. At

SOURCE. "Discussioni della Camera dei Deputati. Tornati del 2 guigno
1887," *Atti Parlamentari* (Sessione 1886–1887), Vol. III, pp. 3156–3161. Selected and translated for this book by Donald A. Limoli.

Dogali the national dignity was not compromised; not at Dogali where 400 valorous men made the sacrifice of their young lives to increase the esteem (the honorable Ricotti has already said it) of Italian arms before the civilized world.

Dignity or interest, it little matters. The Government has talked of an *undertaking*; which?

In the many writings that have appeared in Italy on the African question in recent times, several undertakings have been devised: from the most epic to the most grotesque. . . .

The first which comes to mind is naturally the idea of what I have heard called the great war; an expedition that is, that aims to strike the enemy in the heart, that would be directed to Aduwa, to Aksum, the sacred city, or to any other principle cities of the Tigrè or Amhara.

Given the conditions of the country, especially its economic conditions, would it be wise to undertake such an expedition? What expenses would it bring for the country? What results would come of it? Let us briefly recollect history. . . . I cite facts that ought to be remembered.

Since the European soldier first set foot on Abyssinian soil, that is from the first Portuguese expedition of 1540, over three centuries have now passed, and massacres similar to that of Dogali can be counted by the tens, even more than by the tens. I will pass over ancient expeditions: so many centuries have gone by, the implements of war and military tactics and organization have changed so much, that it does not suit our purpose to talk of them.

But the two Egyptian expeditions took place ten years ago. The first one, of 6000 men, was trained and led by a distinguished Danish officer, Colonel Ahrendropp. . . . Of 6000 men, only 300 survived a massacre that was much more extensive and serious than that of Dogali. The Government of Egypt also wanted to vindicate the fallen, and prepared a second expedition of 20,000 men with 24 pieces of field artillery, which was led by Rathif-Pasha, an eminent officer, who gave proof of his courage and ability in later battles, and by the son of the viceroy, Prince Hassan, who was educated in military art in the academy of Berlin. The Egyptians proceeded toward the interior of Abyssinia constructing three forts, one of which could hold 15,000 men.

The two armies met at Gura, where, given the number of combatants, a battle was fought that was one of the bloodiest of the century; 40,000 men remained dead on the field; of the Egyptians, who numbered, as I have said, 20,000, only 4000 were able to take refuge in one of the forts they had constructed; the other 16,0000 remained on the field where they fell, leaving the Remington rifles with which they were armed in the hands of the Abyssinians.

I recall all this so that we may have a clear idea of the forces the Abyssinians possess, and which in this battle were, according to some, 150,000 and, according to others, 200,000.

But it is said: the Egyptians are the Egyptians: let us talk of England! [The speaker then discussed the English expedition under Lord Napier against the Negus Theodore in 1868. Part of what he said about it follows.]

What forces did England have to employ to obtain the result that it did, that is to say, the death of Theodore and the immediate withdrawal of the expedition, leaving to the present Negus the very artillery of the victors? England sent 41,000 men from her Indian forces to Abyssinia, namely, 14,000 combatants and 27,000 men in suppport of these in the services; 20,000 horses, 7000 oxen, 6000 camels, 44 elephants for the artillery. Despite all this, the English commanders themselves say to you that, although worn down by force, if Theodore had, instead of throwing himself into the narrow pass of Magdala, retreated toward the south, crossed the Blue Nile, blown up, or destroyed in any way whatever the Portuguese bridge that crosses it, the campaign would have been very much longer, and would have cost England four times more, while the English army would have been decimated by hunger and sickness. . . .

Thus, to put it briefly, an expedition of this kind would require Italy to send 50,000 men (I take roughly the English figure); I will not speak of the millions [in money] because the number of these will depend on the duration of the campaign, and because it would not be surprising if Ras Alula did with the Italian army what the Russian generals did not disdain to do in 1812 with the army of Napoleon, that is to say, to retreat and await . . . [it] at that point in which its defeat would be most probable.

We come now to a second idea: to that of a *small war*, to an expedition that would be kept in the most modest proportions; . . . in brief to an expedition that proposes to occupy Keren and a part of the high plain around it.

[After reading the Chamber reports on the difficult mountainous terrain this expedition would have to operate in, and estimating that even for this expedition at least 20,000 men would be needed, the speaker went on as follows.]

Let us say more, briefly, about the *small war:* what sacrifices would it impose on you? Note, I talk to you always of sacrifices, not, of course, because I think that the policy of a great country should be only the calculation of a tradesman. I am convinced that the country will make sacrifices of money and blood when it has before it a high, precise objective. But the national dignity has not been offended and I have the right to look for a proportional relationship between the sacrifice that may by chance be asked of me and the results that it is right to expect from it.

No, to this I trust we will never come. An expedition against an enemy that has nature allied with it, in regions through which you must proceed without the aid of maps, because those you have are not only incomplete, but differ much between them in locations and place names; where water is lacking, where the climate is severe, where you can not even have information services; . . . an expedition through mountain gorges, where a detachment of men can hold back the most well-trained and more numerous companies; . . . such an expedition, either greater or smaller, either kept in small or extended to large proportions, would be more than folly, it would be a crime. The man who plunges the country into one of these wars, which, to say nothing else, are lost with injury and shame, and are won without utility and without glory, would bring down on his shoulders a heavy weight. (*Good.*)

But it is said, let us remain at Massawa. To what purpose? I hear it said: to bring civilization there. Where? To Massawa only?

The other day, the honorable Chiaves expressed the thought

with a more precise phrase: remain at Massawa, he said, if I am not mistaken, to second the desires the Abyssinians might manifest for civilization.

But honorable Chiaves, the desire of Abyssinia, and of its Kings from Oubiè to Negousiè, from Negousiè to Theodore, from Theodore to John, is only one: that of having an outlet on the sea. Nor will you ever win Abyssinia over to civilization, if you do not leave her that outlet that finally connects her to the European continent: the outlet we have gone precisely to deny her.

And then civilization! I do not want incomplete knowledge of certain facts to cause fallacious judgments.

The Abyssinian has nothing in common with the other races of Africa. He has neither the sluggish intellect nor the bloody instincts; he remembers his origins from the great Caucasian family of which he is one of the most vigorous branches. Besides, a people that for centuries has fought at the price of its own blood to prevent its soil from being touched by foreign feet, may be barbarian, but to me it appears that it holds by the principles that are, or should be, the most noble established by the modern world. Barbarian! But it was not so long ago that our king sent gifts to the Negus and received gifts and letters from him, that of the barbarian had neither the form nor the substance. . . .

Leave civilization alone, and speak of things without hypocrisy; say that all the states of Europe practice colonialism and that we must practice it too. . . . Say this, and perhaps even I might agree with you: but on the condition that you also tell me what your aims are, and that you demonstrate to me what useful results will come from the sacrifices the country imposes on itself.

What are the results of our occupation of Massawa? What do you hope from it? Commercial relations? But all the travelers there tell you how it is impossible to establish this without the friendly consent of the Negus. And even if you had this? The last word of the last European traveler who entered Abyssinia is this: "nothing to import, nothing to export." The delegates of the Milanese Committee are less severe, but they do not give you greater hopes; they say to you: you can export a bit of red cotton to adorn the robes of Ethiopian dignitaries, and boxes of matches; you can import only ivory which, alone, because of its high price, can sustain the great expense of transportation; but everyone knows that the production of ivory is very rare in Abyssinia.

[Rejecting expeditions to Abyssinia on the one hand, but holding on the other that it would be useless for Italy just to remain at Massawa, Martini concluded his speech with an appeal for the gradual withdrawal of Italian troops from Massawa.]

But I know that there is an objection that is put forward here to the abandonment of Massawa.

It is said: How? Would it not be cowardice to withdraw? I think that no one who has the soul of an Italian could council his country to commit an act of cowardice. But who asks of you the immediate withdrawal of all our soldiers? My proposal of a decrease of 500,000 lire in this article [of the budget] reflects my thought concretely, which is not of a flight, but of a gradual withdrawal of the troops. . . .

Remaining at Massawa without going either forward or backwards, is for me the worst alternative. I understand the dream of an Ethiopian empire under the protectorate of Italy; I do not understand remaining at Massawa, whether I consider it under the moral aspect or whether I consider it under the commercial and political aspect. . . .

I know that recognizing an error is a duty, but that it is sometimes a painful duty; one should instead experience a feeling of inexpressible satisfaction, when, confessing and recognizing one's own error, one can at the same time assure the increased prosperity and glory of one's own country. (*Very good! Bravo!—many deputies go to congratulate the speaker.*)

4   *Francesco Crispi: Dogali and the Necessity of Revenge and Expansion, Speech in the Chamber of Deputies, Session of June 3, 1887*

SOURCE. Francesco Crispi, *Discorsi Parlamentari*, Rome, 1915, Vol. II, pp. 839–840. Selected and translated for this book by Donald A. Limoli.

The Ministry, when formed, agreed on a common program, and on it we remain agreed.

For African affairs we have taken as our point of departure the *status quo ante;* so I do not think that on this [issue] former and present ministers can be accused of contradiction.

The honorable Martini read a few words of the speech I made on May 7, 1885. I will call back to mind others that seem to me more to the point in this discussion. I spoke as follows: "Italy is at Assab, at Massawa, and at other places in Africa, and there she must remain." I repeated this view on February 4 of this year, when as president of the commission for the bill of five million lire [for Africa], I expressed my opinion clearly.

Gentlemen! As for the past, it is useless to return to it. The Chamber, in three solemn debates, with three solemn votes, judged that past and approved it . . . (Interruptions) . . . approved it, gentlemen; and in the name-call votes that were held then, I find the honorables Toscanelli and Martini among those who voted approval. *(Very good! Bravo!)*

Now, if as my point of departure I take the matter then approved, and I cannot do otherwise because one cannot change the past, no one can or should be surprised if the honorable Depretis is found to be in agreement with me. Parliamentary houses, gentlemen, are not academies, and the votes that take place in them make laws for the future. Therefore, let us look at the present and concern ourselves with the future.

With respect to the future, the minister of war told you what the whole concept of the government is. However, I, and I think I am interpreting the thought of the other ministers sitting around me, might add a few further words, and they are these.

We do not have, nor have we ever had, the idea of conquering Abyssinia. The honorable Martini might well have desisted, in his brilliant exposition, from drawing such a dark picture of the dangers and difficulties which the undertaking might lead to. But, though on the one hand we have no desire for conquests, we do not intend on the other to remain in a state of inactivity, which might be more dangerous than action, and in any case harmful to the name of Italy and to our future. But what action will we take? Gentlemen, and with this I reply to the deputy DiRudini too, the limits in which the minister of war kept his declarations are the only ones you can ask for. *(Bravo! Good!)* *(Voices: Naturally! Very true!)*

We cannot renounce any action whatsoever. That circumstances, accidental chance, or an unforeseen occurance might council to reconstruct our position in Africa and to restore to our arms that splendor that all aim at.

What is our aim? One alone: to assert Italy's name in the regions of Africa and to show to the barbarians also that we are strong and powerful. *(Hear! Hear!)*

The barbarians understand only the thunder of cannons: very well, at the opportune moment, the cannons will thunder, and let us hope that they will thunder with the victory of our arms. *(Good!)* . . . .

For us, therefore, the issue is one of faith [in the government]; the honorable Toscanelli would not grant us this faith; and we are sorry about this *(hilarity)*, but we like to think that the Chamber will not deny it to us when the time comes.

In any event, even if it fails us, we will not be the ones who will recall our troops from Africa; it will be another ministry, of which, perhaps, the honorable Martini will be president.

5   *Francesco Crispi: Amba Alagi—His Innocence, Menelik's "Treason," and the Need to Persist, Speech in the Chamber of Deputies, Session of December 19, 1895*

In the present conditions of the Chamber, a speech is not easy; but for me, a declaration is necessary. Permit me to make it, and have the kindness to listen to me in silence, if only because of my poor health.

The Opposition wants my head: *(Oh! Oh!)* but I feel myself still strong enough to keep it on my body.

What is my crime? It is always repeated, but never proved,

SOURCE. Francesco Crispi, *Discorsi Parlamentari*, Rome, 1915, Vol. III, pp. 871–873. Selected and translated for this book by Donald A. Limoli.

that a policy of megalomania results every time I head the Government. All that has happened in Africa is owing to me; hence, mine is the fault and mine is the responsibility; hence it falls to me to pay for the consequences of the doleful battle of Amba Alagi.

Permit me to say to you that you are not right. The African undertaking is not mine, and if it had fallen to me to execute it, I would not have done what was done.

The African undertaking began without a plan. We went to Assab, buying that territory from one of the petty sultans to whom it belonged. We went then to Massawa, but without having any objective. I lamented and lamented about this, not because I was against Italy having a position in Africa, as our great predecessors have desired, but because if it had fallen to me to advise my government to go to Africa, I would have first advised it to conduct itself differently at the Congress of Berlin, where with respect to possessions in Africa and possessions in the Adriatic all eyes were closed. Only once was I able to express my thoughts, and this was in 1882, when England asked for Italy's participation in the expedition against the Egyptian insurrection. It was refused. My prayers were in vain, and England's hopes were deluded.

In 1885, censuring the Massawa expedition, I concluded my speech thusly: "We are at Assab; we are at Massawa; there the national flag has been raised. There we must remain, and better the conditions of our occupation."

I have said that I took no part in what previously happened in Africa. And, to show what part I had in this, and that I have desired and demanded an African empire, you should have brought here some document that I wrote, some action that I took.

VOICES ON THE LEFT. All your actions! . . .

IMBRIANI. Just the summary will do.

CRISPI. General Baratieri, my companion and friend, is not Governor owing to me. *(Ooh!) (Ooh!)*

My friends, listen to me and don't make noise; be patient and forebearing.

He was appointed Governor February 24, 1892. Taking over the government, I found him in possession of his office; I did not change the instructions that my predecessors had given him; I confirmed them.

The revolt of Batha-Agos and the rebellion of Mangasha occurred, which have been so well expounded to you by the deputy Martini.

All this [that is, all that has happened] was not due to us; there was no preconceived plan; the victories were not mine, and consequently I should not be blamed for the defeats.

IMBRIANI. Uccialli! Uccialli! *(Outcries on the Extreme Left)*.

CRISPI. Let us go back, since Uccialli has been brought up. *(Comments)*.

I have talked about it before. The Treaty of Uccialli is one of those accomplishments that do honor to Italian policy.

Then, King John was on the throne of Abyssinia; Menelik asked for our aid in his struggle against the Emperor, and he got it. The Treaty of Uccialli was concluded, and from that treaty we got the Ethiopian high plain.

Who has failed to be faithful to that treaty? Not us. Menelik failed to honor it, inspired by influences hostile to us; we recalled him to his duty.

The Treaty of Uccialli is one of the most civilized acts concluded in recent times.

Our aim was, as I have said on another occasion, to compel Menelik to give up the slave trade, so much so, that we even got him to go so far as to have Ethiopia represented at the Conference of Brussels for the abolition of the slave trade. This laid a restraint on Menelik, a restraint which he did not like, and this was also one of the reasons why he failed to abide by his obligations.

But let us return to the resumé of events that I was briefly making to the Chamber.

The insurrection of Batha-Agos, the events that followed, the victories of our arms, were neither planned nor foreseen; the latter resulted from the efforts and valor of our forces commanded by General Baratieri.

General Baratieri came to Rome. He was asked what the needs of maintaining the defense were. No limitations were imposed on him because he alone could judge the state of things in Ethiopia, and he alone could know what was needed; he alone was to ask what was necessary. *(Comments and interruptions on the Extreme Left).*

A VOICE. How generous you are!

CRISPI. Listen, gentlemen (and I direct myself to the hecklers): the Convention, whose history you can read better than I, did not, in its famous decree of May 12, 1793, condemn Carnot, who organized the victory, but the generals who did not ask all that was necessary to win.

This is history, gentlemen. *(Outcries and interruptions of various kinds).*

If I had told and ordered General Baratieri to wage a war of conquest at all costs, to go deep into the Tigrè, to go to Shoa, I would have been mad, and I am not mad. Then you would have been right; you would have said to me: you had this utopian dream of an African empire, and having conceived of it, you did not see the means or make the preparations necessary to achieve the end. But I never had this in mind. And when Baratieri was in Italy, and I talked with him, there was no manifestation whatever of this idea, of this view.

VOICES ON THE EXTREME LEFT. He is not here to reply to this.

PRESIDENT. But keep silent!

CRISPI. When he returned to Eritrea, nothing of what he asked was denied him, and the defeat of Amba Alagi, unfortunate as it is, is one of those events that the government cannot be blamed for, because the government learned of it only when everyone else learned of it. *(Comments of various kinds—Interruptions—outcries on the Extreme Left).*

Put the premise first and then draw the conclusion from it.

Now the premise is this: I have never had ideas of expansion, and I have never imposed them on General Baratieri. *(Interruptions).*

Do not make me say what I have not said!

IMBRIANI. But you did speak about the Tigrè!

CRISPI. I spoke of the Tigrè after Baratieri's victories. I did not think of it before that. Its occupation is a consequence of our defense against the enemy; after the battles against the enemy, in which fortune favored us, we occupied those territories in which the victories were won.

Whose job is it to decide what military measures are necessary to hold those territories? The Governor's . . . *(Interruptions—Comments)*.

The Chamber, under my Government, has concerned itself with the African question six times, and it has always supported me.

For the moment, I ask only this: give us the means to reconstruct our position; with, on our part, the promise of no policy of expansion *(Very well!)* but only one of necessary and powerful defense, so that the flag of Italy may always fly in those distant lands. *(Very good!)*

Neither cowardice nor imprudence.

Cowardice dishonors governments, and ruins states; by imprudence they are lost.

Neither imprudence, nor cowardice; the well-being of Italy is what we want. *(Lively approval—Agitation—Comments)*.

PART FOUR

Britain's Nilotic Imperative

MOTIVES

1 Ronald Robinson and John Gallagher: New Frontiers of Insecurity

Whether the British occupation of Egypt precipitated the partition of Africa is still the subject of debate. That the occupation resulted in the British acquisition of West African territories is vigorously disputed. On the other side of the continent, however, the implications of the British presence in Egypt are clearer and more generally accepted by modern scholars. Ronald Robinson and John Gallagher have brilliantly delineated the problems for British diplomacy in East Africa and the Nile Valley to defend the Nile waters, and thereby the very existence of Egypt itself, after Lord Salisbury's decision to retain the British presence at Cairo.

If the strategic reasons for staying in Cairo were strong, the internal Egyptian reasons against withdrawal were overwhelming. By 1889 Baring had convinced the Prime Minister that there could be no stability or security in Cairo without occupation. As the British Agent saw it, the internal crisis which had come to a head in 1882, was still unsolved. Revolution still simmered beneath the surface tranquillity of the occupation. The chances of setting up a reliable Egyptian *régime* and so returning to a supremacy wielded from outside, were smaller than ever. . . .

SOURCE. Ronald Robinson and John Gallagher, with Alice Denny, *Africa and the Victorians: The Official Mind of Imperialism*, London: Macmillan & Co., 1961, pp. 274 and 281–289. Reprinted by permission of St. Martin's Press, Inc. and The Macmillan Co. of Canada, Ltd. Copyright Ronald Robinson, John Gallagher, and Alice Denny, 1961.

By June 1889, Salisbury had come round entirely to Baring's point of view. The British Agent had stated his case in these words:

". . . the real reason why the evacuation policy is well nigh impossible of execution . . . is based on the utter incapacity of the ruling classes in this country. . . . [They] are almost exclusively foreigners. . . . Now, all this class are detested by the people, and they are more disliked now than they ever were before . . . if he [Riaz Pasha] were left to himself he would go far to produce a revolution in six months. . . . Really, the more I look at it, the more does the evacuation policy appear to me to be impossible under any conditions."

Baring warned the Prime Minister that even if the French agreed to give the British a right of re-entry, a withdrawal now would lead to anarchy and disaster for British influence. Moreover he could see another and even worse danger in evacuation. Reopening the entire Egyptian question would shatter any chance of reconciliation between Britain and France and might well lead to war. . . .

Having reached this conclusion by the middle of 1889, Salisbury soon drew others, more momentous still for the future of Africa. Within the next six months he decided at Baring's prompting that if they were to hold Egypt, they could not afford to let any other European Power obtain a hold over any part of the Nile Valley. In so doing, he took what was perhaps the critical decision of the Partition. Henceforward almost everything in Africa north of the Zambesi River was to hinge upon it.

The idea that the security of Egypt depended upon the defence of the Upper Nile was as old as the pyramids; and the government had been reminded of it often enough. Sir Samuel Baker, the well-known explorer and once the Khedive's governor in the Sudan, wrote about it in 1884 and 1888. He pointed at the danger that a hostile Power could readily dam the Upper Nile, starve Egypt of water, and so destroy the country .This had been one of the objections of the forward party to abandoning the Sudan, and for the same reason Riaz Pasha had pressed upon Baring the need to win it back.

". . . The Nile is the life of Egypt. . . . The Nile means the Soudan. . . . If [any European Power] . . . took possession of the banks of the Nile it would be all over with Egypt. . . . The Government of His Highness the Khedive will never willingly consent, not without compulsion, to such an attack on its existence."

But the British Agent was not at this time persuaded. He had strongly advised Salisbury against reconquering the Sudan for the time being; and the Prime Minister had agreed.

"If an unlucky combination of circumstances had not reduced the finances of Egypt very low," he told the Queen, "it might be possible to take this opportunity of restoring the power of the Khedive over the valley of the Nile. But Egypt could not afford an expedition; and the House of Commons would certainly decline to bear the cost."

To their minds, an advance was out of the question until Egypt could afford it; but already they foresaw that one day circumstance might force them to secure Egypt by regaining the Sudan.

So far they had had good reason to be complacent about the Upper Nile and its headwaters in Uganda and Ethiopia. As long as no other Power was in sight of seizing these regions, they could have little bearing on Egyptian security. The Dervishes who held the Sudan could not cut off the flow of the river on which the life and stability of Egypt depended, for they were no engineers. No European Power had yet reached the point of sending menacing expeditions towards the Upper Nile, and it was still possible that Britain would leave Egypt soon.

But things were very different by 1889. The British were certainly intending to stay. Cairo was becoming more and more the pivot of their Mediterranean strategy. A foreign Power astride the Upper Nile would be in a position either to levy blackmail or to lever them out of Egypt. It was the Italians, advancing from the Red Sea towards the eastern Sudan, who presented the first threat of this kind.

In May 1889, the Italian minister, Crispi made the Treaty of Uccialli with Ethiopia—an agreement designed to give Rome great influence in the country of the Blue Nile. He also laid claim to Kassala which commanded the Atbara tributary of the Nile. With

this town as a base the Italians might edge their way towards
Khartoum at the confluence of the White and the Blue Nile.
Crispi's vaulting African ambition and the challenge at Kassala
goaded Salisbury to make up his mind about the Nile Valley as
a whole.

How long he had meditated it before putting on paper the
policy of closing the Valley of the Nile, who can say? But by
August 1889, the Prime Minister was anxious enough about
Kassala to ask Baring what he thought about it. The reply must
have been emphatically against letting foreign Powers into the
Nile Valley, because on 15 November, "[the Prime Minister]
concurred fully as to the inviolability of the valley of the Nile
even in its affluents. . . ." The doctrine was already fully formed.

The reasons for adopting this policy are plainly disclosed in
Baring's correspondence with Salisbury. If the Italians took
Kassala, he wrote,

". . . They would soon strike the valley of the Nile . . . at
Khartoum . . . the establishment of a civilised Power in the Nile
Valley would be a calamity to Egypt."

When Baker and others had put forward similar views in 1888,
Baring went on, he had thought them "unnecessarily alarmist":

"The savage tribes who now rule in the Sudan do not possess
the resources or the engineering skill to do any real harm to
Egypt."

But the Italian threat had now converted Baring,

". . . The case would be very different were a civilised European
Power established in the Nile Valley. . . . They could so reduce
the water-supply as to ruin the country. . . . Whatever Power
holds the Upper Nile Valley must, by the mere force of its
geographical situation, dominate Egypt."

There was already enough discontent inside the country without
inviting Foreign Powers to manufacture subversion by drought.
But Baring the administrator still guided Baring the strategist. He
did not want Salisbury to stop the Italian advance at the expense
of a premature reconquest of the Sudan, for this would dis-
organise the Egyptian finances which the British Agent had been

at such pains to set in order. He urged the Prime Minister to keep 'a strictly defensive policy' for the time being; and to keep the Italians out of the Nile Valley by diplomacy.

Just as the Prime Minister in June had concurred in Baring's counsel to stay in Egypt, so after November he took up Baring's policy of defending the occupation of the Upper Nile.

"In respect to Kassala,"Salisbury wrote in March 1890, "it gives the Power occupying it command over one of the main affluents of the Nile, and therefore a power of diverting a portion of the supply which is vital to Egypt." And he agreed to". . . such measures as may be necessary for the purpose of protecting your Nile Valley against the dominion of any outside Power."

It was, he declared, ". . . essential to the safety of Egypt" that this should be done. The policy was comprehensive. At first it applied specifically to the Italians and Kassala. But Salisbury and Baring had plainly adopted it from November 1889 as a general principle; and the principle held good for all Powers and for all parts of the Nile Valley, indeed as far south as the headwaters of the river in the Uganda country.

Thus the safety of the Nile had now become a supreme consideration, and the policy was quickly put into effect. On 7 March, 1890, Salisbury warned the Italians off the Nile, and later Baring was sent to Rome to try and set safe limits to their advance. The new strategy also forced Salisbury and Baring to reconsider the defensive policy of the past six years in the Sudan. Baring gave three reasons for doing so; in the first place, Egypt's finances had now turned the corner; secondly, "the dervish movement has been going rapidly downhill"; and thirdly, diplomacy could not be relied upon for ever to ward off other Powers. In the end, occupation alone could make certain of the Upper Nile. The Prime Minister agreed that sooner or later the Sudan would have to be reconquered. But like Baring, he preferred to wait— so long as diplomacy would suffice to keep foreign rivals away. Salisbury as usual was against giving the imperialists at the Horse Guards a free hand. More important, he took it for granted that an "imperialist" advance would jar upon the prejudices of the electorate at Home.

"They were so deeply impressed with the disasters of six years ago," Salisbury explained, "and the apparently inexorable necessity which had driven them into situations where those disasters were inevitable, that they shrink instinctively from any proposal to advance into the Egyptian desert. I do not say that this is a sufficient argument to prevent such an advance, if there is a clear balance of undoubted advantage in its favour; but in the absence of any such evidence, it must be accepted as a strong presumption. As far as I can see matters, I should say that until you have money enough to justify you in advancing to Berber, you had better remain quiet."

For the time being, diplomacy must remain the chief defence of the security of Egypt in the Nile Basin. If he was not yet ready to re-occupy the region, he made it plain that he would oppose its occupation by any other Power. Having already warned off the Italians, he quickly gave the French and the German ambassadors a similar message. The new strategy was now operating.

For all the worldly wisdom which prompted this strategy, it flowed less from hard-headed reckoning than from a change of heart. Behind it lay a sea-change in the Victorian spirit and the official mind. A new age was struggling to be born. To the old men who sat at the head of affairs—as old men usually do—it seemed that imperialism was entering on its greatest epoch. But European expansion was already at odds with the new forces of colonial nationalism which it had goaded into life. The dynasts were beginning to lose their way in history. The shadows were falling over the times and themes they knew best. The end of the European age was in sight. Beset with problems for which their historiography offered no solutions, the old men in the chancelleries came more and more to combat their manifestations rather than to grapple with their causes.

Salisbury had said that Ireland must be held, by persuasion if possible, by Indian methods if need be. Persuasion had failed. Baring had said that collaboration would not work freely in Egypt. Collaboration had been too risky to try. Both in Ireland and on the Nile, the Unionists had turned to Indian solutions. Before long, Milner was to apply them to the Transvaal. What was more, the gradual merging of the Unionist and the Anglo-

Indian creeds was helped by new trends of religious and political belief. Changing ideas about the role of the state, the right relationship between races, the likelihood of a new age of violence —all these contributed profoundly to the emergence of the new spirit.

In the event ministers began to fear that Providence and the laws of progress were no longer working on their side. Shocked by nationalist intransigence and Oriental fanaticisms, jostled by new rivals in Africa and new enemies in the Mediterranean, they were losing their nerve. Self-confidence had carried the English to the ends of the earth. Drop by drop it was dribbling out of them.

For the Victorians at mid-century the excellence of moral suasion and free partnership had seeemed self-evident. But now this belief was being shrunk by fears of subversion and disloyalty. Too often the old aspirations to liberate and improve the world had been ungratefully accepted or surlily refused. Orientals and Africans had been shown the way. They had not followed it. Boers and Irishmen had been given equal rights with Englishmen. They had misused them. Step by step, the easy British optimism modulated into an injured resentment and a harsher outlook. Since the Irish bit the hand that fed them, they should undergo twenty years of resolute government. Since the Indians could not be assimilated, the Ilbert Bill and the Indian Councils Bill were Radical treachery to the *Raj*. Since the King of Burma was a bad risk, he should be deposed. Having failed to find willing partners by policy, the Victorians condemned them to be involuntary subjects.

Hence they were driven into abandoning creative policy and replacing it by cold administration and control. Prestige became all important to them. So too did insurance. Policy grew more and more committed to the warding off of hypothetical dangers by the advancing of frontiers. When Salisbury put his Nile strategy into practice, the defensive psychology which kept watch over northern Indian had been transplanted into Africa. The frontiers of fear were on the move.

And so the Prime Minister at the end of the Eighteen-eighties had decided upon an enlarged Egyptian policy. Not that there was any popular demand for it. It had emerged from the sub-

jective calculations of national interest made by the small group
which still decided such matters. To them supremacy in Egypt
was becoming crucial, as the balance in Europe and the Mediterranean shifted. In Salisbury's mind, the pivot of the British position in the Mediterranean, and therefore in the world, was moving
from Constantinople and the Straits to Cairo and the Canal, from
south-eastern Europe and Asia Minor to the Nile Valley and
north-east Africa. The Nile Valley strategy was something of an
anomaly among the traditional concepts of the national interest
handed down from Pitt, Canning, and Palmerston to Salisbury.
He became the first Victorian statesman to discover a vital interest
in the middle of tropical Africa, but if he was the first, he was
not the last, to do so. The decisions of the winter of 1889 to 1890
set the priorities of British policy for the remainder of the Partition, and the Nile Valley headed the list. Salisbury stamped his
new design upon tropical Africa, but it was a new design for an
old purpose. Hitherto Britain had given way to her rivals in both
east and west Africa, in order to protect Egypt. Henceforward,
she could yield only on the west, for the Nile Valley and its
approaches from the east coast were now considered vital to
Egypt. The Mediterranean and Indian interest, like a driving
wheel in some vast machine, was now engaging the lesser wheels
of eastern-central Africa and connecting them one by one to
its own workings. At the turn of Salisbury's strategy, these once
remote and petty interests in the Sudan, Uganda and the northern
hinterlands of Zanzibar were changing into safeguards of Britain's
world power.

THE SCRAMBLE

2 Robert O. Collins: Origins of the Nile Struggle: The Mackinnon Treaty and the Anglo-German Agreement of 1890

Robert O. Collins, Associate Professor of African History in the University of California, Santa Barbara, has long been a student of the Upper Nile. He regards 1890 as the critical year in the contest among the European powers for control of equatorial Africa during which Lord Salisbury successfully kept the Germans from the Upper Nile by utilizing the Mackinnon Treaty to conclude the Anglo-German (Heligoland) Agreement. The Mackinnon Treaty, however, not only gave King Leopold access to the Nile, but also set the pattern by which Salisbury's successors would try to keep out the French.

In 1884–85 Britain had encouraged German colonial adventures and at Zanzibar had even sought to smooth the way for German Empire in those parts of East Africa where no vital British interests were at stake. After the decision to remain in Egypt, Britain did have a large strategic stake in the Upper Nile, and Salisbury could calculate that Bismarck's prudence would not permit him to jeopardize his European alignments for a wilderness in central Africa or the schemes of a "Freebooter" like Peters.

SOURCE. Robert O. Collins, "Origins of the Nile Struggle: Anglo-German Negotiations and the Mackinnon Agreement of 1800," in Roger Louis and Prosser Gifford and Alison Smith, eds., *Britain and Germany in Africa*, New Haven: Yale University Press, 1967, pp. 132–136, 139–142, 144–145, and 150–151. Reprinted by permission of Yale University Press. Copyright 1967 by Yale. University.

Salisbury thus counted on Bismarck's caution. In fact the Prime Minister required it, for in 1889-90 he did not possess the parliamentary strength to ignore the ever-growing influence of the British colonial groups, precisely those people who became most excited about the activities of German nationals in Africa. Throughout the autumn of 1889 and the spring of 1890 the Conservatives were losing ground, and in the Commons they were increasingly dependent upon the Liberal Unionists to maintain their majority. The Irish question had obstructed the march of Tory democracy, and the electorate's frustration with the Conservatives was reflected by the party's dismal showing at the by-elections. On June 17, 1890, the government majority actually plunged to a perilous four votes. Even if Salisbury did not approve of Mackinnon, Rhodes, and their wealthy followers, and was constantly annoyed by the importunities of the missionary groups, he would have to be prepared to keep them all satisfied in Africa in order to keep their powerful support at home.

Moreover, in spite of Bismarck's assurances of cooperation and Salisbury's skepticism about any German design to grab the Nile, both British and German nationals were exacerbating potential difficulties in East Africa to the point where a settlement was desirable before the repercussions of their quarrels damaged Anglo-German relations in general. Zanzibar, the Tana-Juba hinterland behind Witu, the regions west of Lake Victoria and Lake Nyasa were all, more or less, disputed ground which both Bismarck and Salisbury would have liked to have settled—each on his own terms. Throughout the summer and autumn of 1889 the British and German positions on these questions shuttled between London and Berlin. Salisbury's attitude was flexibility on the coast, firmness in the interior. In November 1889 he recognized the German protectorate at Witu, but he specifically reserved the claims of British subjects in the Tana-Juba hinterland beyond. Earlier in the year he had insisted on the rights which the Scottish missionaries had acquired in the interior west of Lake Nyasa. But what Bismarck desired was a settlement of these vexatious questions, and after further representations at Whitehall, the Chancellor was able to induce Salisbury to resolve some of the disputed ground by arbitration, including those very claims he had reserved the previous month in the Tana-Juba hinterland. To abandon British rights in the hinterland behind Witu to the perils of arbitration appears, at first, surprising, particularly when Salisbury refused to arbitrate the other interior questions, Nyasaland and the region west of Lake Victoria. But Salisbury had to include some question of substance in the arbitral schedule or risk alienating Bismarck, whose restraint in these East African squabbles Salisbury would want to preserve. As it was, the arbitral topics were not "a bill of fare that will be tempting to the Germans," and without the Tana-Juba hinterland, or a question of similar importance, Bismarck could hardly have taken seriously Salisbury's consent to arbitrate. If Salisbury had restricted arbitration to petty questions only, Bismarck might easily have been driven to loosen his rein on German nationals in East Africa, thereby precipitating the retaliation of British imperialists, who would have certainly demanded vigorous anti-German action from Salisbury in return for their domestic political support. Of all the interior disputes, The Tana-Juba hinterland was the least risk to arbitration. True, the hinterland pointed directly at the Upper Nile, but Bismarck had by thought, word, and deed repeatedly assured the British that the German government had no designs on the Nilotic regions.

Then suddenly in March 1890, Bismarck ceased to guide the destinies of Germany. The dismissal of Bismarck and the emergence of the Emperor Wilhelm II at the head of German affairs had a profound impact on Salisbury. Wilhelm II had sympathized with Peters' plan for German expansion [in equatorial Africa], but Bismarck had been able to keep the Emperor's "Equatorial enthusiasm" in check. Now Bismarck was gone, and German policy in Africa, as elsewhere, increasingly reflected the Kaiser's erratic and frequently imprudent views. . . .

On April 18, 1890, Salisbury had returned to London after a bout of influenza. Many months before he had decided that the European powers must be kept out of the Nile valley for the security of Egypt and the British position in that country. Before his illness in March, he had even warned the Italians to remain in Ethiopia and not to venture into the Nile valley. Now at the beginning of May, as his suspicions of German intentions deepened, he sought to apply the same policy to Germany. Hitherto he had hoped to resolve Britain's African differences with the

German Empire by arbitration, and Sir Percy Anderson was at that time preparing to go to Berlin to determine the agenda of arbitration with representatives of the German Foreign Office. . . . Thus during the first weeks of May, Salisbury's uneasiness over German activities in East Africa fused with his principle of the inviolability of the Nile valley. Only a comprehensive settlement with Germany, and not just arbitration, could have resolved the East African disputes with Germany, preventing thereby any German threat, real or imaginary, to the Upper Nile and ending the frictions between British and German nationals in the hinterland and on the coast. . . .

No sooner had Sir Percy Anderson reached Berlin to begin his discussions over Anglo-German colonial disputes with Dr. Krauel than Sir William Mackinnon and his supporters were on the move. Since 1889 they had warned of German designs on the Upper Nile, but Salisbury had refused to listen, dismissing Mackinnon as a troublemaker who had "no energy for anything except quarrelling with Germans." Even as late as April 1890, Salisbury had not changed his opinion of Mackinnon, commenting that he and his powerful friends were the obstacle to any agreement with the Germans over African questions, for "any terms we might get for him from the Germans by negotiation he would denounce as a base truckling to the Emperor." But Mackinnon was not to be put off by Salisbury's snubs. In April 1890, Stanley returned to Europe from Africa, stopping at Cannes, where he met Mackinnon and delivered to him there six treaties supposedly signing over to the Imperial British East Africa Company large tracts of territory west of Lake Victoria. From Cannes, Stanley and Mackinnon traveled to Paris and Brussels where, in long conversations with King Leopold, Mackinnon and the King agreed to discuss the division of the spheres of influence of the Company and the Congo Free State. Now the problem, from Mackinnon's point of view, was to persuade Salisbury to declare a protectorate over the territory west of Lake Victoria on the strength of Stanley's treaties. Thus when Mackinnon arrived back in England, the agitation on the part of his company and the imperialist group, including Cecil Rhodes who supported him, shifted emphasis from the Nile to the triangle of territory between Lake Victoria, Lake Tanganyika, and Lake

Albert Edward. To Mackinnon and his friends, this region was of vital importance, not so much because of its relation to the Nile waters, which began its long journey to the Mediterranean in the highlands west of Lake Victoria, but rather because its position was essential to the completion of the Cape to Cairo route. In the beautiful upland hills and valleys between Lake Victoria and the central African rift valley, the question of the Upper Nile and the Cape to Cairo route were fused, and Mackinnon and his ally, King Leopold, joined forces with Rhodes and Harry Johnston to preserve the All-Red Route as well as the Nile waters from German control.

At the beginning of May 1890, Salisbury's diplomacy thus had two principal objectives: one, to save the Upper Nile for the security of Egypt, and, two, to keep the Tanganyika corridor for Mackinnon, Rhodes, and their powerful friends, not because Salisbury personally regarded the Tanganyika strip as strategically vital or of commercial interest, but rather because these politically influential personalities did. On May 6, Salisbury, Stanley, and Mackinnon dined together at Windsor, where the Prime Minister undoubtedly learned of Mackinnon's talks with Leopold as well as the demands of the British East African Company to save the Tanganyika corridor. And within a few days, this seemed impossible to do.

From the first, Sir Percy Anderson appears to have been skeptical about getting the Germans to acknowledge British access to Lake Tanganyika, and during his negotiations with Krauel, he became convinced that they would not do so. On May 9, three days after the dinner at Windsor Castle, he reported from Berlin that the Germans would certainly not concede the region west of Lake Victoria. Salisbury acted decisively. He decided to negotiate directly with Hatzfeldt, the German ambassador in London, leaving Anderson in Berlin to deal with the other petty items. Certainly Salisbury had decided to offer the Germans a "comprehensive bargain" in central Africa. He was none too soon. By the second week in May, British public opinion and pressure from the British press had been whipped up by rumors and reports of the activities of Peters and Emin Pasha in Africa, and by the speeches of Stanley and the influence of Rhodes and Mackinnon in London. On May 13 Hatzfeldt told Salisbury that the hinterland question must be solved soon before it developed into an "insoluble situation." The question of control of the great lakes and the Upper Nile could no longer be delayed. By the second week in May, the "controversy had suddenly become critical— critical for the future of Anglo-German relations and perhaps even for the survival of Salisbury's Cabinent." Happily for the Prime Minister, he had a ready solution—Heligoland.

On May 13 in a conversation with Hatzfeldt, Salisbury presented his comprehensive program to resolve Anglo-German rivalry in the hinterland of East Africa. In return for the island of Heligoland in the North Sea, and full possession of the east African coastal strip which the Sultan of Zanzibar had leased to the Germans, Britain would receive Witu and its hinterland, the Upper Nile, and a division of territory at each end of Lake Tanganyika so that Britain would have access to the lake, preserving the All-Red Route. This was the maximum gain Salisbury could hope to obtain and far beyond anything the Germans had in mind to give. Salisbury must have realized his proposal would be rejected. It was. On the seventeenth, Marschall wrote to Hatzfeldt absolutely refusing any British "wedge" to Lake Tanganyika, which he vigorously exclaimed to Anderson would "close up behind the German sphere." On May 21, Salisbury again met with Hatzfeldt and modified his demands. He withdrew his claim to the region north of Lake Tanganyika, apparently abandoning the Cape to Cairo route and its supporters. In reality he had found another way to keep the All-Red Route British without trying to acquire it from the Germans. Salisbury had personally never been enthusiastic about the Cape to Cairo route, but he was realistic enough to understand the powerful political forces supporting that imperial dream. The Nile was essential to Salisbury's overall imperial strategy—the Cape to Cairo route was not. When he learned that the Germans would not concede both for Heligoland, the Cape to Cairo route had to go. What made its abandonment possible was that Mackinnon had already made its retention feasible. On May 14, the day after Salisbury's first offer of Heligoland to Hatzfeldt, Mackinnon wrote to the Prime Minister that "the King of the Belgians . . . most generously expresses his desire to help us in every way to facilitate our access to [Lake] Tanganyika." Mackinnon may have indicated that Leopold was ready to help when he dined with Salisbury at Windsor on May 6, but on May 20 Salisbury saw the draft of an agreement between Mackinnon and Leopold in which the King had actually conceded Mackinnon a corridor connecting Lake Tanganyika and Lake Albert Edward *behind* the territory Salisbury was about to abandon to the Germans. On the following day, while discussing the hinterland question with Hatzfeldt, Salisbury wrote to King Leopold "that no objections will be raised on the part of the Foreign Office to the engagements which have been entered into by Your Majesty, as Head of the Congo State, and Sir William Mackinnon's Company. . . ."

Once Salisbury had consented to the ratification of the Mackinnon Treaty with its Tanganyika corridor, Mackinnon and his clan could no longer insist upon the inclusion of the Tanganyika territory in the British sphere of the proposed Anglo-German agreement. They could hardly object to an agreement with the Germans which protected the Upper Nile for Britain when they had already received the Tanganyika corridor from the Congo State. But just as Salisbury was freeing himself from the Tanganyikan shackles with which Mackinnon and the colonialist group sought to bind him, the Germans returned with conditions which, now that Salisbury did not have to retain the Tanganyika territory, were quite acceptable. The Reinsurance Treaty with Russia had lapsed and the Wilhelmstrasse had by the end of May decided not to renew the line to St. Petersburg. It would have been much too hazardous to break the line to London as well. Marschall was thus prepared to split the difference, conceding the Stevenson Road in return for the Tanganyika territory west of Lake Victoria. To Salisbury the Stevenson Road was vital, and with the Mackinnon Treaty a reality, he could now cavalierly abandon the territory claimed by Stanley's treaties. On June 5, 1890, Salisbury settled the principal terms of the Anglo-German Agreement with Hatzfeldt. . . .

On July 1, the final draft was signed. In return for Heligoland, for full sovereignty over the coast of German East Africa, and for a boundary between the British and the German spheres west of Lake Victoria fixed at 1 degree south latitude, Britain received Witu and the Tana-Juba protectorate with its hinterland as well as the Stevenson Road connecting Lake Nyasa with Lake Tanganyika. Salisbury had not only removed the many potential danger spots in East Africa where the activities of his more exuberant nationals would clash with the Germans, but he had also sealed the Upper Nile from possible German encroachment. He wrote triumphantly to the Queen that "the whole country outside the confines of Abyssinia and Gallaland will be under British influence up to Khan, so far as any European competitor is concerned"; but more accurately he wrote to Malet in Berlin that:

"The effect of this arrangement will be that, except so far as the Congo State is concerned, there will be no European competitor to British influence between the first degree of south latitude and the borders of Egypt, along the whole of the country which lies to the south and west of the Italian Protectorate in Abyssinia and Gallaland."

Of course, Salisbury did not get the Tanganyika corridor for the Cape to Cairo route, to which he whimsically referred as a "very curious idea which has become prevalent in this country." But then he could afford to be nonchalant, for in effect Mackinnon had gotten it for him, Salisbury merely adding sufficient escape clauses in the event of French or German objections. Perhaps he even thought that the Anglo-German agreement would effectively cancel the Mackinnon Treaty by recognizing a British sphere to the "western watershed of the basin of the Upper Nile." In any case he could console himself in the knowledge that a chartered company could not bargain away sovereign rights, but then in 1890 Salisbury clearly did not envisage a Congolese advance to the Nile. In fact, he appears at this time never to have regarded the Congo State as a serious competitor for the Nile valley.

3   Robert O. Collins: Leopold II and the Upper Nile

Although King Leopold's acquisition of the Congo seems to have been motivated principally by economic factors, his search for the Nile sprang chiefly from pride, prestige, and the political grandeur of being a twentieth century Pharaoh astride the source of that great river. Robert O. Collins attempts to show that Leopold's Nile quest was a personal obsession upon which the King squandered millions of francs for dubious economic advantages.

As the constitutional monarch of tiny, divided Belgium, Leopold II had never possessed a large national population enthusiastic for imperial adventures; nor could he command the military and economic resources of Britain or France. But as sovereign of the Congo Free State, he exercised unchallenged rule over a large and wealthy African territory unhindered by popular demands or constitutional limitations. In Europe Leopold was a restricted monarch; in Africa he was his own master. As the sovereign of the Congo, he need answer to no one except perhaps for some ill-defined obligations to the signatories of the Berlin Act, who had created the Congo. As its enlightened despot he could marshal and maneuver the Congo's resources to carry out his schemes untrammeled by interference from within, alert only to intervention from without. This enormous advantage helped offset the superior power of his rivals, and when it was combined with the astute and venturesome diplomacy he practiced with such flair, the King was indeed a dangerous opponent. Leopold thought big in Africa. His designs were always breathtaking in scope if frequently unrealistic in practice, but the sheer

SOURCE: Robert O. Collins, *King Leopold, England, and the Upper Nile, 1899–1909*, New Haven: Yale University Press, 1968, pp. 28–31, 272–73. Reprinted by permission of the Yale University Press. Copyright 1968 by Yale University.

magnitude of his schemes made their consequences all the more alarming. Thus, Leopold obstinately pursued his goal of control of the Upper Nile, and, caught in the web of his own megalomaniac ambition, he lavishly expended the resources of the Congo on the Nile quest. From the founding of the Congo State in 1885 until his death in 1909, he never abandoned his search for the elusive fountains of the Nile.

Leopold fought for control of the Upper Nile not with vast armies and navies but with legal claims and treaty rights put forward with persuasive skill accentuated by daring expeditions in Africa and bold strokes of diplomacy in Europe. In the end such means to acquire control of the Nile proved more formidable to harried British statesmen than Italian diplomacy in Ethiopia, German designs in Equatoria, or French defiance at Fashoda. Control of the Nile waters, which Kitchener had won at Karari and Salisbury preserved at Fashoda, was nearly abandoned to Leopold's lawyers in Brussels. Leopold, not Marchand, was Britain's most tenacious rival for possession of the Nile and the land beyond.

Despite the intricate and tortuous nature of Leopold's diplomacy on the Upper Nile, its object remained incredibly constant. From the early days of the Emin Pasha Relief Expedition until his death twenty years later, Leopold wanted to be on the Nile. Toward that end he expended vast sums of money and marshalled armies in Africa. To achieve that goal he employed all his skill as a diplomatist in Europe. To win the Nile he was prepared to trade his permanent claims in the Bahr al-Ghazal for his temporary occupation of the Nile shore. True, his insatiable greed for African minerals was aroused by the mines at Hufrat an-Nahas, but a few shallow holes in the western Bahr al-Ghazal never attracted Leopold as did the Nile waters. Like Cromer, Leopold wanted the Nile, and for it he would readily abandon the land beyond the river.

If Leopold's purpose was clear and consistent, his motives were less so. The King was a complex and subtle man. He sought constant ends by inconstant means. His intrigues obscured his motives; his maneuvers confused his priorities. The single obsession of today became the ephemera of tomorrow. Yet behind that façade lurked the King's overwhelming passion for his own glorification

fed by his enormous economic acquisitiveness and his Olympian
cartographic conceptions. Dreams, yes, but dreams that ignited
his energies and fused his determination to transform what might
have been idle speculations into the realities of empire. Without
his creative imagination and his inspiring visions, the economic
acquisitiveness and the megalomania for territory that characterized the King in Africa would have remained unfulfilled.
Leopold was a modern Pharaoh seeking a suitable gateway to
adorn the edifice he had constructed in the Congo. The Nile
represented the triumph of his vision. It was his *panache*. He had,
of course, abandoned his territorial aspirations in the Bahr
al-Ghazal to retain the Nile. He hoped to make a profit with
what was left—the Congo-Nile railway—but the line could never
refund the millions of francs spent in the Nile quest or even pay
for itself. Thus, he had forsaken the territorial imperative in
return for a few more precious years on the Nile. At best he
might leave his successors a Congo-Nile link as a derisive monu-
ment to the days when King Leopold II was a Nilotic power.
Economic imperialism was not the motive power of Leopold's
imperialism on the Upper Nile; it was the residue.

4 J. D. Hargreaves: Survey of the Partition of West Africa

*Although the great drama of the partition centered after 1889 in
the Nile Valley, both Britain and France continued to carve out vast
empires in West Africa. Ronald Robinson and John Gallagher assert
that the scramble in the West continued as it had begun—an offshoot
to Britain's Nile Valley policy. J. D. Hargreaves concurs that West
Africa, at least until 1895, was subordinated to British interests in
eastern and southern Africa but demonstrates that the partition con-*

SOURCE. J. D. Hargreaves, *Prelude to the Partition of West Africa*, London: Macmillan & Co., 1963, pp. 338–349. Reprinted by permission of St.
Martin's Press, Inc., Macmillan & Co., Ltd. Copyright John D. Hargreaves
1963.

tinued in the West for reasons frequently independent of events in the Nile Valley.

The Berlin Conference caused no sudden change in the basic attitudes of the European states. After 1885 as before, pressures for expansion which originated with French or British subjects on the West African coast were counter-balanced in Paris and London by diplomatic caution, by the political instinct to avoid commitment and to economize. The extension of European control along the coasts meant that the administering powers were becoming increasingly involved in the affairs of their new hinterlands; but in practice the inland extension of governmental power was slow and often reluctant.

In June 1885 Great Britain constituted the territories between Lagos and the Cameroons, together with the banks of the Niger up to Lokoja and of the Benué up to Ibi, into the Niger Coast Protectorate; but in principle her governments were willing and even anxious to leave the administration of the area beyond the delta to the National African Company, as "the cheapest and most effective way" of discharging the obligations to maintain free navigation which had been accepted at Berlin. (Had Goldie been able to come to terms with the Liverpool oil traders of the delta, the government would have been delighted to leave the entire protectorate to Company rule.) Negotiations about the terms on which this might be done began early in 1886; they did not run smoothly, and Goldie even threatened wildly to transfer his Company's treaty rights to France; but in July 1886 the Charter was finally issued. The Company was empowered to exercise in the name of the Crown all such rights as it might acquire by its treaties in the Niger; it was allowed to levy customs duties for the purpose of covering administrative costs —a provision which afforded an important loophole for oblique discrimination against the imports of competitors, and which permitted the Company to achieve in practice that commercial monopoly which was forbidden by the letter of the Charter. With the fruits of this monopoly the Royal Niger Company (as it now became) created a rudimentary governmental framework which for several years appeared impressive enough to deter France and Germany from any serious challenge on the lower Niger. In practice Company rule had many grave faults and weaknesses; but the British government, as a recent study emphasizes, was still content to leave its major West African interest beneath this light administrative umbrella, while itself devoting slightly increased diplomatic vigour to defending its interests in East Africa.

But it was not only the British government which gave a low priority to West African policy. The fall of Jules Ferry at the end of March 1885, in consequence of a military set-back in Indo-China, meant a pause in the French advance towards the upper Niger. All colonial enterprises were temporarily discredited by the failure of one; the Chambers became even more reluctant to vote funds for military expeditions, just when French troops on the Niger were meeting potentially more formidable opposition. In February 1883 the French occupied Bamako, which at last brought them near the main centre of Tokolor power at Ségou; but, having clashed with Samori's advanced forces near Siguiri, they were forced to recognize the existence of a second formidable African state in the upper Niger. Moreover their own operations (involving requisitioning of foodstuffs and the use of forced labour) had created resistance in the rear. During the middle 1880's substantial French forces had to be diverted into Cayor, where since 1882 Lat-Dior had again been opposing France over the construction of her railway, and into Galam, where Mamadu Lamina, a well-travelled Muslim scholar, was organizing resistance among the Sarakulé.

Fortunately for the French, their enemies failed to combine. Although Amadu had been re-organizing his dominions with a view to their eventual defence against France, he seemed equally determined to resist the challenge to his authority represented by the rise of rival African empires. Formerly, it is said, he had held Mamadu Lamina six years in prison; certainly he did not wish to encourage a militantly Muslim Sarakulé state within his own sphere of power and influence. He was also on bad terms with Samori, and seems to have made no serious attempt to co-operate with him. Prudently enough, Amadu would have preferred to avoid a battle with the French and their superior technology; when they appeared willing to co-operate with him, Amadu responded loyally, signing and observing a new treaty in 1887. The French were meanwhile more worried about Samori, who in 1885 turned to the British Governor at Freetown, offering to accept British protection and seeking an assured supply of fire-arms. Frightened lest the Niger sources should come under British control, the French in 1886 and 1887 sent envoys to Samori, and on each occasion claimed to have obtained his signature to treaties of protection. Whatever passed on these occasions, Samori certainly did not intend to alienate his sovereign independence; but the British government accepted the treaties in this sense and did not interfere when France eventually undertook the task of bringing this over-mighty protégé to heel.

This temporary shift of French policy was not exclusively due to the difficulty of obtaining money for military operations. During the middle 1880's there was some disillusioned reaction, both in Paris and in St. Louis, against the policies of Faidherbe and Brière de l'Isle. Galliéni, back in the Sudan as military commander, but still impetuously following the swing of his enthusiasms, now proposed the abandonment of the attempt to reach the Niger by way of the Senegal (and the writing-off of the ill-fated railway) in favour of developing alternative routes through Futa Jalon and the *rivières du sud*. From this point of view, the prevention of any alliance between Samori and the British was clearly of prior importance. But other African rulers in the extreme western Sudan might also need to be associated with French policy. In 1886 Galliéni signed a treaty of protection with Amadu's brother and nominal vassal, Aguibou of Dinguiray, and two years later there were new treaties with the Alimamies of Futa Jalon.

Still other possible approaches to the Niger were also being examined by Frenchmen. Between 1887 and 1889 Captain Binger was carrying out the most important journey of West African exploration since Barth, travelling from the upper Niger to Grand Bassam through Mossi and Dagomba, and so exploding the geographical myth that the "mountains of Kong" would always prevent commercial expansion from the Ivory Coast in the direction of the Sudan. Verdier's once-despised holdings now began to assume considerable interest. At Porto Novo too there was some talk of redressing the failure on the lower Niger by establishing commercial contact with Boussa by way of Abeokuta; unsuccessful probes in this direction were made by Viard, a former agent of C.F.A.E. [Compagnie Française de l'Afrique Equatoriale].

These developments redirected attention to the coastal settlements, suggesting to both sides the need for a settlement of pending Anglo-French boundary disputes. At the same time, the French operations against Lat-Dior and Mamadu Lamina in the Senegal raised difficulties concerning the limits of British jurisdiction in the Gambia valley. For a time the old idea of 'comprehensive dealing' revived. In 1887 a new incident in the Porto Novo lagoon led the Intelligence Branch of the British War Office to prepare a paper on West African problems. General Brakenbury (who had served in Ashanti under Wolseley) argued that such places as Appa and Ketenou were of very minor importance, now that the chance had been lost of uniting Lagos with the Gold Coast; but that Freetown, which the Carnarvon Commission on Imperial Defence (of 1879–82) had designated for re-fortification, demanded prior attention. Samori now seemed militarily capable of capturing Sierra Leone, and reports of his treaties with the French had therefore caused great apprehension. In order to ensure the exclusion of French influence from the near vicinity of Freetown, both inland and on the coast, Brakenbury suggested concessions both at Porto Novo and in the Gambia.

Nothing was done immediately, except to negotiate a *modus vivendi* to prevent further conflicts around Porto Novo; Holland, a former official who was now Colonial Secretary, suggested grouping the various pending boundary disputes into a single comprehensive agreement, but refused to consider ceding the Gambia. But next summer the Gambia question was again brought forward by Hutton, now as eager to promote an exchange as he had once been to block one. His friend Harry Johnston, Vice-Consul in the Cameroons, spent a weekend at Hatfield with Lord Salisbury, and urged the exchange of the Gambia as part of a broadly visionary scheme for the planned partition of the whole African continent. Salisbury, impressed, agreed that Johnston should air his views in *The Times*, in an attempt to influence public opinion; and Holland reluctantly agreed to consider an exchange. But conditions were far less favourable than in 1876. The French felt a less acute need for the Gambia route now their railway plans had been begun, and the general climate of Anglo-French relations was frigid. Even in Britain, the abatement of mercantile opposition would not remove all difficulties; opposition was feared from Irish M.P.s and perhaps from the Queen. So in 1889 it was decided to grasp an opportunity to negotiate a comprehensive frontier settlement which would reduce friction and protect Freetown against encirclement, but without attempting an exchange. A Convention of 10 August 1889 settled boundaries, on the coast and for short distances inland, at the Gambia, Sierra Leone, Assinie, and Porto Novo (where Britain at last withdrew from Ketenou and part of Appa).

*   *   *

During the 1890's the policies of the European powers in West Africa became rather more widely and consistently influenced by new political attitudes, best characterized by that overworked word "Imperialist." This is not the place for any serious analysis of these attitudes, nor of the changes in European society which made them so widely acceptable. Their essential features were a new conviction that future economic benefits would follow from the "possession" of colonial territories, undeveloped and unpromising though these might actually be; and a new readiness to justify the deployment of military force in order to compel recalcitrant Africans to collaborate in the "civilizing mission" of the Europeans. This "new imperialism" affected France's African policy earlier than Britain's; its rise is well illustrated by the career of Eugène Étienne, an Algerian-born disciple of Gambetta, who represented Oran in the Chamber after 1881.

Étienne was a friend and former business associate of Rouvier, and served as under-secretary for the Colonies in his government of 1887. He held that office again from 1889 until 1892; it was now re-attached to the Ministry of Commerce, and Étienne himself was given the right to attend Cabinet meetings. Étienne was becoming the leader of a growing colonial pressure-group, which operated inside and outside parliament; he was closely associated with the *Comité de l'Afrique française*, founded in 1890, and in 1892 became chairman of a group of ninety-one colonially-minded Deputies, drawn from all parts of the Chamber. Under his direction the advance into *Soudan français* was resumed. Between 1890 and 1893 Amadu's armies were defeated and the Tokolor empire broken; on 16 December 1893 French troops entered Timbuktu. Thereafter they advanced rapidly down the Niger, and into the lands south of the great bend. Meanwhile in Dahomey the insistence of the new King Behanzin upon the independence of his kingdom and its right to Cotonou (which had recently superceded Whydah as the principal port) drew the French into a series of military campaigns, which led to the occupation of Abomey in November 1892 and the dismemberment of the kingdom in 1894.

Now for the first time the French, advancing from two directions, were in a position physically to test that claim to Hausaland which the Niger Company had still not converted into effective control, and to revive their challenge to the Company's monopoly of the Niger navigation below Boussa. It was true that in 1890, in an unguarded moment, the Foreign Ministry had renounced French claims south of a line from Say to Barruwa (and in 1890 had offered the British an even more favourable demarcation line south of Say), but now that circumstances provided the opportunity to pursue more ambitious aims, ingenious men were able to interpret their commitments rather loosely. The famous "race to Borgu" between Captain Decoeur and Captain Lugard in 1894 opened a new struggle for position on the navigable portion of the lower Niger, a struggle in which really substantial interests seemed to be at stake.

For a time, it seemed that this struggle might become a triangular one. Although Bismarck showed little interest in his African colonies after they had been marked out, and there was even talk of German withdrawal, both Togoland and Kamerun had nevertheless begun to expand inland, under pressure from local traders or administrators; they began to make their own demands upon German policy. Bismarck's successors, less strongly resolved to maintain the priority of continental over colonial interests, thus found themselves drawn into Anglo-French rivalries in West Africa. In November 1893 the British, by an apparently generous recognition of Germany's claims in Kamerun, tried to use her to block France's expansion from the Congo towards both Nile and Benué; in March 1894 France turned the tables. On the Niger, Frenchmen and Germans rediscovered common interests in opposing the regulations made by the Niger Company; in March 1894 Dr. Kayser, who as Colonial Director in the German Foreign Office was securing a stronger voice for colonial interests in the formulation of national policy, warned the British Ambassador that the Niger navigation might become "the next great international question." For a time there was even talk of France and Germany agreeing to give a north-easterly turn to the inland expansion of Togoland and Dahomey, so that both territories might touch the Niger below Boussa; on the other hand Goldie thought of co-operating with Germany in order to seal off French expansion from Dahomey. Nothing important came of these plans for a stronger German role; but they added an extra element of uncertainty to Anglo-French relations during the troubled 1890's.

Until 1895 British governments still tried to limit their commitments in West Africa. Salisbury, who by a decision of 1888 confirmed that British interests in Southern and Eastern Africa should receive higher priority, was successful in imposing 'a selective regulation of the British advance' in the west. He, and his Liberal successors, were under some pressure to be less rigorously selective. During the 1890's merchants and officials on the west coast, supported by Chambers of Commerce in British cities, were increasingly anxious to expand the frontiers of British influence, either by direct action or by supporting Samori in his prolonged resistance to the French advance. But these West African interests represented "an energetic but not a compulsive lobby in British politics," and could not determine policy. Sierra Leone was finally delimited, within modest boundaries, in January 1895, the Colonial Office complaining that the diplomatists had traded its interests for the sake of gains in "the Niger-Congo and Nile questions." To the north of the Gold Coast, some belated efforts were made after 1892 to conclude treaties with the states of the savanna belt; but though most of Gonja, Mamprussi and Dagomba was thus saved for eventual British control, the northern Mossi states could not be kept out of French hands. In Yorubaland the expansion of the Colony of Lagos, though accelerated by Governor Carter after 1892, remained gradual, and subject to restraints imposed from London.

Even on the Niger, where British claims were most valuable and extensive, it was intended to dispose of the revived French challenge by negotiation. But in this as in other aspects of colonial policy there was a notable change of emphasis after Joseph Chamberlain went to the Colonial Office in 1895. This ex-radical business-man saw tropical Africa as an 'undeveloped estate', capable of profitable improvement by energetic and purposeful administration, and by increased public investment. Convinced of the benefits which the discharge of Britain's Imperial mission would bring to all affected by it, Chamberlain insisted on maintaining British territorial claims to the fullest practical extent. In December 1895 he was prepared to protect the lower Niger by a complicated, three-sided, territorial exchange, involving the cession of the Gambia and Dominica to France in return for Dahomey; but when Salisbury preferred a more limited and local negotiation, Chamberlain insisted on some very tough bargaining. As a leader of the Liberal Unionists in a coalition Cabinet, he was powerful enough to veto some of Salisbury's proposed concessions to France, and eventually to initiate a risky policy of replying to French military encroachments in kind. Though increasingly at odds with Goldie over future policy, Chamberlain strongly supported the Niger Company's insistence on keeping the French off the navigable Niger below Boussa, and out of the main part of Hausaland. Salisbury would have preferred to be much more conciliatory over details; however, it seems doubtful whether even he would have conceded anything which he considered essential to the embryonic territory of Nigeria. Despite the growth of anglophobe colonial enthusiasm in France, it was doubtful whether that government would deliberately risk war against the British navy for the sake of the Niger; sure enough, on 14 June 1898, they conceded the essential points of the British demands.

* * *

This agreement virtually completed the diplomatic partition of West Africa, though both Britain and France still had to undertake military campaigns to make their power effective in

Ashanti and in Hausaland, around the middle Niger and on the borders of the desert. One problem which still seemed open concerned the future of Liberia, where there had been frequent rumours during the 1880's and 1890's of impending annexation by either France, Germany, or Britain. Nevertheless this tenacious little Republic, helped by much luck, succeeded in maintaining its national sovereignty. Elsewhere there were frequent proposals for frontier revision, and some succeeded. The most important formed part of the Anglo-French "Entente" agreement of 1904; but even this included only a frontier rectification in northern Nigeria, a smaller one in the Gambia, and the cession to France of the Isles de Los.

On this occasion the French made another determined effort to obtain all the Gambia; they had discovered that their railway was overtaxing the navigable capacity of the Senegal river, and wanted the Gambia as an auxiliary "feeder." They tried again, offering compensation in Asia and the Pacific, and in 1908 Sir Edward Grey apparently agreed that the colony might be ceded without the city of Bathurst, provided the compensation was adequate. In 1911 the French made another overture, sadly mismanaged, asking for huge slices of Nigerian territory at the same time. And even this was not the end of the matter. There is a file in Dakar entitled *Projets d'Échange de la Gambie, 1916–20.* But, apart from the repartition of the German colonies in 1919, the frontiers which had been defined by 1898 were essentially those within which the modern African states have grown to national consciousness and independence. To a very considerable degree, their main configurations had already been foreshadowed by the relations between the European powers and the coastal peoples of Africa before 1885.

*   *   *

Nobody will claim that these frontiers, determined by distant and ill-informed negotiators, were well-adapted to African needs. It is true that their arbitrary nature is often over-emphasized; relatively few were settled by ruler and compasses alone. Since European claims were often based upon treaties with African rulers, there were many cases where the new frontiers coincided with traditional ones; other things being equal, the colonial powers preferred to follow chiefdom boundaries, where these were known. But even these boundaries might still divide Africans of the same language and culture; and once they came under effective European occupation they became harder to cross than would have been the case in the past. And in addition there were numerous cases where European political requirements, such as the desire to have frontiers convenient for the collection of customs duties, led to the deliberate partition of an African state; to take three varied examples, it was so in Samu, in Appa, and in Dagomba.

It was within these new border-lines that the technology, culture, and institutions of the several colonial powers gradually made their impact during the twentieth century. Neighbouring Africans with virtually identical cultural traditions now found themselves subject to different laws, learning different languages and different doctrines in school, using new transport routes which carried them towards different ports and capital cities. These new forces of division were of course felt more quickly and more strongly in commercially-developed areas than in the back country. Distant places without schools or roads often preserved old relationships with their neighbours across the frontier, sometimes to the confusion of colonial officials. Yet even in such places, the new colonial frontiers would in the long run shape the political future.

PART FIVE

French Conflict of Interests

MOTIVES

1 _Henri Brunschwig: Jules Ferry and French Colonialism_

On July 28, 1885, Jules Ferry made his famous speech in which he outlined his economic arguments for the expansion of the French Colonial Empire. This speech marks a great divide in the history of French imperialism. Ever afterward, Ferry's arguments were employed in a variety of disguises to justify French expansion overseas and to convince several generations of historians that the second French empire was founded for fundamentally economic reasons. Henri Brunschwig has quoted the significant passages of Ferry's speech in his French Colonialism, 1871–1914.

On the eve of the meeting of the Conference of Berlin (1885), colonial imperialism was still essentially political. It was not until July 28, 1885 that Jules Ferry made his famous speech, putting forward arguments of a neo-mercantilist nature. Then it was, after Africa and Indochina had been conquered and allocated, that economic doctrines were advanced to justify a policy of expansion. This is the point at which the driving force for colonial imperialism began to come not only from a political generator but from an economic one as well. . . .

Jules Ferry had been overthrown on March 30, 1885 but on

SOURCE. Henri Brunschwig, _French Colonialism, 1871–1914,_ William Glanville Brown, tr., New York: Frederick A. Praeger, 1966, pp. 63–64, 75–81, and 85. Reprinted by permission of Frederick A. Praeger, Inc., and the author. Copyright 1960 Max Leclerc et Cie. English translation by William Glanville Brown. Copyright 1964 Pall Mall Press Ltd.

July 28 he spoke in the Chamber in favour of the credits sought for Madagascar. He took this opportunity of explaining his "system of colonial policy." This was the first time he embodied his arguments in the form of a clear statement of doctrine. He began by denying that he had acted without foresight and merely for the pleasure of expansion, and recalled his principle of seizing the favourable moment. He next developed at length the idea of "investment colonisation" (*colonisation de capitaux*), saying that there was a type of colonisation other than that of emigration.

"It is the type suitable for peoples who have either too much capital or too many products. (*Approval from many parts of the Chamber.*) It is the modern type, the one which is now most widespread and most fruitful, for economists have always rightly questioned whether there was any benefit to be obtained from the emigration of individuals. In learned books I have read calculations detailing the loss occasioned when a man leaves his mother country to become a settler. This matter is possibly open to argument. Yet it is quite clear that a country which allows a large number of its citizens to emigrate is not a happy, prosperous country, and France cannot be criticised for the fact, nor feel it a reproach, that she produces less emigrants than any other country in Europe. (*Approval on the Centre and on the Left.*) But this is not the only matter bound up with the question of colonisation. For wealthy countries, colonies are places where capital can be invested on the most favourable terms. That famous man, John Stuart Mill, devoted a chapter of his book to proving this, and he summed up his argument on this point by saying: 'One of the best things in which an old, wealthy country can engage is colonisation.'"

BRIALOU. "For the capitalists!"

JULES FERRY. "I agree: for the capitalists. Is it a matter of no concern to you, M. Brialou, that the total capital of this country should increase as a result of intelligent investment? Is it not in the interests of labour that there should be plentiful capital in this country? (*Interruptions.*) . . . I maintain that France, which has always had an abundance of capital, a great deal of which it has exported abroad—the exports of capital made by this great country, which is so wealthy, can be reckoned in milliards—I maintain that it is in France's interests to consider this aspect of the colonial question. But, Gentlemen, there is another aspect of this question which is far more important than that to which I have just referred. For a country such as ours, which is obliged by the very nature of its industry to devote itself to exports on a large scale, the colonial question is a matter of finding outlets for those exports. . . . In this connection, I repeat that to create a colony is to provide an outlet. Experience shows that it is enough . . . *(Interruptions on the Right)* . . . —in connection with this particular aspect of things, it is of the greatest importance at this time and in the midst of the crisis which is affecting all European industries, to remember that, when one founds a colony, one is supplying an outley for trade. It has been pointed out—and there are any number of examples of this to be found in the economic history of modern peoples—that provided the colonial link is maintained between the mother country, which is the producer country, and the colonies it has founded, economic dominance will accompany, and to some extent will be subject to, political dominance. . . ."

Ferry went on to give a series of figures showing that the colonies supplied an important outlet for national products. In 1881, France had exported to its empire products worth 126,-523,000 francs, and its imports from the colonies were worth 91,967,000 francs. When the Chamber resumed after an adjournment, he spent some time in emphasising the importance of these outlets, and then went on to develop his argument regarding the second aspect of the system: namely, "the enormous importance of ideas of civilisation."

"There is another matter, another order of ideas, with which I must also deal—as briefly as possible, I assure you—and this is the humanitarian and civilising aspect of the matter. M. Camille Pelletan has been very contemptuous about this. With his own inimitable spirit and finesse, he condemns it and says: 'What sort of civilisation is this which is imposed by gunfire? Is it anything other than another form of barbarism? Are the rights of these inferior races less than ours? Are they not masters of their own countries? Have they asked for your presence? You enter their countries against their will, you do violence to them, but

you do not civilise them.' That is his argument, and I have no
hesitation in saying that it is not a political argument; it is not
history, but rather political metaphysics . . . *(Cries of 'Ah! Ah!'
on the extreme Left, and of 'Exactly' from a deputy of the Left)*
. . . and I challenge you—let me throw you down my challenge,
M. Pelletan—to carry your argument to its logical conclusion,
your argument which is based on equality, liberty and independence for inferior races. You will not carry it to its logical conclusion for, like your honourable friend and colleague, M.
Georges Perin, you are in favour of colonial expansion when it
takes the form of trade."

CAMILLE PELLETAN. "Yes."

JULES FERRY. "You are always citing us M. de Brazza's expedition as the type of colonial policy which you favour and dream
of. I am fully aware that, so far, M. de Brazza has always been
able to carry out his civilising mission without resort to force.
He is a dedicated man who sacrifices himself on his march towards
a lofty and distant goal. He has gained a personal influence over
these peoples of equatorial Africa such as no one else has won.
But who can say that the day may not come in these settlements
created by him, to which such worthy Europeans have devoted
themselves and which henceforth are subject to France—who can
say that the day may not come when the black populations, in
some cases corrupted and perverted by adventurers and by other
travellers, by other explorers less scrupulous, less paternal and
with less power of persuasion than our famous fellow-country-
man, de Brazza: who can say that a moment may not come when
these peoples may attack our settlements? What will you do then?
You will do what all civilised peoples would do, and it will not
make you any less civilised. You will resist by force and, for the
sake of your own security, you will be obliged to impose your
protectorate over these rebel peoples. Let us speak clearer and
more frankly. It must be openly said that the superior races have
rights over the inferior races . . ." *(Protests on the extreme Left.)*

JULES MAIGNE. "You dare to say this in the country where the
rights of man were proclaimed?"

DE GUILLOUTET. "This is to justify slavery and the slave trade!"

JULES FERRY. "If M. Maigne is right: if the rights of man were
intended to cover the black people of equatorial Africa, by what

right do you go and impose exchanges and trade on them? They do not ask you to go there . . ." *(Interruptions on the extreme Left and on the Right; applause on several benches on the Left.)*

RAOUL DAVID. "We are not trying to impose these things on them. It is you who are doing so!"

JULES MAIGNE. "Proposing and imposing are two different things!"

GEORGES PERIN. "And in any case, you cannot carry out forced trade-dealings."

JULES FERRY. "I repeat that the superior races have a right because they have a duty. They have a duty to civilise the inferior races . . ." *(Applause on the same benches on the Left; renewed interruptions on the extreme Left and Right.)*

[This repeated affirmation provoked a storm. When it had eventually subsided, Ferry went on to his third point.] "And then there is the political aspect of the matter. M. Pelletan, who is a distinguished writer, always comes out with remarkably precise formulas. I am going to borrow one which he used the other day to describe this aspect of colonial policy. He said: 'It is a system which amounts to seeking compensation in the East for the caution and self-containment [*recueillement*] which are at the moment imposed on us in Europe. Now I must make it plain that I do not like this word 'compensation'. This word has often been used in a deceitful way—I do not say that it has been so used in this Chamber, but elsewhere it has. If anyone says or implies that any government of this country, that any Republican administration, has imagined that there were any compensations to be found anywhere in the world for the disasters we have met [in Europe], then I consider this to be an insult—and a gratuitous insult to this government. *(Applause on the Centre and the Left.)* I reject this insult with all the strength of my patriotism. *(Renewed applause and cheers from the same benches.)* There can be no compensation, none whatever, for the disasters we have suffered. *(Applause.)* Now, to get to the root of the matter and clear it up once and for all: if the word 'compensation' were used during the discussions and bargaining at the Conference of Berlin, I would have you know that compensation of the kind alluded to in this debate was neither offered, solicited nor accepted in any form whatever. *(Applause on the Left.)*

"The real question which has to be asked, and clearly asked, is this: Must the containment forced on nations which experience great misfortunes result in abdication? Is the fact that a detestable policy, based on hallucinations and the refusal to face facts, brought France to a situation known to you all, a reason for the governments which inherit this unhappy state of affairs to condemn themselves to having no European policy? Should they let themselves be so absorbed by contemplating this incurable wound that they play no part in what is going on around them? Are they going to remain just as spectators and allow peoples other than ourselves to establish themselves in Tunisia, allow people other than ourselves to police the mouth of the Red river and fulfill the clauses of the treaty of 1874, which we undertook to get respected in the interests of the European nations? Are they going to leave it to others to dispute the mastery of the regions of equatorial Africa? Are they going to leave it to others to decide the affairs of Egypt which, from so many points of view, are in reality French affairs? *(Loud applause on the Left and Centre; interruptions elsewhere.)*

"I assert that France's colonial policy, the policy of colonial expansion—that policy which sent us during the period of the Empire to Saigon and Cochin China, which led us to Tunisia, which drew us to Madagascar: I make bold to say that this policy of colonial expansion was based on a truth of which for a moment I must remind you. This is that our navy and merchant shipping in their business on the high seas must have safe harbours, defence positions and supply points. *(Applause from many parts of the Left and Centre.)* Do you not realise this? Look at the map of the world, and tell me whether these bases in Indochina, Madagascar and Tunisia are not essential to the security of our shipping? *(Further applause from the same benches.)* . . . In Europe as it now exists, in this competitive continent where we can see so many rivals increasing in stature around us—some by perfecting their armed forces or navies, and others through the enormous development produced by their ever-increasing population—in a Europe, or rather in a world, which is so constructed a policy of containment or abstention is nothing other than the broad road leading to decadence! In this period in which we are now living, the greatness of nations is due exclusively to the activities

they develop. It is not the 'peaceful radiance of institutions' . . .
(Interruptions on the extreme Left and on the Right.) . . . which
makes them great."

PAUL DE CASSAGNAC. "We won't forget this; here is an apology
for war!"

DE BAUDRY D'ASSON. Bravo! The Republic means war! We shall
get your speech printed at our own expense and distribute it in
every corner of our constituencies!

JULES FERRY. "To radiate without acting, without taking part
in the affairs of the world, to stand on one side from all European
combinations and to regard any expansion towards Africa and the
Far East as a snare and a rash adventure—this is a policy which,
if pursued by a great nation, would, I assure you, result in abdication in less time than you could think. It would mean that we
should cease to be a first-rate power and become a third- or a
fourth-rate power instead. *(Renewed interruptions on the same
benches; applause on the Centre.)*

"Neither I, nor I imagine anyone here, can envisage such a
destiny for our country. France must put itself in a position where
it can do what others are doing. A policy of colonial expansion
is being engaged in by all the European powers. We must do like-
wise. If we do not, then we shall meet the fate—not that we here
shall experience it, but our children and grandchildren will—
which has overtaken other nations which played a great role on
the world's stage three centuries ago but which today, for all their
power and greatness in the past, are now third- or fourth-rate
powers. *(Interruptions.)* The question we have to decide today is
of the highest significance. Not to vote the credits under discussion is to proclaim and pursue a policy of abdication." *(Cries
of 'No! No!')*

In Jules Ferry's case, all the arguments up to that time find
their place: the trade argument, the humanitarian argument, the
political argument. Despite a flight of oratory about the export
of capital, Ferry's exposition of his economic ideas only concerns trade and its outlets. He had not yet thought out the
problem of investments and he made no reference to protection.
It was his political peroration which earned him the Chamber's
applause when he sat down.

2 Stephen H. Roberts: The Economics of French Socialism

The eclipse of Jules Ferry was the nadir of French colonialism, but by 1890 interest in overseas expansion revived in France under the skillful direction of Eugène Etienne. To the glory to be won on African battlefields, Etienne applied the economic arguments of Ferry. In his classic study of French imperialism, Sir Stephen M. Roberts, Vice-Chancellor and Principal and formerly Professor of History in the University of Sydney, has emphasized the importance of economic considerations that were employed to justify the extension of France in Africa.

March 30, 1885, was clearly the nadir of colonization in France. So Ferry fell, and, falling, kept secret news that would have fully vindicated himself, but which, disclosed at that juncture and in that fashion, would have hindered, and probably wrecked, the negotiations then proceeding on the Chinese frontier. He remained isolated on the fringe of the Republican party, he was defeated for the Presidency, he was shot at in the corridor of the Chamber, he was insulted as "Le Tonkinois" whenever he appeared in public, and in the elections of 1889 was even defeated by a Boulangist. Not till 1891 did his ostracism end and the Vosges electors send him back to the Senate; but he died, worn out, if vindicated, early in 1893. He had paid the ultimate price. France sometimes decrees that a statesman has deserved well of his country; more often she crucifies him. But Ferry needed no formal adulation, for the nature of his work was best shown in the very sites of his statues, at Saint-Die, Tunis and Haiphong.

SOURCE. Stephen H. Roberts, *History of French Colonial Policy*, London: P. S. King, 1929, I, pp. 20–24. Reprinted by permission of Frank Cass & Company Ltd., publishers of the New Impression, 1963, and the author.

"Ferry le Traître" was the first of the French colonials, the
creator of the French Empire—that Empire in which the great
forward movement was starting all along the front in the very
year of his death.

But it was some time before his sacrifices bore fruit, for France
in the years after 1885 was whirling back in a storm of Con-
tinentalism. "The vote of March 30 was the condemnation not
only of the greatest living French statesman, but of the principle
which had guided the policy of France since the Congress of
Berlin." The result was that the next six years were negative ones
in so far as colonial expansion was concerned. But the foundations
were being laid for the great onrush of the nineties. Eugene
Etienne, the Under-Secretary for the Colonies from 1887 to 1892,
was orientating and fixing the principles of French colonial
policy, and, although the Deputies were "surprised and alarmed"
and public opinion "still badly prepared to accept them," he
outlined the empire-schemes that events were tending towards
in Africa. Speaking in a famous speech of May, 1890, on the subject of the Dahomey expedition, and answering the anti-colonial
interpellation, he definitely postulated the fact that France had
not only a series of trading-posts in Africa but an African Empire. He made France see the unity and cohesion of her African
efforts, and stood for concerted action as against the *petits
paquets* or desultory efforts of the previous decades. Ignoring the
jeers of the Right, but supported by the Centre and moderate
Left, he claimed the whole of the *hinterland* as, or as becoming,
French. He thus reduced Ferry's generalizations to a concrete
programme, and fixed the course of French activities in Africa
for the ensuing years.

"If you drop a line from the Tunisian border past Lake Chad to
the Congo, you can say that most of the territories between that
line and the sea, excepting Morocco and the English, German and
Portuguese coastal possessions hidden in the immense circum-
ference, are either French or are destined to enter within the
French sphere of influence. We have there a vast and immense
domain which is ours to colonize and to make fruitful; and I
think that, at this time, taking into account the world-wide movement of expansion, at the same time as foreign markets are closing

against us, and we ourselves are thinking of our own market, I think, I repeat, that it is wise to look to the future and reserve to French commerce and industry those outlets which are open to her in the colonies and by the colonies."

Obvious as this may seem now, it was a unique conception in the France of 1890 to visualize an Empire from the Chad to the sea and the Congo to the Mediterranean, and even to postulate any unified plan, still less a constant forward-movement based on the economic *motif* alone. It was singularly fortunate that France, at this crucial moment, had as the guiding force of colonial organization a man with a definite policy and a determination to advocate that policy in the face of strenuous opposition.

This year, 1890, may be taken as the definite turning-point in the history of France's second colonial Empire, in that it marked the commencement of a really constructive interest in colonial questions. Etienne's "Advisory Colonial Council" amply demonstrated this, impossible as such a conception would have been even five years before. The previous period of stagnation, of retreat even, had known no such interest, and it was only the Boulangist adventure and the Panama scandal that attracted public notice. Where colonial progress was mentioned, as in the case of the Sudanese venture, it was only to be assailed. Now, however, when the violence of the Ferry epoch had subsided, and the problem could be approached with clearer minds on the part of the politicians and a kind of jaded acquiescence by the public, progress was possible. To the old positive hostility, a more or less uneasy mistrust had succeeded, but at least allowed of some expansion. The new period thus niggardly allowed was by the pressure of facts largely one of military expeditions,—in Dahomey, Sudan, Timbuktu, Chad, Madagascar, and Upper Tonkin,—and the spectacular shattering of native kingdoms at least associated an element of the always desired "glory" with colonization.

But it would be unjust to characterize this period as solely military: it is true that the colonies now began to be looked on as a school for military training and that the military were amongst the keenest exponents of expansion; but, over and above this, there were so many expeditions because the extent of territory conquered was so vast, and because in every case, powerful native kingdoms, organized almost entirely on a predatory fighting basis, were in the way. It was inevitable, therefore, that colonization in the nineties should partake of a military flavour, but all the time it was clearly realized that there was, in addition, the economic side. Indeed, in the minds of those who directed colonial evolution, there was no doubt but that the soldier was merely the forerunner of the trader and exploiter. After the patrol, and without it if possible, came the *entrepreneurs*. "We must push the traders to the front," argued Etienne, in the Deputies in 1891, and must emphasize pacific missions like those of Monteil and Binger in West Africa. *"La Politique Coloniale"* (that is, the economic conception of Ferry and Etienne) was in the ascendant, as against "the policy of abstention" of the seventies and "the policy of colonial conservation" (implying a standing-still as against expansion) of the eighties. Instead of the negative and unprogressive features of former policies, a reasoned optimism was to be found.

It is true that, until about 1894, this was hindered by the triumph of the Continental ideas of Clemenceau and Déroulède, but the alliance with Russia (1892) and a new *détente* with Germany (1894), by provoking a sense of security, allowed a turn again to the colonies. This was especially the case when Gabriel Hanotaux entered his memorable term of office at the Quai d'Orsay in 1894, because he followed Ferry in believing that, not only was colonial development inevitable, but actually profitable and strengthening to the power concerned. Accordingly, he sponsored a forward policy in northern and central Africa and in Madagascar, and these years (1894–1898) saw the most continuous advance in all parts of the French colonial Empire. The spirit of Ferry's expansion of 1884–1885 was now accepted as directing the movement of French colonization, and there was a steady advance and colonization. These ideas held until the rudder again went to Clemenceau's hand (1906–1909). That vigorous theorist, inflexibly opinionated as he was, was throughout the embittered foe of French colonization.

In the interim, thought on colonial policy was crystallizing in various directions. That colonization was inevitable now seemed beyond dispute: that it was "an imperious duty," to use Etienne's phrase, was not so certain: that it was a wise move economically and politically was believed at least by the directing minds, and, owing to the propaganda of bodies like the "Committee of French Africa" from 1891 on, by a widening circle of outsiders. And, most significant of all, it was coming to be believed that colonization was a supplement to, rather than an antagonist of, the prized theory of "continental solidarity," the parties of the Duc de Broglie and of Clemenceau notwithstanding. Beyond that, there was practically a consensus of opinion that colonization should pay, whether it actually did so or not. No attention was paid to the question of the development of the colonies as individual entities: that was simply unthinkable in the nineties: they were pieces in the wider organism and their sole function was to strengthen France and to serve her needs. They had to develop along the lines France needed, they had to sacrifice themselves if need be for France. "France, which has sacrificed so many lives and so many millions to obtain privileged markets, and which only consented to the sacrifices under this promise, has the right to control the improvement of colonial cultures and industries"—so ran the official history. Again, "the colonies can enrich themselves in selling us cotton, instead of ruining us in making cotton goods." The subservience of the colony to the motherland in every way was thus unquestioned, and France was enforcing the colonial theory that England employed in 1660. In fact, she was building up a gigantic tariff-union, a huge *Zollverein*, with the parts completely secondary to the centre.

As a result of this clearly perceived theory and the consistent forward policy in practice, the French Empire expanded by leaps and bounds. The million square kilometres of 1870 had become 8½ millions by 1914, and the colonial population had gone from five to 50 millions. France was the second colonial Power in the world, and, if the Atlantic-Indian Ocean dream had been shattered by the *débâcle* of Marchand at Fashoda, the Congo-Mediterranean policy was realizing itself more completely every day, and the separate colonies were becoming merged in the wider unity of French Africa. Already by 1906, when the reaction became noticed, conquest and organization had proceeded entirely across the Sahara, and with offshoots as far apart as Wadai and Mauretania. The whole was being galvanized into unity, and

Motives   183

consolidation was taking the place of military conquest. Railway missions and economic surveys were replacing military patrols, and it was Binger rather than Marchand who set the model.

3   Henri Brunschwig: The French Economy and Colonization

Henri Brunschwig has analyzed the economics of French colonial expansion. His conclusions have shaken the firm belief that the products of the colonies could be exploited for the benefit of France, on the one hand, while providing a monopoly market for French industry on the other. The motives and predictions employed by the French colonial movement to justify the acquisition of vast territories in Africa were in reality a myth.

It is difficult to calculate what effect colonial expansion had on the French economy. Statistics are often lacking and the customs figures do not enable one to get a general picture. The official source, the *General Table of External Trade*, traces the course of expansion, but does not deal separately with the various territories before they came to have some economic importance. Thus, in 1885, one table is headed "French Settlements in the Gulf of Guinea (Great Bassam, Assinia, Porto Novo, Gabon)" and another "West Coast of Africa from Morocco to the Cape of Good Hope, not including French and British possessions." A special table is devoted to Senegal as from 1890 and to the French Congo as from 1906. As from 1891, the Table of "French Settlements on the West Coast of Africa" groups together the French Congo, the Soudan, French Guinea, the Ivory

SOURCE. Henri Brunschwig, *French Colonialism, 1871–1914,* William Glanville Brown, tr., New York: Frederick A. Praeger, 1966, pp. 87–96. Reprinted by permission of Frederick A. Praeger, Inc. and the author. Copyright 1960 Max Leclerc et Cie. English translation by William Glanville Brown. Copyright 1964 Pall Mall Press Ltd.

Coast and the Gulf of Benin. As from 1905, the Soudan, French Guinea, the Ivory Coast and the Gulf of Benin are dealt with together under the heading "Other French Settlements on the West Coast of Africa." Under these circumstances it is impossible to compare a particular territory's trade with France, before and after it was occupied. . . .

In view of this, studies based on figures which are accurate only in appearance must be treated with the greatest reserve. The statistics available can be made to prove anything, but it would be dishonest to overlook the fact that these statistics are unreliable. However, my object is not to draw up a table of the economy of the colonies at various periods of the imperialist era, but to show the part played by economic and financial circles in the expansion and organisation of the colonial empire. All I am seeking to learn from the figures is the extent to which trade increased or decreased, and the evidence for this can be accepted as valid when different sources confirm it.

A question constantly under discussion at the time was whether colonial expansion was a paying proposition. The rapporteurs of the Colonial Estimates raised the question in the Chamber and in the Senate almost every year. A few general conclusions can be drawn from the debates on the Estimates. It must be noted that, from the very first, no one ever spoke in favour of giving up the colonies, for colonial policy was never regarded as a purely economic matter. Imperialism, born of nationalism, remained nationalist.

Colonial expansion was unquestionably followed by an increase in trade between France and its colonies. If we refer to the published statistics, starting from the time when the French Empire may be considered to have been complete (Morocco alone being excluded), we observe a marked increase. According to the Office Colonial, the total trade of territories coming under the Ministry for the Colonies rose in value from 838,129,459 francs in 1901 to 1,398,206,449 francs in 1913—an increase of more than two thirds. If to this we add the total trade of Algeria and of Tunisia, the growth over the same period is from 952 million francs to 1,595,917,000—an increase of 67.6 per cent. This increase was not continuous. There were two periods when it was affected by recession: the first—a marked recession in 1903 and 1904—

reduced the value of the total trade of the territories coming under the Ministry for the Colonies to 786,822,052 francs; the second—in 1907 and 1908—was less marked and reduced trade by only 16 million francs.

If this development is compared with the way in which France's trade as a whole was developing, one finds that, during the same period, the value of trade rose from 10,825.9 million francs in 1901 to 19,984.3 million francs in 1913—an increase of 84 per cent. The recession of 1903-1904 is apparent on the graph of general trade; that of 1907–1908 corresponds to a significant fall in France's general trade. The *General Table of France's External Trade* gives us, averaged over a five-year period, the percentage of France's total external trade both with foreign countries and also with its colonies and protectorates.

The following figures are taken from this table:

	Foreign Countries		Colonies and Protectorates	
	Imports %	Exports %	Imports %	Exports %
1882–1886	95.30	93.27	4.70	6.73
1886–1890	93.89	93.46	6.11	6.54
1891–1895	92.45	91.56	7.55	8.44
1896–1900	92.19	90.16	7.81	9.84
1901–1905	91.43	89.38	8.57	10.62
1906–1910	90.85	89.51	9.15	10.49
1909–1913	90.72	89.08	9.28	10.92

So, if one takes imports and exports together, between 1882–1886 and 1909–1913 the percentage went up from 5.71 per cent to 10.2 per cent, which is a negligible amount if one remembers that in France foreign trade was only a small proportion of total trade, internal and external.

What Jules Ferry in 1890 wanted above all were outlets. The colonies undoubtedly provided these. When the contribution of colonial exports and imports to France's total trade is examined, it becomes clear that in most cases, during this period, France exported more to the colonies than it imported from them. Working from the aggregate results already cited, we find that (excluding Algeria and Tunisia) in 1901 the value of French exports to the colonies was 245,198,544 francs, and the value of colonial imports into France was 171,747,266 francs. In 1913 its exports to the colonies were worth 654,087,197, and imports from the colonies were worth 744,121,257. In this latter year, the totals of both kinds of trade were larger and—what was exceptional for the period—colonial imports to France exceeded in value French exports to the colonies. But this imbalance disappears if account is taken of France's trade with Algeria, Tunisia and Morocco, including the port of Tangiers. The total trade between France and its overseas territories in 1913 is then found to have amounted to 3198 million francs, of which 1191 million is accounted for by colonial imports from France and 1507 million by French exports to the colonies.

North Africa, which is not included in the statistics of the Office Colonial, obtained the lion's share of the trade between France and its overseas territories. Trade with North Africa equalled or exceeded that of all the other colonies added together, as is clearly shown by the statistics published each year in the *Table of Foreign Trade*. In 1908, the trade of the colonies amounted to a value of 1,030,152,542 francs and that of Algeria and Tunisia to 1,045,400,000 francs. In 1914, the Institut Colonial of Marseilles drew up the following table:

	Algeria, Tunisia, Morocco (francs)	Colonies (francs)
1909	1,064,259,000	1,090,385,000
1910	1,314,014,000	1,224,426,000
1911	1,556,456,000	1,245,345,000
1912	1,803,483,000	1,287,167,000

The territories of North Africa were also the largest importers. All the statistics agree on this point. "Our sales to Algeria, Tunisia, Madagascar and Guinea exceed our purchases from them."

Where figures relating to the period before French occupation are available, these invariably show that the relationship between imports and exports changed as from the moment of French intervention. All the colonies, from being in the main exporters, become in the main importers. This is explained by the supplies sent to the military and civil establishments there, and later by the

capital equipping of territories which gradually received the
ports, roads and railways needed for their development. This relationship between imports and exports naturally varied from
territory to territory. Some, such as France's Congo colony,
had to wait a long time before receiving capital equipment,
so that, until 1913, its exports to France exceeded its imports
from the mother country. Others, after long being mainly importers, eventually came to supply France with more than they
received. Thus Indochina from 1908 onwards, and Madagascar
after 1909. Algeria, Tunisia and Morocco more or less consistently remained importers. In Senegal, variations in the ground-
nut harvest explain the freakish appearance of the graph.

   Towards the end of the century, French opinion at last awoke
to the fact that the real value of colonies lay less in their supplying outlets for French industries (which had plenty of markets
elsewhere) than in producing raw materials. The partisans of an
active colonial policy consequently changed their views about
protection. The Méline tariff of 1892, while protecting French
agriculture and industry, had placed a duty on most colonial
products on entry into France. But French products were imported duty-free into the colonies, which placed duties upon
imports from foreign countries, and these duties were an essential
part of local budgets. Most loans guaranteed by the state were
made on condition that public works in the colonies should be
executed by French firms, with French supplies carried on French
ships. So the Republic therefore had those specially privileged
markets which Jules Ferry had dreamed of ensuring for France.
However, after a few years, France realised that there was not
such a great need for them, and soon the French colonial party
was solidly lined up against the protectionists!

   In 1899 these latter began to get worried about competition
from industries which had been set up in the colonies, where
labour was cheaper and taxation lower than in France. On
March 8, Jules Méline told the annual congress of the Association
of Industry and Agriculture that, "in order to meet this danger
and in order to discourage in advance possible attempts to set up
industries in our colonies—in short, to compel our overseas possessions to purchase exclusively from us the manufactured goods
they need and, willingly or unwillingly, to perform their natural

function of supplying privileged outlets reserved for French industry," colonial industries ought to be subjected to a compensating tax. A bill backed by Méline, Krantz and Boucher was tabled in the Chamber. It proposed that a licence should be required by industrial and agricultural establishments in the colonies if their products were of a kind to compete with those of France.

This roused the colonial party. In a series of articles in *La Quinzaine Coloniale*, Charles Depincé, the head of the Union Coloniale's department dealing with Madagascar and Indochina, showed that the protective tariff of 1892 was adversely affecting the development of overseas territories.

"Who can say what price has been paid for this increase [in French exports], whether the duties imposed by the General Tariff have not for many years been affecting the economic development of the colonies subject to it, and whether this has not resulted in postponing the day when they may supply our industries with really desirable, valuable outlets; whether, in a word, by seeking immediate gains, the protectionists have not been working against themselves, sacrificing future gains which would be ten or twenty times as great.

"They are aware that the operation of the law of 1892 has not brought them all they expected of it. But the fact that the general movement of our colonial trade, with a few fortunate exceptions, has not progressed entirely satisfactorily, and that this slow progress is indicative of an economic situation which is not all that could be wished—it is not this which worries them and is at the back of their minds. If it were, they might be forced to conclude that this slow progress was due to the tariff system for which they are responsible; they would prefer not to have to come to such conclusions. No: what worries and confounds them is that, notwithstanding all the precautions taken, France has merely a privileged position where they were expecting it to have a monopoly. Despite the duties imposed by the General Tariff, the colonies still buy more from foreign countries than from France. Moreover, some colonies are now being equipped to manufacture certain goods for themselves. In this, and in those natural products of the colonies which are similar to those of France, the protectionists see all the elements of dangerous competition for metropolitan industry and agriculture. This is what they object to."

The Chamber debated the matter in January 1900. Le Myre de Vilers, the rapporteur from the Colonial Estimates, demanded that colonial products should be admitted free of duty. "Colonial products must be admitted to France free of duty, just as our products enter the colonies free of duty. This would be the Colonial Convenant." The expression was taken up by the colonial party's press. Chailley-Bert wrote: "Put the colonies in a position where they can produce. Give them some encouragement. As soon as it is known that you have given effect to this Colonial Convenant, that colonial products are assured of free entry into France just as ours are into the colonies, capital will pour into the colonies for development of all kinds."

The controversy was keen and protracted, and I shall not trace all its stages here. Bienvenu-Martin, the rapporteur of the 1902 Estimates, took up Le Myre de Vilers' scheme for getting rid of duties. This received the support of Noël, the rapporteur of the Customs Committee, who proposed reducing the duties by stages so that goods would be admitted duty-free at the end of ten years; but the proposal was not accepted. After this, the matter was debated every year, protectionists and the colonial party taking every opportunity to appeal to public opinion. Adrien Artaud, vice-president of the Marseilles Chamber of Commerce, pleaded the cause of customs autonomy for the colonies before the Colonial Congress he had helped to organise in Marseilles in 1906. Jules Harmand frequently advocated the same reform, in particular in his book, *Domination et Colonisation*, published in 1910. When the tariff of 1892 was increased by the law of March 29, 1910, all the groups concerned had to unite in a single "Fédération Intercoloniale" to prevent its being applied to the colonies. The Federation first won temporary exemption for the colonies, and then, on July 29, 1913, a provision that the duty should not apply to them was voted, to come into force on January 1, 1914. This provision was made applicable to "colonial products classed as secondary," such as coffee, cocoa and tea, which were thereafter admitted duty-free.

So colonial expansion, which had, at the start, been encouraged by the protectionists, finally led to their finding themselves in violent opposition to those who had acquired overseas interests. This becomes easier to understand if one studies the statistics showing the relative parts played by France and foreign countries in the trade of France's colonies.

Confining myself to the period after 1900 and the completion of the conquest, and regrouping the figures published by the Office Colonial, I have drawn up the following table, which excludes Algeria and Tunisia, these being the territories showing the largest debit balance.

Imports (in francs)

Year	From France	From the French Colonies	From Foreign Countries
1901	245,198,544	20,437,169	208,975,169
1904	194,188,623	13,460,036	203,989,180
1905	225,826,358	12,495,436	250,757,697
1906	201,386,226	14,465,749	239,093,294
1907	219,943,727	16,618,340	292,845,262
1909	230,397,844	15,466,674	267,291,729
1910	238,687,839	—	321,197,472

Exports (in francs)

Year	To France	To the French Colonies	To Foreign Countries
1901	171,747,226	13,715,416	179,055,840
1904	157,587,448	8,406,259	209,190,506
1905	152,421,921	7,123,624	225,311,919
1906	179,276,468	8,568,573	232,483,267
1907	195,317,402	9,014,918	307,778,233
1909	247,562,616	9,876,294	317,955,192
1910	287,389,025	—	377,178,139

It will be seen that, on the whole, the trade of foreign countries benefited more than French trade from France's colonial expansion.

Foreign Trade with French Colonies

Year	Total Trade %	Imports to Colonies %	Exports from Colonies %
1894	46.0	49.0	56.0
1903	49.0	51.0	47.0
1904	52.5	49.0	56.0
1905	55.2	51.1	60.3
1906	46.1	47.5	44.7
1907	60.1	41.5	38.2
1908	56.6	55.2	58.0
1909	53.6	52.0	55.2
1910	56.9	57.3	56.7

I have not found the statistics for the years 1911–1913. According to the Standing Committee on Customs Revenues—the statistics of which, it should be remembered, are appreciably different from those of the Colonial Customs—the total value of trade in 1912, including Algeria, Tunisia and Morocco, amounted to 2857.5 million francs, of which the foreign share was only 1176.5 million francs.

It would be impossible to make this brief survey the basis for drawing conclusions about the economic value of colonies under the Third Republic. This would necessitate a far more thorough enquiry, including replacing the unreliable customs statistics by data obtained from chambers of commerce and from undertakings which made use of or dealt in colonial products, or operated mainly in overseas markets; and no doubt these would be difficult to obtain. Nevertheless, it is possible to draw a few general conclusions from this investigation.

1. The connection which Jules Ferry made between protectionism and colonisation did not really exist. Expansion developed between 1880 and 1892 under a system of free trade, and continued after the introduction of protection under the Méline tariff of 1892. From 1900 onward, the leaders of the colonial party waxed indignant against this protectionist system.

2. The colonies did not supply French industry with a profitable monopoly. They could not have done so because French industry was not in a position to supply them. They were there-

fore obliged to obtain supplies from foreign countries, despite
the customs duties which made these more expensive.

3. The policy of expansion cost France more than it brought
in. Does this mean that those who advocated it should have
desisted? Not necessarily, for they could always hope for future
benefits. This colonial policy essentially consisted of banking
on the future. Credits are voted for the armed forces because
of the dividends which will accrue after the conquest; investments are made because railways and other technical installations
will enable the country to be properly exploited, and hospitals
and schools are built in order to create a profitable labour force
on the spot. There is constant speculation on the future and,
in the last analysis, this speculation leads the colonisers to equip
the colonial dependencies instead of purely and simply to exploit them.

FASHODA

4 Ronald Robinson and John Gallagher: The Meaning of Fashoda

The great confrontation of French and British imperialism at Fashoda climaxed half a generation of colonial rivalry. Although acknowledging that the Fashoda crisis aroused public opinion in Britain for the first time to near hysteria, Ronald Robinson and John Gallagher regard Fashoda as the logical conclusion of the strategic necessity of the Egyptian policy assiduously practiced for over a decade by the men who controlled affairs in Britain.

At first sight there is a certain absurdity about the struggle for Fashoda. The massive advance of Kitchener's army took two and a half years, and it ended by browbeating a few men marooned by the side of the Nile. There was a strange disproportion between ends and means, as there was in building two railways from points two thousand miles apart to run into the deserts of the Upper Nile. A still deeper absurdity seems to lie in the French speculation about damming the river and in the labours of the British to stop them. Even Marchand himself came to see that the scheme was hare-brained, for it turned out that there was no stone within miles of Fashoda. To this extent, the great rivalry

SOURCE. Ronald Robinson and John Gallagher, with Alice Denny, *Africa and the Victorians: The Official Mind of Imperialism*, London: Macmillan & Co., 1961, pp. 376–378. Reprinted by permission of St. Martin's Press, Inc. and The Macmillan Co. of Canada, Ltd. Copyright Ronald Robinson, John Gallagher, and Alice Denny 1961.

for the Upper Nile was based on a myth. The greatest absurdity
of all might seem to be that for two months two great Powers
stood at the brink of war for the ownership of the *sudd* and
desert of the Upper Nile.

It is true that after 1895 there was an irrational fringe to the
British attitude towards the Nile. It is no less true that this attitude
commanded the assent of British opinion during the dramatic
climax of the struggle. Nearly all the English newspapers stood
firm behind the government during the crisis, and their tone was
considerably more strident than that of the French press. The
abstract analysis of editorials is not worth much as an evaluation
of public opinion, but there is no doubt that there was plenty of
warlike spirit in the country. Even the British and Foreign
Arbitration Association let it be known that while they remained
devoted to their doctrine they did not think that it should be
applied to Fashoda.

The aggressive mood of 1898 has often been regarded as an
example of the hysterical passion for aggrandisement which is supposed to have swept through Britain at the end of the century.
This 'new imperialism' is said to have been produced by the
spread of literacy, the coming of the mass vote and the rise of the
yellow press. This may be so, or it may not. At the end of the
century there may have been a new imperial spirit rising in some
sections of English society. Perhaps the new voters and the new
readers may have applauded a policy of swagger and bluster
towards the foreigner. The newly fashionable theories of Social
Darwinism may have introduced a racial arrogance towards lesser
breeds without the law. More people by this time may have come
to believe that Africa could be made into another India.

All this may have been true; but it is not to say that new public
pressures drove the government down the road to Fashoda, or
that popular demand in September 1898 compelled government to
do what it would otherwise not have done. During the Fashoda
crisis the leaders of both parties came out openly in favour of the
Nile Valley strategy. In a speech on 12 October, Rosebery
warned the French not to make a mistake ". . . which can only
lead to a disastrous conflagration"; the next day Asquith spoke in
the same sense; on 28 October Harcourt spoke of the need for
national unity; while Campbell-Bannerman said on 24 November

that ". . . we ranged ourselves as one man in determining to resist
the aggression." This chorus of patriotic union was joined by the
Liberal and Radical press. Among the politicians only Morley,
among the newspapers only the *Manchester Guardian* stood out
against this general line of approval and support for the British
government. At the time of Fashoda opinion in the country was
being exhorted by two political parties both saying the same thing
and both casting it in stereotypes of the national honour and the
civilising mission. It may well be true, as Chamberlain asserted,
that British policy was strengthened by ". . . the spectacle of a
united nation," but it does not follow that the policy was determined by that spectacle. To assert that it was, is to study the
situation of 1898 from the standpoint of other centuries and, it
may be, from the standpoint of other countries.

The Fashoda crisis was not the outcome of a ferocious popular
will then, although it evoked signs of one. It was the logical conclusion of a strategy followed by the Foreign Office for a decade.
Of the calculations and interests involved in this, the public knew
very little. The leaders of both parties understood the strategy,
and most of them approved of it; but time after time they re-
frained from any public explanation of the vital issues it involved,
lest this should hinder British diplomacy abroad and provoke the
intervention of the ignorant at home. Foreign policy was a
matter for an *élite*, and they conducted it according to their own
view of national interest and world policy. The British electorate
found that their country now enjoyed a condominium over the
Sudan, whether they liked it or not. However it may have appeared to the man in the street, to the initiated few Fashoda was
simply the climax to an old policy of imperial defence.

In the eyes of the real makers of policy, there was obviously a
scramble in Africa; but it was hardly for Africa or for empire
for empire's sake. Throughout the partition their over-riding
concern was to claim those regions of the continent which seemed
vital for security in the Mediterranean and therefore in the world.

5   G. N. Sanderson: French Policy on the Upper Nile

For Britain, Fashoda was the product of her Egyptian policy—well defined and relentlessly executed. For France, Fashoda was the result of separate, irreconcilable, and, therefore, conflicting policies within the French government. G. N. Sanderson, Professor of History at Royal Holloway College in the University of London and formerly Professor of History in the University of Khartoum, Sudan, reviews the French march toward Fashoda, seeking to explain how the pursuit of prestige sent Marchand to Fashoda despite formidable opposition within the government to his foolhardy mission. Prestige, not economics, dominated the march to Fashoda. The result demonstrated the folly of a policy motivated by glory and formulated from the crucible of conflicting objectives.

Except for a moment in June 1894, the Germans always kept their action, or inaction, on the Upper Nile subordinate to their general foreign policy. In France, at the other extreme, policy towards the Upper Nile often followed a completely autonomous course which was sometimes in direct opposition to the broader trends of French diplomacy. Indeed, by 1897 the Foreign and Colonial Ministries were pursuing two separate and irreconcilable policies. Something not dissimilar occurred in London during 1897–1898, when Salisbury and Chamberlain differed radically on policy towards France in West Africa. But not even "pushing Joe" ever dared to imitate the off-hand arrogance with which the Pavillon de Flore sometimes ignored the directives—indeed, almost the very existence—of the Minister for Foreign Affairs.[1]

[1] Pavillon de Flore was the location of the French Colonial Ministry and "pushing Joe" was Joseph Chamberlain, British Colonial Secretary. *Ed.*

SOURCE. G. N. Sanderson, *England, Europe and the Upper Nile, 1882–1899*, Edinburgh: Edinburgh University Press, 1965, pp. 386–392. Reprinted by permission of Edinburgh University Press. Copyright G. N. Sanderson 1965.

Between 1889 and 1892 Eugène Etienne [Under-Secretary for the Colonies] had striven to introduce some order into the chaos of French activity and stagnation on the mainland of Africa. His scale of priorities, on which the upper Ubangi and the Upper Nile ranked very low, was maintained by his successor Jamais. But Jamais quite failed to control either the soldiers in West Africa, or the forces which Etienne himself had released. When Delcassé took over in January 1893, the under-secretary's control over expansionist activity was little more than a legal fiction. Mizon was levying private war in Adamawa, a region which London and Berlin regarded as their private bone of contention. In West Africa the *commandant supérieur* Archinard passed on Delcassé's instructions to his subordinate Combes—but with explicit orders not to obey them. On the upper Ubangi the younger men were going as far as they dared in opposition to the "politique de moindre effort" for so long enforced by Paris and by de Brazza. Even Liotard, normally the most loyal of subordinates, had caught the prevailing infection when he advanced on Bangasso in March 1893. In this situation Haussmann, the *Directeur Politique* at the *Colonies*, tended to regard his function as that of a brake on local excess of zeal. In 1893 he was not looking for new adventures, above all not on the Upper Nile, but rather to liquidate old ones, especially the potentially very dangerous Adamawa affair.

To these hazards Delcassé seems to have been quite indifferent. He did indeed recall Mizon, but evidently with the greatest reluctance. He did not get to grips with the *officiers soudanais* until in December 1893 heavy pressure from press and parliament forced him to appoint a civilian Governor-General, Albert Grodet, with the directive that "the period of conquest and territorial expansion must be considered as definitely over." Meanwhile, influenced by Victor Prompt's dangerous hydrological speculations and perhaps by the sudden enthusiasm of d'Arenberg and Harry Alis, Delcassé launched a drive for the Nile. [King] Leopold had promoted this idea through his agent Harry Alis, hoping to enforce a diplomatic settlement on the upper Ubangi as an indispensable preliminary to the French expedition; but to Leopold's dismay Delcassé proposed to challenge the Congolese by armed force as well as to "re-open the Egyptian question" by a threat to the Nile waters at Fashoda. Meanwhile,

Delcassé kept even his own *Direction* as far as possible in the dark. Develle, the Foreign Minister, was no wiser, though he was on record as approving at any rate a mission "towards" the Bahr al-Ghazal. However, Delcassé invoked the assistance of the President of the Republic himself to overcome Monteil's reluctance to undertake the mission; and Sadi Carnot, usually regarded as a model of constitutional rectitude, associated himself completely with a mere *sous-ministre*'s private and unauthorised project to challenge the British occupation of Egypt.

The Monteil Mission of 1893 was not so much a policy as a conspiracy in the margin of policy. It was neatly frustrated when Leopold II, a conspirator beside whom Delcassé was a beginner, inspired the probably unwitting Monteil to insist on a previous agreement with the Congo State as a *sine qua non* of his departure for Africa. Delcassé could not dismiss out of hand the colonialist hero of the hour and a man who still enjoyed the powerful support of Etienne. The Mission therefore languished from August 1893, when Monteil delivered the ultimatum embodying his "conditions," until it was given its quietus by Casimir-Périer early in 1894. Casimir-Périer's suppression of the mission was certainly prompted by his desire to assert his own ministerial authority against Presidential encroachment; he was moreover prepared, from whatever motives, to go to almost any length to please King Leopold. At the beginning of 1894 there were however good objective reasons for putting a sharp curb on adventures in Africa. The British had protested again Mizon's proceedings in language which, if used in any but an African dispute, might have heralded an early ultimatum. In December 1893 there had been an accidental but bloody clash between British and French troops in the hinterland of Sierra Leone. In January 1894 a French column, sent to relieve a junior officer who had advanced to Timbuktu in direct contravention of orders, was ambushed and annihilated. *Le Matin* thundered: "Les Romains, qui furent le modèle des conquérants dans l'antiquité, châtiaient sans pitié l'héroïsme indiscipline."

The early months of 1894 were the high-water mark of "héroïsme indiscipliné." Thereafter the *Colonies* (since April 1894 a full Ministry) seems to have exerted a more effective control over its agents overseas. The details of this process are unknown. Boulanger, despised for his lack of expert knowledge, initiated an internal re-organisation of his Ministry; and this may have had some effect. The appointment of Grodet certainly went far to spike the guns of the *officiers soudanais*, in spite of— or perhaps because of—Grodet's quarrelsome, unscrupulous and generally unpleasing personality. Haussmann's rather ineffective *immobilisme* began to be eclipsed by the influence of younger men, more in sympathy with the forward policy and perhaps for that very reason better able to control it. After his return to the Pavillon de Flore in June 1894, Delcassé no longer seems to have held his *Direction* at arm's length; he evidently worked closely with it in opposition to the proposed Phipps-Hanotaux settlement.

In the second half of 1894 the Colonial Ministry launched a series of successful missions—Decoeur, Toutée, Ballot—through the Dahomey gap towards the middle Niger. These successes, and the *esprit de suite* of the whole operation, showed a professional touch which had been lacking in the planning of the Monteil Mission; and they extorted the rueful admiration of a fellow-professional, Sir Percy Anderson: "It is impossible not to be struck by the admirable way in which the numerous French expeditions are conducted by capable officers." In sharp contrast to these successes, the Liotard Mission to the Upper Nile, author-ised by the French Cabinet in November 1894, made no progress worthy of the name. But compared with the West African ex-peditions, the "Liotard Mission" was little more than a *façon de parler*. There was no independent mission under an experienced military explorer. Instead, the drive to the Nile was entrusted to a rather pedestrain administrator already over-burdened by rou-tine tasks for which his resources were barely adequate. Delcassé's apparent satisfaction with this rather half-hearted arrangement invites speculation; it is at least possible that his policy towards the Upper Nile was no longer so headstrong as in 1893.

Delcassé's successor Chautemps was a clear-headed administra-tor, who took the first and decisive step towards remedying the 'situation anarchique' of conflicting and overlapping jurisdictions in French West Africa. The setbacks to Delcassé's forward policy in the Ivory Coast and elsewhere had raised an outcry in the Chambers; Chautemps insured against a similar danger on the

Upper Nile by simply neglecting to reinforce Liotard. This quiet reversal of Cabinet policy may not have been to the taste of his *Direction*; but no one else objected—least of all Hanotaux, who had in November 1894 openly opposed the Liotard Mission. In September 1895, Marchand, presumably with support from the permanent officials, submitted his proposals to Chautemps. Administratively, the essence of Marchand's scheme was that the Upper Nile mission should be given an organisation and status similar to those of the successful West Africa expeditions. This was a technically sound proposal which Chautemps was prepared to consider; but he was not prepared to act until the political implications of Marchand's plan had been explicitly approved by the Quai d'Orsay. In September 1895 the relations of France with Russia, and of Russia with Germany, were moving Hanotaux actively to seek a rapprochement with England, rather than to initiate action which could, as he well knew, lead only to a violent quarrel. But he seems to have lacked the nerve to kill the project outright. Instead, he hedged and procrastinated. Meanwhile, so long as Chautemps was in office, the *Colonies* took no further action, and the Marchand Mission remained a paper project.

The mission was finally launched, after the fall of Chautemps and Hanotaux, by those who had doubtless supported it from the first—the permanent officials, notably Ernest Roume. Approval was obtained from Guieysse, the new and professionally inexperienced Colonial Minister, when he had been only a week in office. Berthelot, the new Foreign Minister, was if anything even less qualified for his position than Guieysse. Roume found an ally at the Quai d'Orsay, presumably Benoît, the high colonialist *Directeur des protectorats*. Pleading overwhelming urgency—a plea totally belied by their later action—these men rushed Berthelot into approving a project of which the full political implications had never been explained to him. This concealment was almost certainly deliberate; and the mission to the Upper Nile, in 1895 as in 1893, was promoted by methods which can only be described as conspiratorial. But this time the conspiracy was not merely in the margin of policy; it was a conspiracy directly opposed to Berthelot's policy of amicable settlement with England, if possible even in Egypt.

In 1896 the able and aggressive Gustave Binger became *Directeur des affaires d'Afrique* at the Colonial Ministry. Given a tough-minded Minister who would underwrite their policies, the *bureaux* of the Pavillon de Flore could now disregard the directives of a mere non-political Foreign Minister like Hanotaux. The *Colonies* found their tough-minded Minister in André Lebon; and Hanotaux' efforts to assert his control over this formidable combination were pathetically futile. He apparently watered down Marchand's instructions by omitting all mention of the White Nile and of Fashoda, in the attempt to convert the mission from "a pistol-shot on the Nile" to a means of comparatively gentle pressure in the Bahr al-Ghazal. He certainly opposed the Colonial Ministry's foolhardy and irresponsible policy—supported, however, by his own *Direction*—of enlisting the military support of the Negus Menelik. But after he had been over-ruled in full Cabinet on Ethiopian policy in March 1897 he seems to have admitted defeat; and he took no traceable action when early in 1897 the Pavillon de Flore issued instructions quite incompatible not only with Hanotaux' own watered-down version but with the original objects of the Mission as approved by the Quai d'Orsay. While the *Colonies* did its best to set the Nile on fire, Hanotaux pursued an expectant and unprovocative policy in this sphere, presumably hoping that "Marchand n'arriverait pas"—at least, not on the Nile itself.

The Marchand Mission was the last and most spectacular manifestation of the "Imperialism of prestige" which came to dominate French colonial expansion in the eighteen-nineties. In this movement, economic motives played very little part; in the Marchand Mission itself, none at all. Marchand's own motives were those common to the *officiers soudanais* who conquered a sub-continent while Ministers protested and businessmen placed their investments elsewhere: a hunger for action and adventure, ennobled by the concept of 'la plus grande France', and in Marchand's particular case (which was certainly not unique) spiced by a hearty detestation for 'greedy and hypocritical' England. Until 1893 the "imperialism of prestige" had been restrained rather than encouraged, at least in its more extravagant forms, by the Office tradition at the *Colonies*; Haussmann was utterly opposed to its extension to the Nile valley. Moreover Etienne, from motives which can at least in part be justly described as economic, saw French expansion in Africa largely as the creation of a "Greater Algeria." To this vision the Upper Nile was quite irrelevant. But from 1894 the control of policy fell increasingly into the hands of permanent officials who were, in Monson's words, "extremely combative" towards England. To these men, always ready to assert the prestige of France by "inventing and intensifying" difficulties with England, the Nile project was very relevant indeed; for its fundamental object was to restore French prestige in the theatre where national pride had received its most grievous wound since 1871.

Precisely because the British occupation of Egypt was so widely felt as an intolerable affront to national self-respect, the Nile project enjoyed support far outside the ranks of convinced colonialists once its connection with Egypt had been clearly established. In June 1894, at the close of the debate in which Etienne established this connection, the Chamber voted unanimously in favour of what at least appeared to be a policy of active reprisal against the Anglo-Congolese Agreement. In December 1896, when a Deputy queried the inflated upper Ubangi budget which, as almost everyone knew, concealed the credits of the Marchand Mission, even the Socialist Jean Jaurès demanded "une vote nationale"; and obtained one, by an enormous majority. It is hardly relevant to discuss the influence of the Parliamentary Colonial Group in this connection. The Chamber needed no convincing; all that the Colonialists had to do was to make the keynote speeches and to provide any necessary detailed information. In 1882 the French Chamber had shrunk from the largely imaginary hazards of joint intervention in Egypt. In 1885 it had destroyed Jules Ferry because he had become involved in petty hostilities, for the moment unsuccessful, with China. But in 1894 and 1896 the Chamber gave its overwhelming approval to a policy carrying risks beside which those of 1882 and 1885 were negligible. Behind this policy there was little rational calculation. It rested rather on a quite irrational conviction that a successful expedition to the Upper Nile *must* somehow lead to a favourable solution of the Egyptian question; and on the further assumption, less irrational but almost wilfully erroneous, that economic interests would always keep England from making the

Nile a *casus belli*. These views were not confined to an ill-informed public and parliament. Astonishingly, they were shared by French diplomatists and by the professional experts not merely in the Colonial Ministry, but in the Foreign Ministry. Even had Hanotaux' position been stronger than it was, it is doubtful whether, after his return to office in 1896, he could have halted the Marchand Mission against the combined pressure of the permanent officials and of public opinion.

Beneath the surface of events, however, the "imperialism of prestige" was losing ground to the economic imperialism of the *Union Coloniale Française*. The businessmen who formed this organisation relaxed their hostility to further expansion to the extent of regarding Morocco as an indispensable acquisition; but they never had the slightest sympathy for an imperialism of prestige in the Nile valley. They well knew that in Egypt Cromer safeguarded their investments better than any conceivable alternative régime was likely to do; better, indeed, than they were safeguarded by the *fonctionnaires* in some French possessions. As for the Sudan, profits here were obviously a chimaera. In the shock and disillusion which followed Fashoda, the interests embodied in the *Union Coloniale* were able to use the influence which they had been quietly accumulating during the previous five years. If the Marchand Mission was the last grandiose fling of the old imperialism of prestige, its dénouement in 1898–1899 was the first victory for an imperial policy based on more material calculations. It was at a meeting sponsored by the *Union Coloniale* that Eugène Etienne read the obituary of the imperialism of prestige; Marchand had known what he was about when he so bitterly denounced "les coloniaux d'exploitation rationnelle."

French policy towards the Upper Nile was certainly the outcome of a conflict of interests; indeed of a multiple conflict which even included personal interests, not always of a reputable kind. But once the Upper Nile had been publicly linked to Egypt in 1894, French intervention was sustained by a wider enthusiasm which rose to a climax in 1897 and 1898, only to collapse thereafter with a surprising rapidity. In England, too, similar conflicts played their part in the determination of policy; but here too there was a wider enthusiasm for intervention and ultimately for acquisition. Until the end of 1894 this wider enthusiasm scarcely existed so far as the Sudan was concerned; but in 1898 and 1899 it reached a peak from which it did not decline until it had undergone the chastening experience of the South African War. By 1898 it had endowed with strongly acquisitive over-tones a Sudan policy which had in the later eighteen-eighties been gradually and rather reluctantly initiated as a purely defensive strategy to protect the Nile waters and so to safeguard the British position in Egypt.

PART SIX

The End of the Scramble

1   *Roland Oliver and J. D. Fage: The Partition and Africa*

Roland Oliver and J. D. Fage sum up the scramble from the point of view of the historian of Africa. Directed from Europe, shaped in Africa, and frequently bloody, the scramble began a new epoch in the long history of the African continent.

The most remarkable aspect of the first ten years of the scramble for Africa was the extent to which almost everything of importance happened in Europe. Statesmen and diplomats met in offices or country houses and drew lines across maps which themselves were usually inaccurate. Often the lack of geographical detail was such that frontiers had to be traced along lines of latitude and longitude. In Africa itself the reality of partition was slight indeed. A dozen overworked men could make up the local representatives of a Chartered Company. A consul and two assistants might well form the government of a Protectorate. Such establishments were apt to be too busy keeping themselves alive to engage in military collisions with neighbouring governments. Even if rival teams were racing for a treaty in the same area, it was most unlikely that their paths would cross. The conflicting claims would be sorted out a year later round a table in some European capital.

As the scramble passed into its second decade, however, the activities of the men on the spot assumed a new significance. The position of interior frontiers often depended upon which of two neighbouring powers was able to create something like effective occupation. Encounters between the nationals of different European powers became increasingly frequent. They happened especially along the western frontiers of Nigeria, where (after the French had conquered the native kingdom of Dahomey in 1893) fairly substantial military forces threatened to collide in

SOURCE. Roland Oliver and J. D. Fage, *A Short History of Africa*, Baltimore: Penguin Books, 1965, pp. 189–191. Reprinted by permission of Penguin Books Ltd. and the authors. Copyright Roland Oliver and J. D. Fage 1963.

the disputed territory of Borgu. The hurry to reach Borgu before the French also involved Goldie's Royal Niger Company in its first military clashes with the African states lying within its chartered sphere. To forestall the French in Borgu, it was necessary to conquer the emirates of Nupe and Ilorin.

Again, by the later nineties French expeditions were converging on Lake Chad from three directions, from the French Congo, from Algeria, and from the upper Niger, and for a brief time the dream of a vast French empire linking the Mediterranean, the Atlantic, and the Indian Ocean caught the imagination of the French public. A French occupation of the upper Nile would strike a vital blow at the British in Egypt. From 1896 until 1898, therefore, Commandant Marchand pushed a painful passage with a small company of native soldiers all the way from the Gaboon to Fashoda on the White Nile, some four hundred miles south of Khartoum. Britain in 1885 had compelled Egypt to abandon its former dominion in the Nilotic Sudan to the forces of the Mahdi, Muhammed Ahmad, on the grounds that Egypt could not then afford the expense of reconquest. Salisbury, however, had never lost sight of the Sudan; in 1896, after a disastrous defeat inflicted upon the Italians by the French-armed troops of Menelik of Abyssinia, the new Egyptian army trained by Kitchener was ordered to begin the southward advance. The province of Dongola fell the same year, Berber in 1897, Khartoum itself after the battle of Omdurman in September 1898. A week later Kitchener heard of Marchand's presence at Fashoda, and hastened to confront him with a vastly superior force: the "Fashoda incident" brought France and Britain to the brink of war. This well-known fact of history has tended to obscure another, which is that Kitchener's reconquest of the Sudan, at a conservative estimate, cost the death in battle of twenty thousand Sudanese. The partition of Africa, as it approached its logical conclusion, was beginning to be a bloody business.

2 Endre Sík: The Struggle of the European Powers for Africa

Endre Sík is a long-standing member of the Communist Party of Hungary and a former foreign minister. He views the partition of Africa through the writings of Marx and Lenin in which the scramble is regarded as the struggle of monopolistic, finance capital in the developed countries of Europe for control of Africa's markets and raw materials.

Even before the decade of the 1870's, the great European powers were trying to enlarge their colonial bases on the coast of Africa and occupy the adjacent territories. From the 1870's, and particularly during the 1880's, European capitalism, passing into imperialism, began the occupation of the whole continent. The conquest of Africa spread over several decades. Colonial expansion unfolded in a bitter conflict between rival powers which the ardent resistance of the African peoples rendered even more complex.

With the arrival of imperialism, the great powers played a peculiar role in world politics. In effect, this whole policy reflected the economic conflict of monopoly groups of finance capital of the most developed countries for control of the world market. As a result, at the end of the 1870's and even more so at the end of the 1880's, after a century of relative calm, the conflict between the capitalists greedy for new profits took on a particularly extreme form in Africa.

Even so, this conflict differed fundamentally from the "all

SOURCE. Endre Sík, *Histoire de l'Afrique Noire*, Budapest: Publishing House of the Hungarian Academy of Sciences, 1961, I, pp. 291–293. Translated for this book by Nell Elizabeth Painter and Robert O. Collins. Reprinted by permission of the Publishing House of the Hungarian Academy of Sciences and the author. Copyright Akadémiai Kaidó, Budapest 1965.

against all" struggle of the period of the slave trade. It was
different from this latter struggle in regard to its participants,
motives, and objectives, as in its forms and proportions. If it were
entrepreneur capitalists and their little groups (whether private or
government supported) who fought among themselves in the
earlier period, during the period now in question it was the great
monopolies of finance capital of the strongest countries, represented by powerful imperialist governments, which found themselves in opposition.

As the power of the state became that of finance capital in the
bourgeois-developed countries, the governments of the capitalist
states that had penetrated into Africa no longer limited themselves to playing the role of patron, open or disguised, of the
various colonial adventurers, merchants, companies, etc., but became the active organizers of a systematic battle carried on with
the object of occupying and monopolizing the maximum amount
of colonial territory with the view of creating great colonial units
that, taken together, formed *colonial empires*. This struggle, during which as many tried and true procedures were used as new
ones, was waged on two fronts: on the one hand, against the
peoples of Africa, and on the other, against rival imperialists. The
object of the struggle was no longer the conquest of bases or a
few small enclaves, but the possession of the greatest possible
number of African lands and the exercise of control over backward African countries, which were, or could become, sources of
raw materials and profitable areas for investment.

These attempts being inherent to the finance capital of each
imperialist power, the struggle for African colonies was trans-
formed into a struggle for the partition of Africa among the
biggest and strongest powers and essentially between England,
France, and Germany. As far as the smaller powers who also
possessed colonies in Africa were concerned (Portugal, Spain,
Belgium), they were only able to keep their colonies thanks to
the conflicts of interests and disagreements between the great
powers, which prevented their agreement on the division of the
spoils. . . .

The character of the conflict, as well as the methods and procedures employed by the powers in Africa, were totally different
from the methods and procedures used by the adventurers and

merchants of the sixteenth to eighteenth centuries. At that time, the conflicts had an accidental character. In general, the struggle took the form of disagreement between the occupants over the seizure of some quarry, the occupation of some base, for the continuation of brigandage. These pirates, whether they were adventurers acting on their own account or official government agents, attacked each other to carry off the booty. The *conflicts* were uniquely resolved on the spot by the force the adversaries disposed of at any given moment in any given place.

In the 1880's and during the course of the years that followed, finance capital waged its battle in an entirely different manner. In the first place, it had recourse to diplomatic intrigues systematically plotted in Europe, in the form of conferences and secret agreements concluded between imperialist governments against other imperialist governments. These agreements were constantly violated, annulled, or reconcluded. Yesterday's allies became tomorrow's adversaries and vice versa. At the same time, the rivals' armed forces acquired more importance than they had had in the past. No longer thrown into combat to decide minor conflicts or seize a boat or a port, they now constituted the decisive argument for the struggle in Africa for the partition among the imperialists of entire regions, an argument held in reserve in the course of the diplomatic conferences but always ready to be put into action if necessary for the realization of the proposed plans.

The diplomatic struggle between England, France, and Germany, which lasted roughly twenty years, was nothing more in fact than the preparation of the partition of Africa by means of a great imperialist war. Often events evolved in such a manner that the armed forces of the greatest powers stood face to face, ready to act. Thus, for example, in 1884 the warships of England and Germany were on the verge of setting off the battle over the Cameroon on the coasts of West Africa. In 1898 the French and British imperialists in fact began a military campaign in the eastern Sudan (the Fashoda Incident).

But war did not break out and the partition of Africa unfolded between the imperialist powers without military action (if minor incidents are not taken into account).

The extent of *free* territory and the weakness of small imperialist states which had possessions in Africa (Belgium, Portu-

gal), which the great powers could reduce or economically
conquer, permitted the imperialists to agree on conditions which,
at a given point, could more or less satisfy all the concurring
parties.

3   Henri Brunschwig: The Partition and France

Henri Brunschwig concludes that the French scramble for Africa
was motivated by prestige, not profits.

On the eve of the period of colonial expansion, the system of
free trade was giving satisfaction to European merchants import-
ing the products they needed from overseas. Their overseas sales
were on only a modest scale and worth far less than the purchases they made abroad. They found plenty of sales outlets and,
even if some of them were beginning to fear that the day might
come when these markets would be closed to them, these fears
were never realised.

Protectionism, which arose out of these fears, did not seriously
interfere with the exports of industrialised countries. It may have
reduced them for a few years between certain countries but its
general effect was merely to subject trade to new conditions to
which traders quickly adapted themselves. In fact, most of the
powers considerably increased their exports between 1875 and
1914, for the civilised world's consumption of industrial products
kept increasing. The quantity of these which the recently acquired colonies imported remained very small, for their populations had few needs and were little inclined to develop new ones.

SOURCE. Henri Brunschwig, *French Colonialism, 1871–1914,* William
Glanville Brown, tr., New York: Frederick A. Praeger, 1966, pp. 182–186.
Reprinted by permission of Frederick A. Praeger, Inc. and the author.
Copyright 1960 Max Leclerc et Cie. English translation by William Glan-
ville Brown, Copyright 1964 Pall Mall Press Ltd.

The myth that protectionism helped to bring about colonial expansion was widespread, but it was a myth all the same.

The real cause of French colonial expansion was the spread of nationalist fever, as a result of the events which had taken place in 1870 and 1871. Since 1815, France had felt that colonisation was a vital element in its national prestige, particularly in the power-relationship with Britain, and in the aftermath of defeat became even more than ever jealous of this prestige. France could not endure seeing Leopold II intervene in the Congo, or Italy in Tunisia. The French attitude induced the British government to give more active support to missionaries and merchants who, ever since 1815, had been increasing their activities in Africa and Asia. As for Germany: although Bismarck claimed to be adopting British practice in declaring that the state should follow, and not precede, overseas pioneers, the policy he advocated was not adopted. William II wanted to make Germany a world power. These attitudes of the great European powers led to a scramble for colonies in a hectic atmosphere: one in which each country felt that its national existence was at stake, or would be in the very near future.

Yet the argument that expansion was profitable was also nothing more than a myth. It arose, despite evidence to the contrary— as such myths often do—under the pressure of a public opinion which refused to face facts. In the Chamber and in the press, clearsighted politicians and economists proved that colonial expansion did not pay. But the contrary was believed both by those moved by nationalist emotions and also by those opponents of the policy who condemned the capitalists for the profits they were making out of colonial expansion. The same thing had happened when the Senegalese, Malamine, came to be depicted as a hero of France resisting Stanley's advances, when at the same time contemporary travellers were describing how cordial were his relations with the Belgian mission.

Nor were historians, who shared their fellow citizens' beliefs, any more concerned with these facts. There are few serious works on colonial imperialism. Each generation writes history in its own way, chooses the subjects from the past which enable it to project onto the past its own preoccupations, and each generation is usually unaware of its bias. This is why historiography,

which enables one to understand and explain how successive generations and their historians thought and felt, constitutes today
the most solid of historical studies.

1919 is an important date in the history of colonial expansion,
for it marks a turning-point. After the first world war, the leading spirits among the indigenous peoples cited against the colonialists the very principles for which the latter had declared they
had been fighting. And these principles were inconsistent with
imperialism. As a result, the colonial powers lost their clear con-
sciences, though this in no way interfered with their pursuing
a policy of expansion. It is at this point that the expression "colonialism" first comes to have the deprecatory meaning—the meaning it has carried ever since—of the exploitation of colonised
peoples in the exclusive interests of the colonisers. Were profits
greater during the period between the two wars than they had
previously been? Probably not, if one takes account of expenditure on the armed services, of the loans made to the colonies
during the economic crisis of 1930, and of the huge investments
which were subsequently made and which were not always profitable. But this is a matter for future investigation.

What is already clear, when one looks back, is that imperialism
prolonged and crowned the work of the missionaries and the
philanthropists. Whether they were exploited or not, it is a fact
that the colonial peoples have been civilised and westernised.
Even communism came from the western world and was an
agent of change, uprooting individuals and groups from indigenous traditions and beliefs. The new states which have become
independent since 1947 are based on the western model. Their
leaders have been trained by the former colonial powers and are
continuing the colonising work of these powers amongst the
less developed masses. Whether their institutions are democratic,
authoritarian or communist, they are based upon ideas which are
drawn from the western world.

Ever since the fifteenth century, the peoples of Europe have
been becoming masters of ever more improved techniques and
have been seeking to model the world in their own image. An
essential element in this huge westernising movement has undoubtedly been colonial imperialism and this is so whether or

not the peoples of the colonial powers wished it to have this result—as a large part of British public opinion and many French and Dutch socialists undoubtedly did—or whether it was the incidental and unintended result of the manner in which the colonies were economically exploited. This development would probably have occurred even without colonial conquests and the abuses they brought in their train; but it would then certainly have come about much more slowly.

The more we come to have a clearer understanding of the development of the colonised peoples before the era of imperialist expansion, the more it becomes apparent that, in fact, their relations with western countries were already becoming very close. Even in Central Africa—regarded as barbarous by Europeans influenced by the idea of a hierarchy of civilisation which ranged primitive peoples at the base (because, it was argued, they were devoid of the faculty of rational thinking) and placed at the summit the mature peoples who were endowed with juridical concepts of the law and the state—even in this heartland of "darkest Africa" European products had preceded the presence of Europeans, and christian or mohammedan ideas and beliefs had infiltrated from far away. The gradual penetration of alien products and ideas was altering traditional customs.

If Europe had not exported its nationalist passions, this process of acculturation would have continued under its own momentum, variable in intensity from area to area, gradually eroding traditional ways of thinking and living, relegating custom to the level of folklore—in fact, much the same sort of process as had taken place within the western nations themselves.

It is wholly improper, therefore, to attribute to imperialism the "civilising" of the colonised peoples. They would have followed the same path whether or not they had been subject to direct European control. But they would have developed in their own way and according to their own rhythm, each achieving in the form best suited to it a symbiosis of the elements taken from western societies and its own particular traditions. The crime of colonialism has been that of fiercely accelerating an evolution which was already under way, of shattering what was in process of being dismantled and reconstituted—in short, of violating nature. Peoples who were not in a position to benefit from western culture were, under colonialism, deprived of their own cultures, which to European eyes were inferior and outworn. Colonialism has been a major surgical operation on a desperately weak patient. The colonised peoples, subjected, as it were, to having an alien organ engrafted in them, very nearly succumbed to the operation.

The shock induced by the sudden acceleration in their development has gravely disturbed the psychic state of the colonised. The excesses of reprobates who were to be found here and there in the ranks of the administrators, and the abuses of business firms more attentive to their profits than respectful of local customs, have given rise to those complexes of frustration and xenophobic reaction which are at the root of the pressure for decolonisation. Since it is highly questionable if colonisation procured more benefit to the West than would have accrued to it from the evolution which was taking place before the sudden acceleration, it is legitimate to consider colonial imperialism, and nationalism along with it, as a vast error.

It is therefore all the more saddening to observe the nationalist passion of the peoples who today are now attaining their independence. They have so absorbed the spirit of western nationalism—essentially a phenomenon deriving from Europe's past—that they now are striving to construct for themselves a past which can be compared with that of the former colonial powers. These peoples are young in every sense—for western techniques have enabled them to reduce their rate of infant mortality—but they wish to appear old. History, however, depends on written documents; unable to procure these, they are instead evolving myths.

Even so; their situation is not unique in the evolution of humanity. It is comparable with that of the Gauls and the Britons before the Roman conquest and with the state of development of the Teutonic and Slavonic peoples before they were converted to christianity. It is the situation of peoples without writing but who yet may have attained very high cultural levels in the fields of art, music, poetry and religious awareness, and whose social structure may well be highly developed. The taste for history is peculiar to the western world, yet it is not inconceivable that a spirit of nationalism could be based on the rejection of history, seeking sustenance instead in the youth and vigour of the newly independent societies. These have evolved with such breath-taking speed that, though their leaders in the main are thoroughly westernised, the mass of their peoples are not and still retain the qualities peculiar to young peoples. They might take pride in the frank recognition of this fact and so bring to the world the valour and happiness of peoples without history.

4 Ronald Robinson and John Gallagher: The Partition and Britain

Like Henry Brunschwig, Ronald Robinson and John Gallagher conclude that British participation in the partition of Africa was the result of strategic considerations arising from the British occupation of Egypt. Financial, humanitarian, and commercial interests were always present but of less influence on the official minds that made policy.

Did new, sustained or compelling impulses towards African empire arise in British politics or business during the Eighteen eighties? The evidence seems unconvincing. The late-Victorians seem to have been no keener to rule and develop Africa than their fathers. The business man saw no greater future there, except in the south; the politician was as reluctant to expand and administer a tropical African empire as the mid-Victorians had been; and plainly Parliament was no more eager to pay for it. British opinion restrained rather than prompted ministers to act in Africa. Hence they had to rely on private companies or colonial governments to act for them. It is true that African lobbies and a minority of imperialists did what they could to persuade govern-

SOURCE. Ronald Robinson and John Gallagher, with Alice Denny, *Africa and the Victorians: The Official Mind of Imperialism*, London: Macmillan & Co., 1961, pp. 462–472. Reprinted by permission of St. Martin's Press, Inc. and The Macmillan Co. of Canada, Ltd. Copyright Ronald Robinson, John Gallagher, and Alice Denny 1961.

ment to advance. Yet they were usually too weak to be decisive. Measured by the yardstick of official thinking, there was no strong political or commercial movement in Britain in favour of African acquisitions.

The priorities of policy in tropical Africa confirm this impression. West Africa seemed to offer better prospects of markets and raw materials than east Africa and the Upper Nile; yet it was upon these poorer countries that the British government concentrated its efforts. These regions of Africa which interested the British investor and merchant least, concerned ministers the most. No expansion of commerce prompted the territorial claims to Uganda, the east coast and the Nile Valley. As Mackinnon's failure showed, private enterprise was not moving in to develop them; and they were no more useful or necessary to the British industrial economy between 1880 and 1900 than they had been earlier in the century. Territorial claims here reached out far in advance of the expanding economy. Notions of pegging out colonial estates for posterity hardly entered into British calculations until the late Eighteen nineties, when it was almost too late to affect the outcome. Nor were ministers gulled by the romantic glories of ruling desert and bush. Imperialism in the wide sense of empire for empire's sake was not their motive. Their territorial claims were not made for the sake of African empire or commerce as such. They were little more than by-products of an enforced search for better security in the Mediterranean and the East. It was not the pomps or profits of governing Africa which moved the ruling *élite*, but the cold rules for national safety handed on from Pitt, Palmerston and Disraeli.

According to the grammar of the policy-makers, their advances in Africa were prompted by different interests and circumstances in different regions. Egypt was occupied because of the collapse of the Khedivial *régime*. The occupation went on because the internal crisis remained unsolved and because of French hostility which the occupation itself provoked. Britain's insistent claims in east Africa and the Nile Valley and her yielding of so much in West Africa were largely contingent upon the Egyptian occupation and the way it affected European relations. In southern Africa, imperial intervention against the Transvaal was designed above all to uphold and restore the imperial influence which economic growth, Afrikaner nationalism and the Jameson fiasco had overthrown. Imperial claims in the Rhodesias, and to a lesser extent in Nyasaland, were contingent in turn upon Cape colonial expansion and imperial attempts to offset the rise of the Transvaal. The times and circumstances in which almost all these claims and occupations were made suggest strongly that they were called forth by crises in Egypt and south Africa, rather than by positive impulses to African empire arising in Europe.

To be sure, a variety of different interests in London—some religious and humanitarian, others strictly commercial or financial, and yet others imperialist—pressed for territorial advances and were sometimes used as their agents. In West Africa, the traders called for government protection; in Uganda and Nyasaland, the missionaries and the anti-slavery groups called for annexation; in Egypt, the bondholders asked government to rescue their investments; in south Africa, philanthropists and imperialists called for more government from Whitehall, while British traders and investors were divided about the best way of looking after their interests. Ministers usually listened to their pleas only when it suited their purpose; but commercial and philanthropic agitation seldom decided which territories should be claimed or occupied or when this should be done, although their slogans were frequently used by government in its public justifications.

It is the private calculations and actions of ministers far more than their speeches which reveal the primary motives behind their advances. For all the different situations in which territory was claimed, and all the different reasons which were given to justify it, one consideration, and one alone entered into all the major decisions. In all regions north of Rhodesia, the broad imperative which decided which territory to reserve and which to renounce, was the safety of the routes to the East. It did not, of course, prompt the claiming of Nyasaland or the lower Niger. Here a reluctant government acted to protect existing fields of trading and missionary enterprise from foreign annexations. In southern Africa the extension of empire seems to have been dictated by a somewhat different imperative. Here the London government felt bound as a rule to satisfy the demands for more territory which their self-governing colonials pressed on them. Ministers did this in the hope of conserving imperial influence.

Nevertheless, the safety of the routes to India also figured prominently in the decision to uphold British supremacy in south Africa. It was the same imperative which after impelling the occupation of Egypt, prolonged it, and forced Britain to go into east Africa and the Upper Nile, while yielding in most of west Africa. As soon as territory anywhere in Africa became involved, however indirectly, in this cardinal interest, ministries passed swiftly from inaction to intervention. If the papers left by the policy-makers are to be believed, they moved into Africa, not to build a new African empire, but to protect the old empire in India. What decided when and where they would go forward was their traditional conception of world strategy.

Its principles had been distilled from a century and more of accumulated experience, from far-reaching and varied experiments in the uses of power to promote trade and in the uses of trade to promote power. Much of this experience confirmed one precept: that Britain's strength depended upon the possession of India and preponderance in the East, almost as much as it did upon the British Isles. Therefore, her position in the world hung above all upon safe communications between the two. This was a supreme interest of Victorian policy; it set the order of priorities in the Middle East and Asia, no less than in Africa, and when African situations interlocked with it, they engaged the serious and urgent attention of the British government. At the first level of analysis, the decisive motive behind late-Victorian strategy in Africa was to protect the all-important stakes in India and the East.

An essentially negative objective, it had been attained hitherto without large African possessions. Mere influence and co-operation with other Powers had been enough to safeguard strategic points in north Africa; while in south Africa control of coastal regions had sufficed. The ambition of late-Victorian ministers reached no higher than to uphold these mid-Victorian systems of security in Egypt and south Africa. They were distinguished from their predecessors only in this: that their security by influence was breaking down. In attempting to restore it by intervention and diplomacy, they incidentally marked out the ground on which a vastly extended African empire was later to arise. Nearly all the interventions appear to have been consequences, direct or indirect, of internal Egyptian or south African crises which endangered British influence and security in the world. Such an interpretation alone seems to fit the actual calculations of policy. Ministers felt frankly that they were making the best of a bad job. They were doing no more than protecting old interests in worsening circumstances. To many, the flare-up of European rivalry in Africa seemed unreasonable and even absurd; yet most of them felt driven to take part because of tantalising circumstances beyond their control. They went forward as a measure of precaution, or as a way back to the saner mid-Victorian systems of informal influence. Gloomily, they were fumbling to adjust their old strategy to a changing Africa. And the necessity arose much more from altered circumstances in Africa than from any revolution in the nature, strength or direction of British expansion.

Hence the question of motive should be formulated afresh. It is no longer the winning of a new empire in Africa which has to be explained. The question is simpler: Why could the late-Victorians after 1880 no longer rely upon influence to protect traditional interests? What forced them in the end into imperial solutions? The answer is to be found first in the nationalist crises in Africa itself, which were the work of intensifying European influences during previous decades; and only secondarily in the interlocking of these crises in Africa with rivalries in Europe. Together the two drove Britain step by step to regain by territorial claims and occupation that security which could no longer be had by influence alone. The compelling conditions for British advances in tropical Africa were first called into being, not by the German victory of 1871, nor by Leopold's interest in the Congo, nor by the petty rivalry of missionaries and merchants, nor by a rising imperialist spirit, nor even by the French occupation of Tunis in 1881—but by the collapse of the Khedivial *régime* in Egypt.

From start to finish the partition of tropical Africa was driven by the persistent crisis in Egypt. When the British entered Egypt on their own, the Scramble began; and as long as they stayed in Cairo, it continued until there was no more of Africa left to divide. Since chance and miscalculation had much to do with the way that Britain went into Egypt, it was to some extent an

accident that the partition took place when it did. But once it
had begun, Britain's over-riding purpose in Africa was security
in Egypt, the Mediterranean and the Orient. The achievement of
this security became at the same time vital and more difficult,
once the occupation of Egypt had increased the tension between
the Powers and had dragged Africa into their rivalry. In this
way the crisis in Egypt set off the Scramble, and sustained it
until the end of the century.

British advances in tropical Africa have all the appearances of
involuntary responses to emergencies arising from the decline of
Turkish authority from the Straits to the Nile. These advances
were decided by a relatively close official circle. They were
largely the work of men striving in more desperate times to keep
to the grand conceptions of world policy and the high standards
of imperial security inherited from the mid-Victorian preponderance. Their purposes in Africa were usually esoteric; and their
actions were usually inspired by notions of the world situation
and calculations of its dangers, which were peculiar to the official mind.

So much for the subjective views which swayed the British
partitioners. Plainly their preconceptions and purposes were one
of the many objective causes of the partition itself. There remain the ultimate questions: how important a cause were these
considerations of government? What were the other causes?

The answers are necessarily complicated, because they can be
found only in the interplay between government's subjective ap-
preciations and the objective emergencies. The moving causes
appear to arise from chains of diverse circumstances in Britain,
Europe, the Mediterranean, Asia and Africa itself, which interlocked in a set of unique relationships. These disparate situations,
appraised by the official mind as a connected whole, were the
products of different historical evolutions, some arising from
national growth or decay, others from European expansion
stretching as far back as the Mercantilist era. All of them were
changing at different levels at different speeds. But although
their paths were separate, they were destined to cross. There
were structural changes taking place in European industry cutting
down Britain's lead in commerce. The European balance of
power was altering. Not only the emergence of Germany, but

the alignment of France with Russia, the century-old opponent of British expansion, lessened the margins of imperial safety. National and racial feelings in Europe, in Egypt and south Africa were becoming more heated, and liberalism everywhere was on the decline. All these movements played some part in the African drama. But it seems that they were only brought to the point of imperialist action by the idiosyncratic reactions of British statesmen to internal crises in Africa. Along the Mediterranean shores, Muslim states were breaking down under European penetration. In the south, economic growth and colonial expansion were escaping from imperial control. These processes of growth or decay were moving on time scales different from that of the European expansion which was bringing them about.

By 1882 the Egyptian Khedivate had corroded and cracked after decades of European paramountcy. But economic expansion was certainly not the sufficient cause of the occupation. Hitherto, commerce and investment had gone on without the help of outright political control. The thrusts of the industrial economy into Egypt had come to a stop with Ismail's bankruptcy, and little new enterprise was to accompany British control. Although the expanding economy had helped to make a revolutionary situation in Egypt, it was not the moving interest behind the British invasion. Nor does it seem that Anglo-French rivalry or the state of the European balance precipitated the invasion. It was rather the internal nationalist reaction against a decaying government which split Britain from France and switched European rivalries into Africa.

But the cast of official thinking profoundly influenced the outcome of the emergency. Moving instinctively to protect the [Suez] Canal, the Liberals intended a Palmerstonian blow to liberate the progressives and chasten the disruptive elements in Egyptian politics. But instead of restoring their influence and then getting out, the need to bottle up anarchy and stave off the French forced them to stay on. This failure to work the mid-Victorian techniques, by coming to terms with the nationalists and finding Egyptian collaborators, meant that Indian solutions had to be applied to Egypt as well. The disenchantment of the "Guardians" was replacing the liberal faith in voluntary co-operation; and Gladstone's sympathy with oppressed nationalities was hardening into Cromer's distrust of subject races. For similar reasons, official pessimism deepened about the reliability of the Turkish bastion in the Mediterranean; and as the balance tilted against Britain in the inland sea, her rulers realised that they were in Egypt to stay. Weighing the risks of Ottoman decay and the shifts in the European balance, remembering Indian experience and distrusting Egyptian "fanatics," England's rulers pessimistically extended the search for security up the Nile to Fashoda, and from the Indian Ocean to Uganda and the Bahr-el-Ghazal.

The causes of imperial expansion in southern Africa were altogether different. It was essentially unconnected with the contemporary crisis in Egypt and its consequences in tropical Africa; it moved on a different time-scale, and the impulses behind it were separate. Unlike Egypt and tropical Africa, south Africa was to a great extent insulated from the rivalries of European Powers. Unlike them also, it was being rapidly developed by British commercial interests. The crisis which faced British governments was produced by colonial growth, and not by the decay of a native government. It arose from internal conflicts among the colonists, rather than from rivalries among the Powers. But the south African and Egyptian crises were alike in this: neither was precipitated by drastic changes in the local purposes of British expansion; but in both, the late-Victorians strained to keep up their supreme influence against a nationalist threat, and they were drawn at last into reconquering paramountcy by occupation.

South Africa was a case of colonial society receding beyond imperial control. It was also a case of economic development raising the enemies of the imperial connection to political preponderance over the colonial collaborators. By 1895 the new found commercial supremacy of the Transvaal was sustaining republicanism and threatening to draw the colonies into a United States of South Africa.

Here also the subjective appraisals of the policy-makers combined with objective situations to produce imperial advances. British aims in the south were specifically imperial, as they were not in tropical Africa. For years it had been assumed without question that south Africa must eventually turn into another

Canada. But it was not only in London that official thinking was crucial. Their special historiography had taught ministers that with self-governing colonials it was prudent to follow their friends and rash to push or thwart them. As a result throughout the south African crisis, policy had to be warped to the theorems of the British colonial party.

In 1881 Gladstone had hoped to stultify Afrikaner nationalism by conciliation, as he was to try to do in Ireland. He switched policy back to the mid-Victorian technique of resting imperial supremacy upon a responsible ministry at the Cape and indirect influence over the Boer republics. It was assumed until 1895 that British immigrants and business would engulf the republicans and strengthen the natural imperial ties of self-interest and kinship. Nationalism would be killed by kindness. So long as London kept in line with colonial opinion and Britain's collaborators were upheld, south Africa would eventually turn itself into a loyal dominion. In this belief, Colonial Secretaries from Kimberley to Ripon kept intervention to a minimum, so as to avert another war between Boer and Briton and the risk of another Ireland. Hence they went on dismantling the "Imperial Factor." But by 1896 this system of imperial influence at second hand seemed to have broken under the strain of internal conflicts. South Africa had outgrown imperial supremacy in any form; it had passed beyond the power of British influence to compose the rivalry of its separate states. As Chamberlain saw it, economic development and political catastrophe had wrecked the imperial position in south Africa. It was the Rhodesians' thesis that the Transvaal must be brought under the control of an English-speaking majority. Fearing to lose their last allies, Chamberlain and Milner became their prisoners and followed them over the edge of war. Drawn on by hopes of re-integrating the empire, hardened by the recalcitrance of Afrikaner, as of Irish nationalists, and haunted by the fear of declining national greatness, the Unionists feared that free association would no longer keep south Africa in the empire. The nostrums of the Durham Report had not worked with the nationalists of the Transvaal, as they had done with those of Quebec. South African pressure drove ministers into action as anomalous as that taken at Fashoda. Admitting that imperial supremacy over white colonies was fast becoming a fiction, they were drawn into trying to restore it in south Africa by compulsion.

There are many evidences that towards the end of the century the wearing out of well-tried devices and the emergence of so many intractable problems shocked ministers out of their self-confidence and turned them to desperate expedients. The beliefs which had inspired earlier expansion were failing. Palmerston's axioms were giving way to Salisbury's re-appraisals. Liberal values could not be exported to all with cases of Birmingham hardware. Self-government would not always travel. Some nationalisms could not be killed by kindness. The growth of communities into harmonious commercial and political partnership with Britain was not after all a law of nature. The technique of collaborating classes had not worked everywhere. And as difficulties and doubts mounted, the men presiding over the destinies of the British Empire found themselves surrounded by the Eumenides.

Why were these catastrophes overtaking them? All the processes of British expansion were reaching their peak. The metropolitan society was putting forth its strongest energies. It was at this climactic point that the social changes in its satellites were quickest and most violent. Hence it was at this time that their relations with the metropolis tended to move into crisis. The colonial communities were breaking off toward full independence; while anti-western nationalism and social upheaval were estranging the non-European partners of British interests. The effects of growth were also coming back to roost at Home. England's rulers were alarmed by the symptoms of disintegration, the demand for collectivism, the decay of the landed interest and the running sore of Ireland. The late-Victorians were confronted with nationalist upsurges in Ireland, Egypt and south Africa, and with their beginnings in India. They were losing the faith of their fathers in the power of trade and anglicisation to turn nationalists into friends and partners. They were no longer so sure as they had been that revolutionary change worked naturally and inevitably to advance British interests. And so they ceased to foster and encourage change and tended to be content to preserve the *status quo*. They became less concerned to liberate social energies abroad and concentrated on preserving authority instead.

Canning and Palmerston had known that the liberals of the world were on their side. But the late-Victorians had to find their allies more and more among Indian princes, Egyptian pashas or African paramount chiefs. Finding themselves less successful in assimilating nationalists to British purposes, their distrust of them grew. And becoming uncertain of the reliability of mere influence, they turned more often from the technique of informal control to the orthodoxies of the Indian *raj* for dealing with political anomalies and for securing their interests. They were ceasing to be a dynamic force and becoming a static power. They were more and more preoccupied throughout the world to guard what they had won; and they became less able to promote progress, as they lapsed into the cares of consolidation.

Fundamentally, the official calculations of policy behind imperial expansion in Africa were inspired by a hardening of arteries and a hardening of hearts. Over and over again, they show an obsession with security, a fixation on safeguarding the routes to the East. What stands out in that policy is its pessimism. It reflects a traumatic reaction from the hopes of mid-century; a resignation to a bleaker present; a defeatist gloss on the old texts of expansion. Perhaps at the deepest level the causes of the British share in the African partition are not found in strategic imperatives, but in the change from Canning's hopes for liberalism to Salisbury's distrust of nationalism, from Gladstone's old-fashioned concern not to turn south Africa into another Ireland, to Chamberlain's new-fangled resolve to re-forge it into another Canada.

The notion that world strategy alone was the sole determinant of British advances is superficial. For strategy is not merely a reflection of the interests which it purports to defend, it is even more the register of the hopes, the memories and neuroses which inform the strategists' picture of the world. This it is which largely decides a government's view about who may be trusted and who must be feared; whether an empire assumes an optimistic or pessimistic posture; and whether the forces of change abroad are to be fostered or opposed. Indeed any theory of imperialism grounded on the notion of a single decisive cause is too simple for the complicated historical reality of the African partition. No purely economic interpretation is wide enough, because it does not allow for the independent importance of subjective factors. Explanations based entirely on the swings of the European balance are bound to remain incomplete without reference to changes outside Europe.

Both the crises of expansion and the official mind which attempted to control them had their origins in an historical process which had begun to unfold long before the partition of Africa began. That movement was not the manifestation of some revolutionary urge to empire. Its deeper causes do not lie in the last two decades of the century. The British advance at least, was not an isolated African episode. It was the climax of a longer process of growth and decay in Africa. The new African empire was improvised by the official mind, as events made nonsense of its old historiography and hustled government into strange deviations from old lines of policy. In the widest sense, it was an off-shoot of the total processes of British expansion throughout the world and throughout the century.

How large then does the new African empire bulk in this setting? There are good reasons for regarding the mid-Victorian period as the golden age of British expansion, and the late-Victorian as an age which saw the beginnings of contraction and decline. The Palmerstonians were no more "anti-imperialist" than their successors, though they were more often able to achieve their purposes informally; and the late-Victorians were no more "imperialist" than their predecessors, though they were driven to extend imperial claims more often. To label them thus is to ignore the fact that whatever their method, they were both of set purpose engineering the expansion of Britain. Both preferred to promote trade and security without the expense of empire; but neither shrank from forward policies wherever they seemed necessary.

But their circumstances were very different. During the first three-quarters of the century, Britain enjoyed an almost effortless supremacy in the world outside Europe, thanks to her sea power and her industrial strength, and because she had little foreign rivalry to face. Thus Canning and Palmerston had a very wide freedom of action. On the one hand, they had little need to bring economically valueless regions such as tropical Africa into their formal empire for the sake of strategic security; and on the other, they were free to extend their influence and power to develop those regions best suited to contribute to Britain's strength. Until the Eighteen-eighties, British political expansion had been positive, in the sense that it went on bringing valuable areas into her orbit. That of the late-Victorians in the so-called "Age of Imperialism" was by comparison negative, both in purpose and achievement. It was largely concerned with defending the maturing inheritance of the mid-Victorian imperialism of free trade, not with opening fresh fields of substantial importance to the economy. Whereas the earlier Victorians could afford to concentrate on the extension of free trade, their successors were compelled to look above all to the preservation of what they held, since they were coming to suspect that Britain's power was not what it once had been. The early Victorians had been playing from strength. The supremacy they had built in the world had been the work of confidence and faith in the future. The African empire of their successors was the product of fear lest this great heritage should be lost in the time of troubles ahead.

Because it went far ahead of commercial expansion and imperial ambition, because its aims were essentially defensive and strategic, the movement into Africa remained superficial. The partition of tropical Africa might seem impressive on the wall maps of the Foreign Office. Yet it was at the time an empty and theoretical expansion. That British governments before 1900 did very little to pacify, administer and develop their spheres of influence and protectorates, shows once again the weakness of any commercial and imperial motives for claiming them. The partition did not accompany, it preceded the invasion of tropical Africa by the trader, the planter and the official. It was the prelude to European occupation; it was not that occupation itself. The sequence illuminates the true nature of the British movement into tropical Africa. So far from commercial expansion requiring the extension of territorial claims, it was the extension of territorial claims which in time required commercial expansion. The arguments of the so-called new imperialism were *ex post facto* justifications of advances, they were not the original reasons for making them. Ministers had publicly justified their improvisations in tropical Africa with appeals to imperial sentiment and promises of African progress. After 1900, something had to be done to fulfil these aspirations, when the spheres alloted on the map had to be made good on the ground. The same fabulous artificers who had galvanised America, Australia and Asia, had come to the last continent.

CONCLUSION

Many scholars have sought to provide a comprehensive interpretation for the partition of Africa. Unhappily, none have proved completely applicable to the complex and diverse events of the scramble, and the problem remains today to tantalize scholar and student alike in their search for meaning from the actions of soldiers and settlers in Africa and statesmen and diplomats in Europe. Why, after four hundred years of peripheral contact, did the European powers divide the continent in less than a score of years? Clearly, the earlier contacts of traders, explorers, humanitarians, and missionaries had exposed the continent to Europe and without their beginnings in Africa, further encroachment would have been improbable if not impossible. Yet the prelude to partition neither explains the sudden scramble for Africa nor provides a meaningful interpretation of it. In the search, some authors have perceived simplistic, comprehensive conclusions, the generality of which cannot be supported by the evidence. Some regard the partition as the result of nineteenth century nationalism; others think it the product of economic necessity; a few see the scramble as the result of deep-seated psychological drives. More recently, the partition has been explained as the effect of strategic requirements of empire. Although each explanation carries its own intrinsic value—indeed a few have had a profound and widespread impact—not one has been completely vindicated by the evidence.

Even before the scramble for Africa began European writers had pondered the phenomenon of overseas expansion. The English scholars, J. A. Froude and Sir John R. Seeley, the German, Friedrich Fabri, and the Frenchman, Paul Leroy-Beaulieu, considered overseas expansion as the culmination of national greatness in which colonization was the product of historical evolution, usually divinely inspired, the manifest expression of national destiny, the highest stage of nationalism.[1] Clearly, the mother country profited from colonial trade and raw materials, but the economic benefits were more the derivative advantage of colonialism than its driving force. The romantic, even mystical, expansive force of empire not only confirmed a peoples' vitality but was also the very pivot of their history, the measure of greatness that transcended any balance sheet of imperial profit and loss.

The dramatic overseas expansion in the late nineteenth century, particularly in Africa, stimulated a reassessment of European imperialism. The emphasis on nationalism as the motive for empire gave way to the iron determination of economic necessity, and the economic interpretation of imperialism has had wide appeal among those who believe that man is fundamentally dominated and driven by economic needs. Thus, Sir John Scott Keltie attributed the sudden rush for Africa to the explorations of Stanley, the activities of King Leopold, and the intrusion of Germany, but also to the need for protected markets in which to sell the overproduction of European industry and the commercial rivalry it produced sustained the scramble.[2] The first complete formulation of an economic interpretation was J. A. Hobson's *Imperialism*, which was published in 1902.[3] Hobson attributed European imperialism to the manipulations of a small group of powerful monopolists and financiers seeking more profitable investments abroad for surplus capital acquired by overproducing and underpaying workers at home. Supporting but secondary motives were the "moral and sentimental factors" that subtly combined with financial ones to press forward the cause of empire. Bitter and influential, the Hobson thesis unfortunately did not readily apply to the regions of tropical Africa and even in South Africa his economic interpretation was not confirmed by the political facts.

[1] James Anthony Froude, *Oceana; or, England and her Colonies* (New York, 1886); Sir John Robert Seeley, *The Expansion of England: Two Courses of Lectures* (London, 1891); D. Friedrich Fabri, *Bedarf Deutschland der Colonien? Eine politischökonomische Betrachtung* (Gotha, 1884); Paul Leroy-Beaulieu, *De la colonisation chez les peuples modernes* (Paris, 1882).

[2] Sir John Scott Keltie, *The Partition of Africa* (London, 1893).

[3] John Atkinson Hobson, *Imperialism: A Study* (London, 1902).

More implacable and inclusive than Hobson's *Imperialism* was
V. L. Lenin's *Imperialism, The Highest Stage of Capitalism*, which
forms the core of the Marxist interpretation of imperialism.[4]
Marx himself had few comments on overseas expansion, all of
which were made before the beginning of the partition of Africa,
some ambiguous, others embarrassing. Lenin argued that imperialism was the inevitable, final stage of capitalism, leading to
the ultimate breakdown of the capitalist system. Political partition was but the product of the need for monopolistic capitalists
to acquire outlets for profitable investment. The greatest profits
were extracted where the financiers exercised the greatest political
control. The drive for empire, or modern imperialism, was the
result of these economic needs, and economic exploitation the
product of foreign domination. Lenin's doctrine not only has had
great intellectual appeal but also has dominated the debate on
imperialism and shaped the opinions of many who have never
read his work.

The very comprehensiveness of the economic interpretation of
imperialism has produced a host of critics concerned that the
facts do not really fit the theories and who invariably offer alternative explanations for European imperialism. Thus, a well-known
economist, Joseph A. Schumpeter, regarded imperialism as an
"atavism," the result of political and social attitudes acquired
in the primitive past and transmitted into the more enlightened
present.[5] Man's aimless psychological lust for power for its own
sake and not simply economic need created European empire in
Africa. The French scholar, Henri Brunschwig, has argued that
the French occupation of Africa did indeed have the objective
of regaining the national greatness lost in Europe.[6] French imperialism in the late nineteenth century was the revival of French
nationalism in which the quest for prestige and glory was more
decisive than the interests of French merchants and financiers.
Similarly, D. K. Fieldhouse emphasizes the role of political and

[4] Vladimir Il'ich Lenin, "Imperialism: The Highest Stage of Capitalism,"
Imperialism and Imperialist War (New York, 1935).

[5] Joseph Alois Schumpeter, *Imperialism and Social Classes* (New York,
1951).

[6] Henri Brunschwig, *French Colonialism, 1871–1914* (New York, 1964).

military rivalries rather than profit in the struggle for colonies.[7]
Ronald Robinson and John Gallagher see the partition of Africa
as the result of Britain's political, or to be more precise, strategic
need to control the Suez Canal, the defense of which led to the
British occupation of Egypt and the vast basin of the Nile whose
waters were essential to Egyptian security.[8] The strategic requirements of the British empire and the psychological factors
that influenced her statesmen have provided a more defensible
explanation of British presence at Cairo, Khartoum, and Kampala
than appeals to economic inevitability. Less convincing is the
extension of this thesis to explain the partition in west and southern Africa where personal ambitions, national prestige, and economic factors outweigh strategic consideration.

Indeed, the complexities of the scramble for Africa defy a general, comprehensive interpretation. The great diversity of Africa
and its peoples, on the one hand, and the inextricable interests
and motives of the European powers, on the other, precludes any
sweeping application of a total theory to the continent as a
whole. In the end, a more meaningful and accurate understanding of the partition will be found by examining the scramble in
the disparate regions of Africa where the limits of human perception can more easily encompass the complexities of human
motivation.

[7] David K. Fieldhouse, *The Colonial Empires: A Comparative Survey from
the Eighteenth Century* (New York, 1967).

[8] Ronald Robinson and John Gallagher with Alice Denny, *Africa and the
Victorians: The Official Mind of Imperialism* (London, 1961).

SUGGESTED READINGS

The partition of Africa was as fascinating to its contemporaries as it has become for historians today. With the experiences acquired from a current knowledge of events and a confidence yet unshaken by the mass of diverse, complex evidence inaccessible at the time in the archives and government offices in Africa and Europe, the first historians of the partition wrote comprehensive, coherent accounts of the total process which no later scholar, overwhelmed by the materials, has yet attempted to emulate. Thus, Sir John Scott Keltie, *The Partition of Africa* (London, 1893), provides the most sweeping account of the scramble in which he sees the competition for markets as the fundamental cause of the partition. Sir Charles Lucas, *The Partition and Colonization of Africa* (London, 1922), covers the whole of the partition but superficially. Others, such as Sir Harry Johnston, *A History of the Colonization of Africa by Alien Races* (London, 1899), cannot stand the test of twentieth century historiography. No matter how informative, all of these contemporary writers suffer from the same disabilities: a failure to support their theories with the evidence and a preoccupation with events in Europe without appreciating the factors in Africa that conditioned the scramble.

As the documentary evidence began to emerge from the archives of Europe, the historians began to retreat before the complexity of the partition, seeking safety in Olympian discussions about imperialism in general or the comfort of approaching the partition of Africa within the framework of the diplomatic history of Europe. Thus, William L. Langer, *European Alliances and Alignments, 1871–1890* (New York, 1931), *The Diplomacy of Imperialism, 1890–1902* (New York, 1960), and A. J. P. Taylor, *The Struggle for Mastery in Europe, 1848–1918* (Oxford, 1954), all discuss the partition of Africa as an adjunct of European international relations. Miss S. E. Crowe's *The Berlin West African Conference, 1884–1885* (London, 1942), is an exercise in diplomatic history, but it is one of the few to demonstrate the significance of Africa in the deliberations of the Conference. To the students of imperialism, the partition is presented as part of that larger phenomenon in Parker T. Moon, *Imperialism and the Modern World* (New York, 1961), and more specifically but briefly by Halford Hoskins, *European Imperialism in Africa* (New York, 1931). Within the past few years, scholars have returned to the subject of imperialism equipped with the benefit of yet another generation of historical research and a willingness to reexamine old myths and new realities with uncommon vigor. David K. Fieldhouse, *The Colonial Empires* (New York, 1967) has surveyed European imperialism from the eighteenth century with critical comprehension, while in a smaller but incisive essay Raymond F. Betts, *Europe Overseas: Phases of Imperialism* (New York, 1968), discusses European imperialism with succinct observations free from the preconceptions that have bedeviled earlier historians. The same themes have been discussed in reference to Africa alone in the important work by Lewis H. Gann and Peter Duignan, *Burden of Empire: An Appraisal of Western Colonialism in Africa South of the Sahara* (New York, 1967), in which the authors reassess major assumptions that regrettably have acquired the prestige of incontrovertible doctrine.

These latest works have indeed made a great contribution to the problem of synthesizing and analyzing the complexities of the scramble for Africa into meaningful and manageable interpretations. Nevertheless, the serious student who seeks to penetrate beyond general observations and who wants to test the facts against the theories should turn to specific regions or to the role of the individual European countries in the scramble.

First in importance are the regional studies of the partition. J. D. Hargreaves' *Prelude to the Partition of West Africa* (New York, 1963), is a thorough analysis of the motives and actions of, not only the Europeans, but the Africans as well. Unfortunately, Professor Hargreaves does not carry his perceptive account beyond 1885, so that the student must revert to the histories of European enterprise in the whole of the continent to continue the story of the scramble in West Africa. C. W. Newbury's *The West Slave Coast and Its Rulers* (Oxford, 1961), is a valuable supplement to Hargreaves' more comprehensive work. On the Nile, the account of European rivalry and partition is brilliantly analyzed by G. N. Sanderson, *England,*

Europe, and the Upper Nile, 1882–1899 (Edinburgh, 1965). Detailed, lucid, majesterial, Professor Sanderson has combined a probing study of French and British policy on the Nile with full appreciation for the African factor. It is exciting history in the grand manner. The captivating tale of the continuing rivalry between King Leopold and Britain on the Upper Nile has been unraveled by Robert O. Collins, *King Leopold, England, and the Upper Nile, 1899–1909* (New Haven, 1968). The partition of East Africa has yet to find its historian. Reginald Coupland's *The Exploitation of East Africa, 1856–1890* (London, 1939), although written a generation ago, is still the most scholarly and comprehensive work in English, but like Hargreaves in the West, Coupland does not go much beyond 1886. This deficiency is largely made up by F. F. Müller, *Deutschland-Zanzibar-Ostafrika: Geschichte einer deutscher Kolonialeroberung, 1884–1890* (Berlin, 1959). John Flint's "The Wider Background to Partition and Colonial Occupation" in Roland Oliver and Gervase Mathew, *History of East Africa,* Vol. I (Oxford, 1963), is a succinct presentation of German activities and the British reaction. In southern Africa, the partition is not so much a scramble among the European powers but rather a contest between Briton and Boer. For long the classic work was that of Cornelius de Kiewet, *The Imperialist Factor in South Africa, a Study in Politics and Economics* (Cambridge, 1937), but John S. Galbraith's *Reluctant Empire: British Policy on the South African Frontier, 1834–54,* (Berkeley, 1963), is a more recent analysis of the causes for the growing antagonism between Briton and Boer and a confirmation of British aversion to expand their empire in South Africa.

National histories of imperialism in Africa are more numerous than regional works and, with but few exceptions, less useful for a meaningful understanding of the partition. One such exception is the commanding work of Ronald Robinson and John Gallagher, *Africa and the Victorians* (London, 1961), which analyzes with perception and fine writing late-Victorian policy throughout Africa in the age of partition. Although concerned principally with British policy and policymakers, the continental sweep of this work makes it the singular most important book on the partition of Africa despite the praise and blame that has been heaped upon it. German motives and activities in the scramble for Africa have been examined by numerous historians with varying interpretations. Mary E. Townsend, *The Rise and Fall of Germany's Colonial Empire* (New York, 1930); William

O. Aydelotte, *Bismarck and British Colonial Policy: The Problem of South West Africa* (Philadelphia, 1937); A. J. P. Taylor, *Germany's First Bid for Colonies* (London, 1938); Erich Eyck, *Bismarck and the German Empire* (London, 1950), all concern themselves with Bismarck's colonial policy and activities in Africa. Recently, William Roger Louis and Prosser Gifford have been contributors and editors of a collection of essays dealing with Britain and Germany in Africa (*Britain and Germany in Africa*, ed. Roger Louis and Prosser Gifford, New Haven, 1967). Despite the diversity of the essays, this work is a valuable compendium of the most recent research on Britain and Germany in Africa concluded by the comprehensive historiographical essay by Hartmut Pogge Von Strandmann and Alison Smith, "The German Empire in Africa and British Perspectives: A Historiographical Essay."

There is no adequate history of French imperialism in Africa. An older work, Stephen H. Roberts, *A History of French Colonial Policy, 1870–1925* (London, 1927), is a rather critical account of French colonialism and its economic motives. Thomas Power, *Jules Ferry and the Renaissance of French Imperialism* (New York, 1944), discusses the critical role of Ferry in the revival of French colonialism in the late nineteenth century. More provocative is Henry Brunschwig, *French Colonialism, 1871–1914* (New York, 1964), whose highly interpretive analysis of French imperialism has done much to compensate for past emphasis on the economic motives for the scramble. Finally, Jean Suret-Canale, *Afrique Noire: Occidentale et Centrale* (Paris, 1961), although primarily concerned with African civilizations in West Africa provides a provocative interpretation of the scramble in his chapters on the partition.

The driving power of Leopold II's African acquisitiveness has received widespread attention by numerous scholars. Pere A. Roeykens has been the most prolific and the most lavish in his praise of Leopold. P. A. Roeykens, *Leopold II et L'Afrique, 1855–1880* (Brussels, 1958), is a synthesis of his favorable interpretation of the King. In opposition to Roeykens is the work of Jean Stengers, whose numerous articles and reviews have presented a more balanced view of the motives and accomplishments of the King. His essay, "La place de Leopold II dans l'historie de la colonization" in *La Nouvelle Clio* (October 1950), provides a useful beginning to a study of the King. A scholarly and thorough work on the founding of the Congo Free State is R. S.

Thomson, *Fondation de L'Etat Independent du Congo* (Brussels, 1933). Ruth Slade's *King Leopold's Congo* (London, 1962), is a balanced history of the Congo Free State. Roger Anstey, *Britain and the Congo in the Nineteenth Century* (Oxford, 1962), carefully traces British policy toward the Congo, and is supplemented by the work of Sylvanus John Sodienye Cookey, *Britain and the Congo Question, 1885–1913*, (New York, 1968).

'Are you okay?' Ben asked in concern.

'Fine,' she moaned, then looked up. 'Stupid yoga!'

'Are you having a contraction?' He was assessing her; not wanting to just dive in and place his hand on her stomach, he thought he ought to introduce himself first. 'I'm Ben. I'm a doctor.'

'And I'm Celeste…' She blew out a breath and then slowly unfolded. 'And I'm not having a contraction; it's a stitch.'

'You're sure?' he pressed.

'Quite sure!'

He was suddenly slammed back into the past again—just as he was almost every day and every night, not all the time now, but surely, given that it was nearly four years on, *too* many times.

'So long as you're okay,' he clipped, and went to go.

But suddenly she was holding her swollen stomach with both hands, and blowing out a long, slow breath.

'That,' said Ben firmly, 'is *not* a stitch.'

Carol Marinelli recently filled in a form where she was asked for her job title, and was thrilled, after all these years, to be able to put down her answer as 'writer'. Then it asked what Carol did for relaxation and, after chewing her pen for a moment, Carol put down the truth—'writing'. The third question asked, 'What are your hobbies?' Well, not wanting to look obsessed or, worse still, boring, she crossed the fingers on her free hand and answered 'swimming and tennis'. But, given that the chlorine in the pool does terrible things to her highlights, and the closest she's got to a tennis racket in the last couple of years is watching the Australian Open, I'm sure you can guess the real answer!

**Carol also writes for
Mills & Boon® Modern™ Romance!**

ONE TINY MIRACLE…

BY
CAROL MARINELLI

First published in Great Britain 2009
Large Print edition 2010
Harlequin Mills & Boon Limited,
Eton House, 18-24 Paradise Road,
Richmond, Surrey TW9 1SR

© Carol Marinelli 2009

ISBN: 978 0 263 21105 4

Printed and bound in Great Britain
by CPI Antony Rowe, Chippenham, Wiltshire

ONE TINY MIRACLE...

CHAPTER ONE

A NEW DAY.

A new start.

Another one.

Walking along the beach, Ben Richardson was head down and too deep in thought to really notice the glorious pink sky over the smooth waters of Port Phillip Bay. He had been accepted for a position as Emergency Registrar at Melbourne's Bay View Hospital and would be there in a couple of hours to start his first day, only there were no first-day jitters as he made his way along the beach—after all, he'd had plenty new starts before.

This would be his fourth job in the three years

since Jennifer's death...no, it was nearly four years now. The anniversary was coming up soon and Ben was dreading it. Trying and failing not to think about it, trying and failing not to constantly think how life should be, had *they* lived. Had he stayed put at Melbourne Central, had life not changed so dramatically for him, he'd have been starting to apply for consultant positions now. But staying there hadn't been an option—there were just too many memories there for him. After six months of trying, Ben had realised that he couldn't keep working in the same place that he had once worked with his wife and had accepted, after some soul-searching, that things would never be the same again, could never be the same again. So he had moved on to Sydney—which had felt right for a while, but after eighteen months, well, that restless feeling had started again and he'd moved on to another Sydney hospital. Only it had been the same tune, just a different song. The place was great, the people too...

But it just didn't work without Jen.

So now he had returned to Melbourne, but on the outskirts this time, and it was good to be back closer to his family and amongst old friends again.

No, he wasn't nervous about this new start—the difference was that this time he was looking forward to it, ready for it, excited even by the prospect of finally moving on.

It was time.

He had decided to live by the beach and take brisk walks or jog each morning…except on day three after moving in he'd already pressed the snooze button on his alarm a few times!

Ben picked up speed, even broke into a jog, his large, muscular frame belying his deftness, and all too soon he reached his destination—the house that he had had his eye on for a couple of weeks now.

While working through his notice in Sydney, Ben had made the trip down to find a home close to the hospital. Looking online, speaking on the phone with real-estate agents, he had found several prospects to view over the weekend, determined to secure a home before he started his new job—deciding that maybe if he owned a property then he'd be more inclined to settle for longer.

The real-estate agent had been showing him a typical bachelor apartment, a new development along the beach, with gorgeous bay and City views. It was bright and airy and had all mod cons with the bonus of a huge balcony which would be nice when he had friends or family over. It had everything, really, and Ben had come close to purchasing it that day, but, standing on the balcony as the agent sorted out the documents, Ben had seen the house next door. An older house, it jutted out a touch further onto the beach than the apartment block. The garden, which had direct beach access, was an overgrown green oasis compared to the swish decking and clear-walled balcony that he'd stood on.

Instead of looking at the glorious beach, Ben had found himself gazing into his potential new neighbour's garden. A huge willow tree shaded most of it, there was a slide and swing and a trampoline, but what had really caught Ben's eye had been the boat parked along the side of the house—a man in his forties had been hosing it down and he had looked up and waved as they'd stepped out onto the balcony and Ben had given a quick nod back, only realising then that the man had actually been waving to the real-estate agent instead of himself.

'I'll be with you shortly, Doug,' the agent called, then took a seat at the well-positioned glass table, sorting out brochures and papers and finally locating the contract.

'Is it on the market, then?' Ben asked.

'Sorry?'

'The house next door—is it for sale?'

'Not yet,' the agent said with a noncommittal smile. 'Have a seat, Dr Richardson, and we'll go through the small print.'

'But is it coming onto the market?' Ben persisted.

'Perhaps. Though, really, it has none of the specifications you outlined. That house needs a lot of work, it still has the original kitchen and the garden's a jungle…' Only Ben wasn't listening and the real-estate agent suddenly had that horrible sinking feeling that he was losing his grip on his certain sale. 'The apartment complex is maintained, regularly serviced, there's the gym and lap pool for tenants,' he pointed out, pushing what he assumed were the benefits of living here for this tall, rugged-looking bear of a single guy, with the title of doctor. He had been so sure that low maintenance was the key to this sale.

He was wrong.

Ben was fast realising that high maintenance would be fantastic!

This was a garden and a house he could lose himself in, what with house repairs and oiling decking. And how about a boat…? How much better to fill up his limited spare time renovating a house or out on a boat on the bay than to be confined to modern, sleek lines of the apartment or burning off his endless energy in a lap pool? For the first time in a very long time, Ben found himself interested in something that wasn't work, and, staring at the house, he could almost glimpse a future, a real future… So, instead of closing the deal and moving into the plush apartment complex, to the agent's obvious annoyance, Ben took a gamble, put his furniture into storage and rented one of the cheap furnished units at the other end of the street, prepared to sit it out till the house came on the market.

It was win-win really, Ben thought this morning as he walked along the beach access path to the front of the house. In that short space of time, the bottom had fallen out of the housing market and the developers were having trouble selling the luxury apartments. Already the price had gone down a few thousand, so, if nothing happened with the house…

For Sale by Auction

He saw the board and gave a smile as he read that the auction wasn't far off, just a few weeks away, in fact. And there was an 'open for inspection' scheduled at the weekend. Walking back toward the beach, this time he noticed the glorious skies and the stillness of the morning, seagulls sitting like ducks on the calm water, a dog running in and chasing them away. And then he saw *her*, standing in the glassy ocean, the water to her knees, legs apart and stretching, her hands reaching for the sky. She stood still and held the position and then slowly lowered her arms.

And then did it all over again.

God! Ben rolled his eyes. He had a great physique and made a very half-hearted attempt to keep it, relying mainly on walking a thousand miles a day in Emergency then burning it off with a swim, but this new-age, welcome-the-day-type stuff, or whatever she was doing...

Please!

Still, Ben conceded there *was* something

rather spectacular about her lack of inhibition, something about her that made Ben smile as he walked.

And then she turned and his smile vanished as she bent over…doubled over, actually. Ben saw her swollen stomach and realised she was pregnant *and* visibly in pain. Picking up speed, he walked a touch more quickly along the sandy pathway and onto the beach—not wanting to overreact as maybe it was part of her exercise routine. But, no, she was walking uncomfortably out of the shallows now, still bent at an awkward angle, and Ben broke into a light jog, meeting her at the foreshore. He stared down at a mop of dark curls on the top of her head as, still bent over double, she held onto her knees.

'Are you okay?' he asked in concern.

'Fine,' she moaned, and then looked up. She had amber eyes and big silver earrings and was gritting her very white teeth. 'Stupid yoga!'

'Are you having a contraction?' He was assessing her. Not wanting to just dive in and place his hand on her stomach, he thought he ought to introduce himself first. 'I'm Ben, I'm a doctor…'

'And I'm Celeste.' She blew out a breath and then slowly unfolded. 'And I'm not having a contraction, it's a stitch.'

'You're sure?'

'Quite sure!' She stretched and winced and then rubbed the last of her stitch away. 'Stupid new-age stuff!' He couldn't help but smile and then so did she. 'According to my obstetrician, it's supposed to relax both me and the baby. It will kill us both, more like!'

He tensed, standing on the beach on a glorious warm morning, and was slammed back there again—just as he was almost every day, every night. Not all the time now but surely, given it was nearly four years on, *too* many times.

'So long as you're okay,' he clipped, and went to go, but she was holding her swollen stomach now with both hands and blowing out a long, slow breath. 'That,' Ben said firmly, 'is *not* a stitch.'

'No.' Her eyes screwed up just a touch and this

time he did place his hand on her stomach, felt the weak tightening flowing around her uterus, and held his hand there till it passed, satisfied that it was nothing more than a Braxton-Hicks' contraction.

'It's just the baby practising for its big day.' She smiled. 'Honestly, I'm fine.'

'You're positive?' he pressed.

'Absolutely.'

'If they get stronger, or start coming—'

'More regularly, I know, I know.' She gave him a very wide smile. The sun was up now and he could see her tan and her freckly face. She really did have an incredible smile... 'Well, thanks anyway,' she said.

'No problem.'

She turned to walk along the beach, in the direction he was going, and as he started to walk behind her, he half watched her to make sure she didn't stop again, but she seemed fine now. Dressed in white shorts and a white tight-fitting top, she was curves everywhere, and

Ben felt a touch awkward when her head turned around.

'I'm not following you—I live up there,' he explained.

'Good!' She slowed her pace down. 'Where?'

'In the units at the end.'

'Since when?' she asked.

'Since the weekend.'

'We're neighbours, then.' She smiled. 'I'm Celeste Mitchell, I live in Unit 3.'

'Ben, Ben Richardson—I'm at number 22."

'You're at the quiet end, then.' Celeste rolled her eyes.

'Are you sure about that?' Ben said, raising an eyebrow. 'It certainly hasn't been quiet the last two nights. Fights, parties…'

'That's nothing compared to *my* neighbours,' she retorted.

They were there now, at the row of one-bedroom units that were a bit of an eyesore in such lovely setting. No doubt one day a developer would come in and swoop up the lot of them and build a luxury complex or a hotel, but for now they were just an old and rather rundown row of units that offered cheap rental and beach access—and were filled with backpackers looking to settle for a few weeks and the occasional regular tenant, which Celeste obviously was.

As they walked past her unit, it stood out from the rest—the little strip of grass at the front had been mowed and there were pots of sunflowers in the small porch.

Clearly this was her home.

'Thanks again for your concern.' She grinned. 'And if you need a cup of sugar…'

He laughed. 'I'll know where to come.'

'I was going to say you'll have to go next door. The doctor just put me on a diet.'

He laughed again and waved goodbye. Heading up to his unit, he let himself in, put on the kettle and peered around the gloomy interior before heading for the cranky shower, wondering if it would spurt hot or cold this morning.

He hoped her flat was nicer than his. It was an

odd thought to pop into his head, but he just hoped it was, that was all. It was certainly as neat as a pin on the outside—maybe her husband had painted it. And hopefully she had nicer furniture than his landlord had provided. Still, that wouldn't make up for the noise…

Coming out of the shower, he could hear his neighbours fighting again and for Ben the auction couldn't come soon enough.

He made some coffee and smiled again as he spooned in sugar.

She didn't need to be on diet—she was curvy, yes, but she was pregnant. He thought of that lovely round bottom, wiggling up the beach in front of him, and just the image of her, so crystal clear in his memory, startled him, so that he immediately turned his mind to more practical thoughts.

Her blood glucose was probably high. She'd be around seven months or so…

He forced himself to push her out of his head, and wouldn't let himself give her another thought—till he drove out of his garage, feeling just a touch uncomfortable in his slick four-wheel drive, and saw her watering her sunflowers and waving at him.

He waved back—reluctantly. Ben didn't like waving to neighbours or, despite what he had said, dropping in for sugar, or popping over for a chat. Had she not appeared in pain, he'd have kept right on walking, have kept himself to himself—which was just how he liked things to be.

Whoosh!

As he drove past, Celeste could feel her cheeks redden even as she, oh, so casually waved.

He. Was. Gorgeous!

Gorgeous! Well over six feet and broad, his legs were as thick and as solid as an international rugby player's, and that longish brown hair flopping over his eyes as he'd stared down at her on the beach already had her wanting to run her fingers through it. As for those green eyes…why the hell didn't they have doctors like that where she worked?

Then she stopped being twenty-four and single and remembered she had sworn off men for the next decade at least. Also, she was, in a few weeks, going to be a mum.

Funny, but for a moment she'd forgotten. Talking to Ben, chatting as they'd walked, for a moment there she'd forgotten she was pregnant, had just felt like, well, a normal woman! Which she was, of course—there was nothing more womanly or normal than pregnancy. But this morning she'd been one who'd fancied and blushed and said all the wrong things in the face of a very sexy man. Celeste had assumed, though she'd neither read nor been told it, that the 'fancy' switch remained off during pregnancy—that you went into some sort of hormonal seclusion, where men were no longer attractive and you didn't flirt or even look twice. And for six months it *had* been that way...

Would stay that way, Celeste told herself firmly. Not that she needed to worry. A deft kick from her baby reminded her that she had no choice in the matter—she was hardly a candidate for romance!

CHAPTER TWO

'CELESTE, what are you doing here?' Meg, the charge nurse, shook her head as Celeste handed her a return-to-work certificate as she joined the late-shift emergency nurses to receive handover.

'I'm fine to work. I saw my obstetrician again yesterday,' Celeste explained.

Meg scanned the certificate and, sure enough, she had been declared fit, only Meg wasn't so sure. 'You were exhausted when I sent you home last week, Celeste. I was seriously worried about you.'

'I'm okay now—with my days off and a week's sick leave…' When Meg didn't look convinced Celeste relented and told her everything. 'My glucose tolerance test came in high, that's what the problem was, but I've been on a diet for ten days now, and I've been resting, doing yoga and taking walks on the beach. I feel fantastic—some people work right up to forty weeks!'

'Not in Emergency,' Meg said, 'and you're certainly not going to make it that far. How many weeks are you now?'

'Thirty,' Celeste said, 'and, as the doctor said, I'm fine.'

Which didn't give Meg any room to argue and, anyway, here wasn't the place to try. Instead she took them through the whiteboard, giving some history on each of the patients in the cubicles and areas. 'When the observation ward opens, Celeste can go round there…'

'I don't need to be in Obs,' Celeste said, guilty that they were giving her the lightest shift, but Meg fixed her with a look.

'I don't have the resources to work around your pregnancy, Celeste. If your obstetrician says that you're fine for full duties and you concur, I have to go along with that—I'm just allocating the board.'

Celeste nodded, but no matter how forcibly Meg said it, Celeste knew she was being looked out for as far as her colleagues could—and for the ten zillionth time since she'd found out she was pregnant she felt guilty.

Finding out she was pregnant had been bad enough, but the fallout had been spectacular.

Her family was no longer speaking to her, especially as she had steadfastly refused to name the father, but how could she? Having found out that not only was her *boyfriend* married but that his wife worked in Admin at the hospital she worked in, even though no one knew, would ever know, guilt and shame had left Celeste with no choice but to hand in her notice. Then, just as it had all looked hopeless, she had found out that she been accepted at the graduate emergency nursing programme at Bay View Hospital, which was on the other side of the city.

She hadn't been pregnant at the time of her application and the polite thing to do might have been to defer—perhaps that was what had been expected of her—but with such an uncertain future ahead, a monthly pay cheque was essential in the short term, and, as a clearly single mother, more qualifications wouldn't go amiss. Also, moving away from home and friends would halt the endless questions.

It was lonely, though.

And now her colleagues were having to make concessions—no matter how much they denied that they were.

'Cubicle seven is Matthew Dale, eighteen years old. A minor head injury, he tripped while jogging, no LOC. He should be discharged, Ben's seeing him now.'

'Ben?' Celeste checked.

'The new registrar. He started this morning. Here he is now...' Meg waved him over. 'What's happening with cubicle seven, Ben?'

'I'm going to keep him in. Sorry to open up the observation ward so early but...' His voice trailed off as he caught sight of Celeste, but for whatever reason he chose not to acknowledge her, just carried on giving his orders for the patient. Although she had to offer him *no* explanation as to her being here, and though there was absolutely no reason to, again, for the ten zillionth and first time, Celeste felt guilty.

Almost as if she'd been caught.

Doing what? Celeste scolded herself, as she walked round to the closed-off observation ward, flicked on the lights and then turned back a bed for Matthew.

She was earning a living—she *had* to earn a living.

She had ten weeks of pregnancy to go and the crèche wouldn't take the baby till it had had all its inoculations, so if she stopped now she wouldn't be working for almost six months.

The panic that was permanently just a moment away washed over her.

How was she going to cope?

Even working full time it was a struggle to

meet the rent. With no help from her family, she was saving for the stroller and cot and had bought some teeny, tiny baby clothes and some nappies, but there was so much more she needed. Then there was her bomb of a car…

Celeste could actually *feel* her panic rising as she faced the impossibility of it all and she willed herself to be calm, willed herself to slow her racing mind down. But that was no help either, because the second she stopped panicking all Celeste felt was exhausted.

Holding the bed sheet in her hand, she actually wanted to climb in, to lie down and pull the sheet over her head and sleep—and get fatter—and read baby magazines and feel kicks and just *rest*.

'Feeling better?' Celeste jumped at the sound of Ben's voice. 'After this morning?'

'I had a stitch,' Celeste responded just a touch too sharply. 'And, before you ask, I am quite capable of working. I'm sick of people implying that I shouldn't be here. Pregnancy isn't a disease, you know!'

'I was just being polite.' Ben gave her a slightly wide-eyed look. 'Making conversation—you know, with my neighbour?'

She'd overreacted, she knew that, and an apology was in order. 'I'm sorry—I've had a bit of trouble convincing the doctor that I'm capable of coming back to work, and I've got Meg questioning me here. I just…'

'Don't need it.'

'Exactly,' Celeste said. 'I'm hardly going to put the baby at risk.'

'Good.'

She waited for the 'but,' for him to elaborate, for the little short, sharp lecture that she seemed to be getting a lot these days, but 'good' was all he said. Well, it was all he said about her condition, anyway.

'I've booked Matthew in for a scan. He had a small vomit, and I'd rather play safe. He's a bit pale, and I'm just not happy—they should call round for him soon. I've also found a hand injury to keep you occupied…' He gave her a nice smile and handed her the notes. 'Fleur Edwards, eighty-two years of age. She's got a nasty hand laceration, probable tendon, though the surgeons won't be able to fit her in till much later tonight. Given her age, it will be under local anaesthetic, so if you can give her a light lunch and then fast her—elevation IV antis, the usual.'

'Sure.'

'Could you run a quick ECG on her, too? No rush.'

He was nice and laid-back, Celeste thought. He didn't talk down to her just because she was a grad, didn't ream off endless instructions as if she'd never looked after a head injury or hand laceration before. And, best of all, he hadn't lectured her on whether she should be here.

The observation ward was rather like a bus-stop—you were either standing or sitting around waiting, with nothing much happening for ages or everything arriving at once.

Matthew was brought around first, pale, as Ben had described, but he managed a laugh as he climbed up onto the bed as Celeste had a joke with him.

'You do know exercise is bad for you?' His mother and girlfriend had both come around to see him into the observation ward, but now he was there and settled they would be heading home. Celeste did a careful set of neurological observations, warning Matthew this would be happening on the hour, every hour. 'Whether you're asleep or not...'

She told Matthew's family about visiting and discharge times and wrote down the hospital and extension numbers for them. Just as she was about to get started on the admission paper-work, the doors opened.

'Another admission for you...' Deb, a fellow grad, was wheeling round a rather delightful Fleur—with rouged cheeks and painted on eyebrows, she was dressed in a blue and white polka-dot skirt with a smart white blouse, which unfortunately had been splattered with blood. 'Fleur Edwards, 82, a hand injury—' Deb started.

'Ben's already told me about her,' Celeste said, sensing Deb was in a rush. 'Any family?'

'Her daughter's coming in this afternoon.' They flicked through the charts. 'No allergies, she suffers with arthritis, but apart from that she seems very well…'

'I'll sort things out, then,' Celeste said, smiling over at Fleur, who was patiently sitting in a wheelchair, her arm in a sling. 'Is it getting busy out there?' she asked Deb.

'It's starting to—we've got a multi-trauma coming in.'

Though she smiled as she went over to help Fleur, Celeste was hit with a pang as Deb left, just a pang of *something*. She should be out there, would have loved to really immerse herself in this emergency programme, and though she hoped to when she came back from maternity leave, Celeste was also realistic enough to know that her head would be full of other things by then, and that she'd be exhausted for other reasons, namely the baby who was kicking at her diaphragm right now. Still, it wasn't Fleur's problem.

'Hello, Mrs Edwards.'

'Fleur.' Fleur smiled.

'I'm Celeste—I'll be looking after you this shift.'

'You should be the one being looked after.' Fleur clucked. She really was gorgeous. Widowed for twenty years, she was an independent old lady, and she had cut her hand peeling an orange for her morning snack, Celeste found out as she took her history.

'Well, for now we'll get you into a gown and into bed, so that we can elevate your hand on an IV pole. You've had something for pain—has that helped?'

'I can hardly feel it, the bandage is so tight.' Fleur said. 'Would you mind taking me over to the ladies' before I get into bed?'

'Of course.' Only at that moment Matthew sat up, with that anxious, frantic look Celeste knew all too well, and with a quick 'Won't be a moment' to Fleur she raced over, locating a kidney dish just in time and pulling the curtain around him.

'It's okay, Matthew,' she soothed. 'I'll just fetch you a wet cloth…' And run another set of obs, Celeste thought. He really was terribly pale.

'I've got to get work,' Matthew muttered. He wasn't a particularly large 18-year-old, but none the less he was trying to climb out of bed and he resisted as Celeste tried to guide him to lie back down. 'I have to get to work, I'm going to be late…'

'You're in hospital, Matthew,' Celeste said. 'You've had a bang on your head, remember?'

She was trying to reach for the call bell to summon help, worried that if he became agitated he might fall if he did get out of bed and hurt himself further, but as quickly as it had happened, Matthew seemed to remember where he was and stopped trying to climb out of bed and instead lay back down. 'Sorry.' He gave a wan smile and said it again. 'Sorry. I'm fine now.' And he seemed so, except, like Ben, Celeste was now worried.

'Matthew. Do you know where you are?'

'Hospital.'

She went through his obs—they were the same as before, his blood pressure a smudge higher, but his momentary confusion still troubled Celeste and she buzzed on the intercom. 'Can you send a doctor round to the observation ward?'

'Is it urgent?' Meg checked. 'They're just assessing a multi-trauma.' Celeste looked over at Matthew's pale but relaxed face and wavered for a moment. He seemed absolutely fine now and his obs were stable but, still, she just wasn't sure.

'I need the head injury assessed again,' she said, thinking it was likely Meg was rolling her eyes now. 'Let Ben know—he saw him.' She headed back to Matthew and Fleur gave a worried nod when Celeste said, 'I'll be with you soon.'

'Look after him!' the old lady said. 'Don't worry about me.'

Of course, by the time Ben arrived Matthew

was sitting up and joking about his moment of confusion and refusing the oxygen that Celeste was trying to give him. 'Look, I'm sorry to pull you away,' she told Ben.

'No problem. The trauma team is with the patient and he's actually not that bad. So what's going on with Matthew?'

'Nothing!' Matthew said and it certainly looked that way.

'He was fine,' Celeste explained. 'In fact, he seems fine now, but he had a vomit a little earlier and was certainly confused and restless for a moment. He didn't look at all well—' She was trying to think up reasons to justify pulling a registrar out from an emergency, but Ben quickly interrupted.

'I agree.'

He didn't seem remotely annoyed that she had called him. Instead, he was checking Matthew's pupils and his blood pressure for himself as Celeste explained that he had tried to climb out of bed, insisting he had to get to work.

'How are you feeling, Matthew?'

'Fine. Well, a bit of a headache...'

'Okay,' Ben said, 'I'm just going to lay you flat and have a good look at you.' It was Ben who never got to finish this time as Matthew started to retch again, his face more grey than pale now, and he was moaning loudly about a pain in his head.

'How do you get urgent help around here?' Ben asked, and it was only then that Celeste remembered that it was his first day here—he seemed so assured and competent. He was also a lot bigger than Matthew. He ignored the patient's protests to push off the oxygen mask and attempts to climb out of bed as Celeste pressed the switch on the wall. The light flashed above the door like a strobe as one of the team came to the intercom and Celeste explained what was happening.

The trauma team was still with the multi-trauma, so it was Belinda Hamilton, the rather snooty but exceptionally good-looking senior emergency registrar who came, along with Meg and a porter to get the patient to Resus if required. Had Matthew still been on a gurney it would have been easier to wheel him straight to Resus, but time was of the essence and the observation ward was set up, like any other ward, for such an emergency, so instead Celeste wheeled over the crash trolley. Matthew was like a tethered bull now, and it was Ben doing the tethering as he rapidly explained what had occurred to his senior. But he didn't await her verdict, just told her what was required. 'He needs to intubated and sent for a scan,' Ben said. 'Can you alert the neuro surgeons?'

Celeste was busy opening packs for the intubation, her heart hammering in her chest, stunned at how quickly Matthew had deteriorated.

Though Meg had also come to assist, she didn't take over, just guided and advised Celeste, who was setting up for the intubation. Raji, the anaesthetist, arrived just as Matthew started seizing, his body jerking violently. The whole thing was horrible. In a matter of moments Matthew's condition had become critical—his family would have barely made it to the car park.

Raji was shooting drugs into the patient as Ben gave him the lowdown and thankfully the jerking stopped. Matthew was taking long, laboured breaths, but at least he wasn't seizing or fighting any more, though Celeste could feel her blood pounding, surely up near Matthew's as she wrestled to remove the bedhead to give Raji more access to the patient's airway.

'Here.' Ben must have seen her struggle and removed the bedhead easily for her. Raji was a pleasure to work with, a laid-back guy who really just got on with things, checking all the drugs she had prepared and pulling up for himself the others he required. Matthew was on a cardiac monitor, the seizing had stopped, but he was gravely ill and as Celeste watched Raji intubate the patient, Meg liaised with the porters and Imaging.

'Should we let his family know?' Celeste asked. 'They only just left.'

'Let's just worry about the patient for now,' Belinda snapped, and Celeste felt herself redden.

'I'll call them as soon as I can,' Ben said. 'He'll probably go straight up to Theatre from Imaging.'

It took ten, maybe fifteen minutes at the most before Matthew was paralysed and intubated and on a trolley, being wheeled up to Imaging and probably then on to Theatre. All that was left from his time in the obs ward was a mountain of paperwork and a lot of chaos. The suction equipment was still on and gurgling, and would need cleaning, the oxygen tubing and masks would need replacing; the bedhead was abandoned on the other side of the room, there were packs open everywhere. The crash cart was in chaos and there were syringes and vials on its surface. Everything would need to be tidied and checked and replaced and then checked again.

'So much for giving you a quiet afternoon!'

Meg gave her a sympathetic smile, but her pager went off, and there really was no chance of her staying to help.

Letting out a long breath, forcing herself to just get on with it, Celeste turned around and saw Fleur's worried face.

'Will he be okay?' she asked worriedly.

'I think so,' Celeste said, and came over, her heart sinking as the proud, dignified lady burst into tears and said sorry over and over.

'I've wet my pants!'

'I'm so sorry!' It was Celeste saying it to Fleur now. 'It was my fault for not taking you.'

Ben was at the desk ringing the unfortunate family to tell them what had happened to Matthew, and Celeste and Fleur were in the bathroom. Fleur's wet clothes were off and her hand was wrapped in plastic and elevated on an IV pole, with the old lady sitting in a little shower chair.

'Let's both stop saying sorry, shall we?' A lot

older and a lot wiser, Fleur caught Celeste's eyes and smiled. 'You could hardly leave the young man, could you?'

'I know.'

'I just don't want my daughter to know that I've had an accident—she'll be in soon, and she'll think I'm losing my faculties.'

'Of course you're not!' Celeste exclaimed. Still, she'd have been embarrassed too, so she came up with a plan. 'Why don't I rinse out your clothes?' Celeste suggested. 'They're covered in blood anyway. I'll tell your daughter that's why I washed them.'

'What about my knickers?'

'I'll wash them and hang them by the vent.' A little bit ditzy at times, Celeste could also be very practical. 'They'll be dry by the end of my shift—no one will ever know.'

'You're very kind.'

Not really, Celeste thought. Anyone should do it. She still winced when nurses stuffed filthy clothes into bags for relatives, wondering how they'd like it. Still, she couldn't change the world, only her own actions. So she filled a sink with water…

'Cold water for blood,' Fleur prompted, and Celeste did as she was told then set about showering her patient. Firm friends now, Celeste smiled when Fleur asked what was surely a rare favour. 'Would you mind giving my back an good wash?' she asked. 'I can never reach it.'

'Of course.' Fleur's back was indeed grubby from, most likely, years of neglect, as her arthritis simply wouldn't allow her arms to reach it.

'I bought a brush from the chemist,' Fleur said as Celeste gave it a good scrub. 'You know, on a long stick, but I still can't get there.' So Celeste took her time to wash it as thoroughly as she could, wondering how best to approach this proud lady.

'You'll be needing some help with your hand out of action…'

'I will not!' Fleur said, as Celeste wrapped her in towels. 'I'll manage fine with one hand.'

'You probably will,' Celeste said, 'but there are so many aids, like hand-held showers, and there are brushes for your back but with curved sticks. I'm not sure of all the things that could help, but maybe we could get you assessed.'

'I like my independence.'

'Well, this will help you keep your independence.' Celeste shrugged. 'You may as well while you're here… Have a think about it.'

Fleur was right, Ben thought. Sitting at the desk for a moment, having made a very difficult call to Matthew's mother and not ready to head back out there, he'd overheard the conversation between the two women. Celeste *was* kind, very kind indeed.

It was so easy to become hard working in Emergency—he'd seen it happen to so many colleagues. It was necessary almost if you wanted to survive in this area. He had become hardened too—switched off on certain occasions, because at times it was easier to deal with a patient than a person, kinder to yourself not to think about a family and friends and futures that were being obliterated, to just get on with the job in hand, rather than look at the bigger picture. But watching Celeste wheel out a smiling Fleur, all powdered and warm and well looked after, Ben was a mite conflicted.

Because pregnancy was his *thing*. One of his many *things* if he actually stopped and thought about it, which he tried very hard not to do.

Most people had one—Belinda had just told him on the walk back from Imaging how her younger brother had almost died from a head injury. The staff hadn't noticed his deterioration and it had been Belinda herself who had recognised the signs when she had come to visit. Yes, they all had their *things*. And pregnancy was Ben's—the one thing where he just had to detach and deal with a foetus rather than a baby, look at a set of numbers instead of the person.

He didn't want to be hard, didn't want to be bitter—except he was.

Yet watching Celeste rub her back after helping

Fleur into bed, reluctantly watching the shape of her pregnant belly, he resisted the urge to just walk away, to shrug his shoulders and let her get on with it. She wasn't a nurse, or a set of numbers, or a pregnant woman, she was Celeste, who was kind and tired and had had a difficult start to her shift and a lot of mess to clean up.

'I've spoken to Matthew's family...' As he chatted to her, he lifted the metal bedhead from the floor and replaced it, then easily dragged the portable oxygen cylinder back to its spot—just doing a couple of little things that he didn't need to, in the same way Celeste had done for Fleur, only she could never know the effort behind his easy gestures, because being around her was becoming unbearable for Ben. 'They're on their way back. I've told them to come to the front desk, but if they arrive here, just give me a buzz.'

'I will.' She pulled over a linen skip and stripped the bed. 'Do you think he'll be okay?'

'He'll be in Theatre by now,' Ben said, 'so, hopefully, yes. I'll let you know when I hear.'

Her quiet shift was anything but. By the time it came to a close the crash cart was checked and put away, the eight beds had been filled with patients, Fleur had agreed to a visit from Occupational Therapy and now that visiting time was over, the ward was actually neat and in order—at least the night nurse should have a quiet shift!

'Thank you, Celeste.' Fleur smiled as Celeste helped her into clean, dry undies before she headed off home. 'For all your care and for washing out my clothes—my daughter never suspected a thing.'

'That's good. Theatre just called and it shouldn't be too much longer till they're ready for you.'

'And I'll just stay in for one night?'

'If all goes smoothly, which I'm sure it will. I'll see you in the morning.' Celeste smiled. 'I'm back on at seven.'

'You work too hard,' Fleur fussed. 'I know it's what you girls do now. Still, I hope your young man's at home with dinner waiting so you can put your feet up.'

'I shall!' Celeste smiled and then blushed as she realised that Ben had come in. ''Night, Fleur.' She walked over to Ben. 'I don't want her worrying.'

'Sorry?'

Celeste hurried to explain. 'Well, it's just easier to sometimes let people think that there is a Mr Mitchell at home…' Her blush darkened as it was only then she realised Ben would have neither known nor cared that she had just been caught fibbing to Fleur. 'Have you heard anything about Matthew?'

'That's what I was coming to tell you about. I'm heading home, so I just rang ICU. I didn't get a chance till now. Apparently his pupil blew in Imaging. They got him straight up to theatre and evacuated a massive subdural hae-matoma—so I came to say well done. It was a good pick-up—a lot of people might have hesi-tated seeing as his symptoms were so fleeting.'

'How is he now?' Celeste asked, warming at his praise. Matthew's brain had been bleeding, the pressure building inside his skull, causing his symptoms. It was the scary thing about seemingly benign head injuries—and the reason patients were often admitted for observation afterwards. She had read about it, studied it, learnt about it, but now she had witnessed it for herself. The *chore* of regular neuro obs would never be considered a chore again.

'On ICU. It will be a good forty-eight hours before we know anything, but there is hope…'

Which was always nice.

She handed over her patients and headed for home in a car that was making more new and rather worrying noises. She slowed down at the gates and indicated left for the block of units. She climbed out of the car, leaving it idling, too worried to turn off the engine, because one day it surely wouldn't start again! Absolutely bone weary, she opened the gates and then realised someone had pulled up behind her.

'I'll close them,' Ben called out, which he did, and she drove another hundred yards and then pulled on her handbrake and climbed out of her idling car again to open the garage, because the landlord was too mean to put in automatic doors.

'I'll get that.' He walked over from the gates and made light work of the garage door, and even waited till she had driven inside and closed it for her as she walked out.

Which didn't sound like much, but every stretch was one less stretch that she had to do and she was so tired that all she was was grateful.

'Thanks for that.' Celeste was too weary to even summon a smile.

'No problem,' Ben called, heading back to his own car to repeat the ritual for his own garage. And still he didn't deliver a lecture. Still didn't check that she was okay, or ask if she was sure she should be working.

Had he asked, Celeste thought, as she let herself into her little unit, she might just have burst into tears.

She had to eat, but she was too tired to cook, so she had a bowl of cereal instead.

Then a very quick shower. Knowing she'd

regret it if she didn't, she put out a fresh uniform for the morning, checked her alarm and slipped into bed, too tired to worry, too worn out for tears or even to think really.

She had to be back there tomorrow at ten to seven!

CHAPTER THREE

BEN didn't worry.

He was concerned for his patients at times, but he didn't do worrying.

The worst day of his life had happened a long time ago and he knew things could never be that bad again, so consequently he just got on with things, didn't fret or dwell—or, well, worry!

He hadn't in years.

Yet there was this niggle now and, no matter how he tried to ignore it, still it persisted.

His second day at Bay View Hospital and the floodgates had opened.

One drowning had been brought in as well as victims of a multiple pile-up on the beach road. It was over forty degrees and people were collapsing everywhere. It was just one of those days where everyone ran to keep up and everyone worked up to and beyond their limits.

Including Celeste.

He could see her ankles swelling as the shift progressed, see her blow out of her mouth and onto her red face as she stripped yet another trolley and prepared it for the endless list of recipients, could see the *effort* in her movements, and then finally the sheer relief on her face at 3:30 p.m. when her shift ended. As he watched her waddle out, like it or not, Ben *was* worried.

'What are you doing tonight?' Belinda was tapping away on the computer. In her late thirties, and absolutely stunning, she was also witty. With a tumble of black hair, she had almond-shaped brown eyes, full red lips, and dressed like she'd stepped out of a magazine. Thankfully, *very* thankfully, Ben didn't fancy her a jot, which meant there was no trouble sharing a tiny office and they could chat easily about things—which they did as Ben wound up his day and packed up his briefcase. It was only his second day and already paperwork was starting to pile up.

'I'm stopping in at the real-estate agent's, then the deli to buy salad and chicken instead of a burger and then...' Ben thought about it '...I will *make* myself go for a jog this evening. What about you?'

'I'll show you...' She gave a wicked smile. 'Come here.'

Curious, Ben walked over and looked at the screen and stared at the image of a rather ordinary-looking guy.

'A GP, late thirties, has children but doesn't want to involve them yet...'

'Sorry?' Ben had no idea what she was going on about.

"That's good,' Belinda said. 'The last one I saw brought his children along on the second date! We've chatted on the phone,' Belinda explained to a bemused Ben, 'and he seems great—we're meeting for coffee tonight.'

'You're going on a *date* with him?'

'Coffee.' Belinda laughed. 'You should try it—you'd be a hit!'

Ben shook his head. 'Internet dating isn't for me.'

'Don't knock it till you try it.'

'Be careful.' Ben frowned. 'Shouldn't you go with someone when you meet him? He could be anyone!'

'He's who he says is.' Belinda winked. 'I've checked his registration.'

'Well, good luck.'

The real-estate agent was being nice to him again—there had been a little bit of initial sulking when Ben hadn't bought the apartment, but he'd obviously got over it and he was Ben's new best friend again now that he had a genuine prospective client for the house.

'Can I have a look around?' Ben asked.

'Not till the "open for inspection" at the weekend,' the agent said. 'After that, I can arrange a private inspection for you.'

'I'm actually working this weekend,' Ben said, 'so don't worry about it.'

'You will come and have a look, though?' the agent said anxiously.

'Like I said...' Ben shrugged '...I'm working—but it's really no problem. I'm actually going to look at another house tonight.'

That soon got him on the phone! A private inspection was arranged within the hour and Ben wandered through the house he was seriously thinking of calling home. It did need a lot of work—the kitchen was a bomb and the down-stairs bathroom would need to be ripped out, but the master bedroom had already been renovated, with floor-to-ceiling windows that took in the bay view and a fantastic en suite that did the same.

Yes, it was way too big for one, but it just felt right.

He could renovate it, Ben thought, take his time, pull out the kitchen, do up the back garden... Standing in the master bedroom, staring out at the bay, Ben felt the first breeze of contentment he had in years, the first, the very first glimmer of how finally coming home should feel.

Despite his nonchalance with the agent, despite the shake of his head when he found out the reserve price and that the vendor wanted a quick settlement, he was just playing the necessary game. For Ben, the auction couldn't come soon enough.

A wall of heat hit him as Ben opened the door to his unit. He opened the windows, turned on a fan and put his dinner in the fridge then peeled off his clothes and hoped that the shower ran cold this evening—which thankfully it did.

After showering, he pulled on some shorts and nothing else, then headed for the kitchen. Suddenly, out of the blue, there was this sort of long groan as everything ground to a halt.

It had been happening all over Melbourne— the power outages every evening as the lucky people who had air-conditioning selfishly cranked it up to full. Ben just had a fan—which now, of course, wasn't working.

He went outside to check the power box, just in case it was only him, and glancing down the row of units he saw Celeste checking her power box too.

She was in lilac shorts this time, and a black singlet. Her hair was wet and she looked thoroughly fed up.

'Again!' She rolled her eyes, gave him a brief wave and headed back into what would surely soon be a furnace—unlike his unit, Celeste's got the full questionable glory of the afternoon sun.

And that was when that niggle hit him again— an unfamiliar, long-forgotten feeling that gnawed at his stomach as he pulled open the dark fridge and pulled out the plastic containers he had got from the deli—a strange niggle of worry for someone else.

Ben didn't want neighbours who dropped in on him and he had certainly never thought he'd be a neighbour who did just that—but there he was on her doorstep. She had come to the door holding a bowl of cereal and was clearly irritated at the intrusion but trying to be polite.

'The electricity should come back on in a couple of hours—it's been happening a lot lately,' Celeste said, and went to close the door. She wasn't actually irritated with him and didn't mean to be rude, she was just trying not to notice he was wearing only shorts. Which was normal, of course, in the middle of a heat wave. Had he knocked just two minutes later, she'd have had to put her top back on herself before answering the door!

The sight of all his exposed skin made her own turn pink, though, and she didn't want him to notice!

'Have you had dinner?' he said to the closing door, and she paused, glancing guiltily down at the bowl of cereal—which was probably not the best dinner for a heavily pregnant woman and she was instantly on the defensive. 'I can hardly cook with no electricity.'

'No need to—I've got plenty.' He held up the dishes to tempt her. 'Let's go and eat on the beach—it will be cooler there.'

It was. There was a lovely southerly breeze sweeping in and Celeste walked in the shallows. Ben could practically hear the sizzle as her hot, swollen, red ankles hit the water.

'I should have come down earlier.' Celeste sighed in relief. 'I keep meaning to, I mean, I'm so glad I did when I get here…'

'I'm the same.' Ben smiled, and it was so nice after such a busy day to just walk and say not much, to watch the dogs and the boats and the couples—to just *be*.

And then to sit.

Chicken in tarragon and mayonnaise, with a crisp Greek salad, was certainly nicer than cereal, and washed down with fresh fruit salad, it was bordering on the healthiest dinner of her pregnancy. The baby gave an appreciative kick as she sank down onto her back.

'That was yum—thank you!'

'You're welcome.' Ben gave a small uncomfortable swallow. 'Look, I'm sorry if I dismissed you a bit at work.'

'You didn't.' Celeste frowned.

'I did,' Ben said, 'or rather I didn't let on that we'd already met.'

'That's okay.'

'I just like to keep work separate...'

'That's fine,' Celeste said. 'This evening never happened.' She turned and smiled at him where he still sat. 'How are you enjoying your new job?'

'It's good.' Ben nodded.

'You were in Sydney before?' Celeste checked because she'd heard Meg say so.

'Yes.' Ben didn't elaborate. 'How long have you worked there?'

She didn't reply for a moment as she was busy settling herself back on the sand, closing her eyes in sheer pleasure. 'Nearly three months.' One eye peeked open. 'I don't think they were particularly thrilled when I turned up for my first shift.'

Thankfully he wasn't so politically correct that he pretended to have no idea what she was talking about. Instead, he just grinned and Celeste closed that eye and finally, finally, finally she relaxed.

'God, this feels nice,' she sighed after five minutes of lovely comfortable silence.

And it also looked nice, Ben thought, it looked very nice indeed. Her lashes were fanning her cheeks, her knees were up, and her stomach was sort of wriggling of its own accord—like Jennifer's had, Ben thought, and then abruptly stopped that thought process.

'So there is no Mr Mitchell?' he asked.

'Nope.' Her eyes were still closed.

'Do you see him at all, the father of your baby?'

'Nope.'

'Does he know?' Ben asked, even though it was none of his business. 'I mean, is he helping you out?'

'He thought he was,' Celeste said. 'He gave me money to have an abortion.'

'Oh.' Ben stared down at her.

'I was on my maternity rotation at the time I found out I was pregnant, babies everywhere—not that it made me want one, it terrified me actually, but...'

'You don't have to say anything else if you don't want to.'

But she did want to—lying there with her eyes closed, lost and lonely and really, really confused. Maybe, as everyone said it would, talking might help clear her head. It was worth a try, anyway, because yoga certainly hadn't worked!

'He's married.' She opened her eyes then and closed them—and even in that teeny space of time she saw *it* pass over his features. That moment where you were judged, where opinions were cast, where assumptions were made. 'I didn't know that he was, not that that changes anything.'

'Did you go out for long?' he wanted to know.

'Three months.' Celeste sniffed. 'He was my first real...I just believed him. I mean, I knew why we didn't go out much, and why we couldn't go to each other's homes…'

'Sorry?'

'It doesn't matter,' she muttered.

'So where did you go out?'

'For drives, for dinner, to a hotel sometimes…' She gazed up into his clear green eyes. 'He's a bit older than me, quite a bit older actually,' Celeste said, and then she was silent for a while.

Rightly or wrongly, he did judge—he tried not to, but he did.

Why didn't people think? Why were people so careless?

And now there was this baby…

He closed his eyes and thought of Jennifer—of the plans they had put in place, how much they had wanted a baby, and though he didn't say a word, she could feel his disapproval.

'So you've never made a mistake?' she said defensively.

'I've made plenty,' he admitted.

'But no affairs, nothing you regret.'

'Oh, there's a lot that I regret,' Ben said.

'You're single, divorced...?' It sounded like the questionnaire on Belinda's dating site, and he winced inwardly.

'Widowed,' he said, and it was her turn to judge, Ben knew—he had been through it many times before.

'Do you miss her a lot?' she asked gently.

'Yep,' Ben admitted, and that was enough. He ran some sand through his hands, concentrated on the little grains instead of himself then glanced at his watch. 'The power must be back on by now.'

'So what if it is?' Celeste smiled. 'I'm enjoying talking—you were saying how much you miss her?'

God, she was persistent. Really, he should stand up and leave, but she'd said so much about herself and, picking up another handful of sand, he let it run through his closed fist, and admitted some of his truth. 'I miss it for Jennifer too.' Her silence was patient. 'She loved living.' He looked out to the water and could almost see her, blonde ponytail flying as she jogged. 'She'd be out there running or swimming now—cramming some exercise in after work.'

'Was she fit?'

'Very.' Ben nodded, but there was this savage rip of thought there because, despite doing everything right, despite her healthy lifestyle, it hadn't counted for anything in the end.

'What did she do?'

'She was a doctor as well—in Emergency.'

'What happened?' Celeste asked, but Ben shook his head, not willing to go there. 'Come on.' It really was time to go now, and not just because he didn't want to talk about it. He was doing her a favour. A woman in Celeste's condition really didn't need to hear about how Jen had died. So he held her hands and heaved her up and they walked back slowly, idly chatting about not very much at all, till Celeste wormed her way back in again.

'Have you dated again—I mean since…?'

'She died three, nearly four years ago,' Ben said, answering the unspoken question.

'Oh.'

'A bit.' He gave a shrug. 'Though it was probably too soon.'

'Are you still comparing them to her?' Celeste asked, boldly striding in where no one else really dared to go, but Ben just ignored her question and, glad of the diversion, opened the gates to the units, but Celeste stood patiently waiting.

'Are you?' she asked.

'Sorry?'

'Comparing them?'

She was a persistent little thing, like a little woodpecker, peck, peck pecking away—

'I used to,' Ben admitted. 'But not now—that's not fair on anyone.'

'Especially as she sounds like Superwoman,' Celeste grumbled, and her response was so refreshing Ben actually smiled. 'So,' she pushed, 'are you ready now?'

'Perhaps, though not anything serious.'

'Ooh, I'm sure there'll be plenty of takers.' Celeste grinned. After all, she'd heard the giggles and gossip in the staffroom—Ben could take his pick!

'What about you?' They were sitting on her steps now, the conversation, and the friendship, too new, too fragile to snap it by asking him in. And anyway the power was still off, so they sat on the steps and got to know each other just a little bit better.

'I'm hardly in a position to date.' Celeste rolled her eyes. 'Can you imagine me out clubbing?'

'I guess not!'

'And I'm still in that "all men are snakes" place.'

'It's probably a very wise place to be right now,' Ben agreed. 'I've been a bit of a snake myself lately.'

'Do tell!' She did make him laugh, she was so eager for gossip, and so easy to talk to, that somehow he did.

'I went out with someone for a while—she

was great, but even though I told her from the start—'

'She didn't listen?' she finished for him.

'She did at first, said she wanted the same thing—then, well, it got a bit more serious. She started to hint at wanting different things.' He looked into her smiling amber eyes. 'Like moving in.'

'Not for you?' she said wisely.

'Maybe one day, but she also started talking about children. And one thing I do know is that I don't want kids.'

'Never?'

'Never,' he said emphatically.

She got the message and was actually rather grateful for it. Oh, they hardly knew each other, had barely scratched the surface, but there was certainly if not an immediate attraction then at the very least an acute awareness. Which was something she hadn't felt in the longest time— had been sure, after the way Dean had treated her, that she'd never feel it again. But sitting here, looking into Ben's green eyes, hearing his words, Celeste suddenly realised that he felt it too. That he was carefully reading out the rules of any potential relationship should they choose to pursue one.

'We couldn't be less suited really,' Celeste said after a moment's pause. 'I'm not looking at all, you're not looking for serious and…' she patted her large stomach '…this isn't a hernia!'

'I had worked that out!' Ben smiled. 'So how about we just be friends?'

She stared into his green eyes and this time she didn't blush. Oh, she had a teeny crush on him—what heterosexual woman wouldn't?—but her heart was way too bruised and her ego far too raw and her soul just too tender to even fathom going there again. It was simply nice to have an adult to talk to. Her world had changed so much, and with her family not talking to her and her struggle to fit in on her new course, it was just nice, very nice to have Ben in her life, to talk to a person instead of staring at the television. 'A friend would be lovely.'

And still he stayed. Celeste went in and brought out two glasses of water, and then picked at daisies as they chatted, shredding them with her fingers, joining them up, and when she wasn't looking at him, somehow it made it easier for Ben to talk.

'You see, I had it all with Jen…' He pushed his fingers through his hair, tried to sum up how he was feeling, because she was so easy to talk to. Maybe because she hadn't known Jen, maybe because her eyes didn't well up with tears as friends' and family's did when he spoke about her, or flinch in tiny reproach at his sometimes bungling efforts to try and move on with his life. 'I don't want to try to re-create it—I don't want to do it again with someone else. I've already been there and done it.'

'Lucky you, then.' Ben blinked at her response. Really, he felt anything but lucky, but he supposed that, yes, she was right, he had been lucky to have Jen in his life for a while.

'I'd give anything to be able to say to this little one that its dad and I were in love.'

'Were you?' Ben asked.

'I thought so.' She shrugged. 'But looking back it was just infatuation, I guess—it sounds like you had the real thing.'

He didn't answer, because at that moment her television started blaring through the window, a cheer coming from the unit opposite as the power kicked back in.

'I'm going to do some work…' Ben stood up.

'Well, thank you for dinner…' Celeste smiled '…and a thank-you from the baby too.'

'You're very welcome.'

'I'd offer to return the favour, only I'm having enough trouble rustling up dinner for one at the moment,' she said wryly.

'I don't expect you to.'

He didn't expect her to. Celeste knew that and so too did Ben.

But next night when he came home from work

he could see pots of sunflowers on his doorstep, her way of saying thank you, he guessed.

'I have some good news for you,' Ben said as he knocked on her door.

'I could do with some. Come in,' she invited.

'Matthew was extubated this evening,' Ben explained as he followed her into her tiny kitchen. 'He's doing really well—they're hoping to move him from ICU in the morning.'

That *was* good news!

'It could have been a very different story. I've had Belinda patting me on the back and the neuro consultant even came down to Emergency to say well done. I have told them that the credit goes to you.' He watched her face pink up with his praise. 'I know it's tough deciding whether to wait and see or call for help.'

'It can be,' Celeste admitted, as she pulled a vast jug of iced tea from the fridge and poured them both a long glass. 'I mean, you don't want to look like an idiot or that you're overreacting to everything…'

'Overreact!' Ben said simply. 'For now at least—until you've got more experience and your hunch button's working properly.'

'Hunch button?' Celeste frowned at the unfamiliar term. 'What's that?'

'When you have a hunch about something, when you're almost sure but not quite.'

She'd already worked out what he meant even before he explained it, but as he did explain it, she felt that glow in her cheeks darken just a touch, aware that he wasn't quite meeting her eyes. Her hunch button was tapping away, but for different reasons now, and she flicked it off quickly.

She was so not going to develop a crush on *another* man from work!

Look where that had got her!

And it *was* nice to have a friend.

They sat in her little living room, watching the 'weigh-in' on her favourite show, Celeste grumbling that she should be a contestant. Ben was more than a touch uncomfortable and trying not to show it—he could see the little pile of baby clothes all neatly folded on the ironing board and even though it was weeks away, there was a slight baby smell to the house—which probably had something to do with the baby lotion Celeste was rubbing into her hands, but still... So he went to get the jug of iced tea and when he came back, he poured her one into the glass she was holding, and he wouldn't have been human if he hadn't noticed her cleavage—would have to be blind to miss it actually, only Ben wasn't usually a breast man. Except that they were so jiggly and voluptuous that he was suddenly kneed in the groin with an unfamiliar longing.

So he sat down. He realised he couldn't smell that baby smell any more, just the unsettling scent of Celeste. The room was too hot, so of course she kept lifting up her arms and coiling her hair onto the top of her head as she chatted away, and then it would tumble down again, and she'd lift her arms once more.

'I'd better go...'

'Already?' Celeste said, but then they got

talking, oh, just about this and that, and suddenly it was after ten. As he stood at the door to really go this time, Celeste found herself thinking that she'd had the nicest night in a long time.

Too nice, even.

Because of all the stupid things to be thinking, she was wondering what it would be like to be kissed goodnight by him.

Wondering what she'd do if that lovely mouth came a little bit closer.

'Thanks for the flowers, by the way.' Ben broke into her thoughts. 'You shouldn't have done that.'

'It's no problem.'

'No, you really shouldn't have done that.' Ben grinned. 'They'll be dead in two days—I'll forget to water them.'

'I won't.' Celeste smiled. 'Just enjoy.'

It was a relief to close the door on him!

CHAPTER FOUR

THEY ignored each other at work, of course.

Well, they didn't mention their evenings by the television or walks on the beach and sometimes as she sat in the staffroom and listened as Deb rattled on about how sure she was that Ben was going to ask her out (when Ben had already told her that he was embarrassed by Deb's constant flirting), or when the gorgeous Belinda started talking rather too warmly about him, though Celeste sat like a contended Buddha, inside she was fuming and could have cheerfully strangled them quiet.

She liked him.

Which was okay and everything. After all, half the department liked him in that way too, she was hardly in a minority—no, there was a slightly bigger problem than that.

Sometimes, *sometimes* she got that nervous fluttering feeling, which could only be generated by two.

Sometimes, *sometimes* she got this fleeting glimpse that Ben liked her too.

She told herself she was imagining it—as surely as Deb was. Because there was no way Ben could possibly be interested in her.

So why was he acting so strangely?

Coffee break over, she headed back to Cots— and tried to tell her stupid heart to stop beating so quickly at the sight of him, except it didn't listen. It picked up speed half an hour later, only for different reasons as a rather frantic mother handed Celeste a very floppy baby.

She pushed on the call bell even before she unwrapped him.

He was big and chubby and barely opened his eyes as Celeste swiftly undressed him and ran some obs.

'He keeps vomiting...' The mum was trying not to cry. 'He saw the GP yesterday, she said it was gastro and to push fluids into him...'

No help was coming, so Celeste pushed the call bell again. The baby's pulse was racing and his temperature was high, so she put him on some oxygen and pushed the call bell *again* as she pulled over the IV trolley, resorting in the end to sticking her head out of the cubicle.

'Could I have a hand?' she snapped, and shot a frantic look at Ben, who was showing a patient his ankle X-ray. 'Now!'

'Press it three times for an emergency!" Ben snapped back, when he saw the baby.

She was still learning which way was up— only yesterday she had been warned for overreacting and pressing three times for everything remotely urgent and now she was being scolded for doing too little.

Some days this job was just so hard!

'Depressed fontanel.' Ben swiftly examined

the listless baby, as Celeste quickly lifted him off the scales and set up for an IV. She was terrified of putting an IV line in such a sick baby, but it was part of her course and something she had to learn to do. She'd started on big, strapping, muscle-bound men with veins like tram lines, and then on sick adults. She had even put IVs in a few children now and a couple of babies as well, only not one as unwell as this and not with Mum anxiously watching—and now Meg was here too! 'Poor skin turgor.' Ben continued with his assessment then shook his head as he saw the slight shake of her hands as Celeste held the floppy arm with one hand and poised the needle with the other. 'I'll do it.' He took over without further comment and she was glad that he had. As a fat little baby, his veins would be hard to find at the best of times, but collapsed from de-hydration they were proving extremely difficult and even Ben, with very steady hands, took a couple of goes to establish IV access, eventually finding a vein in his foot.

'I'm in.' He took some bloods and held the IV in firm place as Celeste connected it to a drip and then taped and wrapped it, carefully splinting his foot as Mum hovered close. As Ben relayed the IV fluids he wanted the babe to receive, he glanced up at Celeste with a quick addition. 'Could you put on a mask, please?'

She didn't see *him* putting on a mask, and neither was he asking Meg to. She gritted her teeth, for now she did as she was told. It was becoming an all too familiar pattern—in the couple of weeks that they had been working together Ben had become rather—for want of a word—annoying! She was already being looked out for by her colleagues and was uncomfortable enough with that, but Ben seemed to be on a mission to ensure that she saw only the safest, calmest, least infectious patients and if he wasn't suggesting that she put on a mask he was reminding her to wash her hands!

As if she needed reminding!

Still, with Ben now speaking with the mother,

it was hardly the time or place for discussion—
she'd save it for later.

'He's nine months old,' Ben checked with the
anxious mum as Celeste sweated behind her
mask. 'Is that right?'

'Only just nine months,' his mum said. 'I
know he looks older.'

'How long as he been sick?' Ben asked.

'He started vomiting yesterday, three, maybe
four times.'

'And this morning?' He fired questions as he
continued to examine the baby and ordered a
bolus dose of fluids for him. Celeste had
already put him on oxygen and the paediatricians were on their way down, but Ben was examining his abdomen carefully, concerned that
it was the surgeons that they needed. 'What
colour is the vomit?'

'Green.'

'Okay…' He checked the baby's nappy and,
still not happy with the abdomen, asked Meg to
page the surgeons. Having spoken briefly with

the mother, he rang Imaging to order an urgent ultrasound.

'I think it's an ileus,' Ben said, standing on hold on the phone at the nurses' station as Celeste pointedly washed her hands at the little sink there, yet annoyingly as she dried her hands he pushed the bottle of alcohol hand rub towards her.

'Does that diagnosis mean I can go in there without a mask now?' Celeste asked, and then she frowned. 'Or is that suddenly an airborne disease too?' She watched his jaw tighten.

'You just need to be careful,' Ben pointed out. 'At that age, he could have measles, chickenpox, slap cheek...'

'Here.' He pushed the bottle of hand scrub to her again as she climbed onto the stool to write her notes, but she ignored it.

'You should use this,' he insisted.

'Why?' Celeste challenged.

'Because we don't know what's wrong with the baby yet, because you should—'

'Ben.' She clicked off her pen and put it down.

'While I appreciate your concern, I really don't need you to look out for me.'

'I'm not looking out for you—I'm just—'

'Making me paranoid!' Celeste said. 'Ben, I can beat you on the paranoid stakes with this pregnancy any day!'

He doubted that, but bit his tongue.

'I'm just ensuring that you take sensible precautions,' he said instead.

'I've spoken with my obstetrician, with the infectious diseases nurse, with Meg, and I'm using universal precautions. I'm being as sensible and as careful as possible, but dealing with sick people is part and parcel of nursing,' she said calmly.

'I don't see that it can hurt to take a few more precautions,' he muttered.

'I can't walk around in a spacesuit,' Celeste said, 'and neither can the nurses on the children's or oncology wards, neither can the nurses or radiographers who don't even know that they're pregnant but might be…' She could see his frown descending as the grad nurse gave the registrar a stern talking to. 'And all we can be is sensible, *all* the time, not just when we're visibly pregnant, so thank you for your concern and, no, I won't be using this...' she pushed back the bottle of alcohol scrub '...because I happen to be allergic to it.'

'Fine!' Ben snapped, more annoyed with himself than her. If her doctor was happy to let her keep working, and the hospital was still employing her, if Celeste wanted to keep working—well, it wasn't his concern.

So why was he so worried about her?

It niggled at him all day and later into the evening when, confused, he stood at the supermarket, basket in hand, and chose organic steak, because it was better for the baby—which, again, wasn't his concern, but he just stuffed it in his basket and added a carton of orange juice with added iron. He knew he was overreacting and he had every reason to. It was the anniversary of Jen's death in a couple of days, so it was no wonder he was upset. But then he did what he always did—and chose not to think about it.

A very vague routine had developed—not every day, not even every other day but now and then. He'd wander down and ask if she fancied dinner, or he'd hear her watering the sunflowers at his front door and pop his head around and ask her if she wanted to watch a movie, or whatever.

It was company, that was all.

And she was so-o-o glad of it.

So glad not to have to be as bright and bubbly as she pretended to be when she was at work— so nice to chat and moan, or sit with her feet up on his coffee table and watch a movie.

And never, not once, did he lecture her, or question her decision to keep working.

Till at the end of thirty-three weeks, till *that* night, when, full from organic steak and salad washed down with orange juice with added iron, she heaved herself off the sofa, and Ben glanced at his watch.

'It's only eight-thirty.'

'I just fancy an early night.'

'You're on a day off tomorrow.' Ben frowned, reluctantly seeing her to the door. His own company was the last thing he wanted over these next few nights. 'Are you sure you're okay?'

'I've got a doctor's appointment tomorrow. I want to—'

'Make sure that you look well rested, so you can fool him,' Ben said, and then stopped, his jaw muscles clamping, because it was *none* of his damn business what she did.

'I need to work for a few more weeks,' Celeste said, and Ben said nothing. He just forced a smile, and opened the door, telling himself that she didn't need a lecture, just a friend, but it was getting harder and harder to hold his tongue.

Then she burst into tears.

Celeste, who always smiled, always laughed, always came back with a quick retort, crumpled and gave in.

'I can't do it any more!'

All he felt was relief, relief that she'd seen it, relief that she wouldn't be doing it any more, and he pulled her, sobbing, into his arms and let her weep.

'Then don't,' he said gently.

'I can't afford not to,' she argued, but with herself now. 'Only I just can't face going there again…'

'I know.'

'I'm so tired.'

'I know.'

'And I'm scared of the germs too.'

'Come on.' He led her back to his sofa, fetched some cold water from the fridge and then gently he spoke with her, just as he would a patient, and explored her options. She had everything in place, even had some savings, but it would only just cover the rent and not much else. There would be a bit more money once the baby came along, but undoubtedly things were impossibly tight for her financially.

'The car's about to give up,' Celeste sobbed.

'And I haven't got a baby seat for it. I was going to get that with next month's pay…'

'My sister has had hundreds of car seats—the garage is full of them. She had twins…so that's sorted, okay?'

It was just the tip of a very big iceberg, just another thing on her endless list, but it was a relief to tick it off, to share, to finally admit just how drained from it all she really was.

'I need to work, but I really think that if I carry on, it will affect the baby.' She was so glad that he didn't jump in and confirm her fears. 'I've got all this fluid…'

'Look.' Ben was supremely gentle. 'You've done well to get this far.'

'Some women work right to the end.'

'And some women don't,' Ben said. 'Some women can't, and it looks as if you're one of them.'

'I'll speak to the doctor tomorrow.' She nodded. 'I'll be honest.'

'Good,' Ben said, then he paused. And dived

in where he didn't want to, got just a little bit more involved. 'Have you thought of asking the father for help?'

'Never.' Celeste shook her head. 'And please don't give me a lecture saying that he's responsible too, and that I've every right—'

'No lecture,' Ben interrupted. 'What about your parents?'

'I've written to them.' He realised how hard that would have been for her—knew from their chats how outraged their response had been, how they had cut her off. The fact that she had written and asked them for help after they'd done that to her showed she was thinking about the baby.

'Well done.'

It was the nicest thing he could have said. 'I only posted it yesterday, so I haven't heard. I've asked if I can move back, just for a few weeks...'

He'd miss her, Ben realised, but it was the right thing for her now. She needed family, needed someone to take care of her during these last difficult weeks—and it certainly wasn't going to be him.

'I'm going to speak to the doctor tomorrow.' Her voice was firmer now. 'And then I'll tell Meg.'

'Good.'

'And now...' again he pulled her up from the sofa as she went to stand '...I'm really going home to bed.'

He smiled at her as they reached the door. 'You'll get there,' Ben said, 'you really will.'

'I know.'

She was so tired and so weary and lost, trying to be brave in the dark, that this time when he pulled her into his arms, it wasn't because she was crying, it wasn't because she was upset. He didn't actually know why he'd done it, it just felt very right to hold her.

And for Celeste it felt so wonderful to *be* held for a moment.

A lovely, lovely moment to just stand and lean on him, to feel his words in her hair, his assurances that she had made the right choices, that she would be okay, and that she was doing well.

'I'm scared.'

She had never, not once, admitted it to anyone.

Defiance had become her middle name, because if she stopped for just a second, if she questioned her wisdom to keep the baby, to go on working, to not publicly name the father, to admit, even to herself, that she was struggling, then surely, *surely*, all the balls she was juggling would come clattering down. It was easier to cope, to insist she *was* coping, to just get on and do, rather than stop and think.

Yet in his arms she stopped for a moment— admitted the truth and waited for the crash.

Waited for the balls to clatter to the floor, for everything to grind to a halt, for hopelessness to invade, yet as she stood there, held by him, all she did was pause, just this blink of a pause where she told her truth and, safe for a moment, regrouped.

'Scared of what?' After the longest time he asked her.

'The baby deserves better.'

Ben closed his eyes in regret. Shameful regret because he had, at one time, thought the same too.

Two affluent parents, conceiving a baby that was planned, loved, wanted…

It had been his blueprint, his rage at the universe, because if he and Jen, with all they had, with all their plans and dreams, couldn't get there, why should anyone else?

Only now he held Celeste and realised that, despite the circumstances, the woman in his arms met the last two on the list and, despite the odds, she'd make up for all the rest.

'It's got *you*.' He stayed there, still holding her, and thought about it—thought how lucky that little baby was to have her, unplanned or whatever. It had Celeste—and he thought how she'd made him smile so many times, thought of the warmth of her affection and how lucky the recipient of that would be, and his neat blueprint faded from his mind.

'Am I enough, though?' she asked anxiously.

'Oh, yes,' he replied definitely.

She was absolutely enough.

More than enough.

So much more than enough, only he wasn't talking about the baby now, because holding her, for the first time holding her, he forgot what they were talking about, forgot that she was pregnant. She was simply Celeste, funny, kind and terribly, terribly sexy. The scent of her up close, the soft feel of her head against his chest, overcame him, and he was lost in her. As naturally as breathing, he told her how he felt with a kiss instead of words, just pulling up her chin and kissing her. He lowered his head onto dark red lips and confirmed how *enough* she was with his mouth, and as their lips met Ben experienced this heady rush, like sugar dissolving on his tongue, as he tasted temptation.

She was stunned, because this was nothing like she had ever felt before, because in Ben's arms she felt safe, and just herself. Good, bad, whatever, she was herself with Ben. She had admitted to him that she was scared and the world had carried right on moving, only now it was even better than before.

His hands were in her hair and his mouth was moving with hers and she felt sexy—for the first time in her life she felt sexy and cherished and safe. And Ben felt it too, this tenderness and want rushing in that was *finally* without comparison. There was no logical thought to it—it was just a kiss, but one that tasted like heaven, surrounded by the scent of her hair and with her tongue cool from water. It was instinct, just the haven of instinct.

She kissed him back.

Kissed Ben in a way she never had before.

Not a practised kiss, not the type you have to think about—it was all about tasting, sharing, which was just how it should be. Ben's privacy, the isolated place that was him was suddenly hers to explore, and it tasted divine. Celeste had stepped inside the exclusive inner sanctum of this guarded man and she gloried in it.

'Celeste.' He groaned her name into her mouth, so she knew that she was there, knew she *was* the woman he was kissing tonight. One of his hands was on the back of her head, bringing her face to his, the other was on her bottom, her big fat dimply bottom, she vaguely thought, except he cupped it and stroked it till all it felt was fabulous. She hadn't really known what sexy was, yet she was discovering it now, right now, when it should be the last thing on her mind. Yet she was only a woman and, as his hands gathered her closer to him, it was all she wanted to be.

He had never come closer to escape—to a place where it was just him.

It wasn't a selfish escape.

Because also in that place was Celeste, and for a blissful few moments Ben was himself—the real him, the one that had been lost for ages. So he kissed her, tasted her, wanted her, without past or future, just succumbed to the heady taste of the present. He was hard, and he could feel her lovely bottom in his hands; he was in the place where bliss was no longer enough and then you reached for more, so he pulled her into his hardness, wanted to feel her softness against him, to shed her clothes, to drown in her. But instead he felt the solid weight of the baby that had been there only on the periphery of his mind now pressed into him. He could feel the dense weight of it and, tonight of all nights, it felt like a punch to the stomach, and it was Ben who pulled back.

'I'm sorry.' He released her so quickly it felt as if she were falling. 'That shouldn't have happened.'

Maybe it shouldn't have, but it had. It wasn't the kiss that embarrassed her—she was saving that for later. Right now it was his reaction—he was acting as though he was completely appalled at what he had done.

'Forget it...' She attempted casual, with a heart rate topping a hundred, as if shot awake from a blissful dream. Only now she was facing stark reality and just wanted out of there, as soon as she could. 'Really, it's no big deal.'

'Celeste…' Hell, he didn't want to add to her problems—only he just had, Ben knew that. But he had forgotten in that moment that she was pregnant. As he'd held her, all she had been was Celeste. 'Like I said, I'm not looking for—'

'I get it, Ben,' she interrupted. 'And neither am I. It was just a kiss, just…' She shrugged helplessly, because it had been so much more than just a kiss. She could still taste him on her lips, still feel the delicious crush of him holding her, and now he had taken it all away. 'Just one of those things that should never have happened. It doesn't change anything.'

CHAPTER FIVE

ONLY everything changed.

He saw her come into work around lunchtime the next day and speak with Meg. Trying to pretend nothing had happened, she gave him a quick smile as she passed. It had been a kiss between friends, Ben told himself, that had maybe got just a little out of hand. He was certain they could move on from it, so when a little while later he met her in the corridor, he asked how she was.

'Not bad.' She gave him a breezy smile. 'I'm officially on maternity leave.'

'How are you, Celeste?' Belinda clipped past on high heels and stopped to ask.

'I was just telling Ben that I've been signed

off.' He could see it was with great effort she was maintaining that smile. 'So I guess I'll see you both when I'm a mum.'

There was a message for him in there, Ben knew it, and, feeling guilty, he was almost relieved to hear it. He was having trouble believing how stupid he'd been last night. She had enough on her plate without him messing things up, and a waif with a baby was the very last thing he needed right now.

'I hope she's okay,' Belinda said as Celeste waddled off.

'She will be now she's not working,' Ben answered.

'No.' Belinda gave a little shake of her head. 'I meant that I hope she'll be okay on her own with a baby.'

'She's not a teenager…' They were walking back to the office, and Ben was getting more and more irritated with Belinda's gloom. 'She'll be fine.'

'But, still, it isn't going to be easy. I wonder

who the father is? I mean, she's never said, and surely he should be responsible for something...'

'How's your new man?' Ben rapidly changed the subject as they reached their office. 'Still going strong?'

'Paul's amazing,' Belinda sighed happily. 'We're going away this weekend.'

'I know.' Ben grinned. 'I'm covering for you.'

'His ex-wife's got the kids.'

'Have you met them yet?'

'God, no.' Belinda rolled her eyes as she sorted out some paperwork. 'The last thing I need is someone else's kids.'

It was the last thing Ben needed too.

Of all the stupid things to do... As they worked on in silence, Ben was silently brooding. Whether he liked it or not, he was involved with Celeste and her baby up to a point. He couldn't just stop going over to see her while she remained his neighbour...

'Here.' Belinda broke into his introspection. 'I've got something for you.'

Ben went over to the computer and had to laugh as twenty or so female faces pouted back at him from an internet dating agency's website. 'I typed in your details and came up with all these possibilities for you.'

'I'm not interested in dating, and certainly not this way,' he said.

'Oh, get into the twenty-first century.' Belinda laughed. 'At least you know what you're getting this way—I haven't got time to go out to the clubs. And I know Paul's not looking for a stay-at-home surrogate mother for his children—he knows from the start that my career comes first and I absolutely don't want a baby. Look, she's nice.' She brought up a woman's details and Ben read on.

'She says she wants someone with no baggage,' Ben pointed out. 'I've got a truckload.'

'We all have.' Belinda shrugged. 'You just have to lie a little. I mean, if you get to our age and have had any semblance of a life, baggage is the norm. Go on, Ben,' she urged. 'Give it a go.'

'Leave it, Belinda,' he warned. Colleagues he

could deal with, friendly colleagues even, but Belinda was pushing the line. She was in love and hanging off lampposts and wanted to spread her happiness—but she was talking to the wrong guy. 'I couldn't be less interested in starting a relationship now.'

He meant it.

Four years ago tomorrow... He lay on the bed when he got home and closed his eyes.

Four years...

Had it been that long? It seemed like only yesterday—yet it had also stretched on for ever.

Four years... He snapped his eyes open suddenly, knowing that he just had to deal with the present problem that was Celeste before he could get on with remembering and mourning the past.

'I was wondering...' His voice trailed off. It had taken him ages to decide how best to deal with this and finally he had decided to drop by her place, to pretend nothing had happened, and then offer his solution. Except she had taken for ever to answer the door and when she did, it was clear that he had woken her up. There was a huge pillow crease down the side of her face and the usually sunny Celeste was decidedly grumpy and certainly not about to make this easy. 'Were you asleep?'

'Actually, yes, I was.'

'Sorry.' Ben cleared his throat. He didn't want to just drop helping her, but he did want to pull back and this might just be the way! 'I've got a day off tomorrow. I'm going to do a big shop because I'm having too many take-aways, and I wondered if you wanted to make a list. I could grab some stuff for you.'

'I'm fine, thanks.'

'It really is no problem. You said you were struggling to get to the shops—'

'I did my shopping this afternoon online,' Celeste interrupted. 'So I'm all right. I've got a friend coming over tomorrow and we're going to make a load of meals and stock up the freezer.'

'That's...great.'

'And the doctor said that I needed to rest a lot,' Celeste continued, 'so, I don't mean to sound rude, but...' she gave an uncomfortable swallow '...I'm having a lot of trouble getting to sleep, and I'd just nodded off when you knocked.'

'Sorry about that,' he apologised.

'You weren't to know.' She gave a slight smile, only it didn't reach her eyes, and neither did her eyes meet his. 'But it might be better if you don't...' she gave a tight shrug '...just drop over in future.'

'Sure,' Ben said. He should have been relieved. After all, he'd been hoping for the same thing. He was absolved from duty now, so why didn't it feel great? 'What did the doctor say?' he asked, not able to leave it there.

'I told you.' Celeste's usually sunny face was a closed mask. 'I'm to rest... Look, Ben, it's really not your concern.'

Then she closed the door.

He went back to his unit.

And as he had done for the last few years on this night, Ben tried and failed not to watch the clock.

The horrible thing about anniversaries, Ben had found, was the build-up to them—as if you were stuck in a portal, as if by somehow going over and over every detail, you could change the outcome, bargain with God.

Only not this night.

Oh, he did all that, but there was another layer there too.

Guilt.

Guilt, because when he surely should have been drowning his sorrows in whisky and thinking only of Jen, when he should surely be lacerating himself with thoughts of what could have been, this year he couldn't sustain it.

Instead, he found himself standing at the window and wondering about Celeste.

Found himself thinking not about what could have been, but what already was.

And what could be?

* * *

Time did heal.

He'd been told it, had said it himself, but only now was he actually starting to believe it.

It didn't consume him now, it didn't walk with him constantly, there was room in his mind for other thoughts, so on a day that was usually spent locked in mourning, he awoke, showered and dressed, went to the cemetery and told them he loved them—always had, always would— but instead of heading to her parents' home, instead of stopping, he started. He kept his appointment with the bank, saw the real-estate agent, looked around the house again, put a deposit on a boat, went home, saw that his sunflowers were dying, watered them, showered again, and got changed into shorts.

He did really well, actually!

Until Jen's parents rang.

And then so too did his.

Followed by Jen's sister.

And then it all finally caught up with him.

He tried not to look at the clock, tried not to

remember ringing her from work, then tried to remember the *exact* tone of her voice when Jen had said she had a headache.

It had done nothing to alert him.

Well, actually it had, but he was a doctor and his wife was pregnant and also a doctor and between them they could dream up a million and one scenarios if they so wished. So she had told him it was just a headache…and he had told himself the same.

'It's just a headache, Ben.'

Except when he suggested that she take something for it, instead of her usual rebuff, he'd been concerned to find out that she already had. Jen, who never took anything, had taken a couple of painkillers.

'I'll come home,' he'd suggested.

'For God's sake, Ben.' She'd sounded irritated. 'It's a headache, I'm just going to go and lie down.'

Yes, by early evening it had all caught up with him again.

He didn't walk along the beach today, and he didn't jog. He ran. Only the beach seemed too small—he could see Melbourne miles away in the sunset, but he felt as if he could make it in a few leaps, that he would never run out of energy, that he could run all his life and still never leave it behind.

He wasn't wearing a watch, but he knew the time, knew it to the very second.

Ringing Jen and getting no answer, and telling himself she was just lying down.

He pounded the beach. His lungs were bursting but still, *still* he remembered walking up the garden path and trying not to run, because he was surely being stupid, because there was surely nothing wrong, then letting himself in and calling her name. It was five past seven, as he ran, Ben knew that, because suddenly he felt like swearing at the sky for cheating them, five past seven because he'd seen it on the clock as he had walked into the lounge, seen her kneeling on the floor, her hands on her head on the sofa.

So still.
So pale.
So gone.

Pounding on her chest, ringing the ambulance.

He wanted her and if not he wanted a Caesarean—he wanted life to be salvaged from the wreckage he had come home to, except he knew, knew, knew even as he laid her flat on her back that it was too late.

He ran along that beach, not as if the devil was chasing him, because nothing could catch him now. He was the chaser, pounding on anger, and regret and hate and the unfairness of it all.

Temper split his mind.

He didn't want Celeste and her baby.

He wanted *his*!

It was a relief to be off work, but it was also the longest, loneliest time.

Her request to stay at her parents' was met with a curt letter of refusal and a cheque, which

Celeste would love to have not cashed on principle, but she couldn't afford principles right now. Although she'd have loved to splurge and get her hair cut and buy something fantastic and non-essential for the baby, instead she trimmed her hair with the kitchen scissors, bought another two boxes of nappies and paid two months' rent in advance, then crawled back into bed and carried on missing Ben.

And she did miss him.

Missed him more than she had Dean. Which made no sense, but it was how it was. Over and over she took out the memory of his kiss and explored it, remembered the moment that had ended them—and she wished she'd never tasted him, never been held by him, had never kissed him, because in that moment she'd glimpsed a different world. With just one kiss he'd shown her how good life could be—and then he'd ripped it away.

She thought about ignoring the knock at the door—but not for long. Maybe it was her parents to say they'd changed their minds, or the postman, or maybe, just maybe…

It was Ben.

'I hope I didn't wake you,' he said.

'You didn't.'

'And I'm sorry to drop round…' His four-wheel drive was purring behind him, the engine still going, no doubt ready to make a quick escape.

'It's fine.'

Ben wasn't finding this easy. The whole day hadn't been easy, in fact—but it was something he had promised, something he had to do. 'I went over to my sister's to get the car seat for you.'

'Oh!'

'Look.' He ran a hand through his hair. 'I don't want to offend you, so say if you don't want them, really, you just have to say. But she gave me a few things…a crib, a stroller, one of those jogging ones…'

'Do I have to promise to take up jogging?' she asked.

'No...' Despite the strained circumstances, she still made him smile.

'Only I might get challenged under the Trade Descriptions Act if I'm seen with it,' she teased.

'It's good for walking on the beach too,' Ben said. 'Well, according to my sister.'

She couldn't joke any more, really she didn't know what to say. It wasn't a question of being too proud to accept help, it was more that she'd had none, well, apart from her parents' cheque. But this was real help and real thought and that it came from him made it as bitter as it was sweet.

'Thank you,' she said sincerely.

'Do you want me to bring it in?' He gestured to the vehicle behind him and she said thank you again, her nose a bit red from trying not to cry.

She offered to help, but he shooed her away and she sat on the sofa as a lot of wishes were granted—just not the one she wished for the most, because he couldn't even look at her, Celeste noticed. Oh, he was kind and helpful and set up the crib and accepted a glass of iced tea while Celeste opened bag after bag, smiling at teeny tiny baby socks.

For Ben it was a nightmare.

All these things had been promised for him and Jen—the crib he was setting up now he hadn't got to do four years ago. The little socks and vest Celeste was holding up made him sweat, and even driving here had been hard, with an empty baby seat in the back…

Still, she needed it and he never would—it was stupid to let it go to waste and he had promised her the car seat that night.

That night.

'I'll leave you to it, then,' he said gruffly. It was almost more than he could stand to be in the room, surrounded by baby things, her home set up and almost ready now…almost more than he could stand to look at her, because she looked *terrible*!

So terrible, in fact, that he wanted to scoop her up and run—wanted someone to notice just how unwell this woman was. Where the hell were her parents?

'Did you hear from your mum and dad?'

'Yes.' She tried for upbeat but didn't manage to come close. 'They sent some money…' He could see her red nose, see the swirl of tears in her eyes despite the smile.

'And when…' Ben cleared his throat '…do you see your obstetrician again?'

'Next Wednesday!'

It was only Friday.

'When did you see him last?'

'On Tuesday.' Still the smile remained, but it was wavering now. 'If my blood pressure is still up they're going to admit me.'

'No protein in your urine?'

'No protein…' He was trying to be a doctor, trying to assess her practically, only it wasn't working. He knew they would be carefully monitoring her for pre-eclampsia, knew she was being watched, only he wanted her watched more closely, and as coolly as he tried to assess the facts, detachment wasn't working.

'You've got a lot of fluid, Celeste,' he pointed out.

'I know. I'm allowed one gentle walk a day, and I've cut out salt as well as sugar… They're watching me, Ben.'

And with that he had to make do.

Only he couldn't.

'Why don't you ring and get your appointment brought forward? I could take you there now,' he offered.

'Ben,' Celeste interrupted, 'thank you for all the lovely things—and thank you to your sister too. When I'm able, I'll get her a card.'

And with *that* he had to make do.

CHAPTER SIX

'HI CELESTE!' He gave a tight smile as she came over. The whole street had come out to watch the auction and Celeste had bypassed her gentle walk on the beach today and wandered down for a look—it was what people in Melbourne did on a sunny Saturday afternoon when a house was up for auction.

'Hi.' She was polite and said hello and then bypassed him, but Ben halted her.

'You're supposed to be resting.'

'I'm walking around a house instead of a beach!' Celeste pointed out. 'Anyway, I've got cabin fever. I'm going crazy being stuck inside the unit and at least they'll have the air-conditioning on in the house.' And then she gave him a smile. 'Thanks for yesterday, by the way.'

'No problem. I'm glad it's all going to good use.'

'I meant the doctor pep talk. I rang my obstetrician and they're seeing me on Monday now.'

'That's wonderful.'

'I'm going home to pack my case after this— I have a feeling they won't be letting me out.'

Then she moved on, wandered inside with the rest of the crowd, and when Ben's eyes should have been on the competition, instead they were on her.

He wanted her.

As he walked around the house, stared into rooms, walked through the garden. It was Celeste's comments he wanted, not the real-estate agent's, and she gave plenty.

It *was* stunning. Her entire unit could fit neatly in the lounge, and Celeste was quite sure that if she could just lie on that lovely white sofa and gaze out at the water till Monday, with someone peeling grapes for her and massaging her feet, her blood pressure would be down by her doctor's appointment!

She loved viewing houses, wandering around them, pretending they were hers, and wishing it could be so. The kitchen was a hell-hole, though, but the agent steered them past it quickly and on to view the upstairs. The whole place was to die for—every room in the house, even the master bathroom, was angled for water views!

'There are no blinds,' Celeste pointed out, and Ben smothered a smile, because when he'd first looked around the home, he'd said exactly the same thing, only the agent hadn't ignored him! 'How can you have floor-to-ceiling windows in a bathroom and no blinds?' Celeste demanded.

'The glass is treated,' the agent hissed. 'You can see out, but no one can see in.

'Now, moving along, this is the master bedroom!'

'Divine!' Celeste breathed as she stepped in.

A vast bed was in the centre, and there was a balcony set up with a little table and chairs…

'Are the windows treated in here too?' Celeste asked pointedly as the agent sucked in his breath.

She *did* make him smile.

And he *did* miss her.

She was writing on her little list again—just as if she was a serious bidder—and he could see the real-estate agent's lips purse as she stepped out boldly onto the balcony instead of following the pack back along the hall. 'Can you keep up, please?' the agent snapped, and Ben felt his teeth grind together.

'This room would make an ideal nursery…' Despite her obvious condition the agent addressed a loving young couple and ignored Celeste when she asked a question. How she wished she'd won the lottery, and could pull out the winning bid just to wipe that superior smile off his smug face and make him squirm. Ben saw her face redden as the agent ignored her and then caught her eye and gave her a wink.

'My partner asked a question,' Ben said coolly, watching Celeste's beam of delight as the agent practically gave himself whiplash, turning to face her. No, she hadn't won loads of money, but watching that smug smile leave his face was almost as good.

'I'm so sorry,' he simpered. 'What did you want to know?'

'Thanks for that.' Celeste grinned at Ben as they wandered outside.

'Ooh, it was my pleasure,' Ben replied. 'He's obnoxious.'

Celeste loved auctions—the crowd gathered outside the house, the real-estate agent pumping up the action—yet she was always scared she'd put up her hand and outbid someone, like standing on the edge of a cliff and wanting to jump, just to try it.

There was some serious bidding going on, and Celeste watched on in glee. This was the most exciting thing to have happened to her all week.

Ben was trying to concentrate, but his eyes kept wandering to her.

He hadn't put in a bid yet—he would wait and see... God, even her eyelids were swollen. When he should be concentrating, when he should be focusing, instead he was thinking about her, worrying about her—and Ben didn't like the feeling a bit.

The bidding was slowing down now, the auctioneer having trouble eking out even a small raise in bids—and it was then that Ben put in his first offer.

He saw the flare of surprise in her eyes—she'd had no idea that he would be bidding. It wasn't something he had to discuss with anyone, Ben told himself, that was the life he had built for himself. Yet still there was a little pang of discomfort, remembering all the nights when she had spoken about her hopes and fears and dreams for the future, and he realised that he hadn't let her in at all.

The flagging crowd was suddenly interested, and Ben saw her smile. Just a little smile that winged its way over to him, telling him she was pleased.

Excited for him, even.

He was outbid, so he upped his offer.

And again she smiled.

He was outbid again, so he upped it again.

He looked over for her smile, for that bit of encouragement that he shouldn't need but somehow liked, and then he saw she wasn't smiling.

He had been outbid again, the auctioneer passing the bid to him, only Ben wasn't listening.

There was an aghast expression on Celeste's face, as if she had just received some shocking news—only there was no one talking to her and she wasn't on the phone. Her hands were both on her stomach.

He could hear the auctioneer's warning. Confused, but also needing to get over to her, Ben put in a ridiculously high bid, heard the gasp of shock from the crowd. Ignoring the rest of the proceedings, he waded through the crowd towards her.

'I think my waters just broke!'

'It's okay,' he said soothingly.

'No, it's not.' She was shivering, shock setting in as realisation hit. 'I'm only thirty-four weeks.'

'Thirty-four-weekers do very well…' He could hear his calm voice, only the blood was pounding in his temples as he pulled out his phone. 'Come on, let's get you sitting down. I'll call an ambulance.'

'There's nowhere to sit!' she shrilled. The sun was suddenly hot on her head, her mouth filling with saliva. 'Ben, I think it's coming…'

The real-estate agent had come over to congratulate him, the house apparently his now, but Ben wasn't listening.

'We need to get her inside,' he stated.

'Excuse me?' the agent said.

'Ben…' She was moaning now, whimpering in terror. 'I've got pain…'

'She needs to be inside.' Ben was walking her to the entrance at the side of the house, taking her weight. 'She needs some privacy…'

'You can't just go in!'

'I just bought the house!' Ben snapped. 'She's about to give birth. Where do you want her to do it—on the street?' He gave up walking her then and picked her up—and such was his authority that the real-estate agent actually opened the side gate for him. 'Now, call an ambulance,' Ben ordered, 'and tell them it's a premature baby...' He had her beneath the willow tree now and she was wriggling out of his arms, already starting to strain. Ben realised with alarm that there was no chance of getting her inside. 'And say there's a doctor in attendance.'

'Is there anything I can do?' The man he had waved to each morning, the man he had just bought a house from, was now there, being practical and helpful. 'Some towels,' Ben said as his wife rushed off and he struggled to be calm, to be professional. It was a delivery, he told himself, he was more than capable of dealing with that. Only he could see her terrified eyes...

'I need you to listen to me, Celeste.' He had

pulled down her panties and examined her. The baby wasn't waiting for the ambulance, it wasn't waiting for anything… 'This *is* a small baby, so we're going to try and slow it down.' It was important that they did so, as a rapid delivery could cause damage to the fragile brain. 'You're not to push,' he warned Celeste. 'We want this to happen as slowly and as gently as we can…'

She had never been more petrified—the thought of her baby coming so soon and here, no hospital, no shiny equipment… Yet she was suddenly desperate to bear down, to push, only Ben was telling her to just breathe through it, to resist this desperate urge—and she knew why. 'It's too fast…'

'Your body will have been preparing for this for hours, you just didn't know.' He smiled. 'We just need to slow down this last bit.'

He was right. All morning she had felt restless—trying to lie in bed, to read, to rest. She'd had a shower and then gone back to bed, then decided to go and look at the auction…

'It's coming,' she moaned.

It was. Nothing was going to slow down her baby's entrance to the world, and she was so glad Ben was here and terrified that he might not have been.

'What if I'd been at home, what if…?'

'You'd have coped!' Ben cut short her what-ifs. 'And you're coping well now.'

'I'm sorry we're not talking.' She panted with the effort of not pushing. 'I'm sorry to do this to you…'

'I'm glad to be here,' Ben said, 'I've done this pl—' He didn't continue, as he'd just seen that the cord was around the neck, but not tightly, and he slipped it over. Only it wasn't just that which had halted his words. Yes, he had delivered babies over the years, yes, he had done this plenty of times before.

Just not like this.

Not like this, with his heart in his mouth, as he held a tiny head in his hand and guided a pale life into the world.

Not like this, as he delivered the babe onto Celeste's stomach, rubbed at its back, flicked at its feet. He knew it would breathe, the doctor in him knew that it had only been a minute, but for Ben it was one very long minute, the babe floppy and cyanosed, its heart rate tipping almost low enough that if it went down further he would have to commence CPR. He could hear Celeste's pleas and they matched his thoughts, willing the ambulance faster with oxygen for this little one. He turned the baby over, its back now on Celeste's stomach, and felt his head lighten in relief as the tiny baby startled and took its first breath.

'It's not crying,' Celeste sobbed.

'She will,' he promised.

'She?' Ben was no midwife—maybe it should have been for mum to find out herself, except the baby was too fragile and sick for anything other than practicality.

'You've got a daughter,' Ben said, 'and she needs to be kept warm.' He kept the little one on her mother's stomach, and wrapped them both in towels, relieved to finally hear the sirens.

'I got some string….' The woman who had got the towels had been busy and had the ambulance not been pulling up Ben would have cut the cord then. He was seriously worried at the babe's lack of response. She was breathing, but with effort, little bubbles coming out of her mouth with each breath. The paramedics were straight onto it—suctioning her little airway, even the tiniest oxygen mask swamping her tiny features as Ben clamped and cut the cord.

'We might radio through…' The paramedic looked at Ben, a quick decision being made between them without words—to attempt IV access and work to stabilise her here, or to scoop and run and get her to the hospital which was just a short drive away, depending on the traffic?

'Let's get her to hospital,' Ben said, and the paramedic nodded, wrapping her up in towels.

'We'll send another vehicle for Mum,' the paramedic said.

'No, I want to go with her...' Celeste was sobbing, shivering and shaking, stunned at the speed of it all.

'She needs to get to hospital quickly.' Ben's voice was kind but non-negotiable. 'Can you stay with Celeste for a moment?' He spoke with the woman who had been so helpful. She had brought pillows and blankets from the house now and was doing her best to make Celeste comfortable. 'I'm going to help them get the baby settled in the ambulance and then I'll be back.'

'No,' Celeste sobbed. 'Go with her. Please.'

There was a flash of confusion at his own thought process then, only he didn't pursue it— there wasn't time. He nodded his acquiescence and held the infant as the ambulance sped them the short distance to the hospital. Her little lungs were filling up with fluid and Ben held the oxygen mask close to her face, but allowing room for the paramedic to suction. There was a little probe attached to her ear and her oxygen saturation was low but not dire...

The ambulance swept through the streets, slowing down at High Street, which was filled with Saturday shoppers and weekend drivers, and Ben felt his tension rising as it braked and accelerated, the siren blasting out.

Then he looked beyond the mask and the flaring nostrils and he saw the creamy vernix-flattening dark curls, and navy eyes that were nowhere near able to focus, except he felt as if she was looking straight at him.

It was a bizarre moment of connection, and it was Ben who tore his eyes away first.

He was only the doctor.

This baby's mother was just a friend...

Then the hospital was in view, and he could see Belinda waiting outside. As the ambulance opened he didn't hand the little one over, but ran inside to Resus with the precious bundle—the resuscitation cot warmed and waiting, paediatricians and Raji there, and only then did he hand her over...

And only then did he realise how terrified he had been. A cold sweat was drenching him as he saw the urgency in the assembled staff, and he knew that this was no overreaction. He saw how very sick this little baby was and he was unable to speak for a moment as he struggled to get his breath.

He headed over to the sink as the paramedics gave the handover, and Ben took a long drink directly from the tap, before walking back to where they were working.

Raji had placed a tube down her nose and was suctioning her airway more deeply, the paediatrician had just inserted an umbilical line and fluids were now being delivered. She looked a touch more feisty than she had, her face scrunching in displeasure, little fists bunching and legs kicking a small protest...

'She was very flat...' Ben gave the Apgar scores. 'It was a very rapid delivery.'

'Thirty-four weeks, the paramedics said.' The paediatrician was looking her over. 'But she's quite big for thirty-four weeks—do you know where mum was having her antenatal?'

'I'm sure he didn't have time to ask,' Belinda said. 'You were at a house auction, weren't you, Ben?'

'Actually...' he cleared his throat a touch '...this is Celeste's baby.'

'*Our* Celeste!' Belinda blinked and then looked at the admission card that the receptionist had just filled in. 'Baby Mitchell...'

'She lives in the same street as the auction,' Ben half explained, 'and she must have wandered down to watch it.'

'Well, lucky woman...' Belinda breathed out '...that you were there.'

'She had gestational diabetes,' Ben said, which explained the baby's relatively big size for gestation, 'and she had her antenatal care here,' he added to the receptionist, and she rushed off to get the notes.

'Does anyone know if there were any other problems?'

'Hypertension,' Meg said as still Ben struggled just to breathe. 'She was signed off a couple of days ago.'

'Her blood pressure has been up,' Ben said, watching Belinda blink at the depth of his knowledge. 'She looked very bloated today, and I thought she was tipping into pre-eclampsia,' Ben added. 'I think she was going to be admitted on Monday.'

He felt sick.

The resuscitation area was impossibly hot, and Ben felt stifled, hearing the blip, blip, blip of the monitor. Even watching the team at work was incredibly hard. Oh, he knew they knew what they were doing, knew that babies were tough, even tiny ones, only they seemed so rough with their handling of something so very, very small.

'I'm going to go outside for a bit,' Ben said in a strangled voice.

'You might want to change first.' Belinda glanced up and smiled and only then did Ben register the state he was in.

He had a quick shower and selected some theatre blues, only instead of drying and dressing he sat on the wooden bench, dripping wet, with his head in his hands, her words playing over and over. *'What if I'd been at home, what if...?'* Scenario after possible scenario was playing out in his racing brain.

And not just for this morning.

Over and over the years he had beaten himself up with those very words—wishing he'd come home earlier, wondering about the outcome if he had. He'd been told that nothing could have been done for Jen, that even with the best of care she'd have died, or worse, that the brain haemorrhage she'd suffered would have left her a vegetable. But what about their baby? Could it have been saved if he'd been at home?

There was a myriad of conflicting emotions pelting him.

Relief, regret, resentment even, that he had been there for this child and not his own—and yet, even as resentment flickered it faded just as quickly. That tiny life he had held in his hands, he had willed and willed to live, had felt more for than a doctor should—and not just for the baby, but for her mother too.

Then he remembered his own stupidity, that he had contemplated staying with her after the traumatic birth of her baby.

Of course he should have gone with the baby!

Celeste was stable, another ambulance on the way…and yet instinct had overridden logic for a second, and all he had wanted to do was stay and comfort her.

No!

He stood up then and dried quickly, pulling on his theatre blues and making a firm decision. He wasn't going to get involved with Celeste— whatever it took.

He just couldn't go there again.

Wouldn't.

Couldn't.

CHAPTER SEVEN

'WHEN can I see her?' It was *all* she could think about.

The ambulance had arrived a couple of moments after they had taken her daughter, and she had been taken directly to Maternity. The midwives had been wonderful, keeping her up to date on her baby's progress as Celeste was examined and an IV inserted and bloods taken.

'Why do I need that?'

'Your blood pressure's still high,' the obstetrician explained, 'and you've got a lot of fluid retention. We just want to check your bloods and keep an eye on you, make sure everything's settling down…'

The midwives helped her to wash and freshen

up and get into bed and then Gloria, who Celeste had guessed was the one in charge, finally came in with some real news.

'They've just transferred her from Emergency to Special Care. Once they've got her settled and as soon as *your* doctor gives you the okay, we'll take you over to see her. Here.' She handed her a photo. 'One of the nurses took this…'

Oh, she was tiny, with a little pink hat and tubes and things everywhere, but she *was* hers… The few moments she'd had with her daughter were imprinted on her mind and Celeste already recognised her, could walk into the special care unit now and pick out her daughter, of that she was positive…

'Now,' Gloria said, 'she's doing well, and she's on CPAP. That just means she's needing a little help with her breathing, to fill her lungs with air, and she's been given surfactant and medicines to help with lung immaturity…' She went through all the treatment her daughter was receiving till Celeste understood and then she *again* asked a necessary question, one that Celeste had so far refused to respond to. 'Is there anyone we can call for you?' Celeste shook her head.

'I'll ring my parents soon.'

'You shouldn't be on your own,' Gloria said gently. 'Is there a friend…?'

'Later.' Again, Celeste shook her head.

She wanted some privacy, didn't want to share this moment now with parents who hadn't helped, who apart from a terse phone call and a single cheque had done nothing. And neither did she want friends who hadn't really been there around her, or a father who didn't want to know—all of that she would face and deal with, but right now she just wanted to process all that had taken place by herself…

'Hey!' The door opened and Ben's face appeared. He was perhaps the one person she didn't mind seeing right now—after all, he had been there!

'Thank you.' How paltry it sounded, but she meant it from her heart.

'You're very welcome.'

'How is she?'

'I'm not sure,' Ben said. 'They moved her from Emergency half an hour or so ago…'

'Oh!' Of course he wouldn't know, Celeste told herself. As if he followed his patients up to the ward! Once he had handed the baby over, that would have been it for him.

'How are you doing?' Ben asked.

'Not bad…' She didn't elaborate, didn't want to bore him with the tests she was having. He was asking politely, that was all.

'Well…' he gave a tight smile '…I can't stay. I've got the real-estate ringing every five minutes—I need to sign the contract on the house.'

'You'd better go, then.'

'Do you need anything?'

'No.'

'If you need me to drop by the unit I can fetch some stuff. Do you have a bag packed?'

'No.' Celeste gave a weak smile. 'I'm not that organised. Could I ask you just to check the plugs and things?' she asked reluctantly, when he clearly just wanted out of there. 'I think everything is off, but I only went out for a walk.'

'Sure.' He handed over her handbag, which was on her locker, and waited while she gave him her keys. 'Anything else?'

'Nothing I can think of.'

'Well, I'm on a night shift tonight, so I'll drop these back to you.' And even though he was taking her keys, even though he would be going back to her flat and checking her things, his voice, his stance was as formal as if he were just another doctor doing rounds. 'Congratulations, Celeste.'

'Thank you.'

It was an exhausting evening.

There was no rosy glow of motherhood for Celeste to bathe in. She told her parents the news and as expected they arrived a couple of hours later, bringing with them their endless questions and practically blaming her for the stress they were under.

'What were you doing, walking?' her mother Rita scolded her. 'You were supposed to be resting.'

'The doctor said that I was allowed a gentle walk each day.'

'Have you rung him?' Rita asked. 'Whoever *he* is. Have you let him know he's a father?'

'No.'

'Well, don't you think you should? It is *his* responsibility...'

The time or place didn't matter. The same arguments that had ensued since the day she had told them she was pregnant carried on at the hospital bedside. So much for a baby bringing peace, Celeste thought, waving goodbye to the fantasy that the arrival of their grandchild would cast the arguments aside.

'When will we get to see her?' Rita demanded as Gloria came in.

'It's just Mum allowed in for now,' Gloria said, seeing Celeste's strained face. 'They're ready for you, Celeste.'

It was a relief to be wheeled out of the room and away from them.

'You can actually have one of them come in with you,' Gloria said once they were out of earshot. 'If you want—'

'No,' Celeste interrupted. 'I'd rather see her on my own first.'

They had to sit in a little annexe for a few moments until they were ready for them.

'You poor thing.' Gloria gave her a kind smile, as they sat there. 'I bet this is so not how you planned it.'

'None of it's how I planned it,' Celeste admitted.

'You are allowed to cry, you know.' Gloria put her arm around Celeste's shoulders and felt her stiffen. 'It's been such a difficult day…' Celeste wriggled away because if she started crying she wouldn't stop.

And then it was time… She was wheeled in to wash her hands, and then she was wheeled past the incubators and finally she got to see her daughter.

Lying like a little washed-up frog with all drips and tubes and that little pink hat on... Even then she couldn't cry, couldn't give in, because she felt she had to be responsible, so she listened instead as the special care nurse explained all the drips and tubes and that her daughter was comfortable...

'Can I hold her?' Celeste asked, when they didn't offer.

'Not today. We're keeping her very quiet for now, but probably tomorrow...'

So she got to hold her fingers instead and stared at her teeny pink nails and waited for this whoosh of love to come. It was there a little bit, only it wasn't exactly whooshing as she'd expected—because there was this huge plug of guilt lodged in its way.

'Have you got a name for her?'

'Not yet,' Celeste said. 'I wanted to see what she looked like.' She gazed at her daughter and tried to think of a name that might suit her, but her brain was too fuddled for such a big decision. 'I don't know.'

'There's plenty of time,' Gloria said. 'We should get you back—you're not well either, remember.'

She wasn't.

The obstetrician came in and explained that her blood tests had come back and the results weren't great. 'They should all settle over the next few days now that you've delivered, but we will need to keep an eye on you. You've got pre-eclampsia, Celeste.'

'Had.' Celeste frowned. 'Doesn't it go away once the baby is here?'

'Not straight away,' he explained. 'You're still quite sick. You were being observed for it as your blood pressure was raised at your last antenatal, but...well, you had a lot of other stresses that could have accounted for that. It's good that you've delivered. It could have been dangerous for you both had the pregnancy continued.'

It was a long, lonely evening—friends came and visited, but it was as if they were speaking a foreign language. Oh, they cooed and oohed at the photos, but when eight o'clock came and they headed out for Saturday night, Celeste just lay there with her eyes closed, not because she was tired but because she was scared she'd cry. She ignored the footsteps coming into the room, they could take her blood pressure without talking, and then she heard her keys being placed on the locker and screwed them closed more tightly.

Ben could see a tear slipping out of the side of one eye, and could only hazard a guess as to how hard this day had been for her.

He knew he should just put down the bag and walk out quietly. After all, he had resolved not to get involved—a young single mum was the last thing he needed. She was so young and fragile and he was so jaded and bitter, and his heart was closed so tightly. Only sometimes she managed to wedge it open a little...

'I know you're awake!' Reluctantly he broke the silence, smiling a little at her defiant answer.

'I'm not.'

'I packed a few things for you—your tooth-brush and hairbrush...'

'Thanks.'

'Is there anything else you need—a nightdress or anything?'

'No, thanks,' she answered, her eyes still closed. 'Mum said she'd go shopping tomorrow.'

'How were they?' Ben asked, even as he told himself he shouldn't, looking up at the diuretic infusion and the magnesium infusion and then back to her poor, swollen face.

'Cross.' More tears were spilling out the sides of her eyes now, and he picked off a few tissues and put them in her hand. 'They're still cross with me.'

'They're worried,' Ben said.

'And cross,' Celeste said. 'And so are you.'

'Cross?' Ben frowned. 'Celeste, why would I be cross...?' His voice faded as her eyes opened to him, because she was right. Cross was how he felt—or was he just worried?

He truly didn't know.

'Because we kissed…because you think I just go around flinging myself at men—'

'No,' Ben interrupted, 'I'm not cross at you for that, I'm cross with myself.'

'Why?'

'Because…' He blew out a breath, and he couldn't help but admire her for being so open, for just bringing it out. He sat on the bed, because he definitely wasn't a doctor dropping in now. 'Because I'm the last thing you need right now.'

'You don't know what I need.'

'You don't need *me*,' Ben said very firmly, very surely. 'Since Jen, I've had a few relationships and they don't work. You've been messed around enough without getting involved with someone like me, someone who doesn't want children…'

'You think I'm after a father for her?' Celeste asked incredulously. 'Some long-term commitment from you? Hell, Ben, it was only one kiss!'

'That shouldn't have happened,' Ben said.

'I know,' Celeste admitted. He was right, absolutely he was right. 'You're wrong about one

thing, though,' she challenged. 'I'm not after a
relationship. I'm having enough trouble getting
used to being a mum without someone else in
the picture. It's bad enough that her own
father...' She started to cry then because she
couldn't believe how wrong she'd got it, that the
man she had thought she was in love with had
thought so very little of her.

'Have you told him?' And he said it in such a
different way from the way her mum had—not
accusing. He just asked the question and
watched her face crumple.

'I rang just before you came...'

'And?'

'He doesn't want to know.'

'I'm so sorry,' he said gently.

'I'm not,' Celeste sniffed. 'Well, I am for her,
but not for me. At least I know where I stand. I
will be okay on my own, you know!'

'I know that,' he said with a small smile at
her vehemence.

'And I'm not after a partner or a surrogate

father for the baby—it was just one stupid kiss and I regret it, because I really did like having you as a friend and I hate that it's been spoilt.'

'You were the one who told me not to drop round,' he pointed out.

'You were glad that I did,' she accused.

She was so honest, all he could do was smile at her again. 'We should have spoken about it,' Ben admitted. 'Tried to work it out.'

'That's what friends do,' Celeste said.

'That's what we are doing,' Ben replied. 'So I guess that's what we are.'

'Honestly?'

'Honestly,' Ben said, and to prove it he squeezed her fat sausage-like fingers. 'Have you got a name for her yet?'

'Nope,' she sighed.

'Any ideas?'

'About a thousand…'

'I'd better get down to work.' He stood up. He wasn't making excuses, he was already five minutes late. 'I'll drop by soon, but call if you need anything.'

'I will.' She gave him a watery smile, glad they were friends again, and so grateful to him for his skill today and for his honesty tonight.

Yet she had been honest too. She didn't want a father for the baby, neither was there a need for a relationship to survive....

And that thought was confirmed when at midnight she finally got to hold her.

She held this little scrap of a thing to her heart and thought it might burst as finally love whooshed in.

She stared at her daughter.

Just a few hours old and so, so , so raw and vulnerable and so reliant on her. No, she didn't need a surrogate father or a partner to make things work for her baby. She would take care of that all by herself.

She just wanted Ben for himself.

'We've been waiting for them.' The midwife cuddled her a little while later when she was wheeled back to bed and the tears finally flooded in. 'You have a good cry...' So she did, soothed that apparently it was completely normal to weep, to sob, that it was obviously hormones on top of an early delivery, estranged parents and a very new, sick little lady who was lying in a cot in Special Care, with a father who didn't care a jot…

Trying to convince herself that her tears had nothing to do with Ben.

'How is she?'

Ben had washed his hands and put on a gown over his clothes, even though he would only be looking.

'Good.' The special care nurse looked up. 'I'm Bron.'

'Ben.'

'You're the doctor who delivered her?'

'Yep.' Ben peered into the crib. 'I'm a friend of her mum's as well.'

'Well, she had a good first night—she's a restless little thing, aren't you, Willow?'

'Willow?' Ben smiled, because it was the perfect name for her.

She looked so much better than yesterday. Tubes and machines didn't scare Ben. If anything, they reassured him. She was a lovely pinky-red now, and pushing up against the side of the incubator as if she was trying to dig a little hole to climb into.

'I'm just going to change her sheet—do you want to hold her up?'

It would have been appropriate for Ben to help, rather than just stand and watch—and the most natural thing would surely be to just hold her up as the nurse changed the bedding, except, feeling awkward, he declined. 'No, thanks...' He knew he looked arrogant, but it was a price he was willing to pay, so instead he just stood there and watched as the special care nurse changed the bedding, then wrapped bunny rugs into an oval and wrapped them like a little cocoon to help Willow settle. She was a scrap of a thing really, all spindly arms and legs and with a little pink hat covering her dark hair.

She was cute, but no cuter than any of the

others he'd seen as he'd made his way over to her. They could have taken him to any baby and told him that it was Willow and he wouldn't have known any different.

And then she opened her eyes.

Even though she couldn't possibly be doing it, he felt as if she was staring right at him, just as she had in the ambulance. He stared back at her for a moment, and then once again it was he who looked away first.

'Thanks…' He gave a brief smile to the nurse. 'Thanks for letting me see her. It's good to know she's doing well.'

CHAPTER EIGHT

BEN dropped in on Celeste while she was still a patient and occasionally he saw her in the canteen and stopped for a chat and got an update as to how well Willow was doing.

She was doing *so* well.

Every day Celeste saw progress.

And not just with Willow. The ice was thawing with her mother too. She made the journey every other day, initially to see her granddaughter, but bringing in vital supplies for Celeste, then not so vital supplies and sometimes the occasional treat.

It was also Rita who provided an unlikely source of comfort as her milk supply steadily dwindled.

'The more you stress about it, the worse it will be,' Rita said firmly as Celeste sat in tears on the breast pump she hated so much, but at three weeks of age, Willow was only taking the tiniest of feeds from her mother before she became exhausted, and had to be gavage fed through a little tube that ran from her mouth to her stomach. Celeste was struggling to produce enough milk and hated the bland room where she would sit for ages, only to produce a paltry couple of millilitres.

'It's important that she gets my milk.' Celeste gritted her teeth. The lactation consultant had said so.

'It's more important that she gets fed.' Rita refused to back down—she was tired of the pressures that were being placed on her daughter and frustrated on her behalf. 'I couldn't feed you either, Celeste. I had to put you on the bottle when you were four days old.'

'And look how I turned out.'

The weight had fallen off her, sitting there, often teary, jangling with nerves, huge black rings under her eyes thanks to endless two-hourly feeds, broke and a single mum to boot. It was actually her first vague attempt at a joke with her mother in ages and for a moment Rita didn't get it. Then, as she opened her mouth to carry on with her lecture, she did, catching her daughter's eyes and starting to giggle, as did Celeste.

'You turned out just fine,' Rita said when the giggles had faded and the tears that were never very far away these days filled Celeste's eyes. It was the nicest thing her mother had said to her in a very long time. 'Go and get some lunch.' Her mum took the feeble offerings of milk, stuck one of Willow's ID labels on the bottle and popped it in the fridge. 'I'll finish up in here. You go and have a little break.'

Except it didn't feel like a break.

Celeste far preferred the safe routine she had established. Living in the small mothers' area, she was happy with her spartan room and evenings spent chatting with other anxious mothers. Her days were filled with feeding Willow or expressing her milk, gaining confidence with Willow under the nurse's watchful eye and taking for ever to choose what to order from the parents' menu cards that came round once a day. Only every now and then her mother insisted that she 'take a break'. And Celeste loathed it.

There really wasn't much to do.

The hospital *gardens* were a misnomer, the gift shop had long since sold out of her favourite toffees and she'd read each and every magazine at least twice. She'd popped into Emergency a couple of times, but it had always been at the wrong time, the department full and busy, and she'd sat awkward and alone in the staffroom. But mostly she loathed the canteen, where the best way she could describe herself was an 'almost but not quite'.

Almost a member of staff.

Almost a patient.

Almost a mother.

Except she had no uniform.

No ID tag on her wrist.

And no baby beside her.

Worse, her colleagues, if they were there, waved her over and after a couple of moments updating them on Willow's progress, Celeste sat toying with her yoghurt, listening as Deb raved about the wild weekend she'd had and Meg moaned at length about her stint on nights that was coming up.

And then she saw him.

Pushing his tray along as he chose his lunch, Belinda was by his side, dressed in a tight black skirt and red stilettos, her raven curls tumbling down her back as she laughed at something he was saying, and Celeste felt something twist inside her.

Belinda was so ravishing, so sexy and confident and clever and just...so much better suited to Ben.

She was quite sure that if they weren't already together, it was only a matter of time.

'Celeste!' So deep in thought was she that Celeste hadn't even noticed that her colleagues were clearing up the table. 'Did you hear us?'

Meg laughed at her absent-mindedness. 'We've got to get back—you drop in any time.'

'I will.'

'And I'm sure you're not thinking of it yet, but when you feel ready, you come and talk to me. Try not to let too much time pass without coming back...'

'I won't.' She said her goodbyes and sat alone, glad of the break. Belinda and Ben wouldn't come over. Registrars didn't generally sit with the nurses, well, in the staffroom they did, of course, but not in the canteen. Meg had unsettled her—of course it was way too soon to be contemplating returning to work, but in a couple of months' time, that was exactly what she would be doing—it was just impossible to comprehend from this vantage point.

'How are you?' Celeste was slightly taken aback by the warmth in Belinda's voice, and even more surprised when she put down her tray and joined her. 'How's Willow?'

'Marvellous.' Celeste blushed slightly as both Belinda and Ben joined her.

'Do you have any idea when you'll get her home?' Belinda pushed.

'A week or two,' Celeste said, 'if she keeps on doing well.' But she'd lost her audience, Belinda excusing herself to answer her pager and suddenly it was just Celeste and Ben.

'You'll be starting to pack up.' Celeste dragged her mind to something that wasn't about Willow. 'It's just a few weeks till you move into your new house now.'

'Actually, it's this weekend,' Ben said. 'The vendor was more than keen for a quick settlement and I'm all ready to move in.'

'Oh.' She was stirring an empty pot of yoghurt. 'I was going to come home for a few hours on Sunday—the nurses are insisting I take a night off. I was going to pop over and say thank you properly...'

'I won't be there,' Ben said, and then there was a pause. 'Of course, I'm only down the road.' Except it wasn't the same.

They were friends, but mainly by proximity, and though she didn't want to rely on Ben, on anyone really, there had been a certain comfort to be had knowing he was just a few doors down.

'Have you got my phone number?' Ben asked. Celeste shook her head and he scribbled it down. 'Here it is.' Ben handed her a card. 'You call if you need anything.'

'Thanks.' She pocketed it as Belinda returned, but they both knew she wouldn't use it. Oh, they'd stop and chat perhaps if she was walking on the beach, but there would be no dropping round, no dinners in front of the television. Just as he was moving so too had she—she was a mother now, which, by his own admission, rendered her off limits to Ben.

Belinda said something that made him laugh and then they tried to include her in the conversation, but it didn't work. She hadn't read a newspaper in weeks, so she wasn't exactly up on current events, hadn't been anywhere except the special care unit, which meant she hadn't a clue about the new seafood restaurant Belinda was raving about. She was just so out of the loop that it was like watching a foreign film. Celeste was so busy reading the subtitles, she missed out on the humour and laughed too late, and by the time she'd worked out what was being said, they had already moved on.

'I'd better get back...' She was about to add 'to feed Willow,' but it was a detail they didn't need. The entire focus of her life was just a conversation filler to them. 'Good luck with the move.'

'Thanks.'

It was a relief to move.

To be away from her—even if it was just down the road—made him safe. There could be no dropping over, no hearing the baby cry as he walked past the unit.

Celeste got under his skin.

From the very first moment he had seen her on the beach she had entranced him—and every now and then, when she was around, somehow he forgot his rules.

But closing the door on the unit for the last time, there was a pang of something—a wave of homesickness almost for the weeks he had spent there, despite the argumentative neighbours and the lack of air-conditioning. It hadn't all been bad, Ben thought as he picked up his sunflowers, which now were up to his shoulders in height, and loaded them in the back of the hire truck, along with the rest of his belongings.

It had almost passed as home.

'I'm sorry to trouble you…' Ben was instantly awake, but as it was only his first night in his new home he struggled to find the light. He could hear the panic in her voice and it had him searching for his jeans the second it was on. 'My car won't start, and I can't get a taxi for an hour…'

'Wait outside,' Ben instructed, not asking what the problem was, because clearly there was one—Celeste would never ring at two a.m. otherwise. 'I'm on my way.'

Used to dressing for an emergency dash to the hospital, he was in jeans, T-shirt and running shoes in less than a minute. Another two had his car out of the garage and down the street, and she was there outside the units, waiting for him.

She'd got so thin. Even in these last few days the weight had fallen off her and she was as white as a sheet in the glare of his headlights. He pulled open the car door and she jumped straight in.

'Thank you. You'll be sorry you gave me your phone number,' she gasped.

'I'm not sorry at all—I'm glad you rang.' He could hear that she was trying not to cry, trying to stay calm, and he didn't push her with questions, just drove and let her speak and tell him the bits she wanted to.

'The car wouldn't start,' Celeste explained. 'I think it's the battery.'

'Don't worry about that now.'

'They said that she's had a couple of apnoea attacks...they haven't happened in a while.'

'Okay...' He forgot to indicate at the roundabout and cursed himself for his error as a car angrily tooted—hell, he did this drive most nights when the hospital called him in. He *had* to concentrate.

'Her temperature's high as well, so they're doing bloods...' He didn't answer, just stared at the road as she talked nervously. 'I told them to ring...' She gulped and then managed to continue. 'I mean, I told them that they were to ring me for anything. So maybe it's not that serious...'

He doubted it.

Despite trying not to worry about Celeste, Ben was. He'd seen her toying with her yoghurt, seen her dramatic weight loss, her nervousness—and she'd practically told him that the nursing staff had insisted she have a night off, so they wouldn't be calling her in the middle of the night for nothing.

'She was doing so well!' Celeste insisted, even

though he wasn't arguing. 'I wouldn't have left her otherwise.' God, when did the fear stop? Celeste asked herself. When did you stop living in constant worry?

Get past the first trimester.

Get past thirty weeks.

Get her blood pressure down.

Get past a hellish labour.

Get past those first terrible few nights in Special Care.

Her leg was bouncing up and down, jiggling away.

When did it stop? When did she get to live without fear?

They were at the hospital and he could have just dropped her off, only of course he didn't, so they parked in the emergency doctor spot and he used his swipe card to get them in the back way, without having to go through Emergency.

'How is she?' Celeste was shaking so much as she went through the hand-washing ritual. The unit was brightly lit even at night, but some of cots were covered in blankets to simulate night.

Not Willow's.

She seemed to have more tubes and people around her than she had on the night after her birth and Celeste was glad when the charge nurse came straight over and brought her up to date.

'She's stable, Celeste.' Her voice was kind and firm and Ben's arm around Celeste helped, just this quiet strength beside her as she took in the news. 'Willow gave us some cause for concern a couple of hours ago—she had an apnoeic episode, which isn't unusual here, but she hasn't had one for a while, then she had another, and she started to struggle a bit with her breathing. Now she'd had some blood gases and we've put her back on CPAP, and the neonatologist has taken blood cultures…'

'Has she got an infection?'

'There are some patchy areas on her X-ray,' the charge nurse replied, 'so we've started her on antibiotics.' They were walking over to her cot and Celeste felt her heart tighten when she saw Willow, seemingly back where she'd started, all wired and hooked up and struggling so hard to breathe.

All Ben wanted to do was turn and run, but instead he stood with his arm around Celeste and stared at the machines instead of the baby. At every turn he was pulled in closer, dragged further into a world where he didn't want to belong.

'She's been fine...' Celeste sobbed when she saw her, the only relief being that Bron, her favourite nurse, was the one looking after her. 'She was going to be moved to the nursery next week...'

'It's just a setback,' the charge nurse said firmly. 'Remember when you first came to the unit and we explained that these little one have ups and downs. Well, Willow has done exceptionally well...' On she went about roller-coaster rides and all the rest of the spiel that Celeste was sick of hearing and had dared to think might be over now. All she felt was that she was back at the start again, especially when she was told she couldn't pick Willow up.

'Just hold her hand for now,' Bron said. 'We're trying to keep her quiet.'

And with that she had to make do.

'Here's Heath coming now. You've met him,' Bron said.

'He's not her doctor,' Celeste pointed out.

'No, he's the consultant on call tonight. Have a seat in the parents room and I'll get him to come and speak with you.'

'Are you the father?' Heath asked Ben as he came up to them.

'No, just a friend,' Ben explained. Then they could see Heath wasn't listening to him as the charge nurse was urgently summoning him back to the cots again.

Celeste could only feel guilty relief that it wasn't for Willow but for the little one in the next cot. 'Not *just* a friend.' Celeste looked at him. 'There's no such thing as *just* with you.'

Ben tried not to over-analyse that comment

too much. It was just one of those things—she was grateful probably that he'd been there tonight, for his help these past weeks, and no doubt glad she didn't have to sit alone on this hellish night, because it wasn't actually Celeste who'd drawn the short straw.

The wait to speak with Heath was endless, and she couldn't go to Willow because, as well as working on her, they were working intensely on the tiny infant in the next cot. Ben thought his job was agony at times, but when the other baby's parents arrived, pale and shocked and visibly terrified, he wouldn't have been Heath or the charge nurse for a million dollars. Unlike Celeste, they got to hold their baby straight away.

Because it was already too late.

'We're concerned about Celeste,' Heath said.

Ben had sat with Celeste until Heath had taken them through Willow's X-rays and blood results and asked all the questions that Celeste was just too overwhelmed to ask, but would surely regret not asking later. Until finally she was taken in to sit with Willow.

'I'm not Willow's father,' Ben interrupted.

'Her partner?'

'No.' Ben shook his head.

'I'm sorry.' Heath frowned. 'Only Bron said that you'd been in a few times at night to see Willow.'

For the first time in his adult life Ben was coming close to blushing—he felt as if he'd been caught out doing something wrong. Oh, he'd only been up a handful of times—and never when Celeste was around. He'd just wanted to see for himself how the baby was doing.

Clearly, it had been noted!

'I'm a doctor here.' Ben cleared his throat uncomfortably. 'And as I said, Celeste's a friend. I pop in occasionally to check on the baby. I delivered her…'

'I see.' But obviously he didn't.

'You said you were concerned about her?' Ben pursued.

'Look, I thought you were her partner. I'm

sorry, my mistake—it's been a long night,' Heath said.

Ben realised that if he wanted to, he could just walk away now—ignore the slight indiscretion, say goodnight to Celeste and just fall into bed for what remained of the night. But he didn't want to.

'We're very good friends,' Ben said. 'If I can help in any way…'

'She just needs a break. It's exceptionally unfortunate that Willow got sick on the one night we'd persuaded her to go home. And with the baby dying in the next cot she's hyper-vigilant now,' Heath explained. 'It's common with mothers in her situation, but sadly tonight has done nothing to help with that.'

'What can I do?' Ben asked.

'It's not simply an overnight thing,' Heath said, standing up and shaking Ben's hand before heading back out to the unit. 'She needs regular support, needs to be encouraged to take a break every now and then—once Willow's better, of course.'

Which meant getting further involved with mother and child—which Ben definitely didn't want to do. So instead he offered her more practicality as he said goodnight to Celeste. 'Give me your keys. I'll sort out the car for you.'

'I'll sort it out myself tomorrow,' she said.

'Celeste.' He wasn't arguing or debating the point. 'You *need* your car to work, for Willow's sake. So give me your keys, and if it's the battery I'll charge it or get a new one, and if it's something else...' He saw her eyes close in utter despair, as the water rose ever higher. He wanted to pull her out, to wrench her from the rising tide, except he was so very scared to.

Scared to love her.

Except somehow he already did.

Only the problem wasn't Celeste.

It was Willow.

CHAPTER NINE

HE WAS up at six, on a rare day off. He had boxes to unpack and a kitchen to paint, but instead he wandered down the road, Celeste's car keys in hand. He'd have a look at the car, have a run on the beach and then he'd sort out the boxes. Ben opened the garage and after turning the key in the ignition the car grumbled into noisy life—so it wasn't the battery.

At eight he called the mobile mechanic.

'Do you want my advice?' The mechanic stared at what could loosely be called an engine and frowned heavily.

'No.' Ben gave a grimace. 'Just fix it, get it roadworthy, please.'

'The tyres are bald...'

'Get decent second-hand ones,' Ben said, because against that pile of scrap, four gleaming new ones would stand out far too much.

It took the whole day, but by six he was dropping her keys back at the hospital for her.

'How's Willow doing?' he asked her.

'A bit better, thanks.' Celeste looked completely wiped out. Her hair needed washing and there were huge charcoal smudges beneath her eyes, as if she'd been wearing black eyeliner and rubbed them, except she hadn't worn make-up for weeks. 'The first of her blood cultures should be back soon, but she hasn't had a temperature since lunchtime.'

'What about her blood gases?' he queried.

'They're better.' She shook her head in confusion. She wasn't thinking as a nurse but as a mum, listening to the doctors and the special care staff. 'She's to stay on oxygen…'

He wanted more information, wanted to speak with the neonatologist, to see the baby's X-rays and blood results for himself.

'I got to hold her,' she told him tremulously.

His demands had no place here, so instead he smiled. 'That's good news.'

'Mum's in with her now.'

All he could do was take her to the canteen and buy her a hot chocolate and some cereal from the machine, and only when he handed her the car keys did Celeste remember what he was doing here. He wasn't actually here to find out about Willow at all.

'What was wrong with it?' she wanted to know.

'It needed a new battery.' And a starter motor and brake discs and pads and muffler and... But he chose not to elaborate any further.

'How much was it? There's a cash machine here,' she said.

'It wasn't much. We'll sort it out when Willow's better,' Ben said easily. With a baby that sick, Celeste needed a car that started first time every time, Ben told himself. And he was saving his sanity too, he decided. At least he wouldn't be getting woken up at two a.m. any more...

Except he actually hadn't minded.

If the truth be known, he would have hated to have found out from someone else the next day what had happened.

He'd hardly slept in twenty-four hours but, despite that fact, his mind suddenly seemed clear.

Celeste needed a friend—a real one—and maybe he could be that for while, maybe he could be there for her, at least till Willow came home.

'I've been thinking,' Ben said. 'Once Willow's better, how about a day out?'

'Where?' she asked.

'On the water,' Ben suggested, but she immediately shook her head.

'What if something happened? It would take too long to get here,' she protested anxiously.

'We're not crossing the equator, just taking a ride out on the bay! We could have lunch.'

'I don't think so, but thanks anyway.' She shook her head.

'Don't say no,' Ben said. 'Just think about it.'

* * *

She didn't think about it.

There was way too much else to think about.

As Willow got over what had turned out to be a nasty bout of pneumonia and started to regularly put on weight, discharge day started looming. Celeste's milk supply had finally completely dried up and, regretfully for Celeste, Willow was now taking a bottle, but at least it did give her a little bit more freedom and meant she could get back to the flat every now and then—or even visit the doctor for herself!

'Celeste?'

Ben passed her as he was walking through the main entrance corridor. Amidst a hub of people and cafés and a gift shop, there was Celeste, as white as a sheet, and in her own vague world.

'Celeste…' He tapped her on the shoulder to get her attention. 'Is everything okay?'

She visibly made an effort to concentrate. 'Fine,' she finally answered.

'Willow?'

'She's good,' Celeste said without the usual elaboration of the past few weeks. Normally she gushed over every milestone, and Ben saw her lick dry lips.

'You?'

'I'm bit queasy,' she admitted. 'I was going to get a drink but there's a huge queue.'

'Go and sit down, I'll get you one.' That she didn't argue told Ben she really wasn't feeling well.

Of course there was a queue at the café, but he could be arrogant enough at times and he ignored it, going straight to the front and getting two bottles of water and a bottle of juice—oh, and a muffin.

'Here.' He put his wares on the table and Celeste took a long drink of water.

'How did you get served so quickly? I'd given up.'

'Perk of the job.' Ben winked. 'I got you something to eat...in case you're hungry.'

Celeste screwed up her nose. 'How much do

I owe you?' She scrabbled in her purse for some money, but Ben just shook his head.

'Don't be daft.'

'Add it to my slate!' Celeste said, and then leant forward, rested her head on her arm for a moment and let everything pass by, the noise, the traffic of a busy hospital, the glare of the windows, everything except Ben's concerned voice.

'Should I be taking your pulse or something?' he teased gently to hide his real worry.

'No.'

'You're not very good company today.' He lifted her forehead a little, then saw her grey face and put it back down to rest on her forearm.

'They told me to wait half an hour…' came her muffled voice. 'I should have listened.'

'Should I be sending for a gurney from Emergency?' he asked lightly.

'Please don't!' Slowly she sat up and gave him a weak smile.

'Better now?'

'Better.' She blew out a breath. 'That's twice you've saved me from embarrassing myself.'

'Childbirth is hardly embarrassing,' he pointed out.

'In the middle of the road, with a crowd gathered?'

'Okay.' He grinned. 'So it could have been embarrassing—if I hadn't managed to get you into the relative privacy of what is now my garden! As would fainting outside the hospital gift shop. So what happened to make you feel like this?'

'I just had my postnatal check.'

'Oh.' He was a doctor, so why were his ears going a bit pink? He could walk into the staffroom in Emergency this very minute into a gaggle of nurses who wouldn't halt their discussion with him in the room.

'He suggested that I have a coil inserted, in the unlikely event that I want to resume sexual relations over the next five years!'

She *did* make him laugh—even at awkward things.

'You will want to, eventually,' he said.

'I doubt it!' She took another long drink and

then picked at the muffin. 'It seems like a lot of fuss for nothing, to tell you the truth—well, not nothing,' she mused. 'Having had a family fallout, a baby in Special Care…' She broke off the list of her woes—he wouldn't be interested in all that, especially when she came to the part about how Willow's father didn't want to know her. 'Anyway, he also suggested that I lie down for half an hour afterwards.'

'You clearly didn't listen,' he said a little sternly.

'I felt fine.' Celeste shrugged.

'Well, listen next time,' he ordered.

Colour was coming back to her lips now, and to her cheeks. It had been nice to sit and chat but she'd been gone for a while now and wanted to be back to give Willow her bottle.

'I'd better get up to Special Care…'

She was still a touch pale. 'Maybe you should wait another ten minutes,' he suggested.

Which she probably would have, except the pager she wore went off, telling her that Willow was awake and ready to be fed.

'I should go.'

'I'll walk up with you,' Ben offered, still concerned with her colour.

They walked through the corridors and up to the lift, Ben seeing her right up to the entrance to Special Care, and as they arrived, Celeste was suddenly nervous.

'Do you want to come in?' It was, oh, so casually offered. 'You'll see a huge difference in her…'

'I'd love to,' Ben said, and she could hear the 'but' even before it was said, knew it was coming before it was uttered. 'But I really ought to get back to Emergency. Another time, maybe?'

'Sure.' She didn't get him—just didn't. He seemed to enjoy her company, was always there when she needed him, and yet sometimes all he wanted to do was get away from her!

'Hey…' He turned around. 'Have you thought about coming out on the boat with me?'

'I don't think so,' Celeste declined. 'They're saying that Willow might be ready for discharge next Monday, and I've got loads to get ready.'

'Well, I'm off next weekend,' Ben said. 'So the offer's there…just let me know.'

She was ready.

Well, as ready as she would ever be!

All the new baby clothes had been washed in soap flakes, there were nappies and baby wipes and bottles and formula, the crib that Ben had set up and which Celeste had lined with bunny rugs. All it needed now was Willow—and that was happening tomorrow.

The nurses had practically frogmarched her out of the department, insisting she spend a day at home and strongly suggesting she didn't come back till morning—that she should grab one last night of uninterrupted sleep while she still could.

Her parents, having helped her set up, had gone home, and with nothing to do, Celeste had decided to walk down the road to get a magazine, with the intention of sitting on the beach to read it. Or rather that was her excuse for walking past Ben's new house!

It felt strange, being out in the fresh air—strange to be out in the afternoon sunlight instead of in the nursery—but the nurses had given her very little choice in the matter, so she decided to enjoy it.

She was wearing denim shorts and a white halter-neck T-shirt, pre-pregnancy clothes that were actually a bit big for her now. Her feet were wrapped in thin red leather sandals, and it felt nice to have the sun on her legs, nice to walk along the street, though she felt as if she'd forgotten something, kept pulling out her phone to check it in case the hospital had rung and she'd missed it, or kept scrambling in her bag to check she had her keys. It already felt completely weird to be anywhere without Willow.

Still, the world had carried on very nicely without her. Flowers hung heavy on the trees, the bay was blue and still glistening in the background—and there was Ben, with his new boat all hooked up to his four-wheel drive.

'Very nice.' Celeste commented, walking around and inspecting *his* new baby. 'Very nice indeed.'

'I think I'm in love.' Ben grinned, running a loving hand over his new toy, and all Celeste could do was laugh. 'How's Willow?'

'Very well. She looks like a complete fraud— she's way too healthy to be in hospital.'

'All ready for tomorrow?' he asked.

'As ready as I'll ever be.'

'You'll be great,' he said reassuringly.

'So, are you taking her out?' She wouldn't ask to go with him, Celeste decided, but if he happened to offer again…

'I've just got back,' Ben said. 'I went out with a friend—I'm still not sure about launching her on my own yet.'

'Ooh, no!' Celeste agreed, smiling, but her heart sank a little, realising that she had very literally missed the boat with him. 'The boat ramp is not the place to practise.'

'Yeah, I'm still a novice—but it is nice to be out there again. I'd forgotten how good it feels.'

'There's another launching ramp by the creek,' Celeste said, 'for when you do want to take her out on your own. It's probably the quietest one and you won't be holding everyone up.'

'You've done this before, then?' he asked curiously.

'All the time,' Celeste said with a cheeky grin. 'Well, when Dad and I were talking, I used to go fishing with him.'

'You?' Ben raised his eyebrows. 'Fishing?'

'No, daydreaming,' Celeste said. 'But I'm fishing now…'

It took a second for him to get her meaning and when he did he smiled.

'Let's go, then.'

It was the perfect evening to try out a new boat—the bay was calm, with barely a breeze. For a novice, he did a pretty decent job of reversing the boat and trailer down the ramp, then jumped out and dealt with the boat as Celeste took the driver's seat, just as she had when she had been out with her dad. Having parked his four-wheel drive, she then walked down to the water, Ben holding her hand as she stepped in. His new engine purred into life and she was so glad she had said yes, so glad, as Ben weaved the boat, to feel the wind in her hair and to just breathe again after these last few weeks.

Ben watched as slowly, slowly she unwound. The weight had fallen off her since Willow's birth, and seeing her slender frame emerging he'd realised just how ill she'd been, probably since the day he'd met her. Too much time in the hospital, both as a patient and visiting Willow, had given her that pale, unhealthy colour. Still, the sea air was bringing back some much-needed warmth to her cheeks and when she didn't check her phone for a full ten minutes, Ben knew that finally, even if it was just for a little while, the Celeste of old was back.

They stopped and idled and Ben set out the food they had grabbed on a quick stop at the deli. In the distance, Melbourne glittered gold in the setting sun. Willow was coming home tomorrow and all was surely right in the world—even if it felt otherwise at times.

'Scared about tomorrow?' Ben asked.

'Scared but ready,' Celeste admitted.

'You're going to be a great mum,' Ben said.

'I'd better be...' Celeste smiled. 'She'll be home in a matter of hours.'

He unpacked tarragon chicken in mayonnaise, which tasted as good as they first time they'd shared it, washed down with sparkling mineral water. For Celeste it was bliss to just pause, to escape before life changed yet again tomorrow.

'You've got transport and everything sorted?' Ben checked.

'Dad and Mum are coming,' Celeste informed him. 'Come over in the afternoon if you like— I've got some friends coming round and we're going to have a little barbeque...'

'Shouldn't you take it easy the first few days?' Ben asked dubiously.

'That's the plan,' Celeste said with a flash of her old cheek. 'I'll get them all in and out in one hit!'

They could have headed home then, except they didn't. Ben was playing sailor while Celeste lay in the bottom of the little boat, her feet up on the edge, and listened to the dreamy lap, lap of the water. She couldn't remember being this relaxed since Willow's birth, since before Willow was born, since for ever, really...

When she opened her eyes to tell him so, she suddenly wasn't relaxed any more.

Because he was watching her, just sitting quietly watching her. When Celeste's eyes opened, he didn't look away, he just stared, and she stared right back at those contrary green eyes that both reached for her and resisted her. They stared in silence, reliving their one and only kiss in their minds, and all it did was confuse her, because in that second she was sure that without Willow there would be love between them.

Without Willow.

It was an impossible place and one she never wanted to visit. She could see a flash in his eyes and it could have been the breeze or the sun glare, or it might have been tears, because there was regret etched on his features, and regret laced with anger in hers.

Because without Willow, they'd be mere colleagues now.

Without Willow she'd never have been living opposite him.

There could be no without Willow and there could be no them.

'Rotten timing, huh?' She wasn't making a joke, and she wasn't making a stab in the dark as to how he was feeling—because out on the water, when it was just the two of them, with no past, no future, just this moment in time, there was no question of either of them denying it.

'It is,' Ben said, and he didn't have to elaborate—he'd stated his case from the very beginning.

'So I'm not going mad and imagining things, then?'

'You're not going mad…' He touched her hair, just holding one heavy curl in his fingers, and *how* he wanted to tell her, to explain, but how? Heath's warning was ringing in his ears. This was her day off from worrying and he didn't want to darken it with his grief, couldn't burden this very new mum with his fears for her, for her child.

'I just can't do it.' Ben settled for that.

'I know.'

'I said so from the beginning.'

'You did.'

'Can we still be friends?' Ben asked, and her answer was the same as the one ringing inside his own head.

'I don't know.'

Maybe this was their last kiss but it was the sweetest she had ever tasted.

He bent her head and brushed her lips and if real men didn't cry, that excluded Ben, because she felt the brush of damp eyelashes on her cheeks as his mouth met hers. It was the most fleeting of kisses but it was so mingled with regret and love that it would stay with her for ever.

She didn't have to tell him to take her home

afterwards, he just started up the engine, Ben driving, Celeste pulling on massive sunglasses and trying not to cry.

The whole journey home was neither pleasant nor wretched, yet contained no more kisses.

'Do you want to come in?' she offered when he pulled up at her gates. She knew exactly what she was offering, knew because the air was so thick with want, there could be no doubt in either of their minds.

'Celeste…' His knuckles were white where he gripped the steering-wheel. 'Go inside.'

'Just for tonight,' she pleaded. She wanted a proper kiss goodbye, was greedy for more, and was trying to convince herself she could handle the morning after. Rejection was surely her forte—except she loathed it now.

''Night, Celeste,' he replied.

CHAPTER TEN

HE PROBABLY should have popped over.

Set the tone.

Resumed being nothing but friends.

Only it was too late for that now.

Autumn was coming. Every night the wind stripped a few more petals from the sunflowers. Heading for home from work nearly a week later and sick of the constant reminders, Ben pulled out the gangly stalks and went to shove them on the compost. About a hundred seeds scattered in the garden while he did it and Ben gritted his teeth. So much for forgetting! If he didn't get the seeds up he'd need a scythe next year just to get to the front door!

She was everywhere.

In his head, in his dreams, and as he walked into the house, he headed upstairs to change and his eyes moved straight to the beach, to where he'd first seen Celeste, instead of to the picture of Jen on his bedside table.

'What do I do?' He picked up the silver frame and stared into his wife's clear eyes and wished for just two minutes of her time.

Two minutes of her logical, practical advice, which was a stupid thing to wish for—as if he should even be asking Jen about Celeste!

He wanted her to tell him, just a sign, one little sign, only he didn't even know what he was asking for.

And then he looked at the whole picture, not just at Jen.

He ran a finger over the swell of her stomach to where their baby lay, touched *her* only through glass, touched what he'd never, not even once got to hold.

But there wasn't time to wallow. He had visitors that evening, which proved difficult, and then he was called into hospital to deal with an emergency at around 10 p.m. He could hear the pounding music from Celeste's neighbours as he drove past her unit and despite his best intentions, it was difficult to ignore. However, he determinedly drove on, hoping the party would wind down early, or that she'd taken Willow and gone to her parents'. Surely a wild party next door was the last thing a new mum needed only a few days after bring her babe home.

Still, it wasn't his problem now.

'Sorry!' Belinda looked up from a packed Resus as Ben made his way over. 'You're about to get a page saying we don't need you after all.'

'Sure about that?' Ben checked, because the place was steaming.

'We were alerted for two multi-traumas,' Belinda explained, 'and on top of this amount of patients, I thought we should call in some extras, even though you're not rostered on.'

'Where are the trauma victims?'

'One died en route and one's not too seriously injured. I'm just about to ring the parents— who'd have teenagers, huh? Perhaps I should have waited to call you.'

'Better not to wait and see.' Ben really didn't mind being called in, it was part of his job. 'I'll give you a hand now that I'm here.'

'No, you won't,' Belinda contradicted as she looked at some X-rays on the computer. 'Go and get some sleep—this is just a usual Friday night.'

'I really don't mind,' he persisted.

'Well, I do,' Belinda said. 'You're covering for me tomorrow, remember.'

'Ah, yes!'

'And I'm rather hoping that you *won't* be calling me in.' She winked at him.

'Going somewhere nice?' he asked.

'To a fabulous hotel in the City.' Belinda smiled. 'A million miles away from here.'

'You and Paul still going strong, then?'

'Absolutely. You know you really shouldn't knock the internet.'

Ben just groaned—she never let up! 'Okay, then, I'll head home. Just buzz if you do need help, though.'

He would actually have preferred to be working—wished that Belinda had handed him a pile of patient cards and asked him to wade his way through them, because as he turned into his street, instead of slowing down he speeded up a touch and turned up the car radio. Really, whatever was going on at the flats wasn't his problem. There were parties there every other night, and he couldn't forever be checking that Celeste was okay...

A group of teenagers was spilling onto the street, and despite the car radio on loud he could hear the doof-doof of the music. Though he had driven past, regretting it, resenting it even, he executed a hasty U-turn, flashed his lights at the drunken idiots and pulled over. Opening the gates and heading up to her unit, he saw the lights were on. Hearing Willow's screams from inside, he knocked at the door.

When there was no answer he realised how scared she must be.

'Celeste,' he called during a tiny lull in the music. 'It's me, Ben.'

'What do you want?' He could see she'd been crying when she opened the door.

'I heard the noise on my way back from work. You can't settle her in this. You should have rung me…'

'You wouldn't have been home,' Celeste pointed out, but despite her flip retort he could tell she was still close to tears. 'It's only a party…'

Which it was—a very loud party, but next door to a very new baby and a very new mum, who just hadn't needed it tonight.

'I can't get her to feed, and the nurses said it had to be every three hours at the most,' she said forlornly.

'Come on,' he announced. 'Let's grab her things and you can both crash at my place.'

She was about to say no, about to close the door, but a small fight was erupting in the next unit, and, however much she didn't want to need help, tonight she did.

'Please, Celeste…' Even inside her flat the music was just as loud! 'Pack a bag and come and stay at my house tonight,' he begged again.

She would have argued, but she was too relieved. She wasn't sure if it was her own tension or the noise that was upsetting Willow, but after six weeks of tender care in the special care unit, Celeste was scared enough being on her own with her, without the invasive noise and chaos of next door.

She was trying to clip Willow in her little seat to carry out to the car, but Ben had other ideas. 'Just put her in her pram. It will be just as easy to walk…and she can sleep in it.'

She would never have walked outside with the party mob there, but with Ben she felt safe. He pushed the pram and bumped it down the steps as Celeste locked up. The gates to the units were already open and with his arm around her they walked in swift silence away from the noise along the street and only when it faded in the distance did he talk.

'You should have called the police.'

'What, and have my neighbours hate me?' Celeste said ruefully as they walked along the street. There was a nearly full moon, which provided plenty of light, the music was just a thud in the distance and she could hear the welcome sound of the water now. 'It was only a party…' she said again.

'It's no place…' He didn't finish the sentence, but Celeste knew what he'd been about to say.

'It's all I can afford, Ben,' she told him quietly.

'I know that.'

'There was a small house in town for about the same price—I should have rented that, but I wanted to be closer to the beach. The flat seemed fine when I inspected it. I didn't think to ask to see it at eleven o'clock on a Friday night…' She took over the pram, and was walking more quickly now. Willow, overtired, was still crying, and Celeste was both annoyed at him and at herself. She was trying so hard to cope, so hard to do right by her baby, yet at every turn she seemed thwarted, at every turn life tossed her another curve ball… 'I'm doing my best,' she said as they arrived at his house. 'Though, I'm sure you don't think it's good enough—'

'I never said that!' Ben interrupted.

'No, but you think it!' she retorted. She was angry at him and she knew she shouldn't be. It wasn't his fault, he was being perfectly nice, but his home, his order, his everything only seemed to highlight her own inadequacies.

'Why don't you feed her?' Ben suggested soothingly. He carried the pram and the baby up the stairs and past his stunning bedroom to a rather nice guest room, where he parked the pram. 'Rest on the bed, the view's lovely. You can both relax and get Willow calm and settled…'

'And her mum too…' She was just a bit embarrassed at her outburst. After all, it wasn't his fault how he made her feel.

'I'll leave you to it,' Ben said. 'I'll find some sheets to make up the bed.'

'Thanks,' she said awkwardly.

'Come out when you're ready.'

'I need…' He was turning to go and she stopped him, rummaging through Willow's bag. 'Is there anywhere I can warm up her bottle?'

'Sure,' he said.

'Actually…' she picked up the hot little bundle that was her sobbing baby '…could you hold Willow for me?'

'I'll do the bottle,' Ben said, in an annoyingly calm voice that only made her appear more frazzled. 'I know where everything is.'

He took the bottle and she changed Willow while her screams quadrupled. She felt like howling herself. She knew he'd been expecting her to just lie on the bed and flop out a boob, to feed her baby herself…

She felt such a failure, felt so close to crying that she barely managed to thank him as he returned a couple of moments later with a warm bottle. He sort of hovered for an uncomfortable moment as she sat awkwardly on the edge of the bed and took it from him. Then Willow's mouth clamped onto the teat as if she'd been starved for a week and the only sound was of gulps and tears as an overtired baby finally took its bottle from an overwrought mum.

Although Willow was gulping her bottle, she kept jumping and startling while she was doing it. Celeste kicked off her sandals and lay back on the bed, pulling Willow in tighter, but every time she almost relaxed, the baby would suddenly startle as if the noise, the angst, the panic from her mother was all about to start again.

It was nothing unfamiliar to Celeste.

The party had just been the clincher. In the few days since she'd been home from the hospital, practically every time she'd sat down to quietly feed her babe, her mother had 'dropped in', offering all kinds of suggestions—'Change her first,' or 'Change her after she's fed,' or 'Hold the bottle higher,' or 'She needs winding,' each well-meaning suggestion from Rita only exacerbating the tension further.

Celeste desperately wanted to be back in the hospital, wanted to be feeding Willow with knowledgeable staff offering quiet encouragement, or even to put her to bed in the hospital at night and go home, as she had last Sunday, missing her but knowing she was being well looked after—no, that Willow was being *better* looked after than she could manage by herself.

'It's okay, Willow, it's all okay, Willow,' she said softly, over and over again until finally Willow believed it, until finally her little jerks and startles stopped, and the gulps of tears faded. Celeste felt this unfamiliar surge of triumph as her baby relaxed into her, scared to move almost as Willow moved from resisting her to this passive, trance-like state almost— seemingly asleep, but still feeding.

She really was asleep, Celeste realised as she took the empty bottle from Willow's mouth and watched her little eyelids flicker.

So asleep that if the party down the street re-
located to outside the bedroom window,
Celeste was quite sure that Willow wouldn't
wake up.

And she had done it all by herself.

She'd never been so alone with her baby and
felt so much a mum at the same time.

Celeste stared down at the perfect features of
her daughter, dark little eyebrows that looked as
if they'd been pencilled on, her fine pointy nose
and little rosebud mouth, and she thought her
heart would swell and burst there was so much
love inside it for her baby.

A scary love that knew no bounds—yet still
she felt so inadequate.

This little scrap of a thing was just so utterly
and completely dependent on her, there should
be no room to feel anything else.

Except she did.

She didn't want to move, didn't want to put
her down. She just wanted to stay safe on this
bed, holding her baby, watching the bay with

Ben just a call away. To simply hold onto this first ray of peace.

'Don't fall asleep holding the baby.'

She could hear her mother as if she were in the room with them.

And she was right, Celeste sighed, heading over to the pram and gently lowering Willow in.

As she headed out to the lounge, Ben, sprawled on one of the sofas, looked up from the show on the television he was watching and poured her a glass of wine. It was the second little ray of peace she felt. For the first time since Willow's discharge from hospital, she felt as if she were home.

'She's asleep,' she told him.

'Good. How are you?' he asked.

'Better.' She took a seat on the edge of the sofa opposite him. 'You always seem to bailing me out. It won't be for much longer.'

'I know,' Ben said, then suggested that she choose a movie, so she did, kneeling down as she worked through his collection, and as she did she told him her most recent news.

'I mean, you won't have to keep bailing me out because I'm moving back home.'

His wine paused midway to his mouth. 'When?' he asked and then took a long sip, holding it in his mouth until she replied.

'Next weekend.' Huge amber eyes flashed towards him then looked away. 'Mum and Dad are painting the spare room for her and we're moving the stuff throughout next week. It's just not working, living here. You know what it's like, and Mum and I are getting on a lot better now...' She trailed off.

'How do you feel about it?' he asked shrewdly.

Celeste stared unseeingly at the DVD she was holding. 'To be honest, I haven't really stopped to think about it that much.'

So she did. She sank back on her heels and thought.

Out loud.

'It's not what I really want,' she admitted. 'I asked them a few weeks ago, but that was when I was pregnant. I never wanted to live there with a baby—but it's best for Willow. We could manage on our own, but this way...' Celeste took a deep breath. 'She's nearly two months old—it seems unbelievable. I could put her in the crèche next month and start back at work.'

'Is your mum going to watch her for you?'

Celeste nodded. 'Only for work—she's warned me that she's not a built-in babysitter so we've agreed it's just for a year.' And then she told him her other news. 'I've spoken to Meg and she's going to help me with my application to transfer hospitals.'

'Back to your old one?'

'No.' Instantly she shook her head. 'To Melbourne Central...'

'That's my old stomping ground,' Ben said.

'It's much closer to home than here. Anyway, I'm going to be head down finishing the emergency grad year and then I'm going to do as many shifts as I can and save...'

She looked so young sometimes—she *was* so young, Ben reminded himself. Only that wasn't what he meant. She seemed so fey and carefree at times yet there was a deep streak to her that enthralled him—an inherent resilience that belied her apparent fragility at times.

And she'd clearly given this a lot of thought.

'You say you're getting on with your parents now?'

'It's a lot better than it was.' She'd chosen the movie and popped it in. 'I can't imagine living at home again, though. I couldn't wait to leave the first time!' She rolled her eyes and added, 'They're really strict.' She gave him a smile and this time sat on the same sofa as him. 'There'll be none of this…'

'What?'

'Sitting in the dark with a man, drinking wine!'

'You're twenty-four.' Ben grinned. 'And we're watching a movie.'

'I don't care how old you are, young lady.' She wagged a finger at him. 'When you're under our roof, you live by our rules.'

'You're serious?' he exclaimed, half horrified, half amused.

'Absolutely. It will be even worse this time around, given...' She nodded in the direction of upstairs.

'She can't hear you!' Ben laughed.

'I don't care whether she can hear or not. I've told Mum and Dad that there's to be no talk of "the mess I've got myself into" or "accidents" around her—that's *my* only rule if I move home. I'll put up with anything for a year if it gives her a better start, but I'll tell her her story in my own way, in my own time.'

'That's fair enough.'

'It's not her fault I didn't know her dad was married...' She stopped talking then, thankful for the dark room, because her face was red suddenly, not from embarrassment but near tears. They sat in silence for a while—the words that had never been voiced by Ben hanging there between them...

'How, Celeste?' he finally asked. 'How did you not know?'

'I just didn't.'

'What about nights like this?'

'Like what?'

'Like this.' Ben gestured at the simplicity of it all. 'Did you never wonder why it was always at yours?'

'He didn't come to mine.' Her voice was shrill. 'We went out, we were dating...'

He didn't get it, but it wasn't his place to push it, he'd already crossed that line, so Ben chose to leave it, surprised when it was Celeste who broke the strained silence between them.

'I shared with two other students. I knew what we were doing was wrong...' She stopped again and was staring unseeingly at the television screen.

'Wrong?' Ben frowned. 'I thought you didn't know he was married?'

'It's more than that. I can't tell anyone about Willow's father...it would cause so much trouble.'

'You can tell me,' Ben said, because though

he could sense her indecision, he also sensed her burden.

'You won't say anything to anyone?'

'Never.'

'Because gossip…'

'I don't gossip.'

She looked over to him, at those guarded, remote features that occasionally softened into tenderness—and right now she was the lucky recipient of that emotion. She saw the honesty and integrity there too and it made her shame burn harder, so much so that she couldn't look him in the eyes as she shared her truth.

'His name's Dean. He was my lecturer at university.' When Ben didn't say anything, she wasn't sure if he understood the problem. 'It's forbidden for a lecturer to have a relationship with a student…'

'I know.'

'It happens, though,' she attempted to rationalise. 'All the time. I mean, it's between two consenting adults, and it's a stupid rule really…'

He could see tears squeezing out of her eyes, and, as she always did, she closed them, trying to keep it all in.

'Not that stupid a rule, perhaps,' Celeste admitted. 'He must choose his targets—I mean, he had his story all set up. He said he shared a house with another lecturer—that was why we couldn't go back there—and as I was sharing with students, we always went out miles away. Of course, I assumed it was so that no one from uni found out about us. He told me that once I'd qualified, that we could go more public…'

'You never suspected?' He still didn't get it. Even if he and Celeste were only a little bit in each other's lives, that much of each other they already knew.

'I'd never really had a serious boyfriend,' she revealed, giving a tight shrug. 'Like I said, Mum and Dad were really strict, and when I left home, I didn't go wild or anything. Really, I didn't even know if we were going out at first, it was just a drink, or dinner…' She was squirming with embarrassment now. 'And we went to a hotel a couple of times…it should have been obvious to me,' Celeste admitted. 'I mean, he never answered his phone—it always went to voicemail.'

'Oh?' Ben frowned. 'Is that supposed to mean something?'

'He never answered his phone when he was with me either.'

'Okay…' Ben said, not that he really understood it.

'You're too honest.' Celeste managed a watery smile. 'So am I, I guess, because I never assumed he was lying. He never answered his phone in case it was another of his women—or even his wife.'

'How *did* you find out he was married?'

'He was away one day, another lecturer came in—explaining that he was taking over because apparently Dean's wife was ill…'

'Oh, Celeste,' Ben groaned softly.

The commercials for the film were over so

she put her feet up on the table because that was what Ben was doing and took a sip of her wine and sat there, trying to watch the film while remembering the hurt—the very real hurt—and the fear a few weeks later when she'd found out that she was having Dean's baby.

It was a funny movie that she'd chosen, or it had been the first time she'd watched it—only it didn't seem so funny now. Instead, it was a romantic comedy of errors that just made her feel like crying.

Ben was on the sofa next to her, big and solid and so reassuring.

And there was a picture of Jen by the television.

She couldn't see the image, just the outline of the frame—but that made her feel like crying too.

As if the universe had got something terribly wrong, had tossed them all up in the air and they'd landed in the wrong places, the wrong rooms, with the wrong people.

Except she liked being here with him.

She needed a tissue, Celeste realised, had sniffed four times in the past fifteen seconds and it was getting embarrassing now, except she had to reach over him to get them, so she didn't bother. 'Here.' He pulled a wad out of a box on the coffee table and Celeste managed a wry laugh.

'Do you sit here crying at films often?'

'Nope…' Ben smiled at the image she conjured up. 'Jen's sister was over earlier.'

Oh, God!

She didn't say it, but she flinched at her insensitivity. Wallowing in her own problems, he just seemed so together, it was so easy to forget all he'd been through. 'Just for a quick hi, but she hadn't seen the house.'

'It must have been hard for you,' she said.

'Yes, it was,' Ben admitted. 'Thankfully I was called into work.'

'Thank you.' She stared over to him. 'I mean, really, thank you for everything.'

'I was glad to help.'

'And I'm sorry.'

'For what?' Ben asked, but was just a touch uncomfortable as to how she might answer.

'Because of how difficult things are between us...'

'They're not difficult,' he lied.

'Yes, they are,' Celeste contradicted, 'because I *want* to be friends with you, Ben, but I don't know how to *be* one...' He could see the tears rolling down her cheeks now. 'And please don't feel guilty when I tell you this, but it's part of the reason I'm moving home too—maybe things will be easier, maybe we might even manage to be *friends*.'

'I don't think so.' His fingers wanted to touch her hair again, he wanted to hold her, to kiss her, but it would be too cruel to them both.

But then she looked at him, looked right at him, and said the words that sometimes he'd wished too, stuck her toe in that closing door and kept it wedged that little bit open.

'I wish it could have been you. I wish Willow was yours.'

She meant it, she really meant it, and her nose was running because she meant it so much.

She wished it had been Ben, that he had been the one who'd made love to her.

Wished, wished, wished for so much more than the little they'd had.

'It would never have been me,' Ben said then. 'Because I'd have taken so, so much more care of you than he did.'

He couldn't stand that she was moving away, couldn't stand the thought of not seeing her again, couldn't stand not to touch her some more. 'Come here.' He pulled her at her wrist so she was right up against him and it was like climbing into his boat.

Sort of away from everything.

It was nice to have a cuddle with him while she cried—he was so big she *had* to lean against him, or she'd topple overboard! Nice when he hooked his arm around her and secured her there.

Just really, really nice.

It was for Ben too.

So rarely was he indulgent—but next week she was going somewhere she didn't really want to go.

Leaving him somewhere he didn't really want to be.

Tonight they were here.

And it was nice.

Nice to lie on the sofa with *her.*

Nice to hear her sobs recede and to feel her chest move as she laughed at the film.

It had been a hell of a day. Showing Abby and her husband Mick around the house, with Abby tearing up every five minutes, he'd even offered to take them out on the boat.

Except Abby looked too much like Jen and there would be three in the boat instead of four—so he'd been glad when he'd been called in to work.

It had just been one of those days, and it could have been one of those nights too.

Except Celeste was here and all it felt was right.

He was hovering on the edge of indecision, scared but almost ready to really make a new start.

A very new start.

Certain films shouldn't be watched with a supposed friend who was actually a whole lot more.

They were watching a passionate on-screen kiss—and it seemed to go on a lot longer than Celeste remembered from the last time she had seen the film.

It was like the time when at fourteen she'd been watching a serious documentary with her parents and suddenly they had been watching full-on sex.

Just exquisitely uncomfortable—but for all sorts of different reasons tonight.

His hand was hovering over her stomach, but she was too near the edge of the sofa, needed a little shift, a little hoist from him to bring her closer, which he didn't do, so Celeste wriggled back a bit.

Just a bit.

Ever the gentleman, he moved back a fraction and secured her, his hand on her stomach, and she felt like pulling up her knees, because she'd felt him touch her.

She couldn't remember how to breathe,

because there was this feather-light stroking from his fingers on her stomach, just these almost indistinguishable caresses and a slight irregularity to his breathing as they continued to watch the kissing on the screen.

'When you move home….' His voice was hesitant, slightly gruff. 'Suppose we take things slowly…' She could hardly breathe, hardly dared to hope, scared to move in case he stopped talking. 'Suppose we go out…?'

'I won't have a babysitter—Mum only said she'd do it while I worked,' she whispered back.

'You could come here, we could have dinner, just start at the very beginning, get to know each other properly…'

'And Willow?' Her heart was in her mouth.

'If we take it slowly enough, maybe…' He could hear the blood pounding in his ears as he offered so much more than he had sworn he ever would. 'Maybe in time…'

He was offering her hope—offering *them* hope—that the impossible might just happen.

CHAPTER ELEVEN

CELESTE suddenly didn't care about the film, she wanted to see him, so she wriggled around and his legs had to trap hers to stop her falling off the sofa. He could see her lovely eyes shining in the darkness and he wanted to protect her, even from herself, but, God, he also wanted to kiss her, to just dive straight into that pleasure, but he had to make it very clear too.

'We'll just take things slowly.'

'I know.'

And then he could kiss her—properly this time—and she could kiss him too, a lovely slow kiss that wasn't awkward, just took a little adjusting to, because she was lower than him and rather precariously balanced, so he pulled her in a bit so that her bare thigh had to be clamped by his denimed ones, and as his tongue slid into her mouth, as their lips pressed harder, if she wanted to stay on the sofa, her other leg had to wrap around his.

He smelt like Ben…like the kiss from the first time, except she felt sexy now rather than tired, she felt alive rather than weary, and she felt wanted rather than looked after.

It made her feel dizzy.

She was sucking on his bottom lip, her little hand on his broad back and with the roughness of his jeans in her groin.

'Celeste…' He pulled back a bit as she pressed hard into him. 'I thought we were taking it slowly!'

'Not with this part,' she murmured.

Like teenagers, with no real intent, they kissed, except, unlike the rest of his body, his arm was going to sleep, so he pulled her onto her back and lay on top of her, his elbows sinking into the sofa as he kissed her deeply.

It *was* a kiss that was safe, because they weren't going anywhere more serious at the moment. At some level they both knew that, but it had to be verbally confirmed.

'We can't,' Ben said as her thigh slid between his legs and her hand slid up the back of his T-shirt, feeling the silk of his skin, the firmness of muscle, and she arched towards him. 'I haven't got anything.'

'I know,' she breathed. 'But I had a coil inserted…'

'No.' He stopped then, because she was just too precious to risk it. 'You're not to rely on just that.'

'So just kissing, then…' Her mouth was on his, her body this writhing mass of want beneath his. It was already more than a kiss but, God, it felt nice.

'I think we can manage a little more than that,' he promised. His hand was creeping up her top now, her breast soft and warm beneath his fingers. This was *so* much more than a kiss as his fingers skilfully caressed her nipples.

She'd considered her breasts useless, shrunken little failures, having not been able to breastfeed Willow, but now they swelled beneath his fingers, and the feel of his mouth and his tongue on them was sublime.

She was pressing into him, could feel his erection, and she wanted it closer…

'Ben…' she murmured softly. She could feel these little licks of pleasure in her stomach and it startled her, for he was turning her on her side, with nowhere to go except the back of the sofa and the gorgeous weight of Ben pinning her. Her hand crept to the front of his jeans; she felt the lovely solid length of him and heard him moan. 'Ben…' She didn't know why she kept saying his name, but she couldn't help it. Her fingers started working the heavy buckle of his belt, but his hand stopped her.

'No, this is just for you,' he said. He didn't mean it in a martyred way, he was lost too, but somewhere inside he wanted her to know that it could be about her, that it could just be about this…

He was kissing her hard, this lovely wet kiss that was so deep she didn't want to move or breathe again.

Was there any place nicer to be than on a sofa with her?

He was eighteen again—only it hadn't been that good then.

He was peeling open the zipper of her shorts, wriggling them down over her bottom. As he pressed her body against his, his mouth was on her neck, kissing her, trying to remember not to leave any marks, because it was the last thing she needed with her mother. He was glad he didn't have a condom in the house because he so badly wanted to dive into her. He was holding her hips now, guiding her along his hard length still safely under his jeans. He thought he might explode from the delicious pressure building, but was determined that he wouldn't—because even now it was still about her.

For Celeste was lost within herself, savouring and catching up on everything she'd ever missed—those little licks of pleasure inside her were building to a crescendo. She could hear humming, and realised it was her; she was humming as she coiled her legs around him, coming just to his kiss, coming just for Ben.

'Willow...' she gasped, feeling as if she'd been drinking as the piercing tone of her baby's cries brought her back down to a rather nice place. His kiss welcomed her back slowly as she worked out that she could, in fact, breathe, and then on wobbly legs and dishevelled she stood there in front of him, hauling her shorts back up her legs, more than a little embarrassed but at the same time not.

Then she gave him that wonderful smile and he smiled back and she decided that even if that embrace was all it could be for now—it was more than enough.

Quite simply it was the nicest thing that had happened to her.

Ben had never expected to feel again.

Over the years he had tried and over the past

few weeks he had resisted, but feelings didn't listen to logic.

Finally, he was starting to believe.

There were two glasses on the draining board, her footsteps were on the stairs as she came back down from soothing Willow and there was this delicious presence that filled each room. For the first time in years he was glimpsing a future—not in bricks or gardens, or hours filled with work, but hours and—later on—nights with her.

Maybe he *could* get used to this.

'Hey!' She was standing at the kitchen, hands behind her back, her dark brown hair black in the low living-room light. Her eyes were glittering and she was wearing a provocative smile that demanded caution.

'How's Willow?' he asked.

'Asleep again,' Celeste said. 'How are you?'

'Good,' Ben said, because he was. Having Celeste here was making him feel wonderful.

God, she was gorgeous, standing there just

smiling, her cheeks all flushed, eyes glittering, the top button of her shorts undone.

He was hard again so he turned away, made a big show of washing the two glasses, just to give himself time to recover.

She walked over and kissed him on the lips and he kissed her back, his arms wrapping around her, wet, soapy hands holding her, but she didn't hold him back, she just kissed him.

'Which hand?' She pulled her lips away and smiled up at him wickedly.

He frowned. 'What are you up to?'

'Which hand?' she repeated.

He was smiling and frowning simultaneously. He was beginning to get a hint of an idea as to where this might be leading, but he dismissed it, because he'd determinedly discounted it.

'Left or right?' Celeste prompted.

'Left.'

She pulled her hand from behind her back, and offered it to him but didn't reveal what was in it. 'Open it.'

Ben prised open her fingers and saw the little silver package, the key to heaven, and he was *so* tempted to reach out and take it.

'Celeste...'

'Before you say anything...' she laughed '...I didn't even know that I had them—I got a free bag of samples from the hospital, and I was looking for some nappy cream for Willow...' She didn't have to explain any more, so he smiled and interrupted her, reaching for her other hand and opening it to reveal the same contents.

'That's cheating,' Ben said.

'Why?'

'Because I can't lose.'

'Maybe you deserve to win.'

God, since Jen had died, sex had been just that—sex. Good, bad or indifferent, that was all it had ever been.

But with Celeste?

He stared into those amber eyes, his body charged with the memory of before and the possibility of after, her kiss still wet on his lips.

'I don't want to rush you,' he said gruffly.

'I *want* you to rush me,' she murmured back. How could she explain how different he made her feel? Sex had been a mystery for Celeste before Dean, yet how it had been for them was completely different from what she'd so far experienced with Ben. For her and Dean it had been a logical, preconceived act. Booking into a hotel on a Friday night, she had prepared for the occasion all week, nervousness mounting like the waxing moon and disappointment waning after the event.

But tonight, pressed into him, kissing him, ignoring the film like two teenagers necking in a cinema, it had been the closest she had ever come to her body—to the bliss of a kiss and the intimacy of two people blocking out the world and letting someone else in.

It was neither logical nor preconceived.

And she certainly wasn't smooth and spray-tanned!

But all it felt was right.

'You know I'm moving back home, Ben, so we won't be able to see each other that much, but just for tonight...'

'Are you sure?'

She was about to say something flip, but she stopped, looked into those lovely green eyes and there was no question—this was how it should have been, this was what it was all about, because this was Ben, and always, always, she'd wanted him. Now, finally, she could have him. That he wanted to forge some kind of a future with her—however that might turn out—just blew her mind.

'Absolutely,' Celeste said. 'Except...' She screwed her eyes closed.

'Say it,' he urged.

'I don't want to disappoint you.'

"You could *never* disappoint me,' he said emphatically.

'Oh.' She gave a very wry laugh. 'I might just surprise you.'

A mother she may be but she had little more

sexual experience than an amoeba—and most of that had been gained tonight in Ben's living room.

He kissed her to the bedroom and beyond— only that didn't quell her nerves.

As Celeste dashed to the bathroom, Ben took a moment too…quickly turning over Jen's photo.

Celeste stood in front of the mirror, talking to herself and berating her lack of preparation for what was about to happen. Her bikini line stopped at all stations and as thin as she might be, thanks to Willow, bits of her wobbled in a way they never had before. Even if Ben assured her that he wasn't comparing her to his wife, Celeste was—imagining Jen's perfect white sports bras versus her rather faded maternity one.

She sighed heavily, girded her loins and went back into the bedroom, to where Ben was waiting for her. She jangled with nerves and cellulite for every second of the disrobing, torn between shame and want, but then Ben started kissing her again, hands stroking her, seemingly not fazed at all by her post-pregnancy body.

Rather liking it, in fact, Celeste soon realised. So why waste two hands covering yourself when there was six feet three of male pressed against you?

'We'll take it really slow…' he said, laying her down on the bed carefully. He lay down too, facing her, and then he kissed her. His legs without jeans were right up against hers—scratchy, big, muscly legs—and she was suddenly quivering with a mixture of excitement and fear, feeling as if she were about to turn over the page of an exam and hoping to hell she'd studied enough…

'What are you scared of?' he asked, quirking an eyebrow at her.

'I don't know,' she whispered back, closing her eyes once again.

Ben hated the man who had taken her confidence even before it had had the chance to bloom. Hated her self-doubts, but he had assurance enough for them both. But that she was scared of something so very, very wonderful saddened him too.

She was shaking with nerves as he took her in his arms. It felt so very different from before, because this time she knew where it was leading. He was so lovely to lie with, so big and male...and all hers. While they kissed she explored his body slowly, her hands running down his arms, feeling them solid and strong. Then she progressed to his chest—hard and flat and smooth. Her mouth moved there and she kissed the skin as his hands stroked and soothed her. Wrapped in this warm cocoon of skin and muscle and Ben, her hands slid over his hips and met solid thighs. She could feel him caressing her waist and over her hips, and it was Ben's mouth exploring her now, kissing her pale breasts, one hand moving to the front and making tiny circles on her soft stomach. Had there been a muscle working there, maybe she'd have thought about it and held it in, but there wasn't and anyway Celeste wasn't really thinking, her throat too tight with nerves as his hand crept downwards. Then he was stroking her and she made little noises, pretending to like it, but was too embarrassed to really. He kissed her again, so she stopped making all the right noises and kissed him back, concentrating on that, and tried not to resist his fingers slipping deep inside her, as his thumb stroked her softly and rhythmically.

She suddenly couldn't breathe, so she pulled in air and pulled it in again, and made the same sort of noise she'd been making before except now it came from a different place, this involuntary place that also made her sigh and moan and forget everything except Ben and how he was making her feel.

She held a man in her hand for the first time, exploring him, feeling him slide beneath her fingers, just touching and exploring, delighted with what she found. Ben was patient till he couldn't be patient any more. Her inexperience worried him, not for himself but for her—she was far too trusting and naïve—so he handed her the condom, which was something she should know how to do. But he ended up guiding her clumsy fingers as she rolled it down his length but, too eager, too nervous, she ripped it.

'We've only got one more!' she cried, embarrassed with her clumsiness. She wished he'd just do it for her, but Ben was insistent.

'I'll go to the petrol station if I have to and get some more if you rip this one,' he growled. God, he hoped he didn't have to! Practice may not make perfect, but a patient teacher helped and Celeste heard his moan of pleasure as she slipped it on slowly. Terrified of her nails, she unfurled it with her palms and then she was holding him lovingly for a moment, proud of her handiwork, as his fingers slipped deeper into her slippery warmth.

'I don't want to hurt you...' he gasped. He was suddenly right there at her entrance and she was tight with expectancy and fear. But then he was in just a little bit, two hands holding her hips and just gently stretching her till fear abated and she relaxed, willing him in further. But he was so supremely gentle, so strong and sure that there was pure bliss in there being no rush.

Always, in her vast repertoire of twice, there had been an 'is that it?' moment. Is that what the world raves about? Is that all there is to it?

No, *this* was all there was to it.

All she wanted and all she wanted to be…

He was pushing her onto her back now, his huge frame moving over her, and it felt sublime…till she lost her rhythm and Ben dealt easily with that.

'Stay still.' His words were a low whisper in her ear.

'Still?' Wasn't she supposed to be writhing around? Surely lying still…

'Stay still,' he said again, so she did. She just lay and felt the blissful feel of him within her, the scent of him, of them, and she *really* did try to stay still, except her hips kept lifting, her body kept arching to his.

'Stay still…' he repeated, and she tried harder, except she couldn't, and suddenly she was lifting to him, moving with him, just locked in their own rhythm and Ben wasn't telling her any more because with that pause, she'd got it. Without trying hard, suddenly it was easy.

The skin of his chest was against her lips and she licked it, sucking his salty flesh, her legs around his, ankles trying to grip except he was so broad she could barely manage it. Then she felt the shift in him, something she'd never anticipated in the guarded, reticent Ben, because he was locked into this magical place too. There was no way she could define it, nothing specific with which to gauge it, except suddenly he was moaning her name and forgetting, deliciously forgetting to be gentle. Celeste was urging him on, not with words but with deep kisses on his chest and hands that slid over his buttocks and pushed him in harder. He was all over her, and so into her it made her dizzy, this full focus of him on her, until she was coming, a deep, deep orgasm that pleaded for him join her. And he did, giving in and just diving forward, shuddering his release and tipping Celeste to a place where there was no sound or silence or thought or want—just them and the beat of their bodies matching and minds colliding. She'd glimpsed pure magic and she never wanted to come down or go back or move from this place again.

He kissed her out of it, back to the world and then Ben rolled away from her and Celeste was suddenly scared, scared of losing whatever it was they had just found, scared of this place receding. Then it was her kissing him. On top of him, she kissed him hard, her hand threading into his hair, a silent plea for him not to leave her, for him not to retreat again inside himself because she had seen him now, seen *them* perhaps, glimpsed a marvellous possibility of them together, and she didn't want it to disappear.

CHAPTER TWELVE

'BEN RICHARDSON.'

She hadn't heard the phone ringing, just Ben's voice as he answered it. 'Belinda Hamilton is on call this weekend. No, I've seen her, she was there earlier tonight.' She felt the sheets move, Ben climb out, the shower taps on before the conversation was even over, and then two minutes later Ben, still dripping wet, was beside her, pulling on jeans. 'I've got to go into hospital for a bit.'

'Problem?'

'A bit—Belinda's not answering her pager.' He kissed her and it soothed her, but almost on cue, the moment he had gone, her three hours of sleep were up anyway, because Willow woke up. Celeste padded downstairs and prepared her a bottle, then brought her into bed to feed her. It was the easiest night feed Willow had ever taken, so blissfully easy. The bottle was gone in a few minutes and Willow was back asleep. She deserved a cuddle for being such a good girl, Celeste thought, and moved the pillows, cuddled her daughter in and determinedly ignored her mother's voice in her head that told her she shouldn't have the baby in bed with her.

And that was the scene Ben came home to.

Having dealt with the issue at work, he'd stopped at the petrol station, had bought *lots* of supplies and was ready to fall into bed. On the drive home it had all seemed straightforward, and Ben had felt so sure.

Then he'd called at Belinda's. Sure she was home, he had hammered on her door and felt this flicker of fear, the same fear he had when he'd come home to find Jen.

This silent house and the appalling feeling that something was wrong.

'Belinda!' he shouted. 'I'll call the police if you don't open up.'

'I'm sorry!' The door pulled open and he saw her eyes were swollen from crying. 'I just can't go in.'

'What's happened?' he asked, appalled.

'Can you just cover for me?' she whispered.

'Sure.'

'Can you ring the switchboard and tell them to page you if there's a problem?'

'I'll do it now,' Ben said, stopping the door as she went to close it. 'Belinda, what's going on?'

'Gastric flu…'

'Don't give me that!' he exclaimed.

'Please, Ben.'

It was none of his business. So long as she was okay, that was all that mattered, but his heart was still racing as he let himself into his home, the metallic taste of fear on his tongue and he downed a glass of water and then another before heading upstairs.

And then he'd seen them both on the bed, curled up like two kittens, sleeping, so sweet and perfect and innocent. But he'd glimpsed the past tonight, tasted fear again as he'd knocked at Belinda's door—and maybe that, Ben decided, was the sign he'd craved from Jen.

Maybe that was his warning.

Celeste stirred and half awoke, could see Ben sitting on the edge of the bed. 'How was it?'

'Busy enough, I just had to sort out some backlog, as they couldn't get hold of Belinda.'

'That's not like her,' Celeste frowned. 'Do you think she's okay?'

'She's fine,' Ben said. 'Well, not fine, as I stopped by her flat on the way back. She says she'd got gastric flu but my guess is...' He didn't finish. Belinda's personal life was her own and shouldn't really be gossiped about. 'It doesn't matter.'

Celeste knew she'd just been relegated, knew, though it was almost indefinable, that what she had feared—losing what she'd just found—had already taken place.

'I'll put Willow back in her pram.' She thought

Ben might take the baby from her, but he didn't, so Celeste slipped out of bed and down to the guest room where she tucked her daughter into the pram. Then, as Willow woke up and started grumbling, she wheeled the stroller back to Ben's room and parked the baby in the corner as he undressed and climbed into bed.

It took a few moments to settle Willow and by the time she returned to his bed, Ben was asleep.

Or pretending to be.

She stared at his keys and the phone and the little paper bag from the garage, knowing what it contained and realising they wouldn't be needed.

Wondering what, in that short space of time, had changed things so much. She told herself she was imagining it—overreacting.

Maybe he *was* asleep after all and not just pretending.

The view from the bed was magical and it should have soothed her as she got into bed and lay next to him—only it didn't.

They'd agreed to take things slowly, dinners and dating—and the sex certainly hadn't been a problem. Even as inexperienced as she was, Celeste knew that for certain—what she had shared with Ben was so much more than she had ever expected or anticipated. So what had gone wrong between them?

Though cool and sophisticated wasn't really her forte, though she wanted to curl into him, to wake him with the kiss her body was demanding that she give, to roll over in the soft warm bed and feel his arms wrap around her, she resisted the temptation.

This was way too important to misjudge. So instead she slipped a reluctant body out of bed and checked on a still sleeping Willow, deciding to take advantage of the peace and have a shower, because if she'd stayed in bed she'd surely break the strained silence.

He lay still, hovering on the edge of the decision.

Ben knew that she was awake, knew she was

waiting for him, knew that last night had confused her.

It had confused him too.

With Willow in the room, he hadn't slept a wink. It wasn't the little snuffles that kept him awake, it was the silences that killed him.

He walked across the room, checked that she was still breathing, which, of course, she was. In fact, as he looked down at her, she promptly opened her eyes and smiled at him.

Only Ben struggled to return it. Instead, he tried to go back to bed, but she'd seen him now and was starting to cry.

God, he hoped Celeste wouldn't be long in the shower.

Ben headed down stairs and made coffee for them both and a bottle for Willow, gritting his teeth as the cries grew louder, wondering if Celeste would be out of the shower by the time he got back up stairs.

Hoping so.

He walked back into the bedroom and put

down the bottle and mugs, listened at the bathroom door and could still hear the shower— surely she could hear Willow crying?

Surely!

Ben stared into the stroller, picked up the baby's little soother and popped it in her mouth, but Willow spat it out in disgust, her eyes fixed on him, real tears at the edges, pleading with him to pick her up. So he tried, telling himself to pretend that he was at work where he operated on automatic, except this wasn't work.

He wanted to pick her up, even put his hands into the pram to do so…then he pulled back and tried rocking the pram instead, willing Celeste to come out of the shower and tend to her babe.

What the hell was he so scared of?

Cross with himself, Ben paced the room. He would just go right over and pick her up and be done with it.

Then he heard the bleep of Celeste's phone.

Dean

He didn't read the text—just felt the chill of a

shadow, a big black bird in the sky that could swoop down and take them at any given moment…

'Willow!' Shivering wet, wrapped in a towel, Celeste headed straight for the pram, scooping her daughter up in her arms, feeling her hot, red face and turning questioning eyes to him. 'She's been sobbing!'

'I was about to knock and tell you,' he said lamely.

'To knock?' Celeste stared at him open-mouthed. 'Did you not think to pick her up?'

'I was making coffee,' Ben said defensively. 'And her bottle.'

Which sounded logical and reasonable, Celeste realised—except babies were neither logical nor reasonable, and Willow had needed to be held.

'Can you hold her for me?' Celeste's voice held just a hint of challenge. 'I just need to get dressed…'

'I have to shower and get dressed too,' Ben lied. 'Switch just called, I have to go into work.'

'Ben…' For someone usually so emotional, Celeste's voice was ominously calm. 'I'm not asking you to feed her or change her, I'm asking if you could hold Willow for two minutes.'

'Sorry.' He shook his head. 'I've got to get ready.'

'Ben?' She couldn't believe it, couldn't believe the way he was acting. 'I'm not asking for—'

'Look,' Ben interrupted, 'she's not my…' He didn't finish, his mouth snapping closed before this morning turned into the mother of all mornings, but Celeste finished for him.

'Not your *problem*?' That wasn't what he'd been about to say, but it was easier to nod than to explain. 'God.' Celeste gave a mirthless laugh. 'I really know how to pick jerks, don't I?'

Ben didn't answer so she spoke instead.

'Just how *slowly* did you want to take it, Ben? What, by the time she went to school, maybe we could move in with you?' she said scathingly.

'Willow's father just texted….'

'Don't blame this on him!' Celeste retorted.

'You've been off with me since last night.' When he didn't answer that, she asked again, 'Just how slowly did you mean, Ben?'

'I don't know.'

She stared down at her daughter, *the* most important person in the world to her, and she knew what she had to do.

'I'm not putting her through this.' Willow was starting to whimper. Her mother's arms were a nice place, but it would be even better with a bottle. 'I should have listened from the start— you don't want kids and I've got one.'

Her phone bleeped again and Celeste gritted her teeth. What the hell did Dean want?

'You'd better see what her father wants!' Ben was done. She was right, Willow deserved better than him, and the only way out was to end it— really end it. 'After all, she's his responsibility.'

'Correction!' Celeste spat, hating him too much at this moment for tears. 'She's *mine.*'

He didn't respond, just headed for the shower.

'You might be glad to get rid of me and

Willow, Ben,' she called to his departing back. 'But you've no idea what you just lost.' He closed the door behind him and knew, because he knew Celeste, that she'd be gone when he came out, that she wouldn't hang around to debate the point. He turned on the shower full blast, and prayed she'd go soon, because while the water might drown the sound of Willow's tears, it wouldn't drown his.

It wasn't Willow that was his problem.

He sat on the floor of the shower and held his head in his hands.

It was his own daughter.

It was a hurt like she'd never known.

A rejection not just of her—that she could deal with, had dealt with in the past and could deal with again now. It was the rejection of Willow that was as acute as a sting but didn't abate like one.

Was this the price of motherhood—that the man of her dreams could walk away from her so easily?

Well, let him.

'How long will you be?' Her mother hovered at the door, holding Willow.

'I don't know,' Celeste snapped. After weeks of nagging for Celeste to speak with Willow's father, now that the moment was here, her mother was demanding timelines! Did she not realise how hard this was? 'There are bottles made up.'

'You will be coming back to get Willow, won't you?'

That didn't even deserve an answer, so Celeste just gritted her teeth.

'Maybe you should take her with you…'

'Mum!' It wasn't a snap this time, just a plea for her to stop fretting, worrying, fixing… And then Celeste got it, answered the question that she had wrestled with for weeks, no, for months now. Seven weeks into motherhood and Celeste was starting to get the swing of it—this aching, endless worry lasted longer than the pregnancy, longer than the first days or months. She was stuck with this fear for her child for life—as was her own mum—and now when her voice came, it was gentler, more reasonable, friendly even. 'I'm not going to parade Willow in front of him—he hasn't even asked to see her. I'm just going to see what he wants.'

'What do *you* want?'

'I don't know,' Celeste admitted. 'For some sort of father for Willow, I suppose…'

'What if he wants you back?' It was the first real conversation they'd had in years and Celeste was finally able to answer honestly.

'He lost me a long time ago, Mum. I'm only meeting with him now for the sake of Willow.'

'Be careful,' Rita said, and Celeste nodded.

'Don't wor—' The words died on her lips and then Celeste smiled. 'Okay, worry away if you must, but you really don't have to. Whatever he has to say, Willow and I are going to be fine.'

Seeing him again, all Celeste felt was older and maybe, possibly, just a little bit wiser.

There was none of that giddy rush she'd had

as a student when he'd walked into the lecture room—no blushing when he spoke or hanging on to his every word.

Whether she'd wanted to or not, she'd well and truly grown up and could see Dean for what he was now—a rather sad attempt of a man who'd played on her naïvety, who had taken full advantage of a perfectly normal crush when he *really* should have known better.

The rules were there for a reason.

It was a very short meeting, and not at all sweet. He wanted assurances that his perfect life wasn't about to end soon, that Celeste wasn't suddenly going to change her mind and come knocking—an assurance she was only too happy to provide!

'What will you tell Willow?' he asked diffidently.

'The truth.' Celeste looked at him coolly. 'Probably a nicer version of it. I'll miss out the bit where you offered to pay for an abortion— but she'll grow up with the truth. And when she's old enough, what she does with that truth will be her decision, Dean.'

Then there was nothing else to say, nothing at all, so she didn't bother. Just stood up and walked out of the café and took a big breath and then another one.

Until finally she blew the last one out and let him go.

Then Celeste put one foot in front of the other and did it again, just kept on putting one foot in front of the other, which meant she was walking.

Walking away and getting on with the rest of her life.

CHAPTER THIRTEEN

'WHAT'S going on, Belinda?' It took till five on Monday to talk to Belinda. All day she'd been avoiding him and, clearly thinking he'd already gone home, she walked into the office and did an about-turn, but Ben halted her.

'Nothing.'

'I need to know why you didn't answer your pager on Friday night.'

'I'm sorry about that. I honestly felt so unwell, I just...'

'Belinda, I covered for you, but I'm not going to be fobbed off,' he warned.

'He's still married.' Belinda crumpled as she admitted it. 'I found out on Saturday night... that multi-trauma...'

Ben frowned.

'It was his son.'

'Oh, Belinda.'

'I rang his number but ended up speaking to his wife…I recognised the surname, then she called him to the phone…' She could barely get the words out for crying. 'I just couldn't stay in the department and see him, face her. You think I'd be used to it by now…'

'Used to what?'

'Being let down.' He could scarcely believe the change in her from the confident, outgoing woman he'd first met. 'I'm so embarrassed.'

'Embarrassed?' he asked, bewildered.

'I just feel like a fool,' Belinda admitted. 'I knew he was busy, I made so many excuses for him—he was at work, or with the kids…I guess I just gave him a million and one reasons to justify why he could only give me such a little bit of his time.'

'It's not your fault,' Ben said, and it wasn't Celeste's fault either—if the stunning, street-wise Belinda could be taken in, what chance had Celeste had? 'You were just…' he gave an uncomfortable shrug as analysing emotions was not his strongest point '…trying to be happy…'

'Like we all are,' Belinda said. 'Only we just end up hurting a whole lot of people along the way.' She took a gulp of her coffee. 'I feel such a fool,' she said again despairingly.

'*He's* the fool,' Ben insisted.

'That's not how it feels from here.' She gave a watery smile. 'I'll be okay…I just need to lie low for a bit, lick my wounds…'

'I can imagine.'

'But I'll get there.' Belinda blew out a breath. 'Get back out there soon…'

Ben realised he would never understand some people—never get how someone who had been so hurt could, in such a short time, be talking about getting back out there, laying their hearts on the line, only to have them broken again.

Why?

Except he suspected he was starting to know the

answer. It was he who was the fool—he worked that one out as he drove home that evening.

There were all these people out there, searching for happiness, trying not to be lonely, and he'd had it right there, not once, but twice, *right there* for the taking.

He'd just been too scared of getting hurt again to move on and take what was on offer.

He had wanted a world that came with iron-clad guarantees—and because that was impossible, well, he'd stepped right off the planet. Made some half-hearted attempt to move on with his life—only by *his* safe rules. He'd rather have sex than a relationship, and the more meaningless the better, because then you didn't get hurt. And no children or feelings involved either, please, because that could hurt too. As could biological fathers that might pop up…

Only being lonely hurt more than the risk of loving.

And now he'd lost her too.

He got stuck in his street as a small rental

truck pulled out of the units—his big black bird swooping down and taking her away. He could see her car in her drive and knew she was inside her flat, organising the moving of her stuff over to her parents' house in preparation for the coming weekend. If she went to live with her parents, he knew he had lost her for ever.

He finally realised that this was his moment.

That *this* moment was all anyone had.

And he had to start living in it. He took a deep breath and headed for her door.

'It's not a good time, Ben.'

He could hear Willow's cries as she went to close the door on him.

'I need to talk to you.'

'And *I* need to feed my baby!' She opened the door, her face angry. 'So I hope you can stomach being in the same room as her as you say whatever it is that you have to.'

Willow's screams were louder and louder as they walked through her tiny unit. Everything that was them was gone—the crib, the flowers, the throw rugs, the ironing board by the wall. Just the drab furniture remained and as he followed her through the place, the kitchen was empty, except for a kettle and a jug and a bottle warming.

'It's coming, Willow…' He could hear the strain in her voice as she tried to keep it light for her baby. 'The microwave's gone with the removal…' He watched as she tested the bottle on her wrist then placed it back in the water, and then she snapped, 'I'm just going to feed her and then I'll be gone. I've decided to go before the weekend. There's no point hanging around now.'

'Don't go.'

'Just what the hell do you want, Ben?' she asked wearily.

'You.'

'Well, sorry, but I'm already taken…' Even though she was in the lounge, Celeste had to shout over Willow's screams. 'And I wouldn't have it any other way.'

'I don't *want* it any other way,' he said desperately.

'She isn't going to go away, Ben. I'm not going to pretend she doesn't exist so we can sleep together a couple of times a week!'

'I want Willow too...' She had no idea how hard that was for him to say, no idea of the terror of that admission, so she scorned him instead.

'Oh, so you'll *tolerate* her so you can have her mother.'

'No, I'll try harder. I want her too,' he said again.

'Just leave it, Ben!'

'Jen was pregnant when she died.' Real pain demanded respect. Real pain could be felt and heard and acknowledged, even if we don't know how, because even Willow fell silent. 'About the same stage as you when you had Willow.'

'You should have told me,' Celeste said, shocked.

'How?' Ben shook his head. 'It's not something you just slip into the conversation—and especially being pregnant yourself...' he gave a thin smile '...you didn't need to hear it.'

'No.' She admitted the truth of that. She'd been struggling enough as it was.

'I wanted to tell you after you had Willow... but...I lost my baby, Celeste, and I couldn't do it to you. Give you that fear that you might lose yours too.'

'How?'

'A subarachnoid haemorrhage. Just like that.' He clapped his hands and it made her jump, but it seemed appropriate. She'd learnt about them at uni—a sudden, severe, thunderclap headache— and she felt like crying except it wasn't her place to right now. 'I came home and found her...' And then he corrected himself, because it wasn't really Jen that was the problem, he had loved and lost her and would miss her for ever, but in that he had moved on—had almost reached that place of acceptance, just not quite. 'No, I came home and found *them.*

'She was buried inside Jen and I never got to

hold her and I never really got to mourn her—
and I don't know how to start.'

'You just did.'

He nodded, screwed his eyes closed and
pressed his fingers against them as, dizzy with
images, like a roundabout, he willed it to stop.

'Tell me,' she implored.

'I can't go there,' he said, because he truly
couldn't. 'I didn't want to love you, but I do,
Celeste, and I don't want to love Willow, but I
know I will. I'm so scared of losing you...'

'You did, though, Ben.' She was still angry, so
angry with him. 'You don't want to fall in love
in case something happens, so you'd rather just
let us go...'

'I'm here now.'

'Half of you!' Celeste exclaimed. 'And the
other half is stuck in a place where no one can
visit. Well, Willow and I deserve more than that.'

'I'll give you more than that,' he vowed.

'When?' Celeste demanded, and Ben couldn't
believe his ears.

'What are you asking for, Celeste?'

'Your love,' Celeste said, and her heart was breaking, but she was determined to be very, very strong.

'I just did. I told you I love you…'

'No, Ben.'

'And I *will* love Willow.'

'No.' She absolutely meant it.

'I don't know what you want here, Celeste!' It was Ben that was angry now—he'd never been more open, more honest, had never revealed his heart like this since Jen died, and now he knew why. 'What? Do you want me to say that I love Willow?'

'Anyone can *say* it,' she pointed out.

'Okay?' He picked up the bottle. 'Am I to hold her, to feed her?'

'I'm quite capable of that.'

'What, then?' Ben demanded, because he didn't know what she wanted from him, didn't know what test she had in her mind that he had to pass.

'I want you to *let* yourself love her.' All she did

was confuse him, because he *was* going to love her, in time, he knew that it would grow. 'And when you do, we'll both be here waiting for you...'

'I don't understand you, Celeste.'

'Well, *I* don't understand *you*.' She picked up the bottle and walked into the lounge and picked up Willow, feeding her in silence as he stood at the door and watched.

'You can't just demand instant love,' he protested.

'I can,' Celeste came back immediately. 'She's already got one poor excuse for a father—she doesn't need another, hanging around, waiting for love to grow.'

'You're impossible!' he growled.

'I'm very straightforward, actually,' she replied calmly.

'Say goodbye to Ben.' She stood up, held up a little hand and waved it at him. 'We'll see him when he's ready.'

She put Willow in her crib and tucked her in.

'Now, if you'll excuse me, I need to get on with my packing.'

'That's it?' he asked incredulously.

'That's it,' she confirmed.

'I've come over here, I've told you why, I've told you I love you and that I'll do everything I can for Willow, and it's not enough?' He walked over and looked her in the eyes. 'It's not enough for you?'

'No.'

She meant it, he knew that she meant it, he just didn't get it. 'I don't understand you, Celeste,' he said again helplessly, and kissed her on her taut cheek. 'I'll go.'

'Please.'

'I'll *never* understand your mother,' he said, looking at Willow. He stroked her little cheek and again it was Willow who looked into his eyes—the same way she had the day she'd been born and the next morning too.

Once more, Ben closed his eyes, only this time he opened them again, and she was still there, smiling—patiently waiting for him to love her.

He didn't want to do this—he felt as if he were dying—in fact, he was sure it would have been easier *to* have died.

'She was made for you, Ben,' Celeste said softly beside him, staring down at her daughter and understanding the world now. 'Because you'd never have done this yourself—you'd never have done it again.'

She was right—and somewhere deep inside him something aligned. Because even with Celeste, without a certain little lady being born into his hands, under his tree, he would never have taken that chance again, would never, ever have risked having another baby.

Yet he risked it now.

He looked at this little new life and remembered all that hope, all that love, all that promise he'd once had...

'She was never born.' It probably didn't make sense to Celeste, yet it was so vital to him. He could feel the petal of Willow's cheek as soft and white as a daisy and it felt as if he was being hollowed out inside. He still wanted to run, only there was no beach long enough, no universe that could contain the grief that split him. 'There's no birth certificate, and we hadn't chosen a name…' It hadn't felt right to name her without Jen.

He could never separate the two, had grieved for Jen and their baby, but had never actually separated them, had never let himself grieve just for the baby. 'She was never born.'

'She still *was*, though,' Celeste said, her voice there beside him, her arm around him—and if he'd been there for her before, she was there for him now. 'She still *is*.'

'Daisy.'

He stroked Willow's cheek and finally named the daughter he should have had. And just as he had cut Willow's cord, Willow let him cut his daughter's—her little star hands holding his as grief pitted him. In holding Willow he got to hold his own baby, pressed his lips to her soft cheeks, got to hold Daisy just for a moment, and then sent her back to rest with her mum.

'I love you.' He said it to Willow who was there now, only he didn't just say it, he felt it too. He held her close, but he didn't just hold her—he finally let himself love her, finally let himself hope, and he promised her silently that he would always be there for her. 'And I love your mum too.'

'She knows that,' Celeste said.

'Don't go to your parents'.' Holding her baby, he turned to Celeste. 'Come home.'

And it was home—even if she'd never lived there, his house was already her home.

'Well, I'm all packed.' She was smiling and crying, so very, very proud—and safe too—and for the first time in the longest time absolutely sure. 'I'd better ring Mum and tell her. She'll be on her way soon.'

'What will she say?'

'She'll probably be relieved.' Celeste laughed. 'I'm not the easiest person to live with.'

'I can't wait to find out,' he murmured.

He didn't want her, didn't want them in this shabby, bare unit a moment longer. He wanted them home where they all belonged. The boxes and crib and bags and baby baths and car could all wait till later, so Celeste rang Rita and Ben packed a quick bag for Willow, and they walked down the street pushing a pram, only as a family this time. She was *such* a good baby, because she slept for a couple of very necessary hours while Ben and Celeste kissed and made up and cried a bit too, and when Celeste finally fell asleep in his arms, Ben stayed awake, just so he could feel her warm skin. Then he heard Willow, who was starting to stir in her pram, and he finally felt what had been missing for all those years.

Peace.

A peace that wasn't shattered by Willow's lusty cries, a peace that remained as Celeste chatted incessantly on as she brought in the baby's bottle and then handed him an angry bundle as she decided that instead of feeding her daughter, *he* could do it while she explored the spa in her new bathroom!

Peace as, fed, changed and content, he put Willow back in the pram and wound up her mobile for her.

Peace perfect peace, Celeste thought as she lay in the spa, her toes wrinkling, knowing how much he loved the two of them, mother and daughter. She stared out at the glorious view and at a wonderful future too.

'Marry me!' Celeste shouted to the silence.

'I was about to suggest the same thing,' Ben said, standing in the doorway grinning. 'We should get married out there on the beach, where we met...'

'I take it that's a yes?'

'It's a yes...' He looked out to the beach and he could almost see them—see their wedding, Celeste holding Willow, the celebrant, with family and friends gathered around, and he could almost see Jen, holding Daisy and smiling. And it was a blessing, a long-awaited blessing, to be able to think of them both and smile.

'Oh, well, if you insist.' She laughed.

Lost in thought, he had no idea what she was talking about. 'Pardon?'

'I suppose there's no talking you out of it…' She gave a martyred sigh. 'I guess you'd better climb in and ravish me.'

He didn't ever compare, because there was no comparison—two more different women he could never imagine, and yet he loved them both. But it was then, when he least expected it, that he got his sign, the one he had been longing for from Jen, because just for a second he could have sworn he heard Jen laugh, could have sworn he heard her letting him go with grace, urging him on, to live this wonderful life.

And Ben laughed too.

Laughed as he climbed right in to join Celeste to do as the grad nurse ordered.

Ravish her.

EPILOGUE

NEVER, not once, did she wonder or doubt.

Not even a little bit.

Despite her mother's gloomy predictions, despite what she'd read in the 'blended family' section of a baby book, which Celeste had finally thrown against the wall—not once did she think that their baby would change how he felt about Willow.

Because without Willow, there would be no them.

'It won't be long now.' Ben squeezed her shoulder as she lay on the operating table—with all the passion of a doctor to a patient, but that was what he did sometimes.

They'd experienced three pregnancies between them and all of them had been different.

This had been a textbook pregnancy (if you excluded her massive weight gain), and had gone brilliantly till the very last minute—but eight hours of huffing and puffing and still their baby wouldn't come out!

She'd worked part time till seven months, because that was what she did.

She had told him about her backache and sore ankles but had spoken to the obstetrician, rather than him, when she'd had a ripper of a headache.

And he'd massaged her tummy and kissed her bump and done all the right things throughout.

They both had.

Jollied each other along and assured the other it would be fine.

'I'm scared…' She wasn't even sedated—they had been so mean with drugs that she was thinking of writing a letter of complaint. So much for being a doctor's wife! An epidural might numb your stomach, but it didn't numb your brain.

'What if it changes things?'

No matter how neatly folded, no matter where it was stored, your baggage came on the journey with you—and every now and then you had to cough up and pay the excess or watch as Customs ripped open the zipper and demanded to know what a chocolate bar was doing hidden in your bra.

As if you could explain how it got there.

As if you had meant to pack it and haul it to the other side of the world.

Except you had.

'I don't want it to change anything,' she wailed.

'Change can be good,' he said reassuringly.

It was only the three of them, her and him and Willow. And she was scared for them, scared for the coming baby—scared of change. Only it was happening, whether she wanted it to or not.

'I'm scared, Ben,' she said again.

'I know.'

She could see tears swimming in his green eyes.

'Remember Willow—she was so floppy and ill…'

'And look at her now.'

She knew they were making the incision because the OB had told her, but she only had eyes for Ben.

Could hear the gurgle as they suctioned her waters and she was petrified.

'How can I love it as much as Willow?'

'Wait and see,' he suggested gently.

It was a him.

This beefy whopper of a boy that they held up over the drapes, with a flat nose and bunched-up forehead, who screamed and cried and kicked all the way to the little cot set up for him.

'No wonder I needed a Caesarean.' She just had to smile, had to cry, had to gaze in wonder.

And, of course, so did Ben.

He walked over and stared at his son, got the footprints on his T-shirt and then came back to Celeste.

'You should see the *size* of him!' he said in awe.

'Now do you see why I moaned when he kicked?' she gasped.

She got a quick kiss when they brought him over all wrapped up—but so was she, so she couldn't really touch him. But there were too many people around for real tears.

'Go with him…' Celeste said to her husband.

It was all a blur from there. They were a bit more generous with drugs, and she was stitched and sent to Recovery and then to her room. And Celeste sort of remembered her mum coming and Ben's mum too and a lot of noise…

And later, much later, she woke up.

And remembered.

She wasn't scared of Ben's feelings, not even a tiny bit, okay maybe, just maybe a smudge…

But he had his back to her and his son and a fretful one-year-old on his hip who he was showing the moon to, and that left her alone to stare at her new baby.

She was scared of her *own* feelings.

He was so little.

A huge baby, but really so little and new and wrinkly and perfect, and she was so scared she wouldn't get this right. Then he opened his eyes…

Just stared right at her and demanded she love him.

She would very soon, except she was really tired. 'Ashley…'

She was too sore to pick him up, so Ben did it for her, balancing Willow on one side as he scooped up his son and handed him to her.

'It means "from the ashes",' Celeste said. 'I looked it up.'

'I bet you did.'

'Baby!' Willow forgot for a moment how tired she was. Delighted with both her *finally* awake brother and her vocal skills, she'd recently discovered chanting. 'Baby, baby, baby!' And she clambered over the bed and a catheter, coming dangerously close to a Caesarean incision, and then smothered her brother with kisses and germs followed by lots more gooey kisses.

Then Ashley got a kiss from Dad.

And then Celeste got a kiss from a suddenly very needy, tearful Willow.

There was almost too much love to go around, Celeste thought, very near tears herself.

'I'm going to get her home,' Ben told her.

He'd seen her watery eyes and he understood.

Knew when she needed him, even when she didn't admit it.

And knew when she needed to be on her own too.

The midwives walked in on his kiss to Celeste, but that was okay, because there would be lots of kisses later—she needed wise women with her now.

Tonight was for Celeste to meet Ash.

Ben understood that.

Tonight was the time for Celeste to discover that there was plenty of her to go around.

'Push the button…' He stepped in the lift and guided Willow's hand to the 'G' button—but she managed to miss and they headed for the roof instead!

'You're as unpredictable as your mother!' he huffed.

'Daddy!' She'd said it so many times, but she said it again—started up her chant and continued it all the way to the car park where he strapped her in and drove her home. 'Daddy, Daddy, Daddy!'

He was hers and she was his and never let anyone say otherwise.

He made her milk, put Willow in her cot, kissed her goodnight and turned on her mobile.

Then rang uncles and cousins and friends and deleted the text he wanted to send to Celeste in case it disturbed her sleep—he'd tell her himself in the morning.

Then he checked in on Willow and changed his mind and sent the text anyway.

Willow sound asleep—give ash a kiss—i love you.

And amid a frustrating attempt at a feed with an angry, hungry baby, and with nipples that hurt, a midwife smiled and handed her the phone. Celeste read her text, but didn't reply. He already knew she loved him too, so she just did as instructed. She leant forward and placed her lips on an angry forehead, erased crinkles with soft lips, felt the melting in her heart as Ash snuffled towards her and, after just a beat of a pause, Celeste resumed trusting again.

Felt the sweet weight of a new baby in her arms—and wanted it, could do it, was doing it right now...

It really *was* that simple.

Love grew if you let it.

MEDICAL™

Large Print

Titles for the next six months...

September

THE DOCTOR'S LOST-AND-FOUND BRIDE	Kate Hardy
MIRACLE: MARRIAGE REUNITED	Anne Fraser
A MOTHER FOR MATILDA	Amy Andrews
THE BOSS AND NURSE ALBRIGHT	Lynne Marshall
NEW SURGEON AT ASHVALE A&E	Joanna Neil
DESERT KING, DOCTOR DADDY	Meredith Webber

October

THE NURSE'S BROODING BOSS	Laura Iding
EMERGENCY DOCTOR AND CINDERELLA	Melanie Milburne
CITY SURGEON, SMALL TOWN MIRACLE	Marion Lennox
BACHELOR DAD, GIRL NEXT DOOR	Sharon Archer
A BABY FOR THE FLYING DOCTOR	Lucy Clark
NURSE, NANNY...BRIDE!	Alison Roberts

November

THE SURGEON'S MIRACLE	Caroline Anderson
DR DI ANGELO'S BABY BOMBSHELL	Janice Lynn
NEWBORN NEEDS A DAD	Dianne Drake
HIS MOTHERLESS LITTLE TWINS	Dianne Drake
WEDDING BELLS FOR THE VILLAGE NURSE	Abigail Gordon
HER LONG-LOST HUSBAND	Josie Metcalfe

MEDICAL™

Large Print

December

THE MIDWIFE AND THE MILLIONAIRE	Fiona McArthur
FROM SINGLE MUM TO LADY	Judy Campbell
KNIGHT ON THE CHILDREN'S WARD	Carol Marinelli
CHILDREN'S DOCTOR, SHY NURSE	Molly Evans
HAWAIIAN SUNSET, DREAM PROPOSAL	Joanna Neil
RESCUED: MOTHER AND BABY	Anne Fraser

January

DARE SHE DATE THE DREAMY DOC?	Sarah Morgan
DR DROP-DEAD GORGEOUS	Emily Forbes
HER BROODING ITALIAN SURGEON	Fiona Lowe
A FATHER FOR BABY ROSE	Margaret Barker
NEUROSURGEON…AND MUM!	Kate Hardy
WEDDING IN DARLING DOWNS	Leah Martyn

February

WISHING FOR A MIRACLE	Alison Roberts
THE MARRY-ME WISH	Alison Roberts
PRINCE CHARMING OF HARLEY STREET	Anne Fraser
THE HEART DOCTOR AND THE BABY	Lynne Marshall
THE SECRET DOCTOR	Joanna Neil
THE DOCTOR'S DOUBLE TROUBLE	Lucy Clark

MILLS & BOON®